AIRWAR

AIRWAR

★ TERROR FROM THE SKY

★★ TRAGIC VICTORIES

EDWARD JABLONSKI

DOUBLEDAY & COMPANY, INC., GARDEN CITY, NEW YORK

For my friends,
CLAIRE and PETER CLAY
once of the hospitable "George II,"
Luton, Bedfordshire, and now
of the "Coach and Horses," Rickmansworth,
Hertfordshire, England.

Man, have pity on man.
Rain from the outraged sky
drowned the innocent earth
yet the seed did not die.
Flowering from that rebirth,
man, have pity on man
as you hold the fire in your hand
that can destroy mankind
and desolate every land.
If the power and the glory is this,
a flame that burns to the bone,
what shall be left to grow
when you and your fires have gone?
What maimed and desolate few
shall recover life's full span
from among the ashes of time?
Man, have pity on man.
                    Ursula Vaughan Williams

TERROR FROM THE SKY

Contents

Preface

This is the first of four volumes collectively entitled *Airwar*. Originally the intention was to produce a reasonably comprehensive one-volume history of aerial warfare as it evolved during the historically brief but crucial period of the Second World War. The finished work, despite certain omissions and some short shrifting, proved to be a rather large tome indeed.

The practical solution (achieved with a nimble editorial brain and a deft editorial hand) was to break it down into what seemed to be natural divisions and to issue the book as a multivolumed set over a period of time. Each book would be complete in itself and yet a part of a continuing larger narrative. A decided advantage of this solution was that the illustrations could be larger and the individual volumes easier to handle and, hopefully even if only because of a generous type size, to read.

If there is a major theme of *Airwar* it is that evolution of air power already mentioned against the human background. War does not make war, men do. Men also fashion weapons under stress with a fiendish ingenuity (taken for granted at the time) which after the urgency has passed are recognized as appalling expediencies. But once fashioned the weapons cannot be forgotten nor wished out of existence. So it was with the development of airwar

during 1939–45. Certain technical advances occurred during these years, while men endured terrible stresses, suffered misgivings and pain, and many —too many—died. It was a time of unquestioning (at least prevalently) valor and great deeds that contributed to the accomplishment of a weapon of greater potency than anyone concerned had imagined.

This volume, *Terror from the Sky,* is devoted to beginnings: with the rise of the German Luftwaffe, with the eruption of the Second World War (a war that can be attributed to the sickness inside Nazi Germany more than is generally done). The narrative carries the story through the decisive (though little understood) Battle of Britain and what beleaguered Londoners called "the blitz." These beginnings were more tentative than they appeared to be at the time. The Stuka dive bomber, that winged terror, seemed to be the ultimate air weapon; at the same time the early fighting in France was little more than a sequel to the aerial jousting of the First World War—and equally decisive (which was practically nil).

It was not until the Luftwaffe's rebuff in the Battle of Britain and its ineffectual bombing of British cities which followed that a certain pattern began to emerge. For one thing, despite the old dictum, the bomber did *not* always get through. Also, when it did, great numbers of non-combatant civilians were injured or died—and their dying did not inevitably lead to pleas for peace. Humankind, while capable of devising infinite methods of extinguishing (one is tempted to use "extincting") itself, can also draw upon tragically inexhaustible reserves of courage and a capacity for sacrifice. This was equally true, during 1939–45, of airmen, foot soldiers, seamen, civilians, of friend and enemy. It is on this note that this first volume closes, but it is a subtheme that must thread through the entire work.

The second volume, *Tragic Victories,* is an account of groping, of a search for a method of wielding a weapon not fully understood. Its telling is a tale of loss, of great triumphs that were not triumphs at all. The Flying Tigers were abused and sacrificed for a nation only half-concerned with the ethics of the war; the famous Doolittle raid accomplished little militarily and Midway was, we know now, one of America's most poignant victories. The early attempts at reaching the industrial heart of Germany with British and American bombers are sorrowing in terms of great dedication and sacrifice—and scant fulfillment. The volume opens with the most tragic victory of all, Japan's attack on Pearl Harbor, which inexorably led to Japan's own searing destruction.

Outraged Skies, the third volume, is devoted entirely to that orphaned theater of war, the Pacific. It was an infuriating secondhand kind of war in which those who fought had to learn how to make do until they could be supplied with needed equipment, matériel, and men. It was not official policy to deprive these men of necessities, of course, but the ultimate effect was that it just as well might have been. And some of those who fought believed it was. Thus their feats were no mean accomplishments. They fought against natural enemies—the sea and jungle—and a human enemy whose psychology and philosophy of death were incredible to them. But they persevered, despite dispiriting handicaps, and eventually turned the tide of battle. Still there were times, in their darker moments, when all who fought in the Pacific—Allies as well as Japanese—wondered just who their enemies were, not the least of whom seemed to be some angry aerial deity who implacably and without favoritism sought to destroy them all.

Finally, *Wings of Fire,* the last volume, relates how the air weapon came of age in those last hectic months of the war. Although the Second World War, especially in Europe, was decided on the ground (primarily because its high commanders were traditional ground men), the ultimate victory owed much to air power. If unleashed it could have been *the* decisive weapon—but at a cost to mankind that might have been too frightful to consider. As it was, the fiery endings in both Germany and Japan were devastating enough. It would be best that they never be repeated; nor should it be forgotten that those weapons, now refined but yet the same weapons, are poised—hopefully in limbo. But they are poised.

A last general word: My appreciation to all those who contributed to the preparation of this work and a long bibliography appear in the concluding volume, number 4, of *Airwar.* It might be noted, too, that the word "airwar" was not coined by me; it was a term used widely during the Second World War, although as two words. Eliminating the space took no great ingenuity, but the single word, I feel, capsulizes a concept, a type of warfare that is capable of striking anywhere, anytime, and everyone.

EDWARD JABLONSKI

New York, N.Y.
June 1970

Foreword

MILITARY aviation attained dreadful maturity during the Second World War—actually the first war of truly world-wide dimension. Whether or not this coming of age in technology and strategy was in fact a blessing (read: "deterrent") or a scourge remains for history to determine. Or rather, for men to determine in the course of history. This history—from the club to the intercontinental ballistic missile—is a long one, but the major innovation, the air weapon, is peculiar to the twentieth century.

As we all know, the "flying machine" or "aeroplane" was metamorphosed from a sportsman's plaything into a weapon of war during the early months of the Great War of 1914–18. Despite an exceptionally favorable press, a flood of pulp literature, cinematic fatuities, and a latter-day cult (nurtured by young innocents who never suffered a single experience of war), the "aeroplane" contributed very little to the outcome of that war.

The embryo air weapon, however, gave birth to the myth of the "ace," the high-scoring pursuit, later fighter, pilot, the twentieth-century equivalent of the medieval knight in a curiously anachronistic reversion. So much attention was focused upon these gentlemen jousters, their dainty craft, and their in-conclusive "dogfights" that the more deadly transition of the toy turned weapon was scarcely noticed.

There were inklings and intimations. The Germans introduced, with their abortive Zeppelin depredations, the terror bombings upon cities. With the advent of the giant bombers—the Gothas, Staaken, and others—the German war leaders skirted along the edge of the idea of strategic bombardment: the elimination of an enemy's means of making war far from the battle fronts. But this was not systematically pursued and the Giants, like the Zeppelins, were more assiduously employed at destroying civilians than war industries.

Germany was spared by the Armistice the horrors of mass bombings in the Great War. It was a near thing, actually. Two astute airmen, England's Hugh Trenchard and America's William Mitchell, had grasped the potential of aircraft as a weapon and how it might be used in terms of that potential. Had Germany not surrendered, its cities would have been bombed by huge fleets of large aircraft and its industries laid waste. It very well may have changed the course of history.

Between the wars, especially because of a general revulsion to things military in the democracies, the development of air power was minimal. However, Trenchard managed to keep his RAF out from under the thumbs of the established services and thus encouraged the doctrine of the independent air force. Mitchell, dishonored prophet in his own country, also campaigned for an air force free of Army and Navy control with especial emphasis upon the heavy bomber designed to strike at the enemy behind the lines. About the same time also, Giulio Douhet, in Italy, expounded his concept of "Command of the Air," which was based upon the big bomber. Neither Douhet nor Mitchell were popular among their more conservative military peers, who continued to view war through nineteenth-century eyes. Mitchell, in fact, propheted himself into a court-martial because of his outspoken views on the U. S. Navy's attitude toward aviation.

A not very subtle change in military thinking was obvious in the generally realistic theories of Mitchell and Douhet. For centuries the civilian had been permitted to "enjoy" war at a distance. Unless, of course, he happened to live in the path of armies; if he were swept aside, his home and fields destroyed, himself even killed, it was accepted as the "fortunes of war." It was merely bad luck; no one deliberately set out to kill him.

The introduction of the doctrine of strategic bombardment changed all that. The once flimsy, harmless little flying machine brought this change about. It was suggested during the Great War, lay dormant through the between-the-wars period, and came to full bloom during the Second World War. Curiously, the idea of strategic bombardment was nurtured in the peace-loving democracies, England and, to a greater extent, the United States. Mitchell's ideas, for all their unpopularity, were sustained and understood by his young disciples Henry H. Arnold, Carl A. Spaatz, and Ira C. Eaker, among others.

These men were not devoted to killing civilians—the thought was repellent to them—but to the idea of the destruction of enemy war industries by what came to be called "high-altitude, daylight, precision bombing." Their argument lay in the truth that if you eradicate the enemy's means of making war, he will stop fighting. This could be done, they contended, only if targets could actually be seen (this was before the advent of radar) and efficiently struck: that is, virtually erased off the map. Such bombing could be done in daylight with extremely

accurate bombsights in powerful high-flying, self-defending aircraft. This plane was produced by the Boeing Company in 1935 and became celebrated as the B-17 Flying Fortress. That it was not in fact a flying fortress was proved in combat, but that was beside the point; it was the first flying proof of the efficacy of the strategic bomber.

Over this same period, interestingly, there was no parallel development in Germany, Italy, or Japan —nor France, for that matter. All three of the aggressor nations of the Second World War evolved mighty and potent air forces, but they were invariably subordinate to ground command. This was especially true of Germany. Japan depended upon a formidable navy with its major force being the carriers equipped with an outstanding aircraft, the then unknown Zero.

Germany plunged into war with the most powerful air force in the world at the time. Modern-day apologists claim it was not as powerful as was imagined at the time. Perhaps its strength was overestimated by the Allies (and even the Germans themselves) and some of its sweeping impact could be attributed to shock as much as to superior tactics. But like the carrier-based Japanese naval air forces, it was a fearful instrument of destruction.

Because these great forces were subservient to thinking predominated by surface tactics, they were ultimately wasted. As for Germany and Japan—and Italy and France—such thinking lost them the war.

The Second World War opened and closed with aerial attacks: Dirschau Bridge in Poland by a *Kette* of Stukas and Nagasaki in the Pacific by a lone B-29. And yet the war was not a pure air war. It was throughout, to some extent, and especially in Europe, tied to (and often tied down by) ground strategy.

The role of air power, however, was anything but minor in 1939–45: it was decisive. It is a dangerous delusion to pretend that the bombings of Germany did not contribute heavily to the Nazi collapse. That all was not perfection in the strategic bombardment program is true; how could it have been otherwise? The Germans were not cooperating in its prosecution. But without air power it is unlikely that Allied ground forces would have set foot upon the beaches of Normandy when they did, or quite so firmly. It would have been possible to have bombed Germany into submission without an invasion at all; several responsible airmen believed this. Given the B-29 and the atomic bomb, had the war lasted some months longer in Europe, this would have been inevitable.

The aircraft in operation at the beginning of the war and those at its close were quite different. Those nations whose aircraft development stagnated (partially because they were bombed into stagnation) were defeated. Germany, it is true, developed the first operational jet- and rocket-powered fighters, but fortunately they came too late to have an effect upon the war—thanks to that great military philosopher, Hitler, and to Allied bombardment. There was a wide range of development in the progression from the B-17 to the B-29 and from the P-40 to the P-51. There is an even greater one from the early general-purpose bombs to such refinements as the missile and the atomic bomb.

Aircraft, their weaponry and ordnance, contributed to the war's outcome; immeasurably when compared to their contribution in the First World War. This can be attributed partly to mere technical improvement, but even more to application, to *how* the air weapon was employed. The war opened as a kind of sequel to the Great War and, excepting the innovational doctrine of the German blitzkrieg (the tank plus aircraft team), seemed fated to repeating the inconclusive dogfighting of the previous war. The Battle of Britain changed all that and revealed that German bombardment theory was all but ineffectual in a strategic sense.

It was when the British and Americans, for all their doctrinal wrangling, combined to destroy German industry that the fuller implications of modern air war became a tragic realization. The Japanese, though they initiated the lesson at Pearl Harbor, learned the full lesson themselves at Midway. The aircraft had truly revolutionized war, though few were anxious to acknowledge it.

Air war meant that the day of the civilian noncombatant was over. The cozy concept of leaving war to "guilty" soldiers and sparing "innocent" civilians was dead. That millions of innocent civilians were slaughtered cannot be denied, but war being now what it is, neither can it be avoided.

Remember that.

And it should not be forgotten that the air weapons developed during the Second World War (and refined since) make practically every pin point on the globe vulnerable to attack.

In effect, the evolution of air war during 1939–45 also marked the end of land warfare in the future. It also sank the battleship forever.

The Second World War was the last large-scale war out of which individuals, personalities, emerged. As the war progressed, individual exploits were lost in the emphasis upon "formations." It was the last war of the aces. That last rugged individualist, the fighter pilot, became part of a team whose function was not to *joust* but to escort a load of explosives to a specified target. The lone fighter pilot who went into combat with a "daredevil aces" complex did not last.

But as always, alas, wartime was a time of heroes, of incredible sacrifice—of wasteful sacrifice, of pointless sacrifice—for man has an infinite capacity for such deeds. Courage in war is not a rare or exclusive commodity: all people have it and draw upon it when they must. What makes the heroism of airmen so much more romantically fascinating is the otherworldly element in which they perform: the cloud-laden, cerulean, vasty skies. And when the airman "bought it," his going was spectacular to witness; experiencing it was another matter. Still, there seemed something so clean and pure about falling five miles before ramming into the earth in a splash of flame. Perhaps, but no one has ever been able to communicate his thoughts, feelings, and pain during that remarkable final plunge. Nor would anyone who had seen the interior of a stricken aircraft which managed to return from a rough mission forget the experience: flak and flame produced anything but purity and cleanliness.

There seemed something impersonal, too, about loosing bombs into what appeared to be a toy city; certainly it was inconceivable that full-sized humans lived there. But the horror and misery of those bombed cities have been set down and, when war becomes less objective, it becomes more questionable.

The Second World War was inevitable. The German leaders rationalized sufficiently for themselves and their people good reasons for going to war. The Japanese felt justified in attacking Pearl Harbor. Once the stunned Allies found themselves embroiled, the only recourse was to fight back with all they had—and, as time went by, they had more than the enemy. Neither the Germans nor the Japanese had planned on a long war; they had hoped for short, swift victories and timorous opponents. It did not go, simply, according to plan.

The man who maintains that there is such a thing as a science, or art, of war is, no matter who he is, a fool. In the abstract, as a game, where there is true control and when blood is not the argument, perhaps there is a kind of science or art. But not in real war. It is ultimately a form of international murder and now that air war has placed the nearly ultimate weapon at man's disposal and aircraft have so shrunk the earth, all wars are virtually civil wars of extinction.

It was Walt Whitman who chanted:

Word over all, beautiful as the sky,
Beautiful that war and all its deeds of carnage must in time be utterly lost . . .

There must be, as the poet pleads, a reconciliation between enemies. The Second World War provided an overwhelming number of "deeds of carnage" which should be forgiven but never forgotten. Many of these deeds, excepting those committed in Nazi extermination camps, were done by aircraft: Warsaw, Rotterdam, London, Coventry, Hamburg, Dresden, Berlin, Tokyo, Hiroshima. Such deeds were not exclusive to either side; atrocities were committed by all warring nations; war itself is an atrocity. It is not a matter of which nation perpetrated this or that outrage, but the fact that man is capable of such acts, no matter how just or evil his cause.

This history attempts to trace the evolution of air war and the men and aircraft contributing to it. But I hope, too, that it serves as a warning and a reminder. We must not forget the deeds of courage any more than the deeds of carnage. The development of jet aircraft, the missile, and the atomic bomb—all products of the Second World War—make any future world war unthinkable. Imagine a war with few survivors, without heroes, without victors. What consolation lies in knowing that when "we" go, "they" will go too?

There is scant comfort in the knowledge that there will never be a World War IV. What we all know now can prevent the third.

E.J.

New York, N.Y.

TERROR FROM THE SKY

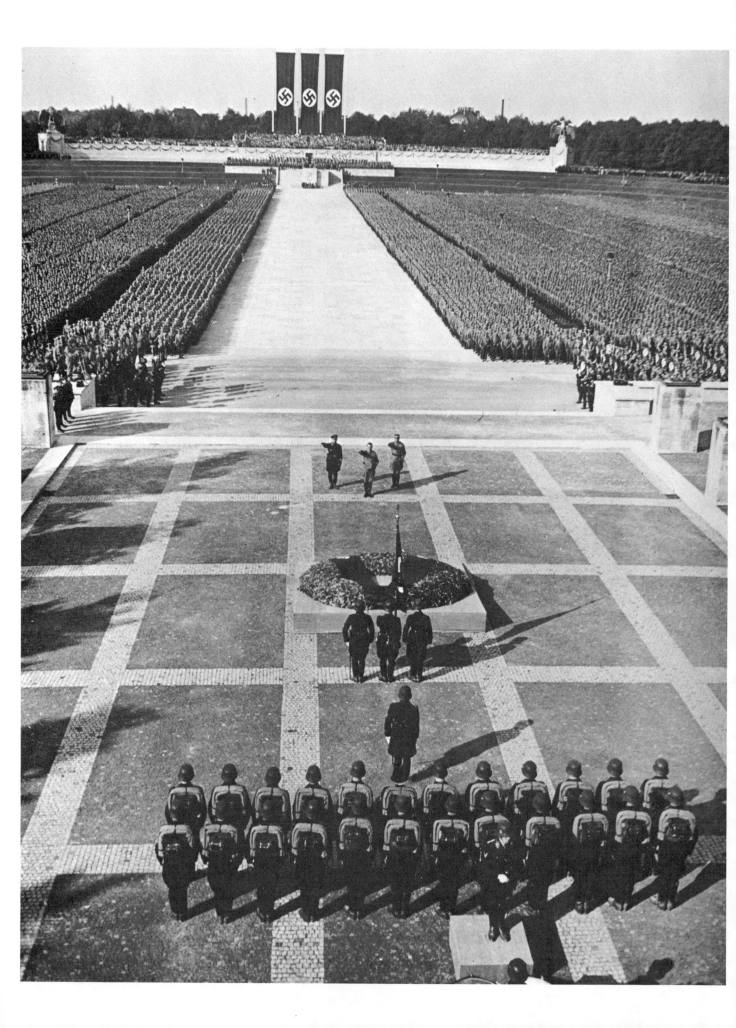

Prologue
PAX GERMANICA

To posterity it will appear like a fairy tale!

—ADOLF HITLER

I

A NATION OF FLIERS

THE BATTLE OF BRITAIN, and perhaps the outcome of the European phase of the Second World War, was predetermined on June 3, 1936, in the smoldering wreckage of a single aircraft near Dresden, Germany. In later years Dresden would acquire immortality as the site of a more dreadful tragedy than the deaths of one German general and his sergeant-mechanic. But the smaller tragedy and the greater one would one day be linked by the inexorable, blind dynamics of history.

The accident that summer day in a world relatively at peace was not impressive enough to make world headlines. The New York *Times* reported it deep inside the paper, on page fifteen. It noted briefly that, during an inspection tour of military bases, Generalleutnant Walther Wever, Chief of Staff of the Luftwaffe, had crashed in a takeoff while piloting his personal plane, a Heinkel He-70, the sleek *Blitz* ("Lightning"). With Wever perished his concept of air power, a concept which, four years later, might have spelled victory for his Luftwaffe in its struggle with the Royal Air Force.

To many an American reader wrapped up in postwar isolation, involved with his own Depression-inspired anxieties and eager to shun Europe's cyclic paroxysms, it came as a surprising revelation that Germany had an air force at all.

The *Times* noted that when "the German Air Ministry was created under the Hitler regime he [Wever] was transferred to that branch of the Army with the rank of major general. He became chief of Section 2 in the Ministry in charge of statistics, with the special task of studying the air forces of foreign powers. It was on his latest assignment as Chief of Air Staff that he was promoted to the rank of lieutenant general."

In 1936 the name of Adolf Hitler meant little to most Americans and the name of Walther Wever even less. Wever had served in the infantry during the First World War and in the Reichswehr (German Armed Forces) until Hitler had come into power. Youthful, dynamic, Wever was an advocate of very modern application of air power.

Had the American scanned the page on which the death of Wever was reported, he would have found little there to disconcert him, although the eventual impact of those events were to alter his life greatly within a few years. Two full columns were devoted to a study of "war rumors" in China which the leaders of that country stigmatized as "a plot." A subhead was terse: "Tokyo Doubtful of War." Another more compact article announced: "Peace Aims Snag on Reich Arming." An attempt to frame an air pact between Germany and Britain had failed. With one wary eye focused upon Moscow, Hitler boasted that his Luftwaffe was superior in quality as well as quantity to the Royal Air Force.

He referred to aircraft and numbers, not men; he was unaware of the fact that with the loss of Wever, much of the quality had already been lost.

II

In 1936 not even Hitler, for all his saber rattling, would have predicted another great war within three years. A master of the big bluff, he was fated, like the Kaiser before him, to blunder into catastrophe, taking millions of victims with him.

There are not any simple causes for war, but the summation of countless variables. But if one single element was required to ignite the Second World War that element was Adolf Hitler. In 1936 Imperial Japan was already on the march in the Far East, but without Hitler's Germany it is unlikely that Japan would have attacked Pearl Harbor. Without its Nazi ally Japan would not have been able to challenge the United States and Great Britain in the Pacific. A Second World War without Hitlerian Germany, therefore, is inconceivable.

An easy rationalization for what occurred in Germany during the two fateful decades 1919–39 has been the hard peace imposed upon Germany by the Treaty of Versailles. The terms of the treaty, however malevolent, did not create the mood and setting for the war to come, they merely supplied the later justifications. The implementation for the next war was set in motion on November 9, 1918—two days before the Armistice was signed, ending four of the most wasteful years in man's history.

This implementation was a secret mutual protection agreement between the newly proclaimed German Republic and the newly discredited German General Staff. It was brought about by a simple telephone call. On that November 9 the call came to Berlin over the secret wire which connected it with the Supreme Headquarters at the Hôtel Britannique at Spa in southeast Belgium adjacent to the German border. The new President, Friedrich Ebert, found himself speaking with Lieutenant General Wilhelm Groener (not the wily Hindenburg, who wished to disown any responsibility for dealing with either the enemy or the new Republic). The general, speaking for the High Command, offered a proposition.

Obviously the new Republic needed help and with the aid of the Army it might have a chance of survival. Ebert, who had known Groener during the war and trusted him despite his military credentials, was moved to tears by this generously offered hand from an unexpected quarter. The Republic, in turn, Groener then stipulated, must shelter the Army from the Allies. It was agreed, secretly of course.

It was an anomalous *mariage de convenance,* for the democratic Republic was avowedly antimilitary and the Army, especially the General Staff, was equally anti-democratic. But they would need each other, they agreed, in the parlous days ahead —the virulent specter of Bolshevism rose like a grimy cloud in the east and vengeance-bent Allies rolled in from the west. This binding of the German government to the military doomed the Reich to a second dance of death—and the old dance was not yet over.

The Allies, hoping to maim Germany's ability to make war again, made the German General Staff one of its chief victims at Versailles. As the repository of Teutonic military philosophy the General Staff was dissolved, along with its fountainhead, the Kriegsakademie (War College). The Army was reduced to a mere hundred thousand men and its instruments of war were seized by the Allies or destroyed. All military aircraft were confiscated and the German Air Force disbanded. How, with all such restrictions, was Hitler in 1936 able to boast of an air force second to none?

The chief architect, the guiding genius, behind the military resurgence of Germany despite the restrictions of the Versailles Treaty and the supervision of the Inter-Allied Commission of Control was the all but unknown Generaloberst Hans von Seeckt. His very anonymity made him acceptable to the Allies to head Germany's token military force; his reputation as a brilliant military thinker delighted the remnants of the General Staff which still remained in the German Army.

What the Allies did not know then hurt them later. Seeckt regarded the so-called Great War as merely the first of a series which Germany might lose. But Germany would rise again, fight again, and ultimately win. Within the limitations of his small army Seeckt began resuscitating the discredited General Staff and building a new, elite,

Hans von Seeckt (1866–1936), brilliant architect of the resurgence of Germany's war machine. Despite the strictures of the Versailles treaty, and with the co-operation of the Soviet Union in the early 1920s, Seeckt created the antecedents of the panzers and the Luftwaffe even before Hitler came to power.

more modern Reichswehr under the very noses of the Allies. New, unwarlike names were devised for certain departments of the Reichswehr. The "Ministry of Pensions," for example, ostensibly under civilian control, was actually under the direction of "retired" Army officers. The function of the Ministry was in fact the collection of data on Germany's manpower potential for the next war. In the guise of "historical research," Seeckt's staff officers (although not designated as such) kept abreast of the latest military developments in the world.

Seeckt was no conservative; he fully appreciated the importance of mobility in warfare (as opposed to the attritional trench war of 1914–18). As for aircraft, nearly everyone in the previous war had been blind to its potential. Seeckt brought several airmen into the Reichswehr. Beginning with only three officers, the air branch of the Reichswehr quickly expanded to fifteen. Among the younger officers were Hugo Sperrle, Albert Kesselring, Hans-Jürgen Stumpf, and Wolfram von Richthofen, a former civil engineer and cousin of the celebrated "Red Knight of Germany." It was a good name for Seeckt's growing circle; in a few years all the names would stand for something.

But names only meant little in 1920, when Seeckt sought to improvise a German military renaissance. With a monocled eye on the greater objective, he managed to keep himself and his burgeoning little army out of the internal strife that erupted in Germany. His military elite was thus nurtured even while Germany's government and economy boiled and festered. Thanks to the agreement between the government and the Army, Seeckt was able to side-step those official inconveniences that might have interfered with his plans.

If he was able to dominate or hoodwink his own Minister of Defense, Seeckt was even more ingenious in solving the problem of how to revive the German Air Force and replenish the supply of aircraft which Allies so wastefully destroyed. If he could co-operate with his own government, which he detested, then why not take aid from a government he truly hated—the Bolshevik Soviet Russia?

Soviet Russia from about the summer of 1922, when an organization called Gesellschaft zur Förderung gewerblicher Unternehmungen (Company for the Advancement of Industrial Enterprises) was formed, contributed immeasurably to the rise of a newly militarized Germany. Known more familiarly as GEFU, the company was formed by a joint German-Russian group, the German members being trusted friends of Seeckt. The existence and function of GEFU was known also to Reich Chancellor Dr. Joseph Wirth and Foreign Minister Walter Rathenau. Wirth was especially essential to the project, for he was at the same time Reich Finance Minister, and Seeckt required additional financing which was not forthcoming from his stringent military budget.

Among the "industrial enterprises" established by GEFU was a Junkers aircraft factory at Fili, not far from Moscow (for Germans were forbidden to manufacture aircraft—in Germany). Another enterprise was named Bersol-Aktien-Gesellschaft, a Soviet-German operation at Trotsk, in the province of Samara. Bersol was to produce poison gas. Several factories for producing artillery shells were projected, and some built, in other sections of Russia. Finally, in the same spirit of dedication to the welfare of the proletariat, the Russians granted to Krupp, the German industrial empire, a large tract of land on the Manych River, a tributary of the Don, for use as an "experimental farm." This was ostensibly for the testing and demonstration of tractors and other farm equipment. A "large-size tractor," it might be noted, produced at this "farm" mounted a 7.5-centimeter gun.

At the same time training schools were established in Soviet Russia—all of this with the blessing of the saintly Lenin—where Germans and Russians could exchange the latest developments in the "art of war."

By 1923 an excellent training ground and tank school was established at Kazan on the Volga; there tactics were devised, vehicles developed, and leaders trained for Seeckt's new army. The seeds of Kazan reached full flower when German panzers smashed across the Polish frontier to open the Second World War and, later, Lenin's legacy to his workers came home too as Hitler's Operation Barbarossa.

The "air weapon," the other element essential to Seeckt's mobility concept, was reforged at the German Air Force Center at Vivupal, near Lipesk about 250 miles southeast of Moscow. The so-called "4th Squadron" stationed there was supplied from Germany through the free port of Stettin, where German customs officials winked when necessary. Military materials of embarrassing bulk were slipped across the Baltic under cover of night. German officers sent to Russia for training were first discharged from the Army. Should anything happen to them while in training, it would happen to a civilian, not a German soldier.

Among the early trainees graduated from the aviation school at Lipesk was Hans Jeschonnek, who would one day serve as Chief of Staff of the future Luftwaffe. Thus were hundreds of airmen trained in Russia during the late twenties—the nucleus of an incipient air weapon. At the same time new—and, according to the treaty, prohibited—aircraft were developed and tested in Russia and other countries.

Inevitable training accidents posed special problems, for there was no simple explanation for the shipment of German bodies from Soviet Russia. The Inter-Allied Commission of Control could not be blind to everything. But the solution was efficiently simple. The bodies of young airmen killed while training at Lipesk were returned to their families in Germany in crates stamped: "Machinery—Spare Parts."

To Seeckt none of this sub rosa activity appeared illicit, nor did it cross his mind that he was disloyal to Germany. He did, of course, scorn the so-called Weimar Republic with all its democratic, anti-military avowals. It was merely the instrument —a temporary one he was certain—for his own ambition to fashion a truly formidable German Army. "The Army," he said, "should become a state within a state . . ." which, under his administration, it certainly was, with its own laws and aims free of internal and international law. "But," Seeckt added, the Army "should be merged in the state through service; in fact it should become the purest image of the state." Thus a state dedicated to the art of war. To Seeckt the excuse of the Versailles Treaty was not necessary; he had begun making his plans long before there was such a treaty. All he needed was a lost war.

"We must become powerful," he declared, "and, as soon as we have power, we will naturally take back everything we have lost."

Meanwhile, civil Germany had become a political cesspool—also attributed to the Treaty of Versailles. Political factions, some of them quasi-military, proliferated as Germany itself sank into economic de-

pression. The central hotbed of German reactionary movements was Bavaria, where the disgruntled gathered to voice their disgust with their government and to curse the treaty. It was in Bavaria's capital, Munich, that Seeckt met with the young leader of one of the more clamorous political groups, the German National Socialist Workers' Party. Seeckt was at the time hoping to put the party's own private army, the Sturmabteilungen, to his own use should he require additional hands to rid the Ruhr of the occupying armies of the Allies.

Seeckt was most impressed with the party's fanatical, ranting leader, who seemed capable of haranguing for hours on a subject dear to the general's heart: the criminality of the Versailles Treaty, the ineptitude of the Weimar Republic, and the eventual emergence of a mighty Reich. The party leader was, of course, Adolf Hitler. "We were one in our aims," Seeckt later said of Hitler, "only our paths were different."

Hitler had no intention of placing his Storm Troopers at Seeckt's disposal—as Seeckt had been misled to believe—for he had other plans for his bully boys. This was revealed in the abortive Bürgerbrau Keller fiasco in a Munich beer hall the following November when Hitler unleashed his elite ruffian band prematurely in a misguided *Putsch*. Among them was no less than war hero Field Marshal Erich Ludendorff, with dreams of glory of his own. Hoping to ride into the role of military dictator of Germany on Hitler's coattails, Ludendorff merely strode through the police firing line— miraculously unhurt—and out of history forever. Sixteen party members lay dead in the street; one party member, second only to Hitler, the ex-fighter ace Hermann Göring, was seriously wounded, and Hitler fled the scene in a thoroughly unmilitary style.

With his rivals out of the way—for Hitler was imprisoned for a while: long enough to dictate *Mein Kampf*—Seeckt could turn his attention to his own plans for a *Putsch* and his own dream of a military dictatorship. But within three years Seeckt himself would fall. Not, ironically, for his remarkable building up of a new German military structure or his all but inexplicable dealings with Soviet Russia—instead Seeckt provided comparatively trivial indiscretions which served as well.

For example, he issued an order entitled "The Proper Conduct of Duels Between Officers," which resulted in a small flurry in the press. Such arrant Prussianism at a time when the Germans were concerned with diminishing that wart in the profile of the national stereotype. With characteristic disdain, Seeckt chose to ignore the criticisms. Whereupon he committed another *gaffe*. During the autumn 1926 maneuvers of the 9th Infantry Regiment Seeckt gave permission to Prince Wilhelm, son of the former Crown Prince, to participate in the exercises. The Prince, as one of the deposed Hohenzollerns, was anathema to the sincere democrats and especially to the vociferous Left. The Socialist paper, *Vorwärts,* declared that Prince Wilhelm's presence, in full resplendent uniform, was "not simply a question of whether parliament or the military shall be the predominant factor in Germany; it is a question of democracy or militarism!"

With the world only recently made safe for democracy, it was obvious that Seeckt would have to go. But what few realized at the time was that by then Seeckt had already succeeded in making Germany safe for militarism. And to some extent his accomplishments were known to insiders. His "military genius," as historian John Wheeler-Bennett has written, was a unique combination: "the precision and accuracy of the soldier" and "the vision and imagination of the creative artist. For such he was, an artist in making bricks without straw, in beating ploughshares into swords, in fashioning a military machine which, though nominally within the restrictions of the Peace Treaty, struck admiration and awe into every General Staff in Europe."

By the time Seeckt made his exit, in October 1926, the presidency of the Republic had been filled by the great hero of the First World War, Field Marshal Paul von Beneckendorff und Hindenburg. Bitter because Hindenburg had not lifted a finger to help him, Seeckt permitted the formation of yet another political party around him, the Deutsche Volkspartei. When he realized, after little success, that his future did not lay in politics, Seeckt diverted whatever power his party had to the party he believed had the most promising future: Hitler's resuscitated Nazis. Seeckt died in 1936, never to know what he had done for that party's ultimate destiny.

Hitler, who had in 1923 appeared to be little more than a loudmouthed incompetent revolution-

ary, had within a decade worked his way into the Hindenburg government as Chancellor. Although the senilescent Hindenburg detested the lowly "Bohemian corporal," he was forced eventually to recognize the power of the Nazis. Hitler—by virtue of verbose spellbinding, blackmail, threat, cajolery, murder, and the aid from German big business, bankers, political conservatives, industrialists, Junkers landowners, and an enormous majority of the German people (who found Hitler's anti-Semitism, anti-communism, and anti-Versailles spoutings very good listening)—had made himself politically inevitable.

So it was that when Adolf Hitler became Chancellor of Germany on Monday, January 30, 1933, he was placed in a position to take over the government of Germany, thanks to Field Marshal Hindenburg. And thanks to General Seeckt he had the superb beginnings of a great war machine. Never before had a mere corporal owed so much to a field marshal and a general, particularly to the latter with his dream of the next war.

"The whole future of warfare," Seeckt had observed, "appears to me to be in the employment of mobile armies, relatively small but of high quality, and rendered distinctly more effective by the addition of aircraft. . . ." Although the term had not yet been coined, Seeckt in the early twenties had already visualized the concept of blitzkrieg.

III

There was no Luftwaffe as such when Hitler became Chancellor of the Reich. Significantly, his first important address, made on the very next day, January 31, 1933, was to the troops of the Berlin garrison. He charmed them all.

As for the Air Force, Seeckt and others had done well by Hitler. In 1926—when Seeckt was forced to resign—the German Air Force consisted of two fighter squadrons, a single bomber squadron, and an auxiliary bomber squadron. By 1931 there were four fighter squadrons, three bombardment squadrons, and eight observation squadrons. While the figures might not have been impressive—and they were not supposed to be—they contained within them hundreds of future air leaders, most of them trained in Soviet Russia.

There were other even less obvious developments. In 1926 also the Deutsche Lufthansa Aktiengesellschaft was created as a joint private and governmental enterprise. Lufthansa combined two of Germany's successful though financially unstable airlines, Deutsche Aero-Lloyd and Junkers Luftverkehr. This consolidation came about under pressure from the German Ministry of Air Transport, supposedly a civil agency, headed by a trusted Seecktian, Captain Ernst von Brandenburg. The captain had attained wartime immortality as the leader of the famed Bomber Squadron No. 3, the *Englandgeschwader,* which had flown the giant Gotha bombers to attack London from the air. One of Brandenburg's functions was to arrange for the training of future military (obviously bomber) pilots in special sections of Lufthansa's Deutsche Luftverkehrschule. In time there were four of these flying schools turning out civil pilots who could double as bomber pilots.

Board chairman of Lufthansa was Erhard Milch, an ex-German Air Force pilot who had been a salesman for Junkers. Milch was an astute, sharp-dealing, well-organized administrator. As an ex-World War aviator he naturally came into the sphere of Hermann Göring, who had found politics more profitable than postwar aviation in Germany. The gregarious, bluff, gross, and well-liked Göring loved to meet with other ex-war fliers and relive the beautiful days of the war. Those were the best years of their lives, when men were men and they fought like knights in single combat in the clean air miles above the trenches.

But when Milch sought out Göring in 1928 it was not to talk about the splendid days of the Great War. No romantic, Milch was concerned with more practical matters. Lufthansa was in trouble and needed government backing to survive. Göring with his reputation as an air advocate was the most likely representative in the Reichstag to approach on this matter. The two old fliers struck up a warm friendship and Göring, though he represented a minor party, did all he could to advance the fortunes of Lufthansa. He boasted to Milch that one day the little Nazi party would run Germany and when it did, Milch would have an important

role to play in the new German Air Force. Milch with his shrewd practical mind could hardly take *der Dicke* ("the Fat One") very seriously; and he did not make any effort to join the party.

When the Nazis did come into power Milch was asked by Hitler himself to serve as Göring's deputy Air Reichskommissar. Milch accepted on the condition that he remain Lufthansa's chairman. By April 1933 Göring was Air Minister and Milch Secretary of State for Air; in effect this signified the convergence of German civil and military aviation. Milch was efficient, ruthless, and ambitious; he obviously would fit into the scheme of things very well. There was, however, one slight hitch. His father had the taint of "Jewish blood" and an important platform of the Nazi party was a virulent anti-Semitism. This was easily remedied considering Milch's aspirations and abilities: his mother simply signed a statement in which she swore she had committed adultery. Milch was, it turned out, a pure Aryan bastard.

The advent of Hitler began to entwine the various strands of German society which had been unraveling since the Armistice. The masses as well as big business were behind him. Seeckt had prepared a military machine for him and Hindenburg put him in power. In truth, however, when Hitler became Chancellor, he had no real social program for Germany beyond a determination to "call to account the November Criminals of 1918" and his own ill-defined power lust. Nor, unlike Seeckt, did he have a military program.

In fact, Hitler, the eternal enlisted man, had little respect for the Officer Corps. On its part, the Officer Corps remained aloof from politics as Seeckt had insisted, smugly content with its privileged lot. Their only concern with Hitler was how they might use him to further their fortunes. Militarily Hitler, the leader of a rabble and such roisterers as the Storm Troopers and his private protective guard, the Schutzstaffel, was an amateur; he would be no great war lord. An intuitionist, Hitler was no practitioner of classic strategies.

But he proved more than the match of the Officer Corps as a tactician. He wooed them with respectful references to their honored traditions and to their important role in the state. He bided his time, as the officers preened, and then he ravaged all of

Adolf Hitler, leader of the New Germany, and Hermann Göring, leader of the newly spawned Luftwaffe, in an early happy hour greeting their admirers, the German people. Two men less capable of planning and *executing an aerial war could not be imagined: Hitler neither trusted nor liked aircraft and Göring did not understand them as a weapon of military strategy. This was their major combined contribution to the outcome of the Second World War.* (NATIONAL ARCHIVES)

them: Hitler transformed the famed German General Staff into an ensemble of lackeys. They were masters of nothing.

IV

The Luftwaffe was Hitler's pet; its leader was Hermann Göring, a good friend and number two Nazi. Beyond the Open Cockpit and Flames in the Sky mystique which Göring advocated, there was no long history, no accumulation of tradition and

privilege for Hitler to contend with, as with the Army. And there too was the proficient Milch, to set a new air force on a sound organizational and administrative basis.

The new Air Ministry, under Milch's direction, was formed from the old Commissariat for Air and the Transport Ministry. This last would naturally include Captain Brandenburg's flying schools for bomber pilots. Among those holding high office in the new Ministry were Oberst Walther Wever, who had been transferred from the Defense Ministry, Albert Kesselring, and Hans-Jürgen Stumpf. Göring, faithful to old comrades and to the glorious days of the Great War, saw to it that posts were found for two of his friends of the old days: Bruno Loerzer and Karl Bodenschatz. Youthful flying personnel were available in limited numbers from the school in Russia and in greater numbers from Deutscher Luftsportsverband, where flying enthusiasts learned the art of gliding under Kurt Student, a member of the Reichswehr Air Technical Branch. The most promising of these sporting pilots were sent to Lufthansa's schools for training on powered aircraft. Among those trained in the schools was Adolf Galland. Although ostensibly prepared for civil aviation Galland and other young German pilots received training also in combat flying, aerobatics, and gunnery.

By the beginning of 1934 Milch had projected an expansion of the aircraft industry and the German Air Force which would require more than four thousand planes. During 1933 the prototypes of the Heinkel 111 and the Dornier 17 were in the planning stage; though little known then these aircraft were to become notorious during the Battle of Britain. Milch's plans called for six bomber, six fighter, and six reconnaissance *Geschwader*. The *Geschwader* was comprised of from ninety to a hundred aircraft as compared to the *Staffel*'s nine. In 1931 the German Air Force was reckoned in *Staffels* (roughly equivalent to squadrons in the American Air Force); three years later Milch quite realistically thought in terms of *Geschwader*. Because Hitler was not yet ready to show his hand, such work was of necessity accomplished in secret.

Not so secret was the growth, under governmental encouragement, of "air-mindedness" among Germany's youth of both sexes. Göring fostered this enthusiasm by initiating annual competitions for civil pilots. On March 8, 1934, following a cross-country contest, he made the awards with characteristic verve. He was aware of Milch's planning and Hitler's dreams for the future, but he could not resist invoking the past in speaking of "the spirit of German aviation." It was a curious point to make: that the individual should become subservient to the state, considering that the fighter pilot of the First World War was an archindividualist.

Göring spoke glowingly of "the spirit that in four years of heroic life proved so successful and singled

out German aviation during the war—the team spirit among the crews.

"My comrades! We must admit that after the dissolution of the old German air service it was impossible to carry on the old spirit of comradeship in disciplined form. Most of us were uprooted from our work and the air service remained only a dream. The terrible longing for flying nevertheless remained in all of you." His next statement revealed a hint of the future. "The new Reich," Göring shouted, "has ordained that flying—even in forms other than sport and civil flying—shall rise again!"

This stirred the audience and Göring told them how they, the youth of the new Reich—one year having passed in Hitler's projected Thousand Year Reich—would contribute. "The young Germany," Göring promised them, "shall be brought up in a passion for flying in order that the German nation shall become a nation of fliers!"

He returned to the subject of the spirit of German aviation. "It is your duty to keep this spirit alive," he told them. "You have this duty to the sacrifices that your comrades have made in the greatest struggle of all times. We have the right to honor our heroes and to hold them up as models to our German youth. In no treaty is there a clause demanding the destruction of this spirit, but the cowards who have made our people unhappy for the last decade and a half have tried to break this spirit."

Göring could not close without a tribute to the Führer, from whom all these blessings came. The young aviators had dropped roses on Hitler's retreat, Haus Wachenfeld, near Berchtesgaden, at the close of the competition. In this luxurious villa Hitler too was able to enjoy some of his blessings among the magnificent vistas of the Bavarian Alps. From his terrace he could observe the young German fliers dropping roses, of which Göring said, "This compliment is the natural thanks. . . .

"For without Adolf Hitler, where would German pilots and German air transport be today? Where would have gone our dream—our longing—if he had not created the new Germany? Therefore, comrades," Göring concluded on a hushed note, "before I award the prizes, we will stand and think a moment in silent respect for our leader—our beloved leader—our people's chancellor!"

A year later, almost to the day that Göring summoned a "nation of fliers," the Führer officially announced to the world—on March 9, 1935—the existence of the Luftwaffe. Hermann Göring was named Commander in Chief, Erhard Milch was Secretary of State for Air, and Walther Wever was Chief of Staff. Within a week Hitler repudiated the Versailles Treaty with the declaration of a German Army of no less than thirty-six divisions (this would require some 550,000 men) and the reintroduction of conscription. The Reichswehr, the Officer Corps, and the underground General Staff were elated. At last they could operate in the open, Germany would once again take her place in the sun.

v

The "Bohemian corporal" was not such a bad fellow, after all. He had, in fact, behaved himself commendably so far as the military was concerned. Even the grisly Blood Purge of June 30, 1934 had certain points to the Army's advantage. The slaughter of Ernst Röhm and some of his unwholesome associates eradicated a serious threat to Army authority by curbing the Storm Troopers. If the Army lost two of its own in the contrived conspiracy, it was but the fortunes of war. But neither General von Schleicher, who had been Hitler's immediate predecessor as Chancellor, nor Kurt von Bredow was involved seriously with Röhm. The power of the Storm Troopers was smashed, however, and the military could make allowance for zeal. Hindenburg even sent congratulatory telegrams to Hitler and Göring, commending them for having "saved the German nation from serious danger." Even so, the Storm Troopers were merely superseded by the SS and Göring's private Geheime Staatspolizei (the "Gestapo"). Estimates of the murders, many of them settling intraparty feuds, ran as high as a thousand, although Hitler admitted to only seventy-seven.

That he and Göring succeeded in such mass slaughter without Army interference attested to the internal impotence of the Reichswehr. Irresolute, self-centered, and indifferent to all except their own small world, the Army had already been trapped by Hitler. This snare was further strengthened when he required them to take the new oath he had devised. It contained no pledge to sustain

the German Constitution, nor to protect the German government. It did not even swear allegiance to the Reich. Instead, it was a personal oath of loyalty to the corporal himself:

I swear before God to give my unconditional obedience to Adolf Hitler, Führer of the Reich and of the German People, Supreme Commander of the Wehrmacht, and I pledge my word as a brave soldier to observe this oath always, even at peril of my life.

The Reichswehr was no more, supplanted by the Wehrmacht, of which Hitler assumed command. That the oath neglected both patriotism and legality did not concern the German generals; they were too preoccupied building up a thirty-six-division Army.

Even the Luftwaffe had grown considerably. Toward the end of March 1935 Hitler boasted to Sir John Simon, the English Foreign Minister, and Anthony Eden that his Air Force had already reached parity with the Royal Air Force. This was not true, but it had its effect. It was a diplomatic victory for Hitler in dealing with England and France. It also confirmed the fears of Winston Churchill, whose lone voice had been raised in warning against the rise of the Luftwaffe. Hitler's vain boast roused the British government enough to begin expansion of the Royal Air Force and to concentrate upon the single-seater fighter aircraft as outlined in Air Ministry Specification F5/34. Among the aircraft this inspired were the Hawker Hurricane and the Supermarine Spitfire.

Having come out into the open with his military plans, Hitler could proudly announce the opening of the Air Warfare Academy at Berlin-Gatow on November 1, 1935. The principal address of the day was given by the Chief of Staff, Generalleutnant Walther Wever, already widely respected and recognized as a leading exponent of the strategic concept of aerial warfare and a disciple of the Italian military theorist General Giulio Douhet. Greatly influenced, as were other military thinkers in Europe, England, and the United States, by Douhet's ideas, especially as expounded in *The Command of the Air* (1921), Wever was a proponent of the independent air force and of the heavy bomber. As such he was not in tune with Göring's Open Cockpit romanticism. Wever was a realist and a powerful, highly regarded officer whose impact upon the growing German air weapon was bound to be an important one.

He opened his remarks with an allusion to 1918 and the Versailles Treaty when "a leaderless nation collapsed internally and dashed the weapons from the hands of the gallant Army." It was the old refrain, The Legend of the German Defeat, still alive late in 1935.

"How will it be in the future now that a new weapon—the Luftwaffe—has appeared?" Wever asked. "Only in a war of the future will it reach full development. The Air Force, which came into existence hardly twenty-five years ago, found its great military origin in the Great War, from which glorious traditions have been handed down to the Air Force of today. Its greatest heroes are shining examples for us; Manfred von Richthofen—its proudest name. . . ."

Popular First World War ace and between-the-wars stunt flier, Ernst Udet. A dashing, ebullient personality, Udet was a superb pilot but had little conception of the meaning of air power in war. He was the advocate in Germany of the dive bomber (an idea picked up in the United States), which resulted in the Stuka concept. (NATIONAL ARCHIVES)

But, Wever emphasized, the air heroes of the Great War strove for something which only Hitler's National Socialism was making possible: ". . . a strong Air Force with independent status in the services." Wever, however, not wanting to slight the Army, was quick to indicate that an independent Air Force could co-operate with the ground forces where necessary, but he visualized a time when it would be possible to avoid "the positional warfare of massed armies," meaning, of course, the wasteful trench warfare of the Great War.

Wever then made his major point: "Never forget that the bomber is the decisive factor in aerial warfare. Only the nation with strong bomber forces at its disposal can expect decisive action by its Air Force."

Under Wever's direction specifications were drawn up for long-range, four-engined bombers. The result was the Dornier 19 and the Junkers 89, prototypes of which were ready for flight trials late in 1936.

Before this took place, however, Walther Wever died at Dresden in the summer of 1936. With him died the development of the heavy bombers. His successor, Albert Kesselring, canceled the Do-19 and Ju-89 to concentrate on medium bombers and the dive bomber, such aircraft as the Heinkel 111, the Dornier 17, and the Junkers 88 in the former category, and in the latter, the Junkers 87, the "Stuka."

In the reshuffling of the Luftwaffe's command following Wever's death another old Great War fighter pilot, Ernst Udet, was placed at the head of the Air Ministry's Technical Branch. The likable, good-humored, dashing Udet was a fine flier but not gifted with organizational or political skills. With his sunny personality Udet was too wholesome for the company he kept. As Germany's number one living Great War ace (with sixty-two "kills" to his credit), Udet's voice meant something to the amateurs in charge of the Luftwaffe after the death of Wever. Unwittingly Udet did them a disservice with his enthusiastic expertise.

In 1933 Udet visited the United States, one of his stops being the Cleveland Air Races. He was most impressed with the performance of the Curtiss-Wright BFC-2, the "Hawk." As the Curtiss Hawk II, the dive bomber was released for export and Udet, with Göring's help, was able to purchase two

The Junkers 52, all-metal commercial transport which was converted into a troop transport and bomber. As a military plane it first was used in the Spanish Civil War in 1936. (LUFTHANSA PHOTO)

A Junkers 87B Stuka of the Condor Legion over Spain. The Ju-87 proved most effective against ill-defended Spanish installations and received more credit than it actually deserved. (NATIONAL ARCHIVES)

of them in October 1933. The German government authorized payment of $11,500 each. In December Udet demonstrated the Hawk at the Luftwaffe's test center at Rechlin. He delighted in kicking the plane into a screaming dive and pointing it vertically at a pin-point target and then whipping it out of the trajectory dangerously close to the ground. Even so, the High Command was not awed by the performance. Major Wolfram Freiherr von Richthofen was especially unimpressed and resisted Udet's proposals for the development of such a plane (a curious sidelight, for Richthofen later commanded a Stuka unit).

Udet did not advance his cause any when in the summer of 1934 he lost the tail of one of the Hawks while stunting over Tempelhof and had to take to his parachute. But despite Richthofen's objections, by January 1935 development contracts for dive bombers were placed with Arado, Blohm and Voss, Heinkel, and Junkers. The designation for this class of aircraft was "Sturzkampfflugzeug," from which the popular term "Stuka" was derived. Although this referred to all dive bombers, it was the Junkers 87 which became widely known as the Stuka. The Ju-87 was selected over its competitor, the Heinkel 118, which Udet had managed to crash during a test because of his unfamiliarity with a small technical detail. Now head of the Technical Branch, Udet was able to proceed with his Stuka campaign.

Around this same time a new fighter, the Messerschmitt Bf-109, was undergoing tests at Rechlin. The Heinkel 111 had already been displayed at Tempelhof as a "commercial" aircraft with ten seats for passengers and a smoking compartment in the bomb bay. Less susceptible of simulation was the Dornier 17, which was rejected as a mail carrier and taken over by the Air Ministry as a bomber and nicknamed "the Flying Pencil." The first Junkers 88 took off on its test flight on December 21, 1936; it too was a medium bomber. Thus was the character of the Luftwaffe established by the close of 1936—a character much different from that envisioned by Wever in his speech at the Air Warfare Academy.

VI

In the summer of 1936 the new Luftwaffe and its young pilots and aircraft were supplied with a testing arena for their theories in Spain. That hapless country soon became an ideological battleground for the forces of the Left and the Right. Russia sent advisers, technicians, and equipment to the "Loyalists," the Popular Front Republican Government of President Manuel Azaña y Diaz. When the "Insurgents," led by General José Sanjurjo Sacanell (who was killed in the early fighting) and General Francisco Franco, sent out a call for aid from the fascist nations, both Mussolini and Hitler responded in his favor. Göring urged Hitler to intervene "firstly, to prevent the further spread of communism; secondly, to test my young Luftwaffe in this or that technical aspect."

Within a week men and equipment were en route to Morocco, where the fighting had begun, and to Cádiz. Among the aircraft were the Junkers 52, the Lufthansa transport converted to a bomber transport, and Heinkel 52s, obsolescent biplane fighters. By November 1936 the "Condor Legion" under command of Hugo Sperrle and with Wolfram von Richthofen as his Chief of Staff was formed. One of the fighter *Staffels* was commanded by the young "civil" pilot Adolf Galland.

Under Richthofen's direction the technique of close support was developed. Thus was Germany's supposedly independent Air Force wedded to the ground forces. That this was a violation of Wever's early plans went unnoticed in the success of the tactics in Spain. By the summer of 1937 more modern aircraft were dispatched to the Condor Legion.

The Messerschmitt 109B-2 began to replace the He-51s. It marked the end of the biplane fighter era. New tactics, particularly as developed by the youthful Werner Mölders (who replaced Galland as *Staffel* leader in the Jasta 88), proved most effective. The old Great War V-formations were abandoned in favor of the *Rotte,* a two-plane unit of great flexibility. (Two *Rotte* made up a *Schwarm* and three *Schwarms* a *Staffel.*) It was learned that in the old close formations the pilots spent a good deal of time avoiding collision and not enough scanning the sky. The lack of radio communications between aircraft, too, was found to be a serious handicap. The *Rotte* technique was eventually used by most air forces during the Second World War in the leader and wingman combination.

Richthofen, in time commander of the Condor Legion, found that the Stuka Ju-87, of which he had not approved originally, was a most terrifying and useful weapon in his close-support tactics. The ugly, bent-winged dive bomber, with the shrieking sirens attached to the landing gear, was hailed as a scourge of the battlefield. Only a few Stukas were sent to Spain, but these were widely used by alternating

Heinkel 111s approaching a Spanish town. When the He-111 was first introduced in 1936 it was passed off as a ten-passenger commercial aircraft. By late 1937 it was functioning as a bomber in Kampfgruppe 88 in Spain. (NATIONAL ARCHIVES)

A Condor Legion He-111 releasing bombs upon a Spanish town. The success of the missions without escort convinced the Germans that the bomber was impervious to fighter opposition. As with the Stuka, this misconception would come to roost during the Battle of Britain. (NATIONAL ARCHIVES)

Guernica: April 26, 1937. The bells in this burning church rang out to warn of the approach of bombers, a warning which was ignored by the people in the village, unaccustomed to air raids. By nightfall more than sixteen hundred lay dead in Guernica's burning streets. (NATIONAL ARCHIVES)

crews and proved most effective in attacks on such port cities as Valencia, Barcelona, and Tarragona. The Stukas also disrupted communications, destroyed bridges, bombed roads, and harassed troops with frightening invulnerability. Franco's Nationalists had by late 1937 achieved air superiority—thanks to the Germans and Italians—which enabled the Stukas to perform most successfully. It was the same also with the medium bombers which had preceded the Stuka to Spain, the He-111s and the Do-17s. Because they were superior to most of the aircraft of the Republican forces, the German planes gained a reputation beyond reality. The most formidable opponent encountered by the Condor Legion was the Russian Polikarpov I-16, the stubby, rugged little fighter—the fastest of its time. The early Condor Legion fighters, the Heinkel 51s, were no match for the I-16; not until the Messerschmitts

arrived in Spain did the *Ratas* ("Rats") meet a better contender.

The Spanish experience taught the Luftwaffe advanced fighter tactics, as well as the use of radio communications in combat, but the seeming invincibility of the bomber formations encouraged overconfidence, for which a dear price would be paid over England. Also the tradition of ground support as the major Luftwaffe function would take its toll in the future.

Still another tradition was established in Spain. On Monday—market day—April 26, 1937, at four-thirty in the afternoon church bells rang out a warning of approaching aircraft in the vicinity of the Basque village of Guernica. Nestling among the gentle hills of the Vizcaya province nearly twenty miles behind the front lines, Guernica had never been bombed although there had been raids in the area

Guernica burns after bombing by German aircraft. History's first senseless terror bombing.

(NATIONAL ARCHIVES)

before. The alarm conveyed by the church bells meant little to the villagers and the farmers gathered in the market place. Ten minutes after the peal of the bells a formation of Heinkel 111s appeared over Guernica. Small, longish objects began to drop from the bellies of the aircraft; within seconds explosions erupted in the crowded streets of Guernica. Their bombs disgorged, the planes descended to low level and strafed the streets. In another twenty minutes Junkers 52s flew over to pour incendiaries upon the smoking terror of Guernica. These lumbering planes too came down to machine-gun the refugees attempting to flee the village. And so it continued, in flaming, dust-embroiled waves, for three hours until Guernica lay shattered and scorched. In the streets, in the broken cottages and houses, there were 1654 dead and 889 wounded—of a population of 7000.

Guernica was only the first name in history to stand for the fiery desolation from the air; others would follow: Warsaw, Rotterdam, Coventry, London. A nation of fliers had found its wings. Guernica symbolized its potent invincibility.

Only history, in the phrase of John Wheeler-Bennett in its "incalculable variations in the tempo of events," would endow it with fuller tragic significance.

BOOK I
Blitzkrieg

Whoever lights the torch of war in Europe can wish for nothing but chaos.

—ADOLF HITLER

2

SCHRECKLICHKEIT

Hardly thirty feet above the fog-enshrouded ground the *Kette* of three Junkers 87B Stukas roared through the slumbrous countryside. Their engines resonating through the river valley, they looked like three ugly predatory birds with gaping jawlike radiators, contorted, splayed wings, and taloned undercarriages. Dangerously close to the earth because of the fog, the *Kette,* led by Oberleutnant Bruno Dilley of Stuka Geschwader 1, sought out its target.

Only minutes before they had taken off from their advance base at Elbing to find the bridges over the Vistula River at Dirschau. They were not, as they had in Spain, to destroy the bridges. Instead they were to keep them open to enable the German Third Army in East Prussia to join with the Fourth Army moving in from the west through the Polish Corridor. The bridges were a crucial supply and transportation link and, it was known, they had been mined by the Poles in the event of a German attack. Once the alarm was given the bridges would be blown and the fine timetable of conquest would be upset.

Dilley's problem was to sever the wires which lay in the left embankment of the Vistula at Dirschau. The fog and the darkness, for it was barely dawn of Friday, September 1, 1939, did not make the mission an easy one. There were trees to skirt and landmarks to seek which disconcertingly slipped past or disappeared in a patch of fog before they

could be properly identified. At least the river was in the right place. For an instant Dilley saw the indistinct forms of the bridges emerging from the mist. Snapping his head from left to right, he noted that the others had seen the bridges also. He kicked the rudder and leveled at the left embankment. It would be a low-level attack, not the classic Stuka peel-off and screeching dive, as Dilley, followed by the other two pilots, plunged at the riverbank, released his bombs, and pulled up in as steep a climb as possible. The engine whined in near protest and that sound was coupled with the explosions. The rear gunners in the Stukas watched as the earth shook and erupted in a gush of smoke and dust.

Dilley glanced at his wristwatch: four thirty-four.

They had begun the Second World War eleven minutes ahead of schedule. It was a portent of things to come. Further: although they had hit their target and had, indeed, snapped the wires leading to the explosive charges on the bridges, the Poles had succeeded, by six-thirty, in blowing one of the spans which sagged into the Vistula. By then the war had officially begun.

The "incident" which had justified the unleashing of *Fall Weiss* ("Case White," the code term for the attack on Poland) had already been staged. On August 31 Hitler issued his "Directive No. 1 for the Conduct of War." Classified as "Most Secret," it read (in part):

1. Now that all political possibilities of disposing by peaceful means of a situation on the Eastern Frontier which is intolerable for Germany are exhausted, I have determined on a solution by force.

2. The attack on Poland is to be carried out in accordance with the preparations made for *Fall Weiss,* with the alterations which result, where the Army is concerned, from the fact that it has, in the meantime, almost completed its dispositions.

   Allotment of tasks and the operational target remain unchanged.

The date of attack: 1 September 1939.

Time of attack: 04:45 [written in red pencil].
This time also applies to the operation at Gdynia, Bay of Danzig, and the Dirschau Bridge.

3. In the west it is important that the responsibility for the opening of hostilities should rest unequivocally with England and France. At first, purely local action should be taken against insignificant frontier violations.

—Adolf Hitler

Harbinger of war: three—a Kette—Stukas *such as began the Second World War in the early morning of September 1, 1939.* (U. S. AIR FORCE)

Terror of the battlefield: with engine whining and propeller screeching, the very sound of the Stuka was frightening as it dived to release its bombs.

(U. S. AIR FORCE)

In his proclamation to the Armed Forces issued on the following day, Hitler stated that "Several acts of frontier violation, which cannot be tolerated by a great power, show that Poland is no longer prepared to respect the Reich's frontiers. To put an end to this madness, I can see no other way but from now on to meet force with force."

He was right about the madness. At the German city of Gleiwitz, for example, Polish troops attacked the radio station in the early evening of August 31. An excited voice interrupted the broadcast and shouted over the air that the time had come for war between Poland and Germany. The sound of shots could be heard also. When the foreign press members were taken to Gleiwitz the next morning they saw about a dozen bodies strewn about the area of the radio station—all in Polish Army uniforms.

They were, of course, dead Germans, condemned criminals who had been promised freedom if they participated in the "incident" and escaped. But even that possibility had been considered: all of the Germans had been fatally injected before the attack on the radio station. The SS leader of the operation, Alfred Naujocks, saw to it that those men who fell unconscious from the lethal drug rather than to gunfire were properly inflicted with gunshot wounds for the visiting newsmen. The entire operation had been planned under the direction of Hitler and Heinrich Himmler, leader of the SS. Polish uniforms and small arms had been supplied through the efforts of General Wilhelm Keitel, Chief of the Armed Forces, and Admiral Wilhelm Canaris, head of German Intelligence. While neither approved, neither did they object to Hitler's plans—which were known to them early in August.

II

It was not to the professional minds of Keitel and Canaris an honorable means of making war, but all this was overlooked in the spectacular thrust of the German blitzkrieg into Poland. It was a kind of war which neither understood—just as neither understood Hitler. Canaris, however, was not the toady that Keitel was (a subservient sycophancy earned him the nickname among his fellow officers of *Lakaitel,* "Lackey"). In fact, Canaris was one of the earliest of the German conspirators who hoped to rid the Reich of Hitler. His conspiracies eventually cost him his life; but on the morning of September 1 Canaris visualized an even greater price when, with tears in his eyes, he said, "This means the end of Germany."

It was a characteristic exclamation, for the professional soldiers had little faith in the war that Hitler had unleashed against their better military judgment. But when Hitler ignited "the torch of war in Europe" the stunning advance of the Wehrmacht behind the Panzer divisions and the Luftwaffe's seemingly ubiquitous Stukas heartened the German generals as much as they shocked a breathless world. All along the German-Polish frontier the wheels of the German juggernaut ground into action. Laughing young, blond soldiers snapped the wooden frontier barrier gates—or smashed through

Hitler's chief military aide, Field Marshal Wilhelm Keitel, whose major function was to agree with Hitler's contributions to the military art. His own final contribution to the war was being present at the surrender ceremonies when the war was over; later he was hanged for his role in the war.

(U. S. OFFICE OF WAR INFORMATION)

in tanks. The Luftwaffe struck at Polish airfields, railroads, and communications lines, crippling aerial defenses from the beginning and rendering troop movements all but impossible.

In Berlin, Hitler watched the blitzkrieg on a massive battle map: the plan, he knew, was foolproof. Two Army Groups were smashing across the Polish plains toward Warsaw. Army Group North, composed of two armies—the Fourth, which flowed eastward from Pomerania across the Polish Corridor and then would turn south for Warsaw; and the Third, which struck westward from East Prussia toward the Polish Corridor, where, it was hoped, on meeting with the Fourth Army, it would race southward to the Polish capital. Attached to Army Group North, under command of General Feder von Bock, was Luftflotte 1, (Air Fleet 1) under Albert Kesselring, who had served as Luftwaffe Chief of Staff immediately after the death of Walther Wever.

Army Group South (Gerd von Rundstedt) was also to push toward Warsaw in a northwesterly direction through Slovakia and Silesia with its three

Hans Jeschonnek, Chief of Staff of the Luftwaffe when the Second World War began. Like many of the Luftwaffe's top echelon, Jeschonnek had been trained at the secret German Air Force center in Russia. A devoted admirer of Hitler, Jeschonnek (who once even begged Hitler to assume command of the Luftwaffe) was unpopular with his immediate chief, Göring.
(NATIONAL ARCHIVES)

armies, the Eighth, Tenth, and Fourteenth. These units were supported by Luftflotte 4 under Alexander Loehr, former commander of the Austrian Air Force, which had been absorbed into the Luftwaffe via Hitler's infamous *Anschluss* in 1938. Chief of Staff of the Luftwaffe was the youthful—forty years old—able Hans Jeschonnek, "graduate" of the school at Lipesk in Soviet Russia, an ardent admirer of Göring, a devotee of Hitler, and an advocate of the high-speed medium bomber and the Stuka.

The two Air Fleets (Luftflotten) were virtually self-sufficient air forces whose components were made up of assorted aircraft types for various assignments as well as antiaircraft batteries (*Flugabwehrkanone*=air defense gun, or more simply *Flak*). The *Geschwader,* the basic tactical unit of the Luftwaffe, took its name from the type of aircraft which

Albert Kesselring, commander of Luftflotte 1 during the Polish blitzkrieg. (H. J. NOWARRA)

The Polish fighter, PZL-11 (for Panstwowe Zaklady Lotnicze-State Aircraft Factory). Designed by Zygmunt Pulawski in the early 1930s, the PZL-11 represented Poland's first line fighter against the Luftwaffe in 1939. (NATIONAL ARCHIVES)

comprised it. The level bombers, mainly Heinkel 111s and Dornier 17s, and later Junkers 88s, were designated *Kampfflugzeug;* the fighters, the Messerschmitt 109 (later the Focke-Wulf 190s), were assigned to *Jagdflugzeug Geschwader (JG)*; the so-called "destroyer" aircraft, the twin-engined Messerschmitt 110 fighter, were termed *Zerstörerflugzeug.* The Junkers 87, and other dive bombers, which included, in the initial days of the war, the Henschel 123, were assigned to *Sturzkampfflugzeug Geschwader (StG)*.

When the war erupted Kesselring's Air Fleet 1 had roughly 800 aircraft with which to support Army Group North (500 level bombers, 180 dive bombers, and 120 fighters). In the south Loehr's Air Fleet 4 had slightly less than 600 planes (310 bombers, 160 dive bombers, and 120 fighters). The Luftflotten total in the east was about 1390 planes (excluding reconnaissance and transport aircraft), which is considerably less than the number generally given as the Luftwaffe strength at the time. In brief, the Luftwaffe was a good close-support air force for

the short war Hitler had in mind; he was hoping too that the French and English would permit him to settle "the Polish question" as they had all the other demands since the *Anschluss,* with little interference.

Compared to the less than second-rate Polish Air Force, the Luftwaffe was indeed a powerful Goliath. The total number of planes in the entire Polish Air Force was slightly over five hundred, of which less than half could be called modern. Even that figure tended toward excessive optimism. There were only thirty-six first-rank bombers, the PZL-37, the *Los* ("Elk"), available to combat squadrons on September 1, 1939. These were used to bomb advancing German armored divisions. The Elk was effective, and the Poles attacked with ferocious courage, but the small band was easily overwhelmed by both numbers and the superior performance of the German fighters.

The backbone of the Polish aerial defense force was the attractive gull-winged PZL-11c—the *Jedenastka* (the "Eleventh"). A product of the State

The Messerschmitt 109E, formidable opponent of the Polish Air Force in 1939. This plane was that of Adolf Galland, one of Germany's outstanding fighter pilots and air commanders. (H. J. NOWARRA)

Contrary to legend, the Polish Air Force was not destroyed on the ground in the opening days of the war. PZLs were dispersed to emergency airfields and camouflaged; Polish pilots succeeded in destroying about sixty German aircraft before the Polish Air Force was wiped out, most of it in air fighting with the superior Me-109s.

(EMBASSY OF THE POLISH PEOPLE'S REPUBLIC)

A Polish road after the Stukas had finished with it.
(EMBASSY OF THE POLISH PEOPLE'S REPUBLIC)

Aircraft Factory (Panstwowe Zaklady Lotnicze, whence the PZL), the P-11, with its fixed landing gear, high wing, struts, and inferior top speed (about 240 miles per hour as compared with the Me-109's 300), was all but obsolete when the war began. Nor could the little fighters climb to the German bomber altitudes to intercept. In all there were about 158 first-line fighter planes in the Polish Air Force when the Germans struck. Of these there were 128 P-11s and 30 of the more outdated P-7s. Even if the Luftwaffe did not contain multitudes, it did easily outnumber the Polish Air Force around ten to one.

Contrary to the widely held belief, the Polish Air Force was not wiped out on the ground. Long before the tanks began to roll and the Stukas began swooping down on the airfields, the Polish planes were moved to well-camouflaged emergency airstrips. While serious damage was done to the runways, hangars, and the planes left behind, what there was of the Polish Air Force was generally untouched by the strafing attacks and dive-bombing.

The first German plane to fall in the Second World War was a Ju-87 Stuka brought down by Lieutenant W. Gnys (who would later serve in the Royal Air Force's No. 302, "Polish," Squadron in the Battle of Britain) piloting a P-11 of the Second Air Regiment, based at Krakow. Despite the victories it was a hopeless battle and typical of the Polish defense. On the ground Polish horse cavalry charged German tanks and armored cars with sword and lances. The cavalry was decimated from the air also when the Stukas attacked men and horses in the vicinity of Wielun, leaving behind an unreal devastation of dead and dying, smoke, flame, and futility. These were delaying tactics—for the blitzkrieg did not always plunge ahead inexorably—and they were disturbing. Heinz Guderian, commanding a Panzer corps, tells of how a section of his advance was held up by a Polish bicycle company. But these were fugitive and tragic efforts. On Hitler's large-scale map, safe in Berlin, the blitzkrieg moved ahead with breath-taking speed.

As the Poles were pushed back from the frontier they retreated inward toward Warsaw, creating pockets of potential resistance in the vicinity of Posen, Lodz, Krakow, and Przemysl. The roads were choked with retreating soldiers and fleeing refugees. Swarms of Stukas screamed down to bomb

Stuka fodder: a Polish girl weeps over her dead sister after the Ju-87s have swept by.

and strafe the highways in another Teutonic contribution to "the art of war," *Schrecklichkeit* (frightfulness). The roads disintegrated into a massive chaos of terror. The great Nazi steam roller crushed all before it, Polish mobilization was stopped before it had really begun, and resistance was dissipated haphazardly along the frontier or in encircled pockets. With no reserves to call upon the Polish Army was overrun by the panzers, motorized infantry, and the booted German Wehrmacht.

All roads led to Warsaw, which was the last stronghold and the prime target. Göring had had to cancel Operation Seaside, the full-scale attack on Warsaw scheduled for September 1, because of the fog which interfered with the aerial operations in the Army Group North area. The Warsaw-Okiecie airfield, home of PZL factories, was bombed by a few He-111s despite the early morning mist. By the late afternoon the weather had cleared enough for more intensive attacks by He-111s and Stukas. *Kampfgeschwader* 27, named for the World War I hero Oswald Boelcke, flew nearly five hundred miles from northern German bases for the first really heavy bombardment of Warsaw. Escorting the bombers were the *Zerstörer,* the Messerschmitt 110, the so-called "strategic fighter" or "destroyer." It was

Veteran of the Spanish Civil War and erstwhile passenger plane, the He-111 looses bombs on Warsaw.

Destruction on the Bzura River. Luftwaffe bombers spared Warsaw momentarily to smash a counteroffensive by the Polish Posen Army, delaying the blitzkrieg. Luftwaffe close support broke the Polish offensive, with the Stukas wreaking the havoc in this photograph.

(EMBASSY OF THE POLISH PEOPLE'S REPUBLIC)

Warsaw, September 25, 1939, bombed out of the war by the Luftwaffe. An He-111 sweeps in to add its bombs to the already burning city.

(EMBASSY OF THE POLISH PEOPLE'S REPUBLIC)

during these attacks on Warsaw that the first air battles of any size occurred between the Luftwaffe and the Polish Air Force. The Polish P-11s climbed in vain to reach the bombers; the Me-110s dived to intercept, the Polish fighters darted away. In a matter of minutes five of the P-11s had tumbled to the ground. In the few short weeks of fighting a total of 116 Polish fighters were destroyed in combat (of these 11 fell to antiaircraft fire, German as well as Polish). Some PZLs were lost when their pilots, in desperation, rammed the German aircraft to bring them down.

But nothing held up the German advance. Within a week the panzers of Walther von Reichenau's Tenth Army (of Army Group South) approached the outskirts of Warsaw. By this time the Polish Air Force had been all but completely expended; most of the first-line aircraft had been lost in the savage, one-sided dogfights. Almost as devastating was the supply problem, for without replacement parts and fuel the planes could not fly; communications, too, had been so disrupted that all military command broke down. Only a few of the Elk bombers continued to operate for a few days and then those remaining and the operational PZLs were ordered to Rumania. By September 17, 1939, the air war in Poland was over.

On that day the Soviet Army marched from the east to seal the fate of Poland. The Red Army met even weaker resistance than the Germans had; the Poles that had escaped the German envelopments were pushed back into the Nazi pincers or were captured by the Russians. With neither an army nor an air force, Poland was finished as a fighting power. "The German Luftwaffe," the Wehrmacht report stated, "has won undisputed mastery over the whole of Poland."

But Warsaw remained, crowded with refugees and fleeing soldiers whose officers rallied to a last-ditch defense. The encircled city became a honeycomb of trenches and improvised barricades as civilians and troops alike prepared for the German attack. The government had already fled to Lublin, and then into Rumania—and internment. By September 13 Operation Seaside, the aerial devastation of Warsaw, was reinstated. In the train of the onrushing German troops, the Luftwaffe had set up temporary airstrips within easy striking distance of the capital.

The first sizable air raid occurred on September 13 when Wolfram von Richthofen ordered an attack on military targets—rail centers, public utilities, military establishments—within the city. Later Richthofen was to say that the "chaos over the target was indescribable." The first major aerial attack of the Second World War was not, by German standards, very worthy of those high standards which they had been demonstrating for the past two weeks to a stunned and frightened world. The bombing timetable went awry and various units came in over Warsaw haphazardly. With more than 180 aircraft converging on the target area there were collisions and confusion. But to the terrorized Poles below it was not confusion of command and timing, but a sky filled with aircraft dropping bombs.

Following this attack, Warsaw was given some respite from the air when the bombers were called off to assist the German Eighth and Tenth Armies under pressure of an offensive suddenly launched by the Polish Posen Army, which had been bypassed during the first week of the war. While the Stukas and He-111s and Me-110s were dealing with the Poles in the Bzura River fighting, the dropping of leaflets pleading for the Poles to surrender began fluttering down upon Nazi-encircled Warsaw. Posters soon appeared upon buildings and trees in Warsaw's outskirts promising those who surrendered food and good treatment. But the pleas went unheeded and all attempts by the Germans to propagandize the Poles into surrendering Warsaw "to prevent useless bloodshed and the destruction of the city" failed. The Poles had already witnessed sufficient German frightfulness along their highways, in the villages and towns, and in some Warsaw suburbs to realize the propaganda promises were delusion. They chose to fight to the end. Those who survived had worse than death in store for them. Behind the Wehrmacht into Poland came Dr. Robert Ley, ex-chemist, alcoholic, and chief of the German Labor Front, who believed that "Germans can never live in the same condition as Poles and Jews." And as he conscripted slaves for German industry, he was as good as his word.

On the day that the Russians began moving upon Poland, September 17, the first real mass attack on Warsaw was canceled when it appeared that the Poles were willing to negotiate for the evacuation of civilians and foreigners. The Polish representative did not appear to negotiate. With the Russians

Warsaw after the air blitzkrieg by Richthofen's bombers. ". . . everything was quiet. Warsaw was a dead city."

swarming in from the east, it was even more important to the Germans that Warsaw fall. For the next several days, until September 24, millions of leaflets rained down upon the beleaguered city promising honorable surrender terms—officers would even be permitted to keep their swords!

At eight o'clock in the morning, September 25, Richthofen unleashed the Luftwaffe upon Warsaw. At his disposal were 8 *Gruppen* (240 aircraft) of the Ju-87 Stukas, some He-111s, and a *Gruppe* of the clumsy Junkers 52 transports. In all Richthofen had about 400 aircraft to deal with Warsaw (the usual accepted number has been 800), not an im-

pressive number once again. But never before in the world's history had 400 planes attacked a single city. Here was the sequel to Guernica modernized, refined, and revised according to the concept of *Schrecklichkeit*. Flying two or three sorties through the day, Richthofen's forces were magnified into a massive destructive weapon.

The Stukas began with their familiar shriek, unleashing their bomb loads into the city. Thirty Ju-52s flew low over Warsaw to deliver the incendiaries into the churning clouds of flame, debris, mortar dust, and smoke. These clumsy craft were not ideally suited for their assignment; the incendiary bombs

General Wolfram von Richthofen (center foreground), cousin of the intrepid Red Baron of the First World War and Stuka specialist of the Second. Although originally cool to the idea of dive bombers, Richthofen learned to use them in Spain and then employed the Stukas with devastating skill in Poland. To his left is General Richard Ruoff, whose V Corps troops Richthofen's dive bombers supported in the conquest of France which came later. (HEINZ J. NOWARRA)

were literally shoveled out of their large side entrances (these were specifically for paratrooper use). The lumbering trimotored aircraft were slow and at least two fell to Polish antiaircraft fire. Also, the method of delivering the bombs did not make for accuracy, for thanks to a strong eastern wind, some of the incendiaries fell among German troops. An

immediate demand was made by Eighth Army headquarters for the cessation of the bombing, but Hitler, who had flown to the battle zone in his own Ju-52, instructed Richthofen to continue over the protests of Brauchitsch.

By late morning Warsaw lay under a pillar of smoke that coiled up thousands of feet into the air. And still the bombers came, although it was practically impossible to find specific targets because of the smoke and destruction. By nightfall five hundred tons of high-explosive bombs and seventy-two tons of incendiaries had been dropped into Warsaw. To this was added the massed artillery which encircled the city. After the planes had left the artillery continued.

The red glare of Warsaw's flames could be seen for miles around, as German and Pole alike stood in awe of what the bloody glow in the sky signified. On the next day Warsaw agreed to surrender; food had all but run out, the water supply was ruptured, and ammunition had been expended. The defenders of Warsaw officially capitulated on September 27, 1939. In less than a month Hitler's blitzkrieg had erased Poland, with the help of the accommodating Soviet Army, from the map.

Walter Schellenberg, a young SS intelligence officer, entered what remained of Warsaw and "was shocked at what had become of the beautiful city I had known—ruined and burnt-out houses, starving and grieving people. The nights were already unpleasantly chilly and a pall of dust and smoke hung over the city, and everywhere there was the sweetish smell of burnt flesh. There was no running water anywhere. In one or two streets isolated resistance was being continued. Elsewhere everything was quiet. Warsaw was a dead city."

Tomorrow the world.

3

"SITZKRIEG"

Forty-eight hours after Hitler had launched his blitzkrieg, Great Britain and France submitted their ultimatums to Berlin. Hitler still had hopes for a swift, tidy German-Polish war to be followed by a breathing spell before he made his next move. But the determined British and the reluctant French had decided to honor their promise to fight if Germany violated the independence of Poland. The policy of appeasement had come to an end and on Sunday afternoon, September 3, 1939, the tired voice of Neville Chamberlain informed the world that Britain had declared war upon Germany to fight against "brute force, bad faith, injustice, oppression and persecution."

When Göring learned of the British ultimatum, delivered at nine in the morning by Nevile Henderson, he exclaimed (echoing the view of Canaris), "If we lose this war, then God help us!"

Hitler's solution to "the Polish question" had now become the Second World War. His partner in the "Pact of Steel," Mussolini, backed down at the last moment and informed Hitler that he could not take part in military operations "in view of the *present* state of Italian war preparations."

If Hitler was unable to count upon Mussolini, he had found a worthy ally in Stalin, with whom he had had the audacious foresight to make a Treaty of Non-Aggression (Nazi-Soviet Pact) before embarking upon the Polish adventure. Thus had Hitler spared his nervous High Command the terrors of

Zweifrontenkrieg (war on two fronts). Thanks to his prescience Hitler had turned this double-front war upon the Poles and the campaign had gone smoothly and at a reasonably small cost. This may have been small comfort to the families of the 13,-981 Germans killed in the Polish invasion and of little strategic import to the 30,322 maimed and wounded. The Polish casualty figures because of the savage fighting, confusion, and destruction may never be known. As for the Luftwaffe, it had lost 734 men and 285 aircraft, over a hundred of which were bombers.

After the partition of Poland by Germany and Russia the period followed which Neville Chamberlain called fittingly a "twlight war" and which many Americans referred to cruelly as the "phony war" (a phrase attributed to the isolationist Senator William E. Borah). Following the devastation of Poland there came a strange pause in the blitzkrieg, a sitting war, or "sitzkrieg," in the press. Along the Western Front it was quiet indeed. Neither the Germans nor the Allies seemed anxious to make the first move. The mood in a still invulnerable America was observed, sadly, by Undersecretary of State Sumner Welles, who found that "many people appeared to feel, like Senator Borah, that the failure of Great Britain and France to undertake the offensive was somehow reprehensible. This feeling was almost sadistic."

Nor were the Germans eager to go on the of-

Hitler and Luftwaffe chief Göring in Poland, September 1939, to survey the results of the blitzkrieg. It was a high moment for both, for Hitler's Fall Weiss had succeeded in answering "the Polish question" and the Luftwaffe had contributed to the bloody solution. (H. J. NOWARRA)

fensive. Just two days before he unleashed *Fall Weiss* Hitler had said, "In two months Poland will be finished and then we shall have a great peace conference with the Western powers." But it had not turned out that way—and besides, the High Command did not feel ready to launch a western offensive. Most seemed to agree with the Commander in Chief of Army Group C (which faced the French opposite the Rhine and the Maginot Line), Wilhelm Ritter von Leeb, who wrote, "The sword does not have the edge which the Führer seems to assume." Leeb had in mind the great number of less than first-rate (older men, ill trained) troops under his command, some of whom were already muttering, "It is the generals who push the war."

But the generals were not pushing the war; even Hitler, speaking is Berlin on October 6, 1939—the day after he had entered a wasted Warsaw—appeared to be pushing peace. "Every German soldier," he told the Reichstag and the world, "has the greatest respect for the feats of the French

Army. At no time and in no place have I ever acted contrary to British interests." He continued with a statement of his aims by saying that his "chief endeavor has been to rid our relations with France of all trace of ill will . . ." and that he fervently believed "even today that there can only be real peace in Europe and throughout the world if Germany came to an understanding . . ."

But when he came to the crux of their misunderstanding, Hitler took another stance. "Why should this war in the west be fought?" he asked. "For the restoration of Poland? Poland of the Versailles Treaty will never rise again." He reminded his listeners that this was assured by Nazi Germany and Soviet Russia. Despite what German newspapers called "Hitler's Peace Offer," the speech contained nothing upon which negotiations could be initiated. Hitler closed with a veiled warning. "And let those who consider war to be the better solution reject my outstretched hand."

It was, as usual, the iron fist in the velvet glove, for ten days previously he had already instructed

A French poilu in the spring of 1940, dug in on the Western Front, during the period described as the "phony war." Writing home, the soldier evokes the stagnation of trench warfare of the First World War. That he does not bother to wear a steel helmet is an indication of the general air of non-belligerence of the time. (U. S. INFORMATION AGENCY)

the Wehrmacht High Command to formulate plans for an early attack in the west, an attack that would strike through neutral Belgium and Holland. The generals were thrown into alarmed opposition. They argued that the steel shortage would seriously affect the outcome of a prolonged war—especially as it concerned the production of aircraft—and that the approaching winter, with its short days and certain fog, would interfere with air support. This argument went on for months between the Army High Command on one side and the Führer on the other during the so-called phony war.

II

During this period, however, there was no phony war at sea, where the German U-boats sank British merchant ships, or where the German pocket battleship *Graf Spee,* after a successful career as the scourge of the south Atlantic, was found by the British Navy and driven into the port of Montevideo, Uruguay, where the German captain scuttled his ship and committed suicide.

Also during the period of Hitler's "command crisis," his partner in war Stalin began activities in the Baltic regions to close off the northern approaches to the Soviet Union. "Treaties" were forced upon Estonia, Latvia, and Lithuania which agreed to the establishment of Russian garrisons, as well as naval and air bases in the Baltic states. Finland, however, refused to be bullied into a treaty. The Russians demanded a strip of the Karelian Isthmus, connecting Finland and the Soviet Union, from which it would be possible to shell Leningrad. In addition, there was the port of Hangö, which the Russians had wanted for thirty years as a naval base. In exchange the Russians would happily cede more than two thousand square miles to Finland along their common frontier. Finland found such demands incompatible with their definition of national sovereignty and neutrality. The predictable ensued: attacks in *Pravda,* broken-off negotiations, and border incidents in which the Finns were cast as villains. On November 30, 1939, Russian bombers attacked Viipuri and Helsinki.

The Winter War of 1939–40 was no blitzkrieg. Although greatly outnumbered, the Finns fought

The Graf Spee, *one of the most formidable of Germany's small battleships which operated in the south Atlantic in the winter of 1939. A float plane is in readiness on a catapult aft of the stack. Damaged in a battle* with British cruisers off South America and unable to escape, the ship was scuttled by its own crew. The captain, Hans Langsdorff, after writing a letter of explanation, committed suicide. (NATIONAL ARCHIVES)

grimly and imaginatively in the cold, heavily forested terrain. Entire Russian divisions were wiped out in the ghostly, white landscapes. But the Russian masses, tanks, and aircraft, and in time, better leadership, made the difference. The Treaty of Moscow was signed on March 12, 1940. The northern approaches to the Soviet Union were secured at great cost: at least 200,000 Russian dead and nearly 25,000 Finnish dead. It was another deadly move in the massive chess game between the two master dictators. Hitler, despite German sympathies for Finland and Mussolini's outspoken criticism of the German-Soviet Pact, needed Russian aid to circumvent the British blockade. It was still a one-front war—even though Russian naval and air bases in the Baltic could only have an eventual, and obvious, function. Stalin trusted Hitler no more than Hitler trusted Stalin.

Hitler, in fact, during these uncertain months of the "twilight war," could hardly have felt much trust in anyone whether ally, friend, or foe. Using the bad weather as justification he continued to postpone the attack in the west while goading his generals to prepare a blueprint for such an attack and to agree to carry it out. By early January it seemed that he would have his way. With clear weather forecast by midmonth, the day of attack was set (for at least the sixth time) for January 17. But then, for even the gods of war have been known to laugh, another hitch in plans came about.

Luftwaffe Major Helmut Reinberger, commander of the paratrooper school at Stendal, was summoned to assist in the planning of air-borne operations in Holland and Belgium. He was on his way to meet with Kurt Student's staff in Cologne but was held up by the congestion in the Ruhr area railways. In Münster he met a Luftwaffe major, Erich Hoenmanns, in the officers' club and explained his problem. Hoenmanns, eager to visit his wife in Cologne, offered to fly Reinberger to his conference the next morning—January 10. Although he was not supposed to fly while carrying highly secret documents, Reinberger was anxious to be on his way.

They took off the next morning in a Messerschmitt 108, the *Taifun* ("Typhoon"), a prewar sportplane converted into a courier and personal transport. The major was familiar with neither the craft nor, apparently, the route. For in the clouds the little monoplane with the two passengers became lost and off

course. In attempting to find his way Hoenmanns inadvertently flicked the wrong switch and turned off the engine.

There was nothing to do but crash-land the *Taifun* near the Rhine River, which Hoenmanns found below the clouds. Except that it was the Meuse, not the Rhine, and they were not in Germany, but in neutral Belgium near Mechelen-sur-Meuse.

When Belgian soldiers arrived at the crash scene they found Reinberger attempting to burn the contents of his briefcase. The fire was stamped out and Reinberger and the hapless Hoenmanns, as well as what remained of the papers, were taken to a nearby army camp. There, too, Reinberger attempted to destroy the papers, which had been placed upon a convenient table, by tossing them into an equally convenient stove. But again the incriminating documents were retrieved from total destruction. Reinberger was certain, as he later reported to Göring, that all that remained were "insignificant fragments, the size of the palm of my hand." He would, naturally, have been most anxious to make that point.

But how much of the papers actually remained? One thing was certain: copies of the fragments which escaped Reinberger's frenetic pyromania were sent to the British and French. There was consternation in all camps. The Germans could not be sure that Reinberger had really succeeded in destroying enough of the evidence. On the other hand, had the Germans, wise war makers that they were, deliberately let the papers fall into the hands of the Belgians? The Allies tended to overestimate the German penchant for adroit skulduggery and leaned toward the latter interpretation. Even the Belgians, who would be among the first to suffer if the plans materialized, did not take the papers seriously enough. Mobilization of the Belgian Army was accelerated, but there was no attempt to unite with the British and French, however, to face the inevitable.

The conferences in Berlin meanwhile were desperate, clouded with doubt and clamorous. Hitler affected an icy calm, always a dangerous sign. Göring, embarrassed by his Luftwaffe, ranted and swore dire retribution. However, it devolved upon Colonel General Alfred Jodl, Chief of the Wehrmacht's Operations Staff, and Hitler's military "adviser" Keitel to determine the next move depending upon how much they thought the Belgians—and the French and British—had learned. The situation was characteristically manic-depressive. One moment all agreed that Reinberger had burned the plans and the next moment they were not so certain. Word had reached Berlin of Belgian troop movements along the frontier. Three days after the incident Jodl noted that a decision had been made: "Order to General Halder [Chief of the Army General Staff] by telephone—All movements to stop."

The Führer was unperturbed (he now had an excuse for another postponement which he could blame on others) as Göring unleashed his vendetta. General Helmuth Felmy, commander of Luftflotte 2, to which Reinberger belonged, and Oberst Josef Kammhuber, his Chief of Staff, were immediately relieved. Felmy, never a Göring favorite, was retired to civil life (though he would later be recalled to serve in Russia) and Kammhuber was sent to Bavaria to command a bomber unit. Kesselring, at the time commanding Luftflotte 1, replaced Felmy.

III

With the attack in the west postponed until the spring (for the weather, too, had turned against the Germans), Hitler turned his eyes northward. The Russians had moved into Finland; it seemed that inevitably the Allies would also invade Scandinavia to cut off that line of approach. Hitler resolved to "save" Norway and Denmark from such a drastic fate. There was the matter, too, of Sweden's supply of iron ore, upon which the German war economy depended so heavily. Equally consequential was the point raised by that stepchild of the Wehrmacht the German Navy. Grossadmiral Erich Raeder insisted that the Imperial Navy could make something of itself if it could operate from bases in Norway, say at Trondheim and Narvik, instead of being bottled up in the North Sea by the Royal Navy.

When Raeder brought up the proposal for a Scandinavian campaign Hitler was in a receptive mood. If he had any fleeting doubts, these were quickly resolved by the doughty and resourceful British.

The auxiliary supply ship *Altmark,* which had been attached to the scuttled *Graf Spee,* had made its way up from the south Atlantic and had slipped through the British blockade into Norwegian waters.

Grand Admiral Erich Raeder, in a prewar portrait. Anxious to make a name for the German Navy, Raeder pressed for an invasion of Norway and Denmark—a move which nearly cost him his fleet. He was later succeeded by Karl Dönitz. (U. S. INFORMATION AGENCY)

The British knew that the *Altmark* carried captured British seamen, survivors of the encounters with the *Graf Spee.* Agents in Norway reported the presence of the *Altmark* and a Lockheed *Hudson* of the RAF's Coastal Command Squadron No. 220 was dispatched to confirm. The *Altmark* was located and soon a British destroyer flotilla converged on the German ship. A Norwegian boarding party inspected the *Altmark* and assured the skeptical British that the German ship was unarmed and carried no prisoners. Winston Churchill, First Lord of the Admiralty, ordered Captain Philip Vian of H.M.S. *Cossack* and commander of the British flotilla, to board the German vessel.

It was night, February 16, 1940, and the *Altmark* had taken refuge in Josing Fiord. With searchlights blazing, the *Cossack,* with Vian aboard, lanced into the narrow inlet. The Norwegian gunboat *Kjell* was first encountered and, with a nod to international law, Captain Vian invited its captain to join him in a search of the *Altmark;* pointedly the British captain made it clear that he intended to board the German ship and release the prisoners he knew were aboard but which the Norwegians apparently could not find. There was no further intervention on the part of the Norwegians.

The *Cossack* then pulled alongside the *Altmark,* which had grounded itself in an escape attempt, the ships were grappled, and a boarding party swarmed over the side. It was like a page out of the career of Francis Drake. There were hand-to-hand combats in which four Germans were killed, several wounded, and a number fled over the side. To the cries of "The Navy's here!" the 299 "non-existent" British seamen were released from locked storerooms and empty oil tanks. In addition to the prisoners Vian also noted several guns, overlooked by

Vidkun Quisling, Norwegian fascist leader, whose name became a synonym for traitor. Quisling assisted the Germans in their invasion of Norway in 1940. Under Nazi occupation Quisling served as premier; after the war he was tried, convicted, and executed for high treason. (NATIONAL ARCHIVES)

the Norwegians, who remained, in the words of Churchill, "passive observers throughout."

Three days later Hitler, who could not remain passive in view of the British resolution, ordered final plans for the "occupation" of Denmark and Norway. "This operation," he stated in a directive dated March 1, 1940, "should prevent British encroachment in Scandinavia and the Baltic. Further it should guarantee our ore bases in Sweden and give our Navy and Air Force a wider starting line against Britain."

Meanwhile the Allies had also been giving serious thought to the strategic importance of Norway and its northern port, Narvik. It was there that Swedish ore was sent via rail for shipment through the North Sea when the Baltic was closed by winter ice. There had even been a plan during the Russo-Finnish War to send troops to help the Finns through Narvik and across Sweden. This raised the question of transit rights across these two neutral countries which the Allies did not actually need to face; the surrender of Finland in March of 1940 made it all academic. Rumors of Allied intentions had already reached Hitler, some through the Norwegian Nazi Vidkun Quisling. Clearly aid to Finland would cut off the Swedish ore, for the English and French would occupy Narvik and the railroad from Narvik to Luleå, Sweden. But the collapse of Finland spoiled Hitler's rationale as well as that of the Allies.

Each side, however, continued with some course of action. Finally, on the morning of April 8, the English began laying mines in Norwegian waters used by German ore ships. What they did not know was that already German warships were under way up the Norwegian coast and troops were ready to move across the border of Denmark. On April 9 Denmark had become a German province and the Luftwaffe had, as Göring insisted, sites for advance fighter bases and air-warning systems. Because the Scandinavian occupation had been prepared in secrecy Göring for possibly the first time had not been informed of *Weserübung* (the code name for the operation) until it had been all but in final form. Göring, whose relations with the other Wehrmacht services had never been good, did not endear himself further by dominating the first meeting he attended on *Weserübung.* The Field Marshal spent most of his time criticizing the already formulated plans, venting "his spleen" as one attendant noted,

A German soldier examines the wreckage of a Norwegian plane, destroyed by Luftwaffe attacks, at Sola.
Bombed, strafed, invaded by German paratroops followed by air-borne infantry, the great air base fell
into German hands the first day of Hitler's invasion of
Scandinavia, April 9, 1940. (NATIONAL ARCHIVES)

Erhard Milch, former board chairman of Lufthansa
Airlines, and one of the architects of the Luftwaffe. A
shrewd administrator, Milch was a greater asset to the
German Air Force than Göring. He was also ruthless
in dealing with his rivals; at the close of the war he
was a field marshal. (NATIONAL ARCHIVES)

Hans-Jürgen Stumpf, whose Luftflotte 5, operating from
Norwegian bases, effectively harassed the British fleet
in the North Sea and British ground and air forces
that attempted to aid the Norwegians.

(NATIONAL ARCHIVES)

and generally disrupting the conference. As a result some changes were made in the plans, putting
heavier responsibilitites on the Army and Navy,
as well as ascertaining the bases. All of Denmark
was conquered in about five hours. The determi-
nant was the vaunted Luftwaffe, although most of
the country was overrun by ground troops. The
threatened bombardment in the style of Guernica
and Warsaw of Copenhagen ended all Danish resistance.

Norway, also invaded on April 9, was not so
readily overcome. The tiny Norwegian Army fought
gallantly, but the Germans in a carefully prepared
operation succeeded in landing troops in a half-
dozen important coastal cities, from Narvik in the
north to Christiansand in the south. Within hours
the great airfield at Sola, a few miles to the east
of the fishing village Stavanger on the southwest

The Focke-Wulf 200 "Condor" as a Lufthansa airliner in the late 1930s and as converted into a Luftwaffe reconnaissance bomber. The Condor was the only long-range aircraft available to the Luftwaffe when war came, and although not designed as a warplane, it was made into one by adding various gun positions and a ventral gondola under the fuselage, which served as a gun position, and eventually a bombardier's position. Though ill suited to its wartime role, with structural weaknesses, and vulnerable to fighter attack, the Condor proved to be surprisingly effective and earned the name of the "Scourge of the Atlantic" after its introduction in the Norwegian campaign.
(LUFTHANSA PHOTO-IMPERIAL WAR MUSEUM, LONDON)

coast of Norway, was in the hands of the Luftwaffe. Early in the morning a half-dozen Me-110s bombed the machine-gun emplacements at Sola (there were no antiaircraft guns). Paratroopers were then dropped to invest the field to be followed by transports (Ju-52s) carrying infantry battalions and a regimental staff. Meanwhile ships disembarked more troops and supplies in the harbor nearby. By the afternoon Sola was a German airfield.

To assure Luftwaffe prestige Göring sent Milch to command the newly formed Luftflotte 5, a temporary command which Milch held for three weeks when he returned to Germany to turn again to administrative details. Milch was succeeded by General Hans-Jürgen Stumpf. From bases established near Oslo, Christiansand, and Stavanger (Sola), the Luftwaffe operated most effectively against Norwegian and Allied troops as well as Allied shipping. The Focke-Wulf 200, the Condor, once the pride of Lufthansa's fleet, was pressed into active service

Junkers 88, the Luftwaffe's all-purpose aircraft. Its functions ranged from that of its original conception as a fast medium bomber through reconnaissance and fighter plane. Designed in 1936 by a German, W. H. Evers, and an American, Alfred Gassner, the Ju-88 served in the Luftwaffe through the entire war.

(U. S. AIR FORCE)

as an armed long-range reconnaissance aircraft. The first important use of the Junkers 88, flown by Kampfgeschwader 30, occurred during the Scandinavian campaign. The He-111 also was employed as was the now infamous Stuka.

The Allies sent small, ill-equipped reinforcements to engage in courageous but doomed ventures. Landings were made at Namsos, in central Norway, under command of Major General Carton de Wiart. The British forces soon came under heavy Luftwaffe attack and within days after the landings Namsos was bombed into an "unforgettable spectacle" of flame. General de Wiart informed London that he "could see little chance of carrying out decisive, or indeed, any operations unless enemy air activity is considerably restricted." The Luftwaffe continued to command the skies, just as their propaganda vaunted.

The aircraft carriers *Glorious* and *Ark Royal* were called in from the Mediterranean to assist in the delivery of aircraft, particularly fighters whose range would not permit their being flown directly from Britain. Since most of the best airfields were in German hands, the Allies were forced to construct their own airdromes under less than ideal conditions. The snow in one Norwegian airfield was packed down by a herd of several thousand reindeer. Bribed by the

The crew of an He-111 about to set off on a bombing mission. The Heinkel 111, a descendant of the single-engined He-70, was designed by Walter and Siegfried Gunther and first saw service in Spain and continued to be operational beyond its time. (NATIONAL ARCHIVES)

medical officer's pure alcohol, the keeper of the herd, a Laplander, drove the herd over the snow a few times to produce a perfect landing ground.

The British field was located on Lake Lesjaskog, near Aandalsnes in central Norway, where two hundred Norwegian civilians appeared to assist in scraping a runway under two feet of snow. Once prepared, the field was ready for the RAF: No. 263 Squadron dispatched eighteen Gloster Gladiators, the last of the biplane fighters, which took off from the deck of the *Glorious*. Led by a Blackburn Skua, an early Fleet dive bomber, the Gladiators flew through a snow flurry for nearly two hundred miles over unknown terrain and actually found the little icy strip on Lake Lesjaskog. Not long after, the ubiquitous Luftwaffe—Ju-88s and He-111s—appeared. Before the day ended ten of the eighteen Gladiators were out of operation. The planes had landed on April 24; by April 27 their effort was over, the Gladiators burned, and the pilots evacuated. The wreckage of some of the Gladiators may be found in the vicinity of Lake Lesjaskog even today.

In the north, at critical Narvik, the Allies were able to hold out longer because they were, temporarily at least, out of the Luftwaffe's effective range. A few airdromes were hacked out of the ice and forests, the most impressive of which was located at Bardufoss, about fifty miles northeast of Narvik. Once again the runways were created by civilians under the direction of British and Norwegian engineers and Royal Air Force technicians. Under the snow lay a six-inch coating of ice—and under that frozen soil, some of which turned to mud under the direct rays of the feeble sun. Work began on May 4 and by May 21 a great hand-carved network of landing strips, taxiways, and shelters was ready for occupancy. Once again No. 263 Squadron with its new Gladiators alighted in Norway. They were later joined by No. 46 Squadron, equipped with the modern Hawker Hurricane, based at another field near Skaanland, which lay closer to Narvik.

The Allied forces were, by this time, under double stress. Not only had the Germans enlarged their holdings in Norway, which included bases closer to Narvik, but Hitler had brought the "twilight war" on the Western Front to an end. Was holding Norway at great cost worth the risk of losing France?

Two Gladiators of No. 263 Squadron, RAF, camouflaged against German air attack at Aandalsnes, Norway, in the spring of 1940.

(IMPERIAL WAR MUSEUM, LONDON)

Flight Lieutenant Caesar B. Hull of the ill-fated No. 263 Squadron, which lost all of its Gladiators in and around Norway—although only two in combat; the rest were destroyed in operational mishaps, to German attack while on the ground, or, finally, when the aircraft carrier Glorious, *evacuating them from Norway, was sunk by the German Navy. Hull, wounded in the fighting in Norway, had not been aboard the* Glorious. *He returned to England and was killed while serving with No. 43 Squadron during the Battle of Britain.* (IMPERIAL WAR MUSEUM, LONDON)

Besides which, the tide of battle had turned severely against the Allies—British, French, and Polish troops. The air war was characterized by a quality of epic tragedy with overtones of the romance of air fighting in the First World War. In objective fact it was a clash of the past and the present with the outcome preordained.

On May 26 three Gladiators of No. 263 Squadron took off from the airfield at Bardufoss and flew south to a temporary field at Bodø. The three biplanes, led by Flight Lieutenant Caesar Hull, came upon a couple of He-111s which fired shots at the English planes but without inflicting damage. The Gladiators put down in the muddy strip at Bodø. While refueling was going on another He-111 appeared over the field. Lieutenant Anthony Lydekker immediately took off and engaged the Heinkel while Hull and the other pilot, Pilot Officer Jack Falkson, were briefed on their mission.

The Allies were retreating northward up a valley to the east of Bodø in an attempt to get to the sea and back to England. As Hull explained, the troops "were being strafed by the Huns all day." The three Gladiators were to interfere with the strafing.

The Heinkel having been chased off, Lydekker landed to refuel and the three British planes prepared to take off. This in itself was a major chore, for mud gripped at the wheels of the planes the instant they touched down. The stickier spots were covered with flat boards. In his report later Hull did not say that they took off; instead they "came unstuck about fifty yards from the end and just staggered over the trees." Falkson was not so fortunate and his plane crashed in the takeoff. Feeling certain theirs was a doomed mission, Hull ordered Lydekker to land and continued on alone.

"Saw some smoke rising," he reported, "so investigated, and found a Heinkel 111 at about 600 feet. Attacked it three times, and it turned south with smoke pouring from fuselage and engines. Broke off attack to engage a Junkers 52, which crashed in flames. Saw Heinkel 111 flying south, tried to intercept, and failed. Returned and attacked two Junkers 52s in formation. Number one went into clouds, number two crashed in flames after six people had baled out."

After attacking another Heinkel which raced south (toward the German lines) with smoke in its wake, Hull returned to Bodø to rearm. "The troops

Norway 1940: Norwegian skiers watch a Luftwaffe crew bomb-up a Stuka. The pilot waits upon one of the wheel pants. (NATIONAL ARCHIVES)

were cheered by the report," Hull wrote, "and I thought another patrol might produce more fun." It took a good deal of persuasion to convince the officer in charge of the strip to permit another takeoff from the viscous field. But Hull was most convincing, more planks were laid down, and he took off again. "This time the valley was deserted, and the only thing I could do was amuse the troops by doing some aerobatics. They all cheered and waved madly every time I went down low—I think they imagined that at last we had air control and their worries were over. Vain hope!"

That night, alternating in the remaining two Gladiators, the three pilots furnished air cover for the ships carrying the troops out of Norway. Fortunately there were no enemy aircraft aloft at midnight so Hull once again amused the troops by "beating up" the vessels as they left. By morning, however, it was agreed that the Bodø runway could no longer be safely used even with planks covering practically all of it. Also, at eight in the morning a jetty near the airdrome came under attack by Messerschmitt 110s and the Stukas. Only Lydekker succeeded in taking off immediately to save the Gladiator, but by the time he arrived at Bardufoss he was wounded and the plane a write-off.

Hull meanwhile had taken shelter in a barn and

Messerschmitt 109E-3 of Jagdgeschwader 77, based at Nordholz, near Cuxhaven, in northern Germany. JG 77 *played an active role in the Scandinavian campaign, during which it was moved northward to Westerland at Sylt on the North Sea.* (H. J. NOWARRA)

watched the dive-bombing for a while before noting that the field itself was not being attacked. He climbed into his plane and took off, climbed and attacked a Stuka at the bottom of its dive. He may have hit it, for the Ju-87 made off slowly over the sea. At that instant Hull was attacked by another Stuka, the shots shattering his windscreen. The force of impact had stunned Hull and he was "thanking my lucky stars" as he came to—only to hear the sound of guns from behind and the thudding of hits in his aircraft. The Gladiator turned into a right-hand dive, which Hull felt he would not be able to get out of, when at about two hundred feet the plane pulled itself out. Hull quickly gunned the engine to clear an outcropping of rocks in his path. This achieved, he was "discouraged to hear the sound of machine guns from the rear again . . . so gave up hope and decided to get her down."

The glutinous mud of Bodø would have been welcome as the screaming, strained engine pulled the Gladiator into the ground. The landing legs snapped and with a crashing roar and a ripping of fabric Hull's plane bounced along the frozen rocky ground in a spray of snow, crunching of trees, and a trail of oily smoke. With an injured head and knee, Hull crawled away from the wreck. The Tom-

mies, whom he had served so well in the hours before, sent him to the nearest British aid station, from which he was later evacuated by air to England. Within hours nothing remained of Bodø: jetty, airstrip, town, and forest blazed after a concentrated Luftwaffe attack.

As Hull had observed, it had all been a vain hope. By June 3 evacuation from Narvik was under way. A merciful stratum of mist and low cloud screened the frantic movement to the seaport from the Luftwaffe, whose planes thronged over the entire area at will, dive-bombing and strafing the troops, destroying communications and generally creating havoc.

The few surviving Gladiators of No. 263 Squadron were flown back to the *Glorious.* The ten remaining Hurricanes of No. 46 Squadron would have to be burned because the planes were not supposed to be capable of landing on a carrier deck. Unable to bring himself to destroy the Hurricanes, Squadron Leader K. B. Cross literally pleaded for permission to attempt the impossible. At this crucial moment every aircraft was priceless and the risk, it was finally decided, was worth it. At midnight, June 7, Cross led a formation of ten Hurricanes out of beleaguered Bardufoss and, after an hour's flight, all ten landed safely on the *Glorious*. Tragically this, too, was a vain hope.

The German Imperial Navy, which had inspired Hitler's Scandinavian adventure, had a final blow to deliver. The two battle cruisers *Scharnhorst* and *Gneisenau,* in Norwegian waters and cruising northward, learned from air reconnaissance and intercepted radio messages of much shipping activity between northern Norway and Scotland. The plane had also spotted a British carrier. On the afternoon of June 8 the German warships sighted the *Glorious* and its two escort destroyers, the *Acasta* and the *Ardent.* Outgunned by the German cruisers, all three British ships were sent to the bottom within two hours. Over fifteen hundred British seamen and airmen were lost in the icy sea—as were the twenty planes, ten Gladiators and ten Hurricanes, so splendidly evacuated from Bardufoss. There were only forty-three survivors, among them Squadron Leader Cross and one other member of his Hurricane squadron. For hours, as they waited for rescue, they saw twenty-five of their countrymen, even

some of their squadron mates, die in the Arctic cold.

It was a triumph for the German surface fleet— but with portentous qualifications not apparent at the time. In the battle with the *Glorious,* the *Scharnhorst* took a torpedo from one of the British destroyers. Within two weeks the *Gneisenau* was hit by a torpedo from the British submarine *Clyde.* Both German ships were under repair, and therefore out of action, for close to six months, a critical half year. In addition the cruisers *Königsberg* and *Karlsruhe* were destroyed in Norwegian waters, the former by Fleet Air Arm bombers and the latter by a British submarine. And during the battles of April 10 and 13 Royal Navy ships accounted for no less than ten of the destroyers which had brought German troops to Narvik. One half of the German Imperial Navy's destroyer strength, therefore, was eliminated within four days, and about a third of its cruisers. As a force at sea the German surface fleet counted for little after the Scandinavian campaign.

It was true, in the short view, Hitler had once

The British carrier Glorious, *which served in the Norwegian campaign, delivering aircraft and evacuating the* *wounded. It was sunk on June 8, 1940, during the withdrawal from Narvik with heavy loss of life.*

again proved himself the supreme war lord, the blitzkrieg concept had proved insuperable, the Luftwaffe incomparable, but at what a price. In order to invade Britain Hitler would need all those ships which lay in dry dock or rusting in the fiords and coastal waters of Norway.

Many missed the full significance of the Scandinavian adventure: that the Luftwaffe had succeeded in disrupting the movement and operations of the most powerful Navy on earth. It was a lesson that would have to be painfully relearned before its implications were fully understood. Even so confirmed a ground soldier as Jodl had glimpsed this truth. His final report to the Führer on the Scandinavian campaign must have been the ultimate shock to Raeder, happy in his moment of hollow victory. "The Luftwaffe," Jodl submitted, "proved to be the decisive factor in the success of the operation."

Foreign Minister Joachim von Ribbentrop, however, spoke the ultimate in cant when he said, "Germany by its action has saved the countries and the peoples of Scandinavia from annihilation, and will now guarantee true neutrality in the north until the war's end."

4

WAS NUN?

Live and let live was still the policy in the Saar," Bernard Fergusson reported from the Western Front, "and anybody who loosed off a rifle was thought to be thoroughly anti-social." In the positions where the British and French faced the Germans in the Siegfried Line the Germans twice in April "went through the motions of an attack, and the second time overran some French posts on our flank; this was considered to be extremely bad form, and not to be imitated."

This idyllic warfare abruptly ended on May 10, 1940, when the Nazi legions struck the Netherlands, Belgium, and Luxembourg. *Fall Gelb* ("Case Yellow"), the assault along the Western Front, erupted at dawn in Holland as the Wehrmacht smashed across the borders, parachutists dropped from the skies on airfields and other vital defense points, and the cry of the Stuka again shattered the peace of the countryside.

This had been preceded by a curious series of tentative and inconclusive actions during the "twilight war." As word of the attack on Poland flashed around the world, President Franklin D. Roosevelt appealed to all belligerents to refrain from unrestricted aerial warfare; in short, the bombing of cities. The British accepted on the same day, September 1, 1939; the French followed on the next day, and the Germans, having already devastated Polish towns and villages and with plans for the bombardment of Warsaw in the offing, accepted Roosevelt's request on September 18. So it was that both sides confined bombing attacks only to absolute military targets: no bombs were to fall upon land lest civilians be placed in danger. Only ships at sea, therefore, were legitimate targets.

The RAF was devoted also to dropping propaganda leaflets, beginning with the first night of the war, when ten Armstrong Whitworth Whitley twin-engined bombers of Nos. 51 and 58 Squadrons delivered "Nickles," as the leaflets were called in code, to Hamburg, Bremen, and the industrial Ruhr. Although there was no interception by German fighter planes, the Whitleys did encounter bad weather, severe electrical storms, and icing. One plane crashed in France.

Nickle raids were not popular with crews, a view shared with them by Arthur Harris, commanding No. 5 Group of Bomber Command when the war began (by war's end he would command the bomber forces of Britain), who felt "that the only thing achieved was largely to supply the Continent's requirements of toilet paper for the five long years of war." By virtue of the irrational sapience rampant in the early weeks of the war, and of which there was little dearth throughout the war, the leaflets were marked "Secret" and carefully watched lest any of the British pilots read them. They were for the eyes of the enemy only, it seems. Harris, who

The Armstrong Whitworth "Whitley"—the "Flying Barn Door" to its crews—was one of Bomber Command's first modern bombers. Employed during the "phony war" in dropping propaganda leaflets, the Whitley accumulated impressive "firsts" during its tenure: it was the first British aircraft to drop bombs on German and Italian soil and the first to fly over Berlin to drop leaflets in what the crews called "bumphlet" raids on October 1, 1939. Earlier "marks" were powered by radial engines; beginning with the Mark IV the Whitley's performance was improved with the installation of in-line Merlin engines. By the spring of 1942 the Whitley was retired from Bomber Command; its day was over.

(IMPERIAL WAR MUSEUM, LONDON)

resented the additional complexity of handling the leaflets as secret documents, regarded them with typical acuity. "Many of the pamphlets," he said, "were patently so idiotic and childish that it was perhaps just as well to keep them from the knowledge of the British public, even if we did risk and waste crews and aircraft dropping them on the enemy."

While hazardous, the propaganda raids were useful in that they provided the air crews with training and reconnaissance flights over enemy territory—all of which would serve a more destructive purpose once the gloves came off. Also it became obvious that, against the "gloves off" day, new operational techniques were required particularly as applied to navigation; the conditions under which the crews were expected to operate required attention.

A typical raid of this type and period took place late in October 1939, when four Whitleys (originally five but one turned back) of No. 51 Squadron took off around dusk from a forward base at Villeneuve, France. The weather forecast was deadly: "rain, hail, and sleet showers, risk of thunder; cloud 7 to 9/10, low base 1000 feet, but 500 feet in showers; freezing level 1500 feet; heavy icing anticipated in shower clouds up to 12,000 feet." Except for the single turnback because of the weather, all planes proceeded to their assigned target areas in the Düsseldorf-Frankfurt region and dropped their Nickles under truly impossible conditions.

The Whitley, at best, could reach about seventeen thousand feet—and through most of the route snow clouds jutted up to eighteen thousand feet. While dropping the leaflets from the "dustbin," (a flare chute in the underside of the fuselage), it was not possible to use oxygen. The "droppers" were forced to walk around, cut the strings binding the bundles, and force them through the dustbin, all without oxygen and with little protection against the freezing temperatures. In one of the Whitleys the droppers—otherwise the navigator and radio operator—collapsed from anoxia. They revived on the way home, however, when the plane began icing up heavily and lost altitude. Controls became all but useless and great lumps of ice were flung back from the propellers and thudded alarmingly against the sides of the plane. Despite these problems and others, the pilot brought the plane safely back to Villeneuve.

Another Whitley had similar troubles, even before reaching Düsseldorf-Frankfurt. On the way to the drop zone the front gun turret and the trim tabs on the controls froze. And as the dustbin was being lowered, that too froze. The leaflets had to be transferred from one side of the plane to the other because of the jammed turret. During this painful operation, the crew discovered that it had taken along only a single charged oxygen bottle—all others were empty. As the Whitley lumbered toward the target, the front gunner passed out from the cold and lack of oxygen. The navigator and copilot relieved the pain of the cold by voluntarily butting their heads against convenient hard surfaces. When they descended to a lower altitude their aircraft came under antiaircraft fire. But they pressed on, despite the pilot's sickness from the cold, anoxia and bucking of the plane. More freezing afflicted the rear gun turrent as well as the air-speed indicator. But the radio operator tripling also as navigator somehow managed to find his way back to base.

As with the other two aircraft, the third Whitley experienced trouble with frozen dustbins, but with variations and augmentation. The leaflets were scattered but only the combined efforts of the crew raised the dustbin out of the slipstream. The navigator passed out from the exertion. The pilot, after five and a half hours of exhausting flight, turned the controls over to the copilot and then joined the navigator in a loss of consciousness. When the pilot recovered it was to the sight of flames shooting out of his starboard engine. A six-inch coating of ice had formed on the wing. In a cloud, the distressed Whitley staggered into a dive. With the tail controls frozen solid, it took the strength of both pilot and copilot to pull the plane out of the plunge. Though leveled out, the Whitley continued dropping; the port engine, the one which wasn't burning, simply stopped under a thick coating of ice.

"The order was given to abandon ship by parachute," one of the crew later related; "as no reply was forthcoming from the front and rear gunners, the order was immediately cancelled. It was afterwards ascertained that the front gunner was unconscious due to a blow on the head from an ammunition magazine, and the rear gunner was unconscious from a blow on the head from the turret due to the dive and subsequent recovery.

"The aircraft then assumed a shallow high-speed dive. We opened the top hatch [all windows were solidly frozen over] to see where we were going, and the second pilot, who was at the controls, opened the side window. The aircraft emerged from the clouds in heavy rain at about 200 feet above the ground. All we could see was a black forest with a grey patch in the middle, for which we were heading; the second pilot pulled the aircraft over the trees brushing through their tops, and the aircraft dropped flat into a field, travelled through a wire fence, skidded broadside on and came to rest with the port wing against the trees on the further side of the clearing."

All climbed safely out of the Whitley and attempted, with little success, to extinguish the burning engine. The pilot climbed into the cabin to get an extinguisher, only to find that the crash had caused it to discharge. Finally the radio operator found another extinguisher and mounting the wing put out the flames. All were safe and unhurt and even managed a laugh when, the next morning, one of the local farmers asked, in French, "What time are you taking off?"

The fourth Whitley had little trouble on the way to the drop area, which was Munich, despite the blanket of hoary ice on the windows and snow underfoot in the front gunner's compartment. It was a cheerful crew, singing on the way to Germany —"Roll Out the Barrel" was an especial favorite —with particular and brilliant solo efforts praised over the intercom system. It was a noisy if frigid Whitley. Over Munich the Nickling was properly accomplished (with the usual freezing of the dustbin, the raising of which eventually exhausted most of the crew). As the plane neared the French border a cylinder head in the starboard engine blew off. With the loss of power the Whitley descended lower and lower into the thick clouds, after which the other engine began to sputter.

"Abandon aircraft," the pilot announced as the plane, flying at two thousand feet, bore down on some hills in the near distance.

First to jump was the front gunner, who entangled himself in the intercom wiring and dangled outside the aircraft, unable to get free, until the navigator gave him a push. The opening of his parachute knocked him out and when he next awakened he was startled at being ringed in by enormous brown eyes. He had dropped into a pasture and became the center of curiosity of a herd of cows.

The radio operator, who had been forced to jump with an oxygen bottle in his hand because his fingers had frozen to the metal, apparently landed in an adjoining field. He also proved that it was possible to cover a hundred yards in record time while encumbered by full flying regalia, complete to boots, and to hurtle a four-foot hedge while being pursued by a bull.

The navigator jumped, with a resultant sprained ankle; the pilot, after setting the plane in a flat trajectory, also jumped and landed gently in a meadow. The Whitley, ostensibly crewless, remained in flight for a few more minutes, plowed into the ground, and burst into flames. In the rear turret Sergeant A. Griffin, whose intercom had gone defective and who had not heard the order to jump, snatched a fire extinguisher and dashed into the front of the plane to save his fellow crew members. Extremely puzzled to find the crew gone, Sergeant Griffin limped to the nearest village, where he found the rest of the crew and learned that he had actually walked away from the crash of the Whitley. They were taken from the cafe in which they met, after being presented with bouquets, to a French hospital for treatment. By the evening all had returned to No. 51 Squadron.

Bomber Command was, however, engaged in more hostile operations during the period of the war's first days and through the twilight war. These incipient efforts were confined primarily to the North Sea approaches to Germany where the German fleet was concentrated. As with the Germans, the British began with good intentions: "The greatest care is to be taken not to injure the civilian population [the original order stated explicitly]. The intention is to destroy the German fleet. There is no alternative target."

Forty-eight minutes after the official declaration of war a Blenheim, with Flying Officer A. McPherson piloting and carrying a naval observer, took off on the first British aerial mission of the war. According to the Operations Record Book of No. 139 Squadron, the duty was "Photo. Reco." and the Time Up 1200 and Time Down 1650. The Remarks read tersely: "Duty successful. 75 photos taken of German fleet. The first Royal Air Force aircraft to cross the German frontier." The last sentence was a small concession to merited pride. It hardly suggested any of the hardships of the four-and-a-half-hour mission.

The Blenheim (a Mark IV, serial number 6215) came in from the North Sea over Wilhelmshaven at twenty-four thousand feet. The men aboard saw several German ships coming out of Wilhelmshaven and entering the Schillig Roads, among them the *Admiral Scheer* and the *Emden*. But they were unable to wire back the information, for, as with the leaflet-dropping aircraft, they were afflicted with the cold. Their radio frozen, McPherson and the naval observer (a Commander Thompson) could relay the intelligence only after they had returned to England. Thus was the first RAF target of the Second World War decided upon.

The major enemy was the weather, with minor contributions from High Command uncertainty. "The war was only 24 hours old," deplored Flight Lieutenant K. C. Doran, "but already the bomb-load had been changed four times. Lunch-time on 4th September found us standing by at an hour's readiness, the Blenheims bombed up with 500-pound S.A.P." McPherson's flight having located some German shipping in the region of the Heligoland Bight, it now devolved upon Doran to lead the bombers carrying Semi Armor Piercing bombs. But these too were changed for five-hundred-pound General Purpose (GP) with eleven-second delay fuses. This was a concession to the weather, which, as Doran noted, was reported as "bloody, and the only attack possible would be a low-level one."

With Doran in the lead aircraft, ten Blenheims (five from No. 107 Squadron and five of 110 Squadron) took off for Wilhelmshaven. Another five from No. 139 Squadron were also dispatched but because of the weather never located their target and returned to base without bombing.

Bristol Blenheims of No. 139 Squadron over France, 1940. Although hailed in the summer of 1936 as the last word in modern fast bomber design, the Blenheim proved vulnerable to the Messerschmitt 109 in France; it was also lacking in armament and protective armor for its crew. "XD" was the code for No. 139 Squadron, whose Flying Officer A. McPherson, in a Blenheim, was the first Briton to cross the German frontier when he photographed the German fleet at Wilhelmshaven on September 3, 1939. The following day, Blenheims of No. 110 Squadron made the first bombing raid of the war on Wilhelmshaven.

(IMPERIAL WAR MUSEUM, LONDON)

"Soon after crossing out over the North Sea," Doran of No. 110 Squadron noted, "we ran into bad weather . . . a solid wall of cloud seemed to extend from sea-level to about 17,000 feet." The formation thereupon dropped down to nearly sea level and flew through the clouds. They flew on instruments and dead reckoning. When they estimated they were over Heligoland, they turned and headed for what should have been Wilhelmshaven. They were barely fifty feet over the water when suddenly "a couple of barges appeared out of the murk and vanished." A dim suggestion of a coast-line also emerged from the fog. "After a bit of feverish map-reading, we decided we were in the approach to the Schillig Roads. By an incredible combination and judgement we were bang on our track."

The Germans were not expecting any action in such dismal weather, and if anyone heard approaching aircraft no alarms were given. As Doran led the flights of No. 110 Squadron into the attack, now divided into two sections of two and three planes each, the cloud base lifted to around five hundred feet. Doran saw a large merchant ship—and just beyond it, the *Admiral Scheer*. The *Scheer* lay in

anchor, away from the shore, protected from the landward side by barrage balloons. Gaining as much altitude as possible—about five hundred feet —without losing sight of the target, Doran led the attack against the *Scheer*. Once the bombs went it would be necessary to make a sharp turn to the left to avoid hitting the cables of the barrage balloons.

Doran recalled seeing the laundry of the German seamen fluttering on the stern as he approached. The sailors seemed to be idling about, watching with little concern the approach of the Blenheims. Not until the first British bomber flashed over the *Scheer*, dropping its bomb, did the Germans realize what was happening. From then on the Blenheims were under heavy antiaircraft fire from both the ships and shore-based batteries. The bombs dropped by the first Blenheim struck the *Scheer* and —thanks to the delayed fusing—bounced off the deck and fell harmlessly into the water. The second plane, its crew under heavy fire, dropped short and the bombs exploded in the water. One Blenheim, its pilot misjudging his height or hit by flak, crashed into the forecastle of the *Emden*. It was the only serious damage done to any German ship in the attack and also killed some Germans and injured several more. No. 107 Squadron lost four aircraft in the attack and No. 110 Squadron one; it was a costly raid for small results. One half of the attacking force was lost in this first bombing attack by the Royal Air Force in the Second World War.

Later in the same day, September 4, 1939, fourteen Vickers Wellingtons, six from No. 9 Squadron and eight from No. 149 Squadron, made an attempt upon the *Scharnhorst* and the *Gneisenau.* Their presence at Brunsbüttel had been noted by the enterprising McPherson on his historic reconnaissance flight the day before. Bad weather and antiaircraft fire again took their toll and two of No. 9 Squadron's planes did not return. One of the bombers lost was attacked by Sergeant Alfred Held in a Messerschmitt 109 of Jagdgeschwader 77. It was the first British bomber of the Second World War credited to a German fighter pilot. Unlike the attack at Wilhelmshaven by Doran and the Blenheims, the Brunsbüttel attack, which was at a greater distance from the United Kingdom, afforded more time for an alarm to be given and a few aircraft to be dispatched to intercept.

In all, seven bombers were lost on the first day of offensive aerial warfare. It had not been a "wizard" day for the RAF—although it did mean much in terms of civilian morale and it did show what British aircrews could do under extremely difficult conditions. The "restricted bombing" policy naturally kept them from attacking the more likely target: the factories in the Ruhr. The Air Staff, however, waited, feeling that "this delicate and difficult problem may well be solved for us by the Germans, who are perhaps unlikely to refrain for more than a limited period at most, from actions that would force the Allies from all legal restrictions." The expression in vogue in the Air Ministry was that all were waiting for the hated "Hun to take off the gloves." When this occurred Bomber Command, too, would remove the gloves and unleash its force against more important targets than the ships of the German Imperial Fleet. But, in truth, the Bomber Command's bared fist consisted of less than five hundred aircraft, many of which were the out-of-date Battles and the hardly better Wellingtons, Whitleys, and Hampdens. The most effective bomber was the Blenheim, and its early

operations, as already described, were hardly comforting. Against the five hundred British bombers, the Germans, when ready to discard the gauntlet, could muster three times the number.

Nor were the Germans, certainly not the Luftwaffe at least, anxious to violate the restricted-bombing agreement. The Germans, like the British, were most active mining their respective coastal waters or bombing enemy warships.

This policy was in force when the first German bombers, Heinkel 111s and Junkers 88s of Kampfgeschwader 30, appeared over Britain. The bombers had been dispatched to attack the *Hood,* supposedly in the neighborhood of Rosyth in the Firth of Forth. On the morning of October 16, 1939, German reconnaissance aircraft had passed over Rosyth and the possibility of a raid on the port was noted. No. 607 Squadron was sent north from its home base closer to Rosyth. But the early-warning system broke down and No. 607 Squadron was not alerted to the approach of the German bombers until late. On the other hand, the Germans suffered some surprise, for they had been informed by intelligence that there were no fighters in the vicinity of Rosyth. There were two additional units, No. 602 (City of Glasgow) and No. 603 (City of Edinburgh), within striking range of the Firth of Forth.

Kampfgeschwader 30 found the *Hood* docked at Rosyth, therefore too close to land, and consequently civilians, to serve as a target. The small force of nine bombers was forced to select other targets as they approached Rosyth at twelve thousand feet. Captain Helmut Pohle, piloting a Ju-88, picked the *Southampton* for his attack. There was some tardiness in the reactions from antiaircraft gunners in the area, so that the bomb run was reasonably unmolested. One British gun battery was engaged in a practice drill when they saw German planes coming over. The gun crew hurriedly changed dummy ammunition for live, and began firing at the bombers.

By this time bombs had begun raining down on the ships. One bomb cut through three decks of the *Southampton* and careened out the side before exploding against an admiral's barge, sinking it. Damage was done to the *Edinburgh* and the *Mohawk.* Pohle, leading the attack on the *Southampton,* found himself in a good deal of trouble. His Ju-88 was struck by flak and the top housing of the pilot's compartment blew away in the dive. Worse, as he headed out to sea in a race for home he came under attack by a trio of Spitfires—the first he had ever seen. The German aircraft, crippled and yawing, staggered under the heavy gunning of the British fighters, which swarmed in three times. Pouring smoke and carrying two dead crewmen, the Junkers splashed into the sea near Dalkeith, Scotland—the first German aircraft brought down over Britain since the First World War. Captain Pohle survived and was taken prisoner. Another German plane, reported as a Heinkel, also fell into the sea. The credit for bringing down the first German plane was given to No. 603 Squadron, led by Squadron Leader E. E. Stevens.

Like the British raids on German naval ports, the German attacks on Rosyth and other havens for the Home Fleet were tentative, meager, almost haphazard skirmishes. They did not lead to great aerial battles, as had been visualized in the pulp magazines the young fliers had read in school. But they took their toll and the losses were bitter if not spectacular. The missing element of drama was finally provided on December 18, 1939, when two dozen British Wellingtons, of Nos. 9, 37, and 149 Squadrons, set out on an "armed reconnaissance" of the Heligoland Bight, specifically the vicinity of the Schillig Roads and Wilhelmshaven. (Armed reconnaissance eliminated the process of sending out one plane to spot targets and then sending out the bombers to strike them. The Wellingtons were bombed up and ready in the event that worthwhile targets were found.)

It was a perfect day, cloudless and sunny, with superb visibility. Two of the Wellingtons turned back because of mechanical trouble and the remaining twenty-two approached from the north, having kept away from the flak guns stationed on ships along the way. The four formations, at twelve thousand feet, then came in over Heligoland. It was about at this moment that the Messerschmitt 109s of Jagdgeschwader 77 intercepted the British bombers. Doggedly pressing on, the Wellingtons continued their reconnaissance, unable to drop their bombs upon the warships below because they were docked or in harbors and thus not to be attacked. The gunners in the Wellingtons did the best they could to fight off the darting Me-109s, which seemed to be coming in from all directions. The tail guns

of the Wellingtons gave the Germans the most trouble, but the bomb-laden Wellingtons, slow compared to the Me-109s, were terribly mauled. For about eighty miles from Heligoland until they were well out to sea the Wellingtons suffered the attacks of the Me-109s, as well as those of Me-110s which had also joined the battle. Taking advantage of the blind spots in the Wellington's defense, that is, where the guns were unable to traverse, the Messerschmitts accounted for no less than twelve of the British bombers (the claim was, however, for thirty-four) at a cost of two Me-109s (British gunners claimed twelve). Worst hit of the British units was No. 37 Squadron, which lost five of its six aircraft dispatched.

The surviving crews reported that many of the Wellingtons had crashed, burning and with fuel streaming from their tanks; it was a memorable argument in favor of self-sealing tanks. In time these would become standard equipment on all aircraft, but the lessons were always tragic and costly. It was learned also that bombers were susceptible to aggressive fighter attacks. If "the bomber always got through," so did the modern fighter get through the bomber's defenses. It was after this battle over the Heligoland Bight that the British High Command gave serious consideration to switching to night operations, when fighter attacks could be expected to be almost negligible.

Bomber Command's crews endured the worst of the Luftwaffe's effectiveness; but the fighter pilots, too, were subjected to the lessons to be learned in a new kind of warfare.

II

Contemporaneously with the attack on Poland, the northern invasions, the halfhearted bombings and Nickling raids, RAF units were sent to France to fight the Germans.

As in 1914, British aircraft crossed the English Channel shortly after the official declaration of hostilities. Ten squadrons of Fairey Battles of what was termed the Advanced Air Striking Force left for France in the afternoon of September 2. One of the Battles fell into the Channel because of engine trouble; it was the only incident of the crossing. The crew was saved and so the transfer was unremarkable and uncontested. The bomber squadrons were reinforced by four Hurricane squadrons of the Air Component attached to the British Expeditionary Force.

The Air Component, as its name implied, was to work with the BEF, as had, in a sense, the Royal Flying Corps a quarter of a century before, as cover for the troops and protective element for the reconnaissance and photo squadrons (Blenheims and Lysanders), also a part of the Air Component.

The Advanced Air Striking Force was to be employed in the more or less strategic bombardment of targets inside Germany with its Battles and Blenheims; the French, it had been agreed, would supply the fighter protection. The facts of war in its new form hindered the mission of the AASF. The

the French Air Force. Before the war regarded as one of the greatest air forces in the world, the Armée de l'Air was in reality antiquated, afflicted with an effete, defeatist command—in short, ineffectual. The young pilots were able and eager, but they had been betrayed. Neither their aircraft nor the policy under which they were expected to operate was anywhere near equal to the task before them.

Burdensome also were the kid-glove bombing rules, observed equally by the Germans and the Allies. Neither side wished to unleash a bomber war on the cities. The French were particularly sensitive to the possibilities of an aroused Luftwaffe and did little to encourage strategic bombardment. It was a policy of kill and let kill just so long as

Fairey "Battles" of No. 218 Squadron, Advanced Air Striking Force in France, 1939–40. The Battle, although obsolete by 1939, was used in front-line service as a reconnaissance bomber during the "phony war" (when this photograph was taken), and as a bomber when the war in the west erupted in May 1940. It was shortly after used as a trainer.

(IMPERIAL WAR MUSEUM, LONDON)

Westland "Lysander," five squadrons of which operated as tactical reconnaissance and photo-survey aircraft for the British Expeditionary Forces in France. Slow, with a top speed of barely two hundred miles an hour (the Me-109 could do well over three hundred), the Lysander was maneuverable but vulnerable and not suited to modern air combat.

(IMPERIAL WAR MUSEUM, LONDON)

impact of the blitzkrieg, especially after the twilight war expired, necessitated the diverting of the bombers to attack the advancing German troops and armored vehicles rather than "strategic" targets behind the lines. The Battles proved less than suitable for modern war.

Late in September 1939, for example, five Battles of No. 150 Squadron were dispatched to reconnoiter ten miles inside the German frontier. They encountered a flight of Messerschmitts and in the battle that followed four of the Battles were destroyed and the surviving aircraft was a write-off on returning to base.

Another handicap was France's Armée de l'Air,

the war remained remotely "civilized." It was also a war of boredom. While the Germans reduced and decimated Poland and then instituted a new order, the French and the British dug in, hoping for the best.

These were tragic, equivocal days which stretched into the months of the twilight war.

The first British fighter squadrons to land in France, and which endured both the boredom of the "phony war" and the frantic humiliation of being pushed out of France, were Nos. 85 and 87 Squadrons of the Air Component and Nos. 1 and 73 Squadrons of the AASF. These Hurricane squadrons were among the first to engage the Luftwaffe, the first British airmen to face the German fliers since 1918. Thanks in part to the press, the opening of the Second World War, at least in the air, was but a sequel to the earlier war. Some of the traditions of that more romantic epic were revived as newsmen sought out aces, colorful characters, human interest stories. The lone fighter pilot engaged in aerial combat high in the heavens furnished good copy—this despite the official negative British attitude toward the glorification of the individual.

Among the first celebrities of the war was a husky, tall, young New Zealander, Flying Officer Edgar J. Kain, of No. 73 Squadron. The friendly, sportive twenty-one-year-old was best known by his

into the equally "impassable" Ardennes Forest. A mere four- or five-minute flight carried the British pilots over Germany. Despite the proximity of "Jerry" (a term which served the British for either the Germans or a chamber pot), the eager fighter pilots found little action in their sector. This was true also of No. 1 Squadron, nesting some thirty miles to the south of Verdun at Vassincourt airdrome near Bar-le-Duc.

At both bases, primitive by RAF standards, the Hurricanes proved their sturdiness, thanks to their rugged construction. Also the wide-track landing gear of the plane was capable of coping with the hazardous, often muddy condition of the landing strips. As for action, apparently the Luftwaffe de-

Among the first to arrive in France were the Hurricane pilots of No. 1 Squadron (left) and No. 73 Squadron. Although they endured the boredom of the

"phony war" they fought furiously after May 1940. Among the No. 73 Squadron members grouped around the antique vehicle is Cobber Kain (on right without hat). (IMPERIAL WAR MUSEUM, LONDON)

nickname "Cobber," an Australian-New Zealand term for "pal" or "chum." With his ready grin, his tousled hair, his crumpled uniform, and his fearless, almost madcap flair for fighting and flying, Cobber Kain seemed a reincarnation of the spirit of Albert Ball or Billy Bishop of the Great War and was the squadron's star performer.

By October No. 73 Squadron was stationed at Etain-Rouvres airdrome near Verdun. The base lay just behind the famed "impregnable" complex of fortresses, the Maginot Line, facing Germany's West Wall. The Maginot Line at this point petered out

voted itself chiefly to reconnaissance and dived into cloud cover and ran for home before the British could intercept.

Not until October 30—the war was nearly two months old—did an RAF fighter bring down its first German plane. Almost directly over No. 1 Squadron's field three German aircraft, Dornier 17s, were seen at high altitude. The airdrome defense section took off immediately in pursuit and Pilot Officer P. W. O. Mould (in Hurricane L1842) overtook the Dornier. The twenty-year-old pilot, the squadron's youngest—a distinction which

King George VI on a visit to an Air Component base in France. The three Hurricanes in foreground belong to No. 85 Squadron (VY), the others to No. 87 Squadron (LK), which like Nos. 1 and 73 Squadrons were the first of the fighter units to serve in France. In the left background are a Blenheim and two Gladiators. (IMPERIAL WAR MUSEUM, LONDON)

Destroyed German bomber in France. At left is the tail section (possibly of an He-111). French soldiers have begun to gather souvenirs from the scattered wreckage. (FRENCH EMBASSY)

A Hurricane I landing at Vassincourt, France. The aircraft, belonging to No. 1 Squadron, was then equipped with a wooden propeller. Pilot Officer Mould of this squadron, flying one of these early Hurricanes, scored the first RAF victory when he destroyed a Dornier on October 30, 1939.

(IMPERIAL WAR MUSEUM, LONDON)

earned him the nickname "Boy"—surprised the Germans and shot the Dornier down without a fight.

Two days later, November 2, 1939, Cobber Kain scored the first victory for No. 73 Squadron. The young giant had been lying sprawled on the ground scanning the skies through field glasses when he suddenly leaped up shouting, "I've spotted a Jerry!"

He ran for his Hurricane, which was in readiness, leaped in, and gunned the fighter down the field. Within nine minutes he had climbed to about twenty-seven thousand feet, above a lone Dornier 17, the "Flying Pencil," on a reconnaissance mission. As Kain closed in upon the German plane the rear gunner began firing at him. A few tracers flashed past the Hurricane's cockpit before Kain "squeezed the teat." One sudden flash of fear came into his mind: he hoped that his armorer had not forgotten to arm the eight machine guns in the Hurricane's wings.

The entire plane jolted as the eight guns burst into action—and it was over. Kain dipped onto one wing to watch the Dornier plunge to earth and strike near a small village not far from Rouvres. The German plane had, as described by Charles Gardner of the BBC, "dug a trench four feet deep across a village street, and all that was left of it was a flaming heap of rubble. Gruesome bits of the crew dangled from nearby trees, and the French children were running round with bits of fingers and hands which they had found lying around."

Kain, meanwhile, dived for home and jumped into a vehicle as soon as he had landed to cheers and back-pattings. On arriving at the crash site Kain had to be reassured that no one in the village had been injured by the Dornier. Kain walked over to the twisted, smoking tangle of metal. Three fellow humans had been horribly mangled in the wreckage. It was difficult for Kain to determine which was worse: the sight of the French children playing with bits of Boche or the head of one of the crew, lying at his feet, intact in the helmet and eyes wide open. Kain stood at the edge of the smoldering trench, his face drawn and grimy. Turning away he was heard to say softly, "Well, it was either them or me."

It was not to be a cinematic, pulp-fiction war after all. And it would become grimmer. This was apparent in the build-up of the German fighter squadrons along the Western Front in preparation for Hitler's frequently postponed and permutated *Fall Gelb*. The Messerschmitt 109 squadrons, free of the Polish campaign, and soon outnumbering the French and British squadrons, proved to be more aggressive than they had once been. By the first of the new year 1940, despite the fact that the invasion of France for which the Allies thought they were ready had not yet come off, there was clearly something in the wind. Up to the end of 1939 the RAF had succeeded in destroying about twenty German aircraft—not an impressive number.

The tenor of the air war was, however imperceptibly, changing. Among the first to experience this was the doughty Cobber Kain. While leading a three-Hurricane flight on patrol, Kain spotted a dozen Messerschmitts. With characteristic dash, he announced to the other two pilots, "Get going, chaps," and dived into the middle of the German formation.

In the first minute or so of the attack, Kain blasted one of the Messerschmitts out of the melee. But he also watched one of the by then crippled Hurricanes racing for the ground and a forced landing. The other Hurricane, Kain noted, was the center of attention of five Messerschmitts. He pulled back on the control stick and came up under one of the German planes, squeezing the gun button. Another Messerschmitt fell out of the battle, streaming black smoke.

It was now Cobber Kain's turn: rushing toward him was a Messerschmitt with guns twinkling. In his rear-view mirror, Kain saw another German plane pouring shells into the Hurricane. Ignoring the rear plane for an instant, Kain activated the eight guns against the oncoming fighter. Nothing happened—Kain had used up his ammunition supply. Luckily his companion knocked the Messerschmitt off Kain's tail—but not before a shell rammed into the engine of Kain's aircraft. There was a burst of flame and thick black smoke filled the cockpit—the air filled with colorful New Zealand profanities. In desperation Kain attempted to ram a German fighter which loomed ahead of him in the thick smoke. But his engine was rapidly dying and the Messerschmitt whisked away.

Cobber Kain was at twenty thousand feet, his plane aflame and he himself choking in the oily smoke. He jerked the stick forward and pushed the nose down. The flames spread and Kain rammed

Squadron scramble by No. 87 Squadron, France 1940. Second plane in the foreground is a Hurricane fitted *with the de Havilland three-bladed propeller, an improvement over the old wooden prop.*

(IMPERIAL WAR MUSEUM, LONDON)

the cockpit hood open and was about to bail out. Then he remembered, when he had taken off he hadn't bothered to fasten his chute properly. He sank back into the smoky cockpit hoping to correct the oversight. He then noted that the dive had smothered the flames, although the cockpit leaked oil and effused smoke. And then the engine came back to life. Hoping to save the precious Hurricane, Kain sought out a place to land and quickly found a spot just at the edge of an airdrome near Metz. He brought the plane down and then hopped out of the tattered Hurricane and, as he himself said, "I fell flat on my bloody face. Passed right out, like a sissy boy."

Kain's cavalier attitude toward regulations (he should have properly adjusted his parachute before ever leaving the ground) had nearly cost him his life. He might easily have been court-martialed for his breach of discipline. As it was, Squadron Leader

Brian Knox would from time to time vent his Dublin Irish on the young New Zealander—this was known as "tearing off a strip" (presumably, and metaphorically, of flesh).

The strip tearing might be earned for some slighting of military courtesy or bearing—the RAF pilots had already begun to fashion curious variations in dress. Kain affected uncreased trousers stuffed into flying boots. Around his neck he generally wore a scarf; a small chain dangled outside his jacket— this carried his identification disks and a small green tiki, the image of a Maori god, as a good luck charm. Like other pilots, Kain liked to wear turtleneck sweaters. Another shared characteristic was the dashingly wind-blown mop of hair. Members of the Senior Service, the Royal Navy, frowned upon this unkempt noncomformity with some disdain, referring to the bulk of pilots as "the Brylcreem boys." The raffish, tradition-free fighter pilots further dis-

A trio of Hurricanes in attack formation—German-eye view. These aircraft are in a neater formation, however, than was possible in combat. But several German fighter and bomber pilots undoubtedly had a glimpse of Cobber Kain leading a couple of his chaps into a fight in a formation that for an instant may have looked as it does here.

(IMPERIAL WAR MUSEUM, LONDON)

turbed the "naval types" when aboard ship by referring to the bow as "the pointy end of the boat."

Drinking became an off-duty pastime, as it had during the First World War, for the young fighter pilots. Every squadron had its favorite "boozer" in nearby French villages. It was quite unlike their local pubs, back home, with the traditional dart board and the pints of bitters. Champagne was easily obtained in the boozers and it was a reasonable substitute for the delectable English beers. It was, of course, dubbed "giggle water."

Victories were celebrated either in the local boozer or in the squadron mess. And, since victories were few in the early weeks, the officer pilots were frequently invited to the sergeant's mess for a blow. Or else a group of men from one squadron visited another squadron. After much imbibing of giggle water such blows became rather destructive and lacking in decorum. Visiting dignitaries were requested to stand on their heads, as a kind of squadron initiation. Or a playful wrestling match resulted in a battle royal and the eradication of the supply of chinaware, chairs, and even tables.

It was following one of these parties that four members of No. 1 Squadron poured themselves into their car to return to their squadron. Two, in the rear seat, were completely out. The other two, the squadron leader—whose car it was—and a pilot, Paul Richey, manned the forward seat.

Soon they were racing through the darkened French countryside. The following (authentic) conversation took place:

"Not so fast, Paul," cautioned the squadron leader.

Edgar J. "Cobber" Kain of Christchurch, New Zealand, and No. 73 Squadron, RAF. The first official British ace of the Second World War with seventeen victories, Kain was killed while "beating up" his airdome in France just before he was to have returned to England to become a flying instructor.

(IMPERIAL WAR MUSEUM, LONDON)

"OK."

A few minutes later the squadron leader spoke again, "Ease off a bit, old boy."

"OK," Richey hazily agreed.

Three minutes later Richey addressed the squadron leader.

"Hey, I'm not driving, you bloody fool, you are!"

"Am I?" said the squadron leader. "Oh, so I am."

The Brylcreem boys were forming their own traditions and Cobber Kain represented them in the first months of the war. The subject of discipline was not taken too seriously. He smiled (if only inwardly) when Squadron Leader Knox tore off a strip, but rebelled when Knox went a step beyond and grounded him. A really drastic punishment was to put Kain in charge of the operations tent, where

he heard the sounds of the battle over the radio to his discomfiture and frustration.

On March 26, 1940, after completing a full day in the operations tent, Kain had reached the limit. On hearing of much enemy activity over the frontier, he sprinted out of the tent and pulled away in his Hurricane in company with two other No. 73 Squadron men.

"In the Luxembourg corner," Kain later reported, "I saw a number of enemy aircraft and proceeded to investigate at 2:30 p.m. I gave a message on R/T [radio telephone] to Flying Officer Perry and Sgt. Pilot Pyne, who were with me—'Enemy aircraft ahead'—and proceeded to attack. I turned into the enemy which had started to climb and gave a burst at the leader who pulled up, turned on his back and spun away in flames. I then noticed 5 more M.E. 109's working round behind me, so I turned hard right and took a sight on the near machine. I fired a burst at him, he dived away and I took three deflection shots at another M.E. 109 which was slowly turning ahead of me. I got behind this aircraft and gave it a burst. He turned on his starboard side and dived right down towards earth."

Suddenly the sky was clear of aircraft, except for Kain's, so he searched for the other Hurricanes. Seeing nothing, he turned south just as his Hurricane was struck by two shells, one hitting the cockpit and the other the fuel tank.

"The explosion of the hood of my cockpit rendered me unconscious," Kain reported, "but I came to diving steeply. After a while I managed to pull out of the dive and tried to bend down and turn off the petrol, but the flames burnt my face. I headed towards France to gain as much ground as possible and when the flames got too intense I decided to abandon my aircraft."

Heaving himself out of the burning plane, Kain pulled the ripcord at twelve thousand feet. At ten thousand feet he emerged from the clouds where he found that it "was all very still and I thought I was in heaven." Afraid that he would land in Germany, Kain yanked at the strings of the parachute, slipping the air and hastening the descent. He painfully struck the ground near Ritzing in the vicinity of a woods. He gathered up his chute, ran for the woods, hid the chute, and set out in a southerly direction hoping he would find himself in France. He was soon challenged by a French captain and after being properly identified, Kain was sent to Evendorff for first aid. He had been burned and was limping badly. The captain informed Kain that he had dropped into No Man's Land, between the French and German positions.

A French staff car returned Kain to Rouves where the squadron medic, Flight Lieutenant R. M. Outfin, spent two hours cleaning up the burns. Kain's uniform was in tatters and had to be abandoned. As he stood up to leave, Kain winced.

"What's wrong with your leg, Cobber?" Outfin asked.

"I don't know, doc," Kain replied. "Some things went in and I don't think they came out." Whereupon Cobber Kain collapsed. The doctor proceeded to remove over twenty pieces of shrapnel from his leg.

Two hours later, when the officers prepared to go to the sergeant's mess as guests for an evening of "fun and games," Cobber Kain's shouts echoed through the village. He would not be muzzled until he was taken in a stretcher by the doctor and a medical orderly to the sergeant's mess. Kain drank to his comrades' good health. They returned the compliment and the happy Kain was carried back to his billet through the village.

Upon recovery Kain was given a ten days' leave in London, where he was awarded the Distinguished Flying Cross, the first bestowed upon a British airman in France. On rejoining his squadron on April 11, Kain seemed to have changed slightly. He was as good-humored and as eager to fly as ever, but he was more businesslike, even neater. Cobber Kain had become engaged while in London and was to be married in June. Soon he was back in action and had scored about twelve official victories. Even so, the days were short on combat despite the improvement in the weather. What was Jerry up to?

III

At dawn, May 10, 1940, they found out. Massive Nazi columns surged over Dutch, Belgian, and Luxembourg's frontiers as Luftwaffe assaults smashed and scorched the airfields behind the lines. It was the third, and to date the most effective, demonstration of blitzkrieg. The twilight war erupted into a nightmare of panzer and Stuka: *Fall Gelb* had finally come.

The extent of this nightmare was soon obvious in air battles such as were not experienced during the first eight months of the war. Typical was the tragic epic of the Maastricht bridges, which furnished the Germans crossing over the Albert Canal in Belgium. Once secured these would serve as bridgeheads for pouring German troops into northern France.

The desperate Belgians had failed to blow the bridges and appealed to the Allies for aid. Counterattacks by ground troops did not drive the Germans away from the bridges, which by May 11 carried streams of armored vehicles, troops, supplies, and ammunition across the Albert Canal. On this same day the Germans carried out one of the brilliant coups of the war: the capture of Fort Eben Emael, reputed to be the most modern, strongest fort in Europe. It was situated a few miles south of Maastricht overlooking the juncture of the Meuse River and the canal. This formidable position was taken from above, by air-borne troops flown in silently by glider. These were towed by Ju-52s from Cologne and released over Aachen, about twenty miles from the fortress. Nine gliders gracefully landed atop the fort and specially trained troops proceeded to put the fort out of action with explosives, grenades, and flame throwers. Reinforcements arrived by parachute and by the afternoon of May 11, with additional help from the Stukas and ground troops, the Germans had taken Fort Eben Emael. Simultaneously with this, air-borne troops also dropped upon the bridge sites to the north of the fort. One, at Canne, was destroyed by the Belgians, but two, at Veldwezelt and Vroenhoven, fell into German hands.

The task of denying the use of these two bridges to the Germans fell to No. 12 Squadron, known as the "Dirty Dozen." Air Vice-Marshal P. H. L. Playfair, commanding the Advanced Air Striking Force, although realizing the mission was undoubtedly foredoomed, asked for volunteers. Characteristically, the entire squadron stepped forward, but only six Fairey Battles were scheduled for the attack, three for each bridge. Leading one section, Flying Officer Norman M. Thomas was to strike at the concrete bridge at Vroenhoven while Flying Officer Donald E. Garland led the other section against the metal bridge at Veldwezelt. That their four 250-pound bombs could do much damage, especially to the concrete bridge, was questionable. So was their breaking through a Luftwaffe-infested sky, let alone the flak. But they would try.

"You British are mad," a German officer later told one of the Battle pilots, I. A. McIntosh. "We capture the bridge [in this instance the one at Veldwezelt] early Friday morning. You give us all Friday and Saturday to get our flak guns up in circles all around the bridge and then on Sunday, when all is ready, you come along with three aircraft and try and blow the thing up."

But they did try, although "at all costs," as the orders had read.

Early on Sunday morning six Battles warmed up on the tarmac at Amifontaine. Then it was discovered that one of the planes in Thomas's section had a defective radio; the crew switched to another Battle, which, it developed, had a malfunction in the hydraulic system. Only five aircraft took off for the bridges. Thomas led his section, consisting only of one other Battle, piloted by Flying Officer T. D. H. Davy. Garland led his full section, the other two planes of which were flown by Pilot Officer I. A. McIntosh and Sergeant F. Marland.

Thomas and Garland had disagreed upon the tactics of the mission. Thomas believed that the approach should be from a high level while "Garland was determined," as Thomas explained, "to carry out a low-level attack, thinking it not only the best form, but the safest.

"My parting words to him were 'it will be interesting to see the result, and may we both be lucky enough to return.'"

An escort of six Hurricanes from No. 1 Squadron had been supplied to clear the air of German fighters. Thomas and Davy flew at six thousand feet—at a thousand feet seven-tenths cloud cover obscured the ground and afforded some protection from flak batteries. While the Hurricanes tackled the Messerschmitts Thomas led the attack on the Vroenhoven bridge. Enemy fighters bore in upon Davy's plane, however, and a brief exchange of fire ensued in which the gunner of the Battle shot down one Messerschmitt. Other German planes went down in the battle, but five of the six Hurricanes were lost.

Over Vroenhoven the two Battles ran into a wall of flak and machine-gun fire. Diving through this murderous barrage, through the clouds, the two Battles raced for the concrete bridge. Fragments of both planes whipped back into the slipstream as the flak hammered at them. The determined British dropped their bombs on the bridge, some of them from so low that the Battles were endangered by their own bomb blasts. Almost negligible damage resulted to the bridge.

When Thomas pulled his Battle out of the dive he realized the plane was too battered to remain in the air. The engine quickly sputtered out and he had to land. Thomas found an open field and brought the Battle in for a wheels-up landing. Within minutes Thomas and his crew were taken prisoner.

Davy too had engine trouble and a badly sieved aircraft. But he hoped to return to base. When it appeared that the Battle might drop out of the air at any moment, he ordered the other two men to jump. This was in the vicinity of Liége, where one of the crew was captured (mistakenly as a German) and manhandled by Belgian civilians until the police arrived. Davy, even with the lighter load, could not keep the Battle air-borne all the way to Amifontaine. He crash-landed inside Belgium.

Garland's section, meanwhile, had proceeded to the Veldwezelt bridge. Determined to carry out a surprise attack from low level, Garland ordered the fuses on the bombs to be set at eleven-second delay. Thus Garland planned to swoop down, drop the bombs, and just have time to get away. As the three Battles approached the bridge the screen of flak fire roared into a frightful crescendo. McIntosh's plane was the first to be hit and the Battle burst into flame. The pilot kept it on its bomb run as long as possible until the observer released the bombs (although with scant if any accuracy). The burning plane crashed shortly after and the crew pulled the near-unconscious McIntosh from the wreck. The three men found refuge, momentarily, in a ditch.

The air over the bridge was an inferno. The twenty-one-year-old Garland, just newly commissioned a flying officer, was resolute. He led his section, now consisting only of his plane and Sergeant Marland's, into the fury over Veldwezelt. He carefully lined up the Battle on a suicide run and accelerated the slender bomber into the barrage. Just as coolly, his observer, Sergeant Thomas Gray, took meticulous aim before releasing the small bomb load. Whether or not these men saw that their bombs scored direct hits upon their target is not known. The terrific flak onslaught ripped the Battle to pieces. Marland also may have scored hits on the bridge but possibly neither he nor anyone else ever knew.

From the ditch in which he was sheltered, McIntosh saw one Battle still in the air, the focus of the relentless flak guns. "We saw this Battle trying to get away," he said. "Then it suddenly stood on its tail, climbed vertically for about a hundred feet, stalled, and nose-dived to earth." They did not know whose plane it was. It hardly mattered, for all three Battles had been knocked out of the sky and only McIntosh and his crew survived. For their efforts in the attack Garland and Gray received the Victoria Cross, posthumously, Britain's supreme award and the first given to RAF personnel. But the third crew member, Leading Aircraftman L. R. Reynolds, radio-gunner, inexplicably received no award at all. Davy, who tried to bring his plane back to base, was given a Distinguished Flying Cross.

All five aircraft had been lost, two crews of three men each had been killed, two crews had been captured, and one had made it back to Allied lines. This expensive, almost quixotic, show of valor had achieved only slight damage to the bridge and cratering of the approaches at Vroenhoven. The Veld-

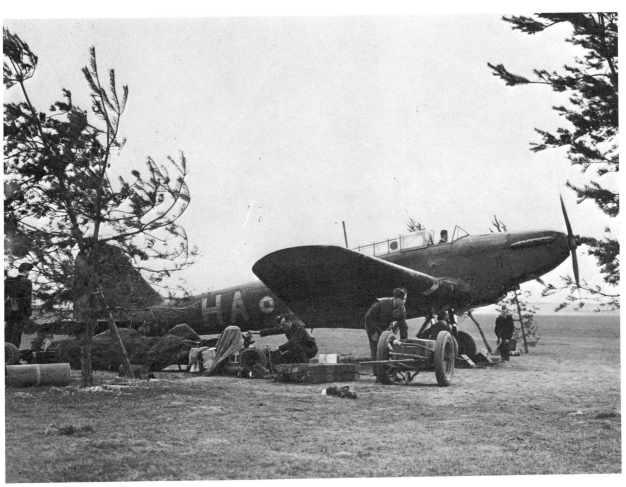

A camouflaged Battle of No. 218 Squadron, Advanced Air Striking Force, in France, 1940. The ground crew prepares the aircraft for combat which, during the "Phony War" never materialized but which, following the unleashing of Fall Gelb (Plan Yellow) *on May 10, 1940, became devastatingly sufficient. Ten out of the eleven Battles of No. 218 Squadron which had been sent to help hold up the German advance at Sedan were destroyed on May 14 in a futile attempt. Despite losses of more than half the RAF bombers which participated in the attack at Sedan and despite the concerted effort by both French and British Air Forces, the Germans rolled on into France.*

(IMPERIAL WAR MUSEUM, LONDON)

wezelt Bridge suffered serious damage to its western truss and was out of use—temporarily.

The Maastricht carnage was but a prelude. As the seemingly invincible German armored forces overran the Netherlands and Belgium, the French—to the south—were shocked by the unexpected materialization of a German vanguard in the form of Ewald von Kleist's Panzer group thrusting through the "impassable" Ardennes Forest. Soon German armored cars and tanks had crossed the Meuse at Sedan. Even earlier, on May 13, General Erwin

Now, on the morning of May 14, 1940, an attempt was made to stop the flood of Hitler's troops passing over pontoon bridges at Sedan. Ten Battles were dispatched from Nos. 103 and 150 Squadrons of the Advanced Air Striking Force. They attacked their targets and, encountering no fighters or flak, all planes returned safely. Air Marshal A. S. Barratt, in command of all British air forces in France, then planned to send bomber forces to deal with Rommel's panzers at Dinant. He was requested by the French to lend all-out effort to a counterattack at Sedan. Because of the command situation in

A Battle of No. 150 Squadron shot down during the Battle of Sedan, during which forty (mostly obsolete) aircraft vainly attempted to stop the Wehrmacht from crossing the Meuse. (H. J. NOWARRA)

A Ju-52 drops men of Fallschirmjäger-Regiment 1— paratroopers—upon Waalhaven, near Rotterdam, as Hitler began the blitzkrieg into the Low Countries. (H. J. NOWARRA)

Rommel, leading his 7th Panzer Division (attached to Günther Hans von Kluge's Fourth Army), had breached the Meuse at Dinant. The stunned French called for aerial interference of the establishment of German bridgeheads at Monthermé and Sedan.

The latter town had particularly tragic overtones in French history. It had been at Sedan, in 1870, where the Germans defeated Marshal Patrice MacMahon's army, captured Napoleon III, and brought an end to the Second Empire. During the First World War, Sedan, a town of about thirteen thousand people, situated on the north bank of the Meuse on the edge of the Ardennes Forest about five miles from the Belgian frontier, had been occupied by the Germans.

France, Barratt was forced to comply. Instead of Dinant, they would attack at Sedan.

His bomber force had dwindled in just the few days since the blitzkrieg had reignited. On May 10 there had been 135 operational AASF bombers on hand; by the evening of May 12 only 72 remained.

But the early morning bombing of Sedan boded well. Around noon the second wave of Allied bombers was sent in; this consisted of a few French aircraft, which were so badly mauled that the French air effort for the day was ended. Then, beginning at three in the afternoon, all available RAF medium bombers—Battles and Blenheims— were hurled at Sedan.

By this time of the day, which the Germans at

the time called "the day of the fighters," the air over Sedan was alive with German fighters (Messerschmitt Bf-109Es), which were superior in speed to the Hurricane. The Battles and Blenheims were so many sitting ducks. Among the elite units the ill-fated British planes encountered were Jagdgeschwader 2, the "Richthofen" unit named for the First

of the eight planes sent on the mission). More than half the Battles did not return to their bases: No. 12 Squadron lost four out of five planes; No. 88 one out of ten; No. 103 three out of eight; No. 105 six out of eleven; No. 142 four out of eight; No. 150 all four of its planes; No. 218 Squadron ten out of eleven; and No. 226 three out of six. A total of

Flood tide: Ernst Udet, Adolf Galland, and Werner Mölders. During the Battle of France Udet was head of the Luftwaffe's Technical Office, Galland the op- *erations officer of Jagdgeschwader 27, and Mölders the top-scoring ace of Jagdgeschwader 53 ("Richthofen").* (NATIONAL ARCHIVES)

World War ace, and Jagdgeschwader 53, in whose third *Gruppe* (i.e., III/JG 53) was the famed Hauptmann Werner Mölders. On May 14 Mölders added another victory mark to the tail of his Me-109: it was his tenth.

As relentlessly as the British came in to attack Sedan, just so relentlessly did the Luftwaffe take its toll. In all, eight Battle squadrons were dispatched along with two Blenheim squadrons (which lost five

thirty-five Battles were destroyed of the sixty-three sent. Counting the Blenheims, the British lost forty aircraft out of the seventy-one they had been able to muster for the attack on Sedan.

There was but a momentary pause in the German thrust across the Meuse; by nightfall Heinz Guderian's panzers crossed the bridgehead and seized the bridges over the Ardennes Canal. The way was open for a drive toward the north and the English Channel; it would outflank the British Expeditionary Forces and the French armies backing up the Dutch and the Belgians. The beaten, demoralized French Ninth Army fell back from an ever widening German front.

By this same morning of May 14 the fate of the Netherlands had already been decided and reached a grim climax in the bombing of Rotterdam. Within four days after the German attack it was clear that the Dutch were beaten. Queen Wilhelmina and the government had fled to England. Some pockets of resistance held, and they were troublesome, but obviously the small, "neutral" country was no military match for the Germans. Still their stubborn fight interfered with the rapid German advance toward France through Belgium, also neutral.

Orders had come from General Georg von Küchler, commanding the small but potent Eighteenth Army, that resistance in and around Rotterdam must be broken "by every means." By eight o'clock in the morning of May 14 surrender negotiations had begun although not without hairsplitting demands on the part of the Dutch commander in Rotterdam, Colonel P. Scharroo. He refused to deal with Dutch civilians sent by Oberstleutnant Dietrich von Choltitz, whose forces were attempting to cross the bridges into Rotterdam. A stickler for form, Scharroo rejected another, this time more official, capitulation proposal from General Rudolf Schmidt (commanding the XXXIX Corps) because it did not carry the proper "rank, name, and signature."

This same ultimatum, however, carried the threat of an aerial attack upon Rotterdam unless Scharroo surrendered. The plans for this attack had already been formulated: one hundred Heinkel 111s of Kampfgeschwader 54 would bomb the center of Rotterdam. The first bombs fell at around three o'clock in the afternoon even while surrender negotiations were under way.

Immediately before the German bombers took off they had been informed of the possibility of a Dutch surrender. If this came about before they reached the target in Rotterdam red Very pistols were to be fired from the ground and the bombers were to return without dropping their high-explosive bombs. While this may seem a humane precaution on the part of the Germans, it is difficult to understand how it was expected that the bomber crews might discern from bombing altitude the red lights in the haze and flame of the battle below. At best, it was a halfhearted precaution.

The crucial question of time reveals the split-second development of the calamity. It had been around noon that General Kurt Student, leading the air-borne troops in Holland, radioed Schmidt's XXXIX Corps headquarters that "bombing attack Rotterdam postponed owing to surrender negotiations." The attack was set for 3 P.M. Just five minutes before, at 2:55 P.M., General Schmidt sent yet another communiqué to Scharroo outlining surrender terms, giving the Dutch commander three hours in which to come to a decision—that is, until six o'clock.

Obviously communications between the German ground and air forces had become inefficient. The Dutch courier hastened across the Willems Bridge. He had barely reached the other side when a hundred Heinkels appeared over the city.

Recall orders had obviously been sent from Luftflotte 2, but as the planes were on their bombing run, and their receiving antennas having been retracted, the messages were not heard by the bomber radio operators. According to German accounts, desperate attempts were made to divert the bombers by discharging Very pistols into the air, but either the crews did not see them or mistook the signals for Dutch antiaircraft fire. Bombs began falling into the heart of Rotterdam.

Just as his plane's bomb load was dropped, Oberstleutnant Otto Hohne, commander of III/KG 54, spotted two red flares ascending through the smoke below. He shouted the recall order code word to his radio operator, who wired to the rest of the formation and prevented the dropping of all but a few bomb loads. It did not matter a great deal to the Dutch by this time, however.

Just over half of the hundred Heinkels had dropped hundred-pound and five-hundred pound bombs into the center of the old city: a total of ninety-seven tons. Within hours Rotterdam was in

Rotterdam after the May 14, 1940, "error" bombing by the Luftwaffe. Although the bombing mission had been called off because surrender negotiations were in progress, more than fifty aircraft dropped ninety-seven tons of explosives into the city, which burned uncontrollably.

(PRESS & INFORMATION SERVICES, ROTTERDAM)

flames: the small fire department was all but help-less because a bomb had hit a margarine factory. Burning oil spread to the timbered buildings and the heart of Rotterdam disintegrated in smoke. A twelve-year-old boy wrote that "There is a funny smell in the air like burned meat and a funny yellow light all over the country from the incendiary bombs. [This is an error. No incendiaries were used.] . . . I went out for a while and they were taking dead people out of the bombed houses. . . . It is awful to watch the people standing by their bombed houses. They don't do much. They just walk around and look at them and look sad and tired."

Rotterdam on that May 14, 1940, became a sym-bol of German *Kultur* like Guernica and Warsaw. The casualties, turned to propaganda uses by the Allies, were exaggerated. The official Dutch figure at the time—and it may have been an honest er-ror—reached thirty thousand dead.

The actual figure would be closer to a thousand men, women, and children—killed in the seven and a half minutes the Heinkels remained over Rotter-dam. In all, twenty thousand buildings were de-stroyed by bombs and the ensuing fires; seventy-eight thousand people were rendered homeless. A square mile of the city smoldered for days. By six o'clock in the evening the Dutch had capitulated. The blitzkrieg had crushed the Netherlands in five days.

Belgium was next on the Nazi timetable. The Belgians, led by King Leopold and reinforced by French and British troops, fought bitterly. The pat-tern was repeated and within eighteen days—on May 27, 1940—Leopold asked for a German peace. This action, however inevitable, was taken without proper consultation with his allies, and placed the French and British forces in serious jeopardy and possible annihilation. Already under pressure by the German forces which had broken through at Sedan, the beleaguered Allies, falling back into France, were left with their left flank exposed. The exhausted armies were rapidly encircled in steel, the panzers, the Stukas, and the Wehrmacht, drawing them closer to the sea at their backs, until the entire British Expeditionary Force, the French First Army as well as units of the Seventh and Ninth Armies, along with Belgian and Polish troops converged upon the French port of Dunkirk.

IV

There were two miracles at Dunkirk, one British, the other German.

The German "miracle" came to pass in the eve-ning of May 24 when from the headquarters of Von Rundstedt's Army Group A an order was issued halting the armored thrust from the south and the west. Panzer Group Kleist and Guderian's 19th Corps pulled up roughly on the line of canals run-ning from Gravelines on the Channel coast and southeasterly through Saint-Omer to Bethune. Rund-stedt had convinced the Führer that the tanks, after the surprising swing through France from the breakthrough at Sedan, should be rested for the major battle of France to come. With the Führer's backing there was no questioning the stop order, despite the objections of Commander in Chief Wal-ther von Brauchitsch. Hitler, who waxed manic-depressive, was one moment decisive and the next cautious. The success of the Lowlands campaign and the breach in the Ardennes was difficult to as-similate. And then Göring promised to destroy the fleeing allies on the Channel with his Luftwaffe. Why exhaust and deplete the Panzer forces if the Air Force could do the job? It was this con-sideration, not the fatuous one that Hitler had elected to spare the British, which resulted in the stop order.

Göring's vanity prompted him to offer more than the Luftwaffe could deliver. Many of the bomber *Geschwader* were still based far from the Dunkirk area, which fact would require long-distance flying and little time over the target. But the Wehrmacht and the panzers had been snatching most of the glory in the Lowlands, while the Luftwaffe con-tinued in a subservient role. Göring longed for a Luftwaffe coup, pure and simple, with no portion of the credit to the Army or Navy.

That the British had already begun to plan Opera-tion Dynamo, the evacuation, was not known to the Germans. That the British would attempt to evacu-ate from such ports as Calais, La Panne, and Dun-kirk seemed likely, but to the land-loving Ger-mans and to Hitler especially, for he had no sea sense at all, any large-scale withdrawal was un-thinkable.

The beach at Dunkirk: troops of the British Expeditionary Forces awaiting deliverance by "the little boats" and the Royal Navy after being driven into a pocket by the Wehrmacht. During the nine days of Dunkirk more than 300,000 men were rescued from the beaches of Dunkirk despite the efforts of the Luftwaffe. (NATIONAL ARCHIVES)

An RAF Coastal Command Lockheed Hudson flies over the beaches of Dunkirk. Oil storage tanks have been set aflame by Luftwaffe bombers.

(LOCKHEED PHOTO)

The British miracle (without qualifying quotation marks) was a stunning accomplishment of flexible planning, courage, civilian participation, imaginative improvisation, and sheer British doggedness. History's most heterogeneous armada gathered along the southeast coast of England. At Dover Vice-Admiral Sir Bertram Ramsay took charge of Operation Dynamo. Besides the craft of the Royal Navy, the Admiralty had pressed civilian motorboats into service. "At the same time," Winston Churchill has written, "lifeboats from liners in the London docks, tugs from the Thames, yachts, fishing-craft, lighters, barges, and pleasure-boats—anything that could be of use along the beaches—were called into service. By the night of the 27th a great tide of small vessels began to flow towards the sea, first to our Channel ports, and thence to the beaches of Dun-

kirk and the beloved Army." A total of 860 vessels of every description took part in the "Dunkirk deliverance," as Churchill called it. Seven hundred were British ships, the rest were French, Polish, Belgian, and Dutch. Nearly 250 ships of the armada were sunk, most of them by the Luftwaffe.

As the men of the British Expeditionary Force limped or were carried ashore, their eyes revealed the harrowing experience they had undergone. Their hollow-cheeked faces were begrimed by the smoke of oil fire, burning vehicles, and shells. These wearied men, returned with only what they wore—for their weapons were abandoned on the beaches at Dunkirk—grateful for their deliverance, brought a bitter question with them.

"Where was the bloody RAF?"

The infantryman, whose concern is generally confined to the few feet of ground he occupies, has little conception of the airman's war. On the Dunkirk beaches the infantryman was only aware of the bombing and strafing of the Luftwaffe. Rarely did he see or recognize a British aircraft overhead. He did not see the Blenheims of No. 107 Squadron bombing the advancing German columns on May 27—the day the evacuation officially began. Coincidentally, it was also the day on which the Rundstedt-Hitler stop order was withdrawn, after a two-and-a-half-day pause.

At dawn on Monday, May 27, the Heinkels began the bombardment of the defense perimeter around Dunkirk; then came Richthofen's Stukas to pin-point the targets. The Dorniers followed. These last were surprised on being attacked by Spitfires of No. 74 Squadron—the first major encounter with this new fighter. Hurricanes of No. 145 Squadron also joined the battle, but the British were always outnumbered by the Messerschmitt 109s and 110s. However, it was soon obvious that the Spitfire was a match for the Me-109 and superior to the Hurricane as a high-altitude fighter.

Even so, great numbers of German bombers broke through the Spitfire and Hurricane formations and bombed the beaches and the ships in the Channel. Oil storage tanks on the western outskirts of Dunkirk were set afire and the black smoke rose as a thick, curling beacon to friend and foe alike. But when the weather turned damp and the ceiling descended this same oily smoke combined with the smoke from the fires in the town and mist to afford cover for the evacuation.

A pilot of No. 43 Squadron described the scene as he saw it from above: "All the harbour at Dunkirk seemed to be on fire with the black smoke from the oil dumps," he said. "The destroyers moved out of the pall of smoke in a most uncanny way, deep in the water and heavily laden with troops. I was flying at about 1000 feet above the beach and the sea. And there I could see the *Brighton Belle,* and the paddle steamers, and the sort of cheerful little boats you see calling at coastal towns on Sunday. Hundreds of boats! Fishing boats and motor boats, and Thames river craft and strings of dinghies, being towed by bigger boats. All packed with troops, and people standing in the water and awful bomb craters in the beach, and lines of men and groups of people sitting down. Waiting, I suppose. And I could see rifles—stacked in threes. And destroyers going back into the black smoke. And wrecked ships on the beach: wrecked ships of all sizes, sticking out of the water. And a destroyer cut in halves by a bomb. I saw it!"

On the beach itself all was a horror. A British gunnery officer sensed "a deadly evil atmosphere . . . a lurid study in red and black. . . . A horrible stench of blood and mutilated flesh pervaded the place. There was no escape from it. Not a breath of air was blowing to dissipate the appalling odour that arose from the dead bodies that had been lying on the sand, in some cases for several days. We might have been walking through a slaughterhouse on a hot day. The darkness, which hid some of the sights of horror from our eyes, seemed to thicken this dreadful stench. It created the impression that death was hovering around, very near at hand. . . ."

The aerial battles generally occurred out of sight of the besieged ground troops. Although German planes did attack mercilessly, the Luftwaffe did not gain mastery of the air over Dunkirk because of the defense afforded by the Hurricane and Spitfire squadrons of No. 11 Group under the command of Air Vice-Marshal Keith R. Park. To contend with the massive formations of German fighters and bombers Park had only sixteen squadrons available —that is, about two hundred fighters. From their bases in southern England the fighters would have to be flown at least fifty miles to the battle area—without the advantage of radar to pin-point the

"Where was the bloody RAF?" The Hurricanes (and the Spitfires) operated above the clouds in fighting the Luftwaffe and so were rarely seen by the beleaguered ground troops at Dunkirk. Although RAF fighters intercepted German bombers, some broke through to bomb the beaches. (U. S. AIR FORCE)

German attacks. This meant that fuel limitations enforced about a forty-minute stay over Dunkirk for the Hurricanes and Spitfires.

To send all sixteen squadrons to cover the entire evacuation area was impossible (it was attempted on the first day, May 27, but the wasteful fuel consumption rendered such tactics infeasible; it also left England open to air attack, and the defense of the home islands was the major function of Fighter Command). Beginning on May 29, Park devised a patrol system over Dunkirk, using four squadrons at a time. Consequently there were stretches of time when no RAF fighters patrolled directly over Dunkirk. Also, while attempting to attack the bombers, they were in turn attacked by the Messerschmitts. Two very large formations of German bombers, including the vulnerable Stuka and the vaunted Junkers 88, assaulted the beaches while no British fighters were present. Three other formations, however, had been mauled by the British fighters.

In the turmoil as much, possibly more, shipping was lost through collision as to German bombs. Also owing to the confusion of battle—and faulty aircraft recognition, especially on the part of the Royal Navy—the men in the Dunkirk perimeter fired indiscriminately at friend and foe alike. All aircraft were taken to be hostile by the harassed troops crowding into the sea. Rear Admiral William Wake-Walker recalled several such incidents on June 1, the sixth day of the evacuation. Spitfires flying low over the beaches received the same attention from the British guns as did a Messerschmitt—even after Wake-Walker hoisted the cease fire flag. Later he witnessed a similar piece of action as he stood talking with Captain W. G. Tennant, the senior naval officer in charge of shore operations, when "a Lysander Army Co-op plane came over very low and flew over the pier. It was fired at by several Bofors guns and Tennant said, 'I'm sure that damn fellow is a Hun—he has been flying over here all day.' I then realized," Wake-Walker reported, "it was the plane flying over at my request to see if the pier was being shelled, and I felt sorry for the poor chap; though he seemed none the worse."

Not all the errors were made on the ground, for Spitfires and Hurricanes attacked each other above the clouds also.

The Luftwaffe attacks on June 1 had been so vicious—Stukas by the dozen not only attacked the ships but also came in low to strafe the struggling figures in the water—that Ramsay realized that the evacuation could be continued only at night. The German ground forces had also begun to press in on the perimeter and the sands of Dunkirk erupted with the shelling from German artillery.

The fighting in the air too had become desperate; the initiative belonged to the Luftwaffe, which could muster great numbers of bombers with escorts. As the battle progressed, and as the German infantry closed in, the Luftwaffe gained airdromes closer to battle site. Only the weather and the RAF interfered. But from time to time, such as on May 29 and June 1, the sun broke through and cleared the mist, and the Germans concentrated with fury on Dunkirk. And so it went, intermittently for the nine days.

"Well, another day is gone," wrote Flight Lieutenant R. D. G. Wight of No. 213 Squadron to his mother, "and with it a lot of grand blokes. Got another brace of 109's today, but the whole Luftwaffe seems to leap on us—we were hopelessly outnumbered. I was caught napping by a 109 in the middle of a dog fight and got a couple of holes in the aircraft, one of them filled the office with smoke, but the Jerry overshot and *he's* dead. If anyone says anything to you in the future about the inefficiency of the R.A.F.—I believe the B.E.F. troops were booing the R.A.F. in Dover the other day—tell them from me we only wish we could do more. But without aircraft we can do no more than we have done—that is, our best, and that's fifty times better than the German best, though they are fighting under the most advantageous conditions."

On the morning of June 4, with the Germans within two miles of the beaches, Operation Dynamo was officially closed. About forty thousand French troops remained behind to hold off the Germans —just as they had during the nine days at Calais and Cassel. Theirs had been an enormous contribution to the miracle of Dunkirk—a contribution frequently slighted in view of the performance of the "little boats" and their own political and military leaders subsequently.

Dunkirk was no military victory. The Germans had permitted practically the entire British Army to escape. True, they were weaponless and most of their equipment lay abandoned along the beaches

German troops haul in a trophy from the English Channel, the tail section of an RAF Hurricane shot down during the desperate fighting of the last weeks of the Battle of France. (NATIONAL ARCHIVES)

at Dunkirk, but it was a tough, experienced army. The Luftwaffe had not been able to achieve—if, indeed, they were achievements—a Warsaw or a Rotterdam. This despite the ease with which the smoking, water-outlined target could be found even in bad weather.

The cost of Dunkirk in shipping was high: 6 destroyers were sunk, 8 personnel ships, 5 minesweepers, 17 trawlers, a hospital ship, a sloop, 3 tugboats, 3 yachts, and 182 other assorted craft. The RAF lost over 100 aircraft and 80 pilots in the Dunkirk battles. The Luftwaffe lost about 150 planes, although claims were made for twice that number.

Churchill reminded the British that "Wars are not won by evacuations. But there was a victory inside this deliverance, which should be noted. It was gained by the Air Force. . . ."

If it was not a spectacular victory, even an almost negligible one, it was, on a small scale, a prologue to the coming battle over Britain. It might have served as portent to the Luftwaffe of things to come.

Dunkirk had not been a victory for the British, although 338,000 men had been snatched out of the jaws of the devouring blitzkrieg. But it was a triumph of the British spirit, best expressed by Churchill during the nine days when he said, "Of course, whatever happens at Dunkirk, we shall fight on."

Churchill had been handed the reins of government, taking over from the ailing and tottering Chamberlain, in the early evening of May 10, 1940 —that morning the Germans had struck in the Low Countries. Reveling in crisis, defying adversity, and spoiling for a fight, the once discredited Churchill, whose warnings of a burgeoning military Nazi Germany had not contributed to his popularity, was the embodiment of the British spirit. He watched the fighting in France with concern, but never with the loss of hope so evident in the French government and High Command.

When the Germans attacked there were eight Hurricane squadrons in France, the Air Component's Nos. 3, 85, 87, 607, and 615 Squadrons and the AASF's Nos. 1, 73, and 501 Squadrons. By May 12 these were joined by Nos. 79 and 504 Squadrons sent to the dwindling Air Component taxed with the support of the BEF. Under the onslaught of the blitzkrieg in the north of France the seven squadrons of the Air Component had been reduced to about three on May 17; four days later the remnants were ordered back to England.

The fighter pilots who had complained about the "phony war" and the scanty air activity had little cause for gripes after May 10. Their fields were bombed and strafed and they were air-borne from dawn till dusk. The bombers of AASF were spent in bombing the advancing Nazi columns while the Hurricanes furnished fighter cover. There was plenty of action for eager fighter pilots, German as well as British and French.

On May 12 Adolf Galland, one of Germany's outstanding airmen, scored his first "kill," a Belgian Hurricane. Flying with a wingman in an Me-109E, Galland had stolen some time away from his desk job. The two Germans spotted a formation of eight Hurricanes flying at nine thousand feet near Liége. Diving from above, Galland opened on an unsuspecting Belgian. The first burst from Galland's guns startled the Hurricane pilots and the formation scattered. The German concentrated on his victim, now clumsily trying to evade the guns of the Messerschmitt. The poorly trained pilot in the antiquated Hurricane had no chance. Galland's second burst shot away the Hurricane's rudder and the plane spun away. Before striking the ground the aircraft shed parts of its wings. Galland then turned to the remaining Belgian planes. Finding one Hurricane attempting to dive away from the battle, Galland in his superior Me-109 pulled up to within a hundred yards of it. The plane whipped away in a half roll and through an opening in the clouds. But the experienced Galland remained locked to the Hurricane's tail. A burst of gunfire and the Belgian plane pulled up for a moment, stalled, and dived straight into the ground. In the afternoon of the same day, while on a routine patrol flight, Galland accounted for another Hurricane—his third victory of the day.

On the day after the Dunkirk evacuation, June 5, Werner Mölders, the leading German ace with twenty-five "kills" to his credit, joined a battle in the vicinity of Amiens. The contenders were French Dewoitine 520s, the best—and rarest, because of the inefficiency of the Production Office—fighter the Armée de l'Air could muster. Only one group had been supplied with the D-520s before the Germans opened their attack on France. It was the group's planes which Mölders came upon fighting off the Messerschmitts. He fired at one of the French planes and lost it in the general melee: there were nine French aircraft standing off more than two dozen Messerschmitts. Mölders turned back to the center of battle. Suddenly his cockpit burst into flame and smoke, his throttle was shot out of his hand, and the Me-109 flipped into a vertical dive. Struggling inside the smoky cockpit, Mölders found the release catch and sent the cockpit hood off into the slipstream. Unexpectedly the Messerschmitt leveled for a second from its dive, which had pressed Mölders into the cockpit, and he jumped. Mölders, floating down into France, watched his plane crash into the ground. Thus it was that Germany's hero-ace was taken prisoner of war. When the French surrendered subsequently, however, Mölders and all the other German pilots taken prisoner in France were released.

On June 5 also the Germans opened their new offensive, *Fall Rot* ("Case Red"), across the Somme and the Seine. Before long their armor had crossed the Marne—the familiar names of an earlier war echoed the sound of disaster. Refugees filled the roads, fleeing from northern France to the south: these too were familiar scenes. The Luftwaffe contributed innovations by strafing and dive-bombing the clogged highways. By this time there were too few targets to keep them occupied.

The British pilots remaining in France, the rem-

Werner Mölders, who was shot down over France after the Dunkirk evacuation and taken prisoner; with the fall of France he was released and served later in the war as commander of Jagdgeschwader 51 on the Eastern Front. Mölder's official victory score for the Second World War was sixty-eight (and fourteen in Spain); he was killed in an air crash later in the war. (H. J. NOWARRA)

The French Dewoitine 520, the best of the few French fighters operational during the Battle of France. The German ace Mölders was shot down by a French pilot in a D-520. (MUSÉE DE L'AIR)

nants of Nos. 1, 73, and 501 Squadrons, later joined by Nos. 17 and 242 Squadrons, fell back to emergency landing strips southwest of Paris. The constant nervous strain, exhaustion, and high-altitude flying took its toll along with the German fighters. Individual pilots flew patrol after patrol until fatigue caused them to fall asleep in their cockpits while they were refueling and being rearmed. When their Hurricanes were ready, the ground crew had to punch the pilots awake. One pilot reported that he had fallen asleep three times while flying over German-occupied territory. Another pilot landed and fell asleep in the cockpit. He was lifted from the plane and when all attempts to awaken him failed, he was shipped to England. He awakened forty-eight hours later wondering how he had ever got back home.

Meanwhile, France lay broken and without hope in the path of the overwhelming German armies, now being lent close support by the Luftwaffe. Even small pockets of resistance were crushed under the Stukas working with the panzers. The French demanded more British fighter squadrons to deal with the Stukas. But the outcome of the battle was obvious and Churchill, after sending additional Hurricanes, relented and sent no more. Of the necessity of this decision he had been forcefully convinced by Fighter Command leader Air Marshal Hugh Dowding. The latter had estimated that fifty-two fighter squadrons would be required to defend Britain from the attack that must come once France was defeated. On hand were a mere twenty-five; if an additional ten squadrons were sent to France, only to be destroyed in the French holocaust, Britain too must fall. As early as May 15, 1940, Dowding had warned the Air Ministry that "if the Home Defense Force is drained away in desperate attempts to remedy the situation in France, defeat in France will involve the final, complete and irremediable defeat of this country."

Churchill, who was romantically inclined and could not leave a friend or an ally in trouble, was seriously tempted to send an additional ten Hurricane squadrons to France. The French were calling for no less than twenty. The dispatch of ten squadrons was being seriously considered when Chief of the Air Staff Air Chief Marshal Cyril Newall learned from Air Marshal A. S. Barratt, commanding the two British air forces in France,

that even if ten squadrons were sent there would be bases for no more than three.

Instead, at Newall's suggestion, six squadrons based in the south of England rotated to France: three each morning and three to relieve them in the afternoon. Soon after, upon witnessing the chaos and hopeless desperation in France himself, Churchill concurred and no further fighter squadrons were sent to France.

The extent of the disorder and near paralysis of the French High Command was revealed when Benito Mussolini, concerned that his German colleague had so brilliantly outdistanced him in the race for conquest, declared war upon France and Great Britain. With the German Army within thirty miles of Paris it was safe no doubt for the Duce's legions to attack the Riviera. On May 10, 1940, Hitler had himself a partner in war: it would, in time, cost them both dearly.

It had been agreed in the French and British Supreme War Council that in the event of a declaration of war by Italy British aircraft were to be bombed-up to attack industrial targets in northern Italy.

So it was that in the early afternoon of May 11 No. 99 Squadron (Wellingtons) landed in France, near Salon, to refuel on the way to bomb Genoa. The longer-ranged Armstrong Whitworth Whitleys of Nos. 10, 51, 58, and 102 Squadrons accompanying the Wellingtons were to refuel in advance bases in the Channel Islands (instead of France) and proceed to targets in Genoa and Turin.

The Wellingtons had barely landed when Group Captain R. M. Field, in charge of the bomber force at Salon, was informed by the French that the planes were not to take off for Italy. Still wondering what this was about, Field received an order from the Air Ministry to send the bombers to Italy. The phone rang; it was the French commander again reiterating that bombing operations against Italian targets were forbidden.

From three-thirty in the afternoon till almost midnight Field was involved in a whirl of order and counterorder; it seemed his phone never stopped ringing. The French High Command had even gone to Barratt, at British Air Forces in France headquarters. Barratt called London attempting to get Churchill. He learned that the Prime Minister was in France. Churchill was, in fact, just sitting down

Symbol of the French Air Force during the Battle of France, May–July 1940. This French bomber was destroyed in an air battle with an Me-109.

to dinner with French Premier Paul Reynaud, Supreme Allied Commander General Maxime Weygand, General Charles de Gaulle, and members of Churchill's party including Anthony Eden and Chief of the Imperial Staff Sir John Dill.

Churchill was reached through General Hastings Ismay, at Weygand's headquarters, and the Churchillian view was constant: "All our [that is, English] minds ran much more on bombing Milan and Turin the moment Mussolini declared war, and seeing how he liked that."

Insofar as he was able to judge, after sifting the various orders, views, and opinions, Captain Field must dispatch the Wellingtons to bomb Italy. The Whitleys in the meantime had already taken off from the Channel Islands.

As the Wellingtons taxied for the takeoff at Salon, the distracted French added the final touch. French trucks, lorries, and carts were driven onto the airfield and stalled strategically in the path of the British bombers. Thus effectively blocked, and not wanting to fight it out with his allies, Field canceled the mission to Italy. The Whitleys, however, continued on and of the thirty-six sent only thirteen bombed their targets. Bad icing conditions and storms over the Alps greatly curtailed the mission.

It required four additional days of discussion before the field at Salon was cleared of the French obstructions. Eight Wellingtons took off to bomb Genoa but again storms interfered and only one plane found the target.

The situation in France had deteriorated so thoroughly by this time that such missions seemed without point. On June 14 the triumphant Germans marched into Paris. On June 17, 1940, Marshal Henri Pétain, succeeding Reynaud as Premier, asked for an armistice. On the afternoon of June 21 Hitler appeared for less than a half hour in the Forest of Compiègne, some forty-five miles north of Paris, the site of the hated German surrender of 1918. Hitler literally danced at Compiègne and then left the technicalities of the signing of the new treaty to others. France was finished and the British were driven off the Continent again. Cobber Kain's No. 73 Squadron, after covering the final evacuations from Nantes and Saint-Nazaire, was the last to leave. On June 18, as the surviving six Hurricanes thundered down the runway, all non-operational

A representative selection of aircraft that fought in the opening phases of the Second World War—from the blitzkreig in Poland to the Battle of Britain.

From top to bottom, *left*: Junkers Ju 87B (9th Staffel, Stukageschwader 1); P.Z.L. P11 (1st Air Regiment, No. 112 Squadron, "Swallows"); Hawker Hurricane I (No. 1. Squadron, markings of

Pilot Officer P.W.O. Mould); *Center*: Junkers Ju 88A (3rd. Staffle, Kampfgeschwader 51), Heinkel He III (Kampfgeschwader 100); *Right*: Supermarine Spitfire A (No. 54 Squadron, markings of Flight Lieutenant A. C. Deere); Dornier Do 17 (Kampfgeschwader 77); Messerschmitt Bf 109E (III Gruppe, Jagdeschwader 26, markings of Captain Adolpf Galland).

Joseph A. Phelan

Where do we go from here? Göring (fifth from right) and his staff gazing from the coast of France across the English Channel at Dover, England. Hav- *ing won a quick victory the Luftwaffe—and the Wehrmacht—had made no real plans to cross that Channel.* (NATIONAL ARCHIVES)

aircraft, supplies, and equipment were set ablaze. France had become a vast funeral pyre.

Looking down upon his stricken country from six miles up, author-pilot Antoine de Saint-Exupéry saw the devastation and the futile burning. "But how many villages have we seen burnt down," he speculated, "only that war may be made to look like war? Burnt down exactly as trees are cut down, crews flung into the holocaust, infantry sent against tanks, merely to make war look like war. Small wonder that an unutterable disquiet hangs over the land. For nothing does any good."

Hitler was jubilant; Versailles was truly avenged. In an outburst of largess he created a flowering of field marshals: Brauchitsch, Bock, Kluge, Leeb, Rundstedt, Reichenau, Witzleben, and Keitel. The Luftwaffe too was honored as Kesselring, Sperrle, and Milch were given their batons.

But there was an unutterable disquiet in the German camp too. The forces of National Socialism, the great German Reich, the Wehrmacht, the immortal Führer himself had achieved incredible heights.

Was nun? "What now?" was the question all the conquerers asked as they stood peering through their glasses across the English Channel. *Was nun?* they wondered as they studied the stark chalk cliffs of Dover.

Was nun? Victory had come so quickly. Poland: twenty-six days; Norway: twenty-eight days; Denmark: twenty-four hours; the Netherlands: five days; Belgium: eighteen days; and France, with its Maginot Line, its great Army and Air Force: thirty-five days.

As they stood arrogantly, assured but questioning the next move, the invincible victors had no idea that, in truth, not even the Führer knew. The tottering British must be added to the victory timetable. All agreed to that.

But how?

BOOK II
The Battle of Britain

Men like these saved England.

AN AIR MINISTRY ACCOUNT OF THE
GREAT DAYS FROM AUGUST 8–OCTOBER 31, 1940

5

ADLERANGRIFF

THINKING now of those days," an English flight lieutenant said in recollection of July–October 1940, "I find that what remains most clearly in my memory is not the sweating strain of the actual fighting, not the hurried meals, the creeping from bed at dawn, not even the loss of one's friends; but rather those odd stolen moments of peace in the middle of all the pandemonium—the heat haze lying lazily over the airfield while we sat munching a piece of grass, waiting to take off; that curiously lovely moment of twilight after the last Spitfire had landed, after the last engine had been switched off, and before the first night fighter took the air, the first search-light split the darkness and the first wail of the siren was heard again—that moment when the evening lay spread out against the sky, giving for an instant a mocking glimpse of stillness and peace before night fell suddenly like a curtain and the whole hideous cacophony of war broke out afresh.

"But, above all, the thing that remains most clearly imprinted on my memory is the spirit which then existed—the same spirit which inspired everybody from the Station Commander to the lowest air-craft-hand. . . . For that was the first trial, the first flush of battle, and it was a great hour."

Another pilot remembers: "We always had a devil-may-care sort of happiness. Lying in the sun waiting at readiness, there were moments of great beauty; the colours in the fields seemed brightest and the sky the deepest blue just before taking off for a big blitz. At dusk everything became peaceful. We were all happy at the thought of another day accomplished, our Hurricanes standing silhouetted against the sky, looking strong and confident, the darkness hiding their patched-up paintwork. In the morning whilst it was still dark, the roar of engines being tested woke us for another day's work."

"They were wonderful, weird, exciting days," a squadron leader recalled. "Days when aircraft left beautiful curving vapour trails high in the sky, days when some of our friends took off and never came back, when others came back maimed and burnt, never to fight again."

It was, despite the pervading ubiquity of death, an exhilarating time. The warriors were young—the average age was twenty—they were vigorous, and they felt they would never die, at least, perhaps, not today. They were a small band of men, Winston Churchill's "few," who must hold back Hitler's con-querers. They were the despised "soft English," the comic "weekend pilots," the unprofessionals, and surely they must soon be overwhelmed by the un-beatable Luftwaffe. In their Hurricanes and Spit-fires they took off from airfields in Kent and Sussex. And here lay some of the root of the spirit: the gen-tle, trim English countryside—home for so many —was the last thing they saw before climbing five miles up to do battle.

The people of Britain too exhibited a spirit of mordant defiance, a quality of tough fatalism, of

Fighter types: typical RAF men of the Battle of Britain. Standing (right), wearing a "Mae West," is Peter Townsend, who on February 3, 1940, shot down the first German aircraft that fell on England—long before the Battle began. Later Townsend went to France to command No. 85 Squadron and returned to fly in the Battle of Britain, during which he became an ace. (IMPERIAL WAR MUSEUM, LONDON)

Command, Members of Parliament. The subjects ranged from wicked—often impractical—devices of war to the defense of London. The common refrain was one of challenging preparation. To Mr. Josiah Wedgwood, M.P., Churchill wrote that "You must rest assured that we should fight every street of London and its suburbs. It would *devour* an invading army, assuming one ever got that far. We hope, however, to drown the bulk of them in the salt sea."

Finally in the German camp on July 2, 1940—eleven days after the signing of the armistice with

recognizing that they would soon be fighting for their very survival—and finding a fearful elation in the thought. In their small island—*their* small island and they intended to keep it—arose a mood of Shakespearean poetry-drama. Winston Churchill gave voice to this mood and was the living paragon of the Briton whom Hitler must defeat before he could win the war in the west.

With the defeat of France came an easy temper of complete victory in the German Army; plans were made for a victory parade in Paris and lists were drawn up of divisions to be dispersed home.

But the final days of June slipped away and there was no indication that London was seriously considering the peace feelers Hitler had sent through neutrals. This was puzzling, for surely, Hitler thought, the British were beaten. The ex-corporal, now the greatest living field marshal, looked with a wistful corporal's heart at the cold, treacherous English Channel. Certainly the British must come to terms.

Instead the contentious Prime Minister dictated reams of warlike minutes, pithy bits of advice, questions, assurances, demands, criticisms, and suggestive comments to his War Cabinet, the High

Waiting: pilots of No. 611 Squadron, with a ready Spitfire (note parachute on wingtip), enduring one of war's characteristic experiences, tedium. During the Battle No. 611 Squadron, then based at Digby, suffered numerous casualties.

(IMPERIAL WAR MUSEUM, LONDON)

The Ditch, the English Channel from thirty-five thousand feet. Calais is at lower left and Dover's white cliffs above. Only the Ditch—and the RAF—stood be- *tween Hitler and, in the phrase of Wehrmacht Chief of Staff Jodl, "The final German victory over England . . ." which he believed to be "only a question of time."* (ROBERT C. CHAPIN)

France—Keitel issued instructions to all three services to prepare for an invasion of Britain. Hitler did not make his own directive No. 16 for the Conduct of the War, official with his signature until two weeks later. Directive No. 16 opened with these words: "As England, in spite of the hopelessness of her military position, has so far not shown herself willing to come to any compromise, I have decided to begin to prepare for, and if necessary to carry out, an invasion of England.

"This operation is dictated by the necessity of eliminating Great Britain as a base from which the war against Germany can be fought, and if necessary the island will be occupied." This was to be

Operation *Seelöwe* ("Sealion"), and Hitler's own equivocal posture is revealed in the conditional phrases closing each paragraph.

Colonel General Alfred Jodl, Chief of Staff of the Wehrmacht, was more definite when he wrote that "The final German victory over England is now only a question of time. Enemy offensive operations on a large scale are no longer possible." He was correct in the last sentence, but in the first he raised "the question of time." And it was time which the Germans were all but deliberately bestowing upon the British. Jodl too could wax happy, for he knew his army would be spared the initial phases of dealing with the British. The major burden must fall upon the Imperial Navy and the Luftwaffe. Admiral Raeder, as early as November 15, 1939, had instructed the Naval War Staff to look into the chances of invading England. At that time he had not expected to pay so heavily for the conquest of Norway. The loss of half his cruisers and destroyers placed Raeder in no position to deal with the British in the Channel—the German Navy had not even been able to interfere very effectively with the Dunkirk evacuation. Operation Sealion would be spread over a sea front of more than two hundred miles, from Lyme Bay to Ramsgate. How the German Navy could clear, protect, and convoy over so large an area was a serious and, Raeder knew inwardly, an impossible question.

On July 19, 1940—a full month after the last Hurricane took off from France and three days after he had signed the *Seelöwe* directive—Hitler appeared before the Reichstag. The German press was to hail the speech made that day as a "peace offer," Britain's last chance before the blow fell.

"In this hour," Hitler said, "I feel it to be my duty before my own conscience to appeal once more to reason and common sense in Great Britain as much as elsewhere. I consider myself in a position to make this appeal since I am not the vanquished begging favors, but the victor speaking in the name of reason. I can see no reason why this war must go on.

"It almost causes me pain to think that I should have been selected by Fate to deal the final blow to the structure which these men have already set tottering. . . . Mr. Churchill ought perhaps, for once, to believe me when I prophesy that a great Empire will be destroyed—an Empire which it was

never my intention to destroy or even to harm. . . .

"Possibly Mr. Churchill will brush aside this statement of mine by saying it is merely born of fear and doubt of final victory. In that case I shall have relieved my conscience in regard to the things to come."

Göring, who had drawn up an ambitious plan for dealing with the British "by attacking the enemy air force, its ground organizations, and its own industry" on June 30, hoped too that the stubborn British would realize the precariousness of their position. He took little interest in the invasion studies being made by the Army staffs. He found little comfort, as the days passed and no word of surrender came from Britain, in watching the emphasis of "the things to come" devolving upon the Luftwaffe. But then his bravado prevailed and he was certain, after the successes of the Luftwaffe since the beginning of the war, that England could very well be blasted out of the war by air power alone.

From the Führer's headquarters on August 1, 1940, was issued the "Top Secret" Directive No. 17 for the Conduct of Air and Naval Warfare Against England:

In order to establish the conditions necessary for the final conquest of England I intend to continue the air and sea war against the English homeland more intensively than before.

Therefore, I order the following:

1. The German Air Force is to overcome the English air forces with all means at its disposal and as soon as possible. The attacks must at first be directed at flying formations, their ground organizations, and their supply organizations; secondly, against the aircraft production industry and the industries engaged in production of antiaircraft equipment.

2. After we gain local temporary air superiority the air war is to be directed against harbors, especially those important to the food supplies, and also against inland food storage facilities. Attacks carried out against the south coast harbors must bear in mind future operations we may wish to carry out and must therefore be restricted to the minimum.

3. The war against enemy warships and merchant ships must, however, take secondary position in the air war unless such ships present attractive opportunity targets, or is an additional bonus to attacks carried out under paragraph 2 above, or where it may be used for training of crews for specialized tasks.

4. The increased air war is to be carried out so that the Air Force can support naval operations on satisfactory opportunity targets with sufficient forces

as and when necessary. In addition, the Air Force must remain battleworthy for Operation Sealion.

5. Terror raids as reprisal I reserve the right to order myself.

6. The intensified air war may begin on August 5. The opening date may be selected by the Air Force itself upon completion of preparations and taking weather conditions into account. The Navy is authorized to begin intensified operations on the same date.

—Adolf Hitler

On the following day an order alerting Luftflotten 2, 3, and 5 was issued. They were to begin preparations for *Adlerangriff*—"Eagle Attack." No date

land would surely bring out the RAF and then, perhaps, the legend would fade.

Finally, with the help of Milch, also present at Karinhall, it was decided that *Adler Tag* would take place on August 10, weather permitting. But the weather turned for the worse and *Adler Tag* was postponed until August 13.

The main burden of the attack fell upon Luftflotte 2, with headquarters in Brussels and whose units were deployed in northern Germany, Holland, Belgium, and France north of the Seine, and Luftflotte 3, with headquarters in Paris and units based in western France. Luftflotte 5 would make its

The armourers . . . Give dreadful note of preparation: while Hitler offered Britain his truculent "peace offer" and Göring wished that Britain might sink into the sea,

the Luftwaffe got ready for its next objective. Lehrgeschwader 1 (left) ground crews check their Ju-88s and armorers of Jagdgeschwader 51 load the guns of the Me-109. (H. J. NOWARRA)

was set for the first day of the intensified attack. High-level, and argumentative, meetings were held at Göring's Karinhall to determine general policy and set an *Adler Tag* ("Eagle Day"). There was disagreement between Sperrle (Luftflotte 3) and Kesselring (Luftflotte 2), the former advocating the operations against the RAF, the ports, and supply centers, as Hitler had outlined. Kesselring leaned toward a concentration on a few targets (he had earlier suggested attacking Gibraltar rather than take on the RAF over England). He was soon shown the light and reluctantly agreed, though he had wanted to maintain the legend of the Luftwaffe's invincibility. A direct attack upon the British home-

thrusts from bases in Norway and Denmark. Two *Fliegerkorps* (air corps), 2 and 8, were assigned to establish air superiority over the English Channel and to disrupt, if possible to stop, all shipping into Britain. Fliegerkorps 2 (more correctly designated with Roman numeral), based on the Pas de Calais within Stuka strike of the Straits of Dover, was under command of General Bruno Loerzer, Göring's old First World War best friend. Loerzer's units would operate within the boundaries assigned to Luftflotte 2—an imaginary line, not always observed, which ran across the Channel northerly from Le Havre, cut the English coast near Portsmouth, and continued upward passing slightly to the west of Oxford and, farther north, to the west of Birmingham up through Manchester. All targets to the left of this line, theoretically, were the responsibility of Luftflotte 2; those to the right belonged to Luftflotte 3.

The other *Fliegerkorps*, number 8, based just south of the *Luftflotten* boundary at Deauville, was commanded by Generalmajor Wolfram von Richthofen. Once the chief critic of the Stuka, Richthofen was celebrated as the master of close support and a Stuka virtuoso. His *Fliegerkorps* consisted mainly of Ju-87s.

Ringing the British Isles and poised for *Adler Tag*, therefore, were three massive German air fleets —bombers, dive bombers, single-engined and twin-engined fighters, reconnaissance craft—about 3500 aircraft. Normally about two thirds of the total strength might be serviceable for any given day, however. As of August 10, 1940, for example, Luftflotten 2 and 3, the major units participating in *Adlerangriff*, had at their disposal 1232 long-range bombers (875 serviceable), 406 dive bombers (316 serviceable), 813 single-engined fighters (702 serviceable), 282 twin-engined fighters and fighter-bombers (227 serviceable), as well as about 50 long-range reconnaissance planes.

Across the Channel Air Marshal Sir Hugh Dowding prepared his Fighter Command for the onslaught he knew was coming. The presence of Dowding, like that of Churchill, at this time and at this place, was providential. A brilliant administrator, a sound strategist, and a shrewd tactician, Dowding was, in personality as well as a leader, the opposite of his opponent Göring. For that matter, the aloof Air Officer Commander in Chief, Fighter Command (to use his correct title), shared little in common with his own fighter pilots, who called him "Stuffy," a term of rakish affection rather than scorn.

The words of Churchill must have spurred Dowding, as he took full advantage of the seven weeks between the end of the Battle of France and the opening of the Battle of Britain. "The whole fury and might of the enemy must very soon be turned on us," Churchill had said. "Hitler knows that he will have to break us in this island or lose the war. If we can stand up to him, all Europe may be free and the life of the world may move forward into broad, sunlit uplands. But if we fail, then the

Air Chief Marshal Sir Hugh C. T. Dowding—"Stuffy" to his irreverent but affectionate pilots. For all his diffidence Dowding was a brilliant strategist and proved it as leader of Fighter Command during the Battle.
(IMPERIAL WAR MUSEUM, LONDON)

whole world, including the United States, including all that we have known and cared for, will sink into the abyss of a new Dark Age, made more sinister, and perhaps more protracted, by the lights of perverted science.

"Let us therefore brace ourselves to our duties," Churchill concluded, "and so bear ourselves that, if the British Empire and its Commonwealth last for a thousand years, men will say, 'This was their finest hour.'"

Dowding had sixty squadrons on hand in time for *Adler Tag* with 704 operational aircraft at their disposal (and 289 in reserve). Of these aircraft 620 were Hurricanes and Spitfires (about 400 of the former and 200 of the latter). The rest were Bristol Blenheims, two-engined light bombers em-

The backbone of Fighter Command during the Battle of Britain: the Hurricane. The Hurricane's performance was limited and was no match for the Me-109 at high altitudes. (HAWKER SIDDELEY AVIATION, LTD.)

ployed as fighters, and the Boulton Paul Defiant, a two-seat fighter which resembled the Hurricane. Over Dunkirk, where the Defiant went into action for the first time, it had proved most successful. German pilots, mistaking it for the Hurricane and not realizing a second crew member manned the rear-firing machine guns, attacked from the rear and were shot down. This advantage lasted briefly, for soon the Germans realized the Defiant was a different plane and dealt with it harshly, for it was no match for the Me-109. Nor was the Blenheim; even less the Gladiator, of which a single flight (six planes) remained operational in one squadron.

The Hurricane was obsolescent by August 1940, though a sturdy fighter and a good aircraft. It was Dowding's plan to have the Hurricanes attack the German bombers, which were slower and less maneuverable than the fighters, and leave the Messerschmitts, the 109s and the twin-engined 110s, to the faster, more nimble Spitfires. The Spitfire was a better high-altitude performer than the Hurricane—and the German fighters too fought well above twenty thousand feet.

Dowding's major concern at the Battle's inception was not aircraft, but pilots. Churchill had appointed newspaper publisher Lord Beaverbrook (William Maxwell Aitken) to head the Ministry of Aircraft Production in May 1940. Beaverbrook's disdain for red tape, his dynamism and highly charged personality contributed to the rise in aircraft production. In this he was, of course, helped by the urgency of the time, the robust defiance that vitalized all Britons after Dunkirk. Beaverbrook's son, John William Aitken, had served in France with No. 601 Squadron and was flying a Hurricane with the same unit based in Tangmere near the coast of southern England.

The air fighting in France had taken a heavy toll —320 RAF pilots killed or missing and 115 taken prisoners of war. Of the 959 planes lost in France, 229 had been fighters. British workers could replace the planes. The young men, "the effete, pleasure-mad youth of Britain," as Hitler called them, had to be trained, and this took time.

A fraction of the deficiency was alleviated by the "loan" of fifty-eight pilots from the Fleet Air Arm. In time No. 1 Squadron Royal Canadian Air Force joined in the battle and refugee pilots from Poland and Czechoslovakia were formed into squadrons. The latter two proved especially savage fighters.

II

When *Adler Tag* finally dawned Dowding could call upon 1253 pilots—almost 200 short of his authorized establishment. These pilots were deployed throughout the main island of the British Isles, in England, Wales, and Scotland. The greater concentration of squadrons were based in south England —in the counties of Sussex, Surrey, and Kent. To reach London from the bases in northern France the Luftwaffe fighters and bombers would have to cross this area, most of which lay in the province of No. 11 Group, Air Vice-Marshal Keith Park, Air

Lord Beaverbrook, William M. Aitken, who as head of the Ministry of Aircraft Production during the Battle of Britain slashed through red tape and made certain that Fighter Command did not lack Hurricanes or

Spitfires. With him is his son, John ("Max") Aitken, a fighter pilot with No. 601 Squadron. At war's end Aitken's victory score stood at sixteen.

(*Daily Express,* LONDON)

Officer Commanding. To the west of this area lay No. 10 Group's domain, Air Vice-Marshal Sir Christopher Brand, AOC. To the north, into Essex and Suffolk counties, Air Vice-Marshal Trafford Leigh-Mallory commanded No. 12 Group. Scotland and the northern tip of England were the responsibility of No. 13 Group under Air Vice-Marshal Richard Saul.

The bulk of the heavy air fighting was to take place over the domains of Nos. 11 and 12 Groups. No. 11 Group consisted of twenty-two squadrons (fifteen Hurricane, six Spitfire, and one Blenheim) and No. 12 Group of fifteen squadrons (seven Hurricane, five Spitfire, two Blenheim, and one Defiant).

To contend with the attack the Air Ministry also established antiaircraft divisions, a Balloon Command with its barrage balloons (a throwback to the First World War), an Observer Corps, and, of the greatest import to Fighter Command, a network of so-called Chain Home Stations operating Radio Direction Finding equipment. In time this RDF came to be called "*ra*dio *d*etecting *a*nd *r*anging," which by mid-war the Americans had abbreviated to "radar." The brain child of Robert Watson-Watt, radar was a decisive factor in the outcome of the Battle of Britain.

In the summer of 1940 a system of radar stations stood along the northern, eastern, and southern coasts of the main island. The spindly masts of the

Radar towers on the English coast, an early detection system that contributed greatly to the outcome of the Battle of Britain.

(IMPERIAL WAR MUSEUM, LONDON)

transmitting and receiving towers were concentrated in the southeastern counties opposite France. Additional stations were erected inland. At the time of the Battle's opening there were twenty-one operational CH stations and thirty CHL (Chain Home Low) stations. The former were capable of picking up objects at a distance of 120 miles but missed low-flying aircraft; the CHL stations supplemented the CH stations on low-flying aircraft up to fifty miles distant. By no means absolutely perfect or foolproof, the English radar system was superior to anything the Germans had developed. And because they had not been able to devise a good system the Germans characteristically assumed the British had also been as unsuccessful.

With radar detecting the Luftwaffe forming up while it was still over France, the RAF was able to send its fighters to meet the German formations. Radar would locate the German formations and enabled the British to ignore diversionary sweeps and concentrate on the main point of attack. It also saved the RAF from wasteful patrols. Pilots were scrambled only when necessary—at least in the ideal situation. Pilots could also keep informed of the rapidly shifting air situation by radio from the ground radar stations tracking and plotting the oncoming Germans. Furthermore, pilots could talk with each other in the air. The German communications system was not as well developed. There was no ground control with radar and while pilots could talk with each other within their own units there was no intercommunication in formations except by signal: the fighters had no radio connection with the bombers. In general this meant operations were dependent upon the orders issued before they had taken off; there was little leeway for the unexpected.

Thus the situation stood when the Germans impatiently girded for *Adler Tag*. Göring, warming up to what was to be the world's first great air battle, expected that the defenses of southern England would be shattered in four days and that the Luftwaffe would take four weeks to eliminate the Royal Air Force. After this, Operation Sealion could be launched and a triumphant Third Reich would be free for more important conquests (especially that of the Soviet Union, which Hitler now seriously considered).

Although the all-out assault was set for the August "Eagle Day," the Luftwaffe ventured over the English Channel before this. On the night of June 5/6 about thirty German bombers flew over the east coast dropping bombs on airfields and upon the vicinity of airfields. Nighttime accuracy, even with the help of a radio beam (code-named *Knickebein,* and quickly jammed by the British), left much to be desired. Such harassment raids were of little military value except to provide the crews with night-flying practice. Also, the raids kept the British on their toes, although they interfered somewhat with production as the workers sought shelter upon the sounding of air raid sirens.

The scattered raids of June were of no great consequence, although some damage was done, and there were a number of casualties, as well as small

Before the curtain rose on the Battle of Britain the Luftwaffe began scattered raids against various port cities on the southeast coast of England and upon vital British shipping in the English Channel. On the left

German bombs fall on Portland, which was attacked for the first time on July 11, 1940. On the right, a view from the nose of an He-111 of English ships under attack in the Channel. (NATIONAL ARCHIVES)

German losses. July saw the beginning of more intensified daylight attacks, particularly upon the port cities—Portland, Falmouth, Plymouth, Dover—and upon shipping in the Channel. By the end of July daylight passage through the English Channel, even for convoys, became hazardous under the attacks of the Stukas, the Messerschmitt 110s, the Dornier 17s, and escorting Me-109s.

Loerzer had selected Johannes Fink as Kanalkampfführer (Channel Battle Leader) to lead a small battle group, Kampfgeschwader 2, to attend to shipping through the Straits of Dover; Richthofen's Stukas did the same to the west. In addition to his own *Geschwader*'s Dorniers, Fink could call upon two *Gruppen* of Stukas (Ju-87s) and two fighter *Geschwader*, JG 26, led by Adolf Galland, and JG 51, led by Werner Mölders. The two

Jagdgeschwader, commanded by the stars of the Luftwaffe, were equipped with the latest Messerschmitt 109Es. Mölders, a great tactician and teacher, was then the high-scoring Luftwaffe ace. He was, interestingly, an ardent anti-Nazi, an aberration for which he was tolerated because of his achievements as a fighter pilot.

If the early July Channel encounters were not conclusive, they were no less deadly for the participants. Flight Lieutenant Alan Deere, leading B Flight of No. 54 Squadron on a convoy patrol—the fourth scramble of the day—crossed the English coast at Deal. At this point the English Channel, that is, at the Straits of Dover, is barely twenty miles wide. Deere, a New Zealander, had been flying since he was nineteen and was a confirmed ace with five official victories to his credit. Shot down over Dunkirk, Deere had joined the "brown jobs" (Army men) and was evacuated by ship back to England.

Leading his flight of six Spitfires, Deere had spotted a silvery plane flying low, escorted by a dozen Me-109s at about a thousand feet and another five serving as top cover. The silver seaplane was a Heinkel 59 decorated not only with the traditional black crosses of the Luftwaffe, but also with a red cross identifying it as an Air-Sea rescue plane. Obviously it was searching for German pilots who had crash-landed in the Channel in the day's early fighting. The RAF had orders to attack the He-59s, red cross or not, for while they rescued the pilots they also reported the British convoys in the Channel.

Ordering half of his flight to attack the seaplane, Deere led two Spitfires to deal with the top-cover Messerschmitts. The German fighters immediately formed into a defensive circle. Diving through the circle Deere shot down one of the German planes and then, as he tells it himself, "straightening out from my favorite defensive maneuver of a tight turn, I found my self head-on to another [Me-109].

"As we sped towards each other at a combined speed of over 500 mph there was little time to think. For my part, the thought of a collision did not enter my head—had it done so I have no doubt I would have tried to avoid it—and when I realized it was to be the inevitable outcome it was too late for evasion action. At one moment the Me-109 was a blurred outline filling my reflector sight and the next it was on top of me blotting out the sky ahead as it passed marginally above, avoiding a direct collision perhaps by a last-minute alteration of course by the German pilot.

"But collide we did; propeller hit propeller, the shock of the impact throwing me forward in my seat, saved only from being crushed on the dashboard by the restraining cockpit harness which bit cruelly into my shoulders.

"The next few moments I recall as a panic-stricken blur as I fought to regain some control over my now vibrating, pitching Spitfire already gushing ominous black smoke into the cockpit. Gain control I did, but sufficient only to keep the aircraft in a too-fast-for-comfort dive towards the English coast, with throttle jammed open but a happily unresponsive engine seized solid by a propeller which under the impact had bent double and dug itself progressively into the engine housing before finally ceasing to turn."

But now fire had begun licking out of the smoke in Deere's cockpit and he knew he had to jump.

The Heinkel 59, which, despite the red crosses painted on its sides (not on this one, however) because of its function as an Air-Sea Rescue plane, was consistently shot down by the RAF. Churchill believed they were used also to make reconnaissance observations during rescue operations. (H. J. NOWARRA)

The Messerschmitt 109, the standard single-seater Luftwaffe fighter during the Battle of Britain. Superior to the Hurricane, it was an even match for the Spitfire. Air battles between the Me-109 and the Spitfire were decided either by pilot skill or luck.

(U. S. AIR FORCE)

Heaving at the cockpit hood he was dismayed to learn that the collision had jammed it shut. Nor could he jettison it mechanically. There was no choice; Deere had to stay with the burning Spitfire, bring it down, and hope to get out somehow on the ground.

"Half-choked by the smoke, licked at by flames I somehow kept the Spitfire heading inland and under a measure of control. I could see nothing directly ahead and only a little to the side as my now burning fighter plunged towards a resting place in the Kentish fields, barely discernible through the smoke and flame. . . .

"I must have prayed, but I don't remember. What I do remember is the crunching sensation as the aircraft hit the ground, fortunately in open country, launched itself in the air again, returned to earth and ploughed a skidding and erratic passage through a field studded with wooden posts, put there as a deterrent to an enemy airborne glider force, shedding bits of fuselage en route."

When the shuddering, bouncing Spitfire finally came to a stop Deere desperately hammered at the perspex of the canopy, broke it open, dived over the side, and ran from the burning wreckage. The Spitfire had come to rest in a cornfield now resounding to the firing of the plane's guns, which had become heated by the flames.

By some miracle, except for slightly burned hands, singed eyebrows, bruised knees, and the cuts from the shoulder harness, Deere was not seriously injured and was back in the battle the next day. His plane, named *Kiwi,* was a total loss, however.

The Me-109 with which he collided had not shared Deere's luck. The tail of the German fighter had been sheared off and, trailing bits of fuselage, the plane fell into the Channel.

August brought a quickening of the tempo of Luftwaffe attacks; by the end of the first week the bombing became heavier and more fierce. Göring waited for an improvement in the weather, however, to launch the all-out attack, set for August 10. Dowding, meanwhile, held his fighters in check, not wishing to waste pilots and aircraft in the preliminary phases of the big battle that must inevitably come. Fighting over the Channel was a risky business; wait for the Luftwaffe to come farther inland to the limit of their range, Dowding wisely cau-

The Messerschmitt 110, the ill-fated Zerstörer (*destroyer*), *which was supposed to operate in the dual role of fighter and bomber and proved to be neither.*
(H. J. NOWARRA)

tioned. Avoid combat as much as possible with fighters—get the bombers; they carried the lethal burden.

But the English weather proved to be characteristically unreasonable. On the evening of August 9, with the Channel socked in with cloud and with Britain under cloud and rain, Göring canceled the large-scale attack of the following day. *Adler Tag,* weather permitting, then was set for August 13.

On the twelfth the prelude to *Adler Tag* took place. While continuing to harass shipping in the Channel and the ports, the Luftwaffe attacked airfields and radar installations. The expanding battle was moving inland.

Spearheading the assault was an *Erprobungsgruppe* (Experimental Group) 210, a mixed unit of fighters, Messerschmitt 109s and 110s, converted to fighter-bombers. The formation, led by Hauptmann Walter Rubensdörffer, consisted of eight Me-109s, some carrying five-hundred- or thousand-pound bombs under their bellies, and a dozen Me-110s, similarly armed. Their targets were the radar antennas along the Kent and Sussex coast. The steel structures, 350 feet tall, rose up out of the marshes and apple orchards of Kent like strange devices from another world.

These spindly antennas were Fighter Command's ace in the hole. Their existence eliminated the Luftwaffe's element of surprise.

On this day the Messerschmitts split up and sped

Me-110s in flight. According to the original conception, these planes were supposed to be able to fight off attackers while on bombing missions, or to serve as escort for heavier bombers. They proved to be sitting ducks for the guns of the RAF. (MUSÉE DE L'AIR)

toward their individual targets upon reaching the English coast. Except for patches of mist the weather was good and the Messerschmitts dropped down out of the sun and raced toward the masts at Pevensey, Rye, Dover, and Dunkirk (the latter on the south bank of the Thames near Canterbury). Although the radar stations had picked up the approaching bombers, the formations appeared small enough to require little more than watching. Almost at the same moment all of the radar stations came under attack and all bombers loosed their bombs on target. The earth shook, buildings collapsed, smoke rose into the air—but, as the Messerschmitts wheeled around for home, the men saw that the masts remained standing.

At Dunkirk two huts had been destroyed but the station continued operating. At Rye all the huts had gone up in the explosions, but by noon the station was back in action. Bombs cut the main electric cable at Pevensey, putting it out for two hours. At Dover the aerials took slight damage and the working quarters were smashed to bits—but Dover continued to operate. These stations were "manned," so to speak, by young women of the Women's Auxiliary Air Force who endured the bombings with exemplary calm.

Though triumphant on returning to their base at Denain, the pilots and crews of Experimental Group 210 found their jubilance premature. Luftwaffe

Communications Chief General Wolfgang Martini learned through detection devices that the radar stations continued to operate despite the on-target attacks by the fighter-bombers.

There was an exception. Just before noon, while more than sixty Ju-88s attacked Portsmouth Harbor, fifteen aircraft veered off and dived toward the radar installation at Ventnor on the Isle of Wight. The heavy bomb concentration destroyed most of the buildings, caused fires which could not be put out because of a lack of water, and seriously damaged the site. Ventnor was out of action for eleven days.

While the radar stations were recovering from the morning attacks the afternoon opened with assaults upon British airfields. Even as the pilots of No. 65 Squadron ran for their Spitfires, the bombs from the Dorniers fell upon Manston, an advance base near the coast. Another airfield, Hawkinge, was also bombed. The fleeing Ju-88s left two hangars destroyed, the workshops afire, and the landing strips cratered. Five people had been killed and four aircraft damaged. For the second time in the day, the airfield at Lympne (actually an unimportant emergency landing field) was bombed. Manston was hardest hit, although like the other stations it was back in operation by the following day. *Adler Tag* eve had cost the RAF 22 fighters and the Luftwaffe 31 aircraft. The toll from July 10 through this August 12 was 150 RAF fighters and 286 German aircraft, including fighters and bombers. And the Battle proper had not yet begun.

Kanalkampfführer Johannes Fink—whose friends lightly called him *Kanalarbeiter* ("Sewer worker") —did not take his position lightly. By seven in the morning of August 13—*Adler Tag,* at last—his Dornier 17s of Kampfgeschwader 2 were air-borne. Fifty-five aircraft roared toward the airdrome at Eastchurch on the south bank of the Thames estuary. All along the coasts of France, Belgium, Holland, and Norway aircraft of the three great *Luftflotten* would converge upon the stubborn British for the Attack of the Eagles.

As was its wont, the weather had turned bad overnight—there were clouds over the Channel and mist and drizzling over the target. Eastchurch, Fink did not know, was a Coastal Command station— not a fighter field. The target of the Luftwaffe was RAF Fighter Command. This was not the only slip of the morning.

When he arrived at the rendezvous point with the fighter escort, the Messerschmitt 110s of Oberstleutnant Joachim Huth's Zerstörergeschwader 26, Fink was annoyed with the behavior of the fighters. Huth's Messerschmitt bore down upon Fink's Dornier, dived, turned, and came back at him. Fink good-naturedly attributed it to the typical fighter pilot's high spirits in celebration of *Adler Tag*. The performance of the Destroyers was ridiculous but understandable. Fink proceeded toward Eastchurch. After cutting through a cloud bank, Fink was further piqued to note that no Messerschmitts were visible anywhere. They had lost one another in the clouds. There was nothing before him except the forbidding coast of England and scattered clouds.

In their stations the radar operators had begun tracking Fink as soon as his planes formed up over Calais. The still inexperienced operators could not predict the Dorniers' destination.

The cloud had thickened so Fink ordered the planes to loosen the formation in order to lessen the chance of collision. When the Dorniers broke through the mist Fink was delighted to see Eastchurch about three miles ahead—and ten thousand feet below. Anxiously peering out of the cockpit, Fink ascertained an unfortunate truth: no fighter escort. The cautious, fifty-year-old leader found some consolation in the sight of the aircraft on the field below neatly lined up, wingtip to wingtip, waiting for them.

Fink led the Dorniers to the attack. At about the same moment some Spitfires of No. 74 Squadron, the only unit dispatched to deal with "a few aircraft," pounced upon the rear of the formation. Oberleutnant Heinz Schlegel's Dornier bucked under the scattered fire from the Spitfire's eight guns. The right engine ground to a stop and began smoking, and Schlegel had trouble keeping the plane from pulling to the left. Another burst from a diving Spitfire solved that problem: the other engine was damaged and, because two of his crew were wounded, Schlegel crash-landed the Dornier in an English meadow. Schlegel and his crew were taken prisoner.

Fink, unaware of the attack going on behind him, dropped his bombs upon Eastchurch. The men on the base below reacted with astonishment as explosions erupted in the early morning. Five Blenheims of No. 35 Squadron went up in smoke. Twelve

men died in the rubble and fire and forty were injured. A direct hit destroyed the operations building. When Fink ducked his plane into the clouds and raced for France, great black clouds of smoke rose up from Eastchurch.

But some of the smoke may have been that of his own planes, for during the fighting Fink lost four aircraft.

Furious because he had had no fighter protection, Fink called Kesselring at Luftflotte 2 headquarters as soon as he had landed. The tone and language of the usually mild Fink prompted a visit from Kesselring, who brought a personal explanation.

A Spitfire harries a Dornier-17, the "Flying Pencil," over England. (NATIONAL ARCHIVES)

Adler Tag had been postponed because of the poor weather. Fink's mission had been canceled although word had come only after he had taken off. The fighters had been informed, which explained not only their absence, but also the odd behavior of Huth's Messerschmitt 110. Fink learned that as he was attacking Eastchurch other uninformed aircraft, the Ju-88s of Kampfgeschwader 54, with Me-110 escort, attempted to bomb the Royal Aircraft Establishment at Farnborough. Fighter interception from No. 11 Group prevented the attack and at least five of the Me-110s, Göring's pet Destroyer, went down under the Spitfire guns. The rest fled for home. The same occurred with a formation of more than eighty Stukas—only they fled before attacking and thus were spared, temporarily, a full-scale encounter with the British fighters. Only Fink's resolute, and vulnerable, formation had succeeded in the morning of Eagle Day.

An attempt to save the glory of the day was made in the afternoon despite the worsening weather. A fighter formation (Me-110s) was sent to the vicinity of Portland to draw off the English fighters. While these engaged the Hurricanes and Spitfires it was expected that the Ju-88s might break through the defenses and bomb the docks and warehouses at Southampton. Most of the bombers got through, causing serious damage while the Me-110s, possibly

Channel near Cherbourg, hoped to find airfields in the Portland area. But cloud cover again interfered —and so did No. 609 Squadron. Diving through the Me-109 escort formation, scattering them, the Spitfires pounded at the "dreaded" Stuka. The slow, clumsy craft was no match for the Spitfire and within minutes five of them lay smashed on the countryside below.

In the same encounter Pilot Officer D. M. Crook of No. 609 Squadron fired at an Me-109, which burst into flame and joined the hapless Stukas in a fiery dive to the ground. The fleeing Stukas spread their bombs over three counties.

The Ju-87 Stuka, once the scourge of the air, reached the end of the road over England in the summer of 1940. (U. S. AIR FORCE)

Aroused Spitfires of No. 65 Squadron take off to confront the Luftwaffe. On "Eagle Day" this squadron drove off an attack by the Stukas.

(IMPERIAL WAR MUSEUM, LONDON)

mistaken for bombers, engaged the fighters. The more sprightly Spitfires dived and twisted through the defensive circle which the Messerschmitts had formed under attack. In the savage fighting, five Me-110s fell. Clearly, the escort required an escort.

During the afternoon attacks also Richthofen's Ju-87s had succeeded in bombing the airfield at Detling, while its fighter escort dueled with the British fighters. Another formation of Ju-87s, aimed at a fighter base at Rochford, could not find it because of cloud cover. When attacked by the Spitfires of No. 65 Squadron, the Germans jettisoned their bombs across Canterbury and fled.

Farther west and south, more Stukas, crossing the

As evening fell the Attack of the Eagles subsided into the scattered detonations of wasted bombs and the desperate scream of the Stuka, the onetime Scourge of the Blitzkrieg, running for home. Small night attacks by bombers did not add to the accomplishment of the day. The eagle's wings had been clipped. The German pilots had not lacked courage, only that required efficiency in the High Command which makes sense of complex, large-scale operations.

When *Adler Tag* officially closed, the Luftwaffe had lost forty-five aircraft—thirty-nine to the British fighters—and the RAF Fighter Command had lost thirteen planes, but only seven pilots in combat.

It was not an auspicious beginning.

6

TARGET: RAF

THE FAT ONE was in a sour mood. His Eagle Day had not gone off as planned, what with the breakdown in command which set it off piecemeal. It was that damned English weather, unpredictable, obstinate, capricious—now bright and sunny, then moody and threatening: like the English themselves. Göring was not at all pleased with the course of the battle. The weather on the day following Eagle Day, August 14, had proved too poor for large-scale operations, although the Luftwaffe flew 489 sorties with the concentration upon the airdromes in southeastern England.

On that morning Göring called a conference at Karinhall with his staff and the *Luftflotten* commanders for the next day, August 15. He was obviously not in a joyous temper. He was concerned with the vulnerability of the Stuka and ordered increased fighter escorts for the dive bombers: as many as three *Gruppen* of fighters per *Gruppe* of Stukas.

As for the heavy bombers, he sarcastically invoked one of his pet comments of the period. Göring suggested that they attend to the British aircraft industries and "not the lightship off Dover."

He waxed serious: "We must concentrate our efforts on the destruction of the enemy air forces . . . including the targets of the enemy aircraft industry allocated to the different *Luftflotten*. . . .

"For the moment other targets should be ignored. . . .

"Our night attacks are essentially dislocation raids, made so that enemy defenses and population

shall be allowed no respite; even these, however, should wherever possible be directed against air force targets. . . ." That was the heart of Göring's master plan: the great German Air Force would erase the British Air Force.

Having committed his air force to the extinction of the RAF, Göring then proceeded to do the same to the Luftwaffe with a series of blunders in High Command. "It is doubtful," he concluded, "whether there is any point in continuing the attacks on radar sites, in view of the fact that not one of those attacked has so far been put out of action." Even as he said this repairmen were working against time to put the Ventnor station back into operation and not succeeding very rapidly. Göring, however, had no comprehension of radar's significance. It was yet another one of his decisions which would cost others their lives.

At almost the same moment Göring spoke and decreed, once again the order to postpone the day's missions because of weather had gone astray. In the absence of Loerzer, who was with Göring and the others at Karinhall, his chief of staff, Oberst Paul Deichmann, upon personally viewing the weather conditions—bright, sunny, with some cloud over the Channel—initiated the day's operations. Picking up the field phone, he dispatched the Stukas for England.

For the first time all three *Luftflotten,* based from Norway in the north to Brittany in the south, engaged in co-ordinated daylight attacks. In terms of

Göring with two aides who unconsciously let him down. On the left is the Chief of Air Intelligence, Josef "Beppo" Schmid, whose appraisal of the enemy's air power was frequently inaccurate; in the center, Chief of the Technical Branch of the Luftwaffe, Ernst Udet, who preferred flying airplanes to theorizing about them. Göring, however, betrayed both of them and the Luftwaffe as well by virtue of simple incompetence.

(H. J. NOWARRA)

numbers it was a more impressive German showing than Eagle Day itself.

The day began serenely enough with a few reconnaissance patrols by the RAF. Air Vice-Marshal Park dispatched a squadron from No. 11 Group to keep an eye upon two convoys just off the Thames estuary, but without incident.

That something big was to be expected was noted on the radar screens when just before eleven o'clock large formations were detected. These were the Stukas, with Me-109 escort, meeting over Calais for the twenty-minute flight across the Straits of Dover to attack the RAF airfields in Kent. When the German formations reached the English coast at eleven-thirty, they were met by a squadron each of Hurricanes and Spitfires. Of the nearly fifty Stukas participating in the attack, only four fell to the British fighters. The rest pushed through the defenses to bomb the airfields at Lympne and Hawkinge. The latter, a fighter base, was not seriously damaged, but Lympne, actually a secondary field, was knocked out for two days. Clearly the Luftwaffe was out to get the Royal Air Force Fighter Command.

While this fighting continued, and radar screens blipped with German air activity in the Channel

Stukas en route to their targets—and, more often than not, their doom.

(EMBASSY OF THE POLISH PEOPLE'S REPUBLIC)

area, another development to the north was unfolding on the screens in the Operations Room of No. 13 Group. Shortly after noon "twenty or more aircraft" were reported approaching from the North Sea. This estimate was increased soon after to three distinct formations aimed at Northumberland: "thirty plus," was the new figure. In reality, the radar operators were plotting a *Gruppe* of seaplanes on a diversionary flight toward the Firth of Forth, to the north of the true path of the other aircraft groups.

Unfortunately for the attacking Luftwaffe, the second group, the bombers of Kampfgeschwader 26,

cort planes with adequate range for the flight from the Luftwaffe base, four-hundred miles distant, at Stavanger, Norway. In his high-flying Messerschmitt, Restemeyer planned to direct the battle against the British fighters.

The forewarned Spitfires of No. 72 Squadron had climbed above the approaching Germans. From out of the sun they pounced upon the German formations. Among the first planes to come under attack was Restemeyer's Messerschmitt. With its eight guns firing, the mottled, graceful Spitfire struck the German fighter. The Messerschmitt staggered momentarily in mid-flight, shedding bits of metal, and then

Spitfire takeoff with wheels beginning to tuck into the wing. Early Spitfires required the pilot to crank the

wheels up (and down) manually; later models were equipped with automatic wheel gear.

(IMPERIAL WAR MUSEUM, LONDON)

sixty-three He-111s with an escort of twenty-one Me-110s of Zerstörergeschwader 76, were off course. Instead of approaching their targets, British Bomber Command bases at Dishforth and Linton-on-Ouse, the German bombers converged upon the English coast at almost the same point as the seaplane feint.

Having been stirred up by the seaplanes, No. 72 Squadron's Spitfires intercepted the formation of Heinkels and Messerschmitts about thirty miles off the English coast. The bombers droned along at about fifteen thousand feet. A thousand feet above them flew the Me-110s, led by Hauptmann Werner Restemeyer. The heavy fighters were the only es-

with an orange flash exploded. The mangled aircraft spun burning into the North Sea.

While some of the Spitfires engaged the Me-110s, which quickly formed into their customary defensive circle, the others flitted through the bomber formation. The suddenness of the attack, and perhaps the sight of Restemeyer's stricken plane descending, unnerved many of the crews in the Heinkels. Bombs were jettisoned harmlessly into the sea as the Heinkels lightened the loads for evasive action. Many ducked into cloud bank over which they had been safely flying just moments before.

After the first shock of the Spitfire attack had

worn off, the German planes pushed on toward their assigned targets. The fighters had to contend with yet another squadron (No. 79) of Spitfires which had been vectored to the heaving, lofty battleground. The Germans were outnumbered and fought with courage, although handicapped by their aircraft, none of which equaled the Spitfire in maneuverability. Once again the Zerstörer proved itself no match for the darting Spitfire. Although hits were scored by the German fighters and many claims made for "kills," British records do not reveal any losses of any of No. 13 Group's aircraft in the day's battle. Besides Restemeyer's plane, another eighteen

some homes in Portland, destroyed by the loosed bombs.

The surviving German planes turned and scuttled for home. Eight bombers did not return. The "surprise" flank attack by Luftflotte 5 cost twenty-seven aircraft and their crews. The expenditure was high for little return.

The other formation contributed by Luftflotte 5, unescorted Junkers 88s from Aalborg, Denmark, had been detected almost simultaneously with the Heinkels and Messerschmitts farther north. This flight made landfall at Flamborough Head, north of the Humber River. These were fifty aircraft of

He-111s over a German base. (NATIONAL ARCHIVES)

Me-110s were shot down and others returned to their bases in Norway badly shot up, with wounded aboard and crews demoralized.

Meanwhile, also under attack, the Heinkels pressed on for England. Spitfires now harassing the bombers were joined by Hurricanes of No. 605 Squadron. More bombs fell into the sea, joined by smoking Heinkels. Those that passed over the beaches and flew inland were then put upon by antiaircraft guns, further adding to the Heinkel's torment. Bombs scattered willy-nilly across the coastal villages—Seaham Harbour, Portland—but to no military point. The most serious damage was to

Kampfgeschwader 30—their target: the airfield at Driffield, home of No. 4 Group of Bomber Command.

This attack fell into the province of Leigh-Mallory's No. 12 Group. Around one o'clock—while the battle raged to the north—No. 12 Group's Spitfires, Defiants, and Hurricanes were ordered up. No. 13 Groups, though heavily engaged, dispatched a squadron of Blenheims to this battle also. It might be noted that the Defiants were specifically dispatched to patrol a convoy in the Humber River. Neither the Defiants nor the Blenheims could have been expected to fight on equal terms with German

Heinkel bombers heading out for targets in Britain.
(H. J. NOWARRA)

An He-111 disintegrates under the eight-gun assault of an RAF fighter attack.
(IMPERIAL WAR MUSEUM, LONDON)

Ju-88, the Luftwaffe's best bomber of the Battle of Britain. (U. S. AIR FORCE)

fighters; however, if, as it was hoped, the German formation contained only bombers the obsolescent aircraft might fare reasonably well. Even so, the Ju-88s were more capable of dealing with Blenheims.

The Spitfires of No. 616 Squadron intercepted the Ju-88s just offshore at Flamborough Head. Instead of breaking up for combat, the German formations dived into the clouds and eluded the British planes—at least temporarily. Then a flight of Hurricanes joined the battle as the Junkers crossed the coast line. The air over Flamborough Head was crisscrossed with machine-gun fire and from time to time the sky became smudged with oily smoke and flame as a Junkers fell under the eight-gun fighters.

Despite the heavy opposition about thirty German bombers broke through and found their targets. With amazing accuracy, considering the harassment, their bombs fell upon Driffield. Four hangars erupted under the onslaught, three blocks of buildings burst open and fell burning, and ten Whitley heavy bombers were destroyed under the heavy bomb concentration.

One of the Junkers was shot down by antiaircraft. But the formation had split up and while the larger one bombed Driffield another dropped its bombs on Bridlington, destroying some houses, and hitting also a nearby ammunition dump.

Then the Junkers turned and ran for Denmark, pursued by the Hurricanes and Spitfires a hundred miles out to sea. The Blenheims joined the pursuit but could not catch up to the swifter Junkers. Ten of the Ju-88s, however, remained smoking and tangled on the Yorkshire countryside or at the bottom of the sea.

Luftflotte 5 had lost, in its first—and last—full-scale daylight attack almost one eighth of its bomber force and one fifth of its heavy fighters. Nor had the feint succeeded in drawing the British fighters away from southeast England. Dowding had not permitted that and as the German bombers of Luftflotten 2 and 3 launched their attacks upon Kent, Essex, and Suffolk, the Spitfires and Hurricanes of No. 11 and No. 10 Groups rose up to meet them.

Even so, Me-110s of Erprobungsgruppe 210, accompanied by swarms of Me-109s and Stukas—about a hundred aircraft in all—slipped across the Channel northeast of London to strike the airfield at Martlesham Heath in Suffolk. While the Messerschmitt 109s held off those few British fighters which

Hurricanes of No. 85 Squadron on patrol awaiting the word to vector in on approaching Luftwaffe forma- *tions. Ideally, the Hurricanes took on the slower bombers while the Spitfires mixed with the Me-109s.*
(IMPERIAL WAR MUSEUM, LONDON)

had come upon them, the Stukas dive-bombed a radio installation and the Me-110s concentrated upon the airfield itself. No. 17 Squadron, part of which was based at Martlesham, had been sent off to intercept a formation of attackers and then suddenly vectored back to their station. The Hurricanes arrived only in time to see columns of smoke rising from Martlesham. It was too late; the German planes had already left for their bases in France.

The Operations Rooms in the sector stations were swamped with German activity in the vicinity of Calais and the Channel. Hundreds of Me-109s swept across the Straits of Dover, contributing to the confusion on the radar screens. And then, around the same time the Me-110s and Stukas freely dealt with Martlesham, the Dornier 17s of Kampfgeschwader 3, with Me-109 escort, had made landfall and were speeding westward over Kent. Almost a hundred bombers made up this formation, plus even

more fighters. Four British squadrons (forty-eight aircraft at best), then patrolling in the general area of penetration, were sent to deal with the Germans. They were easily held off by the high-flying Me-109s. Even the added strength of three more British squadrons did not improve the odds, and the Dorniers continued on to their selected targets. One was the Coastal Command station at Eastchurch; others were radar stations along the southeast coast.

A formation of more than thirty Dorniers pushed on to Rochester, where the most serious strike was successfully made. Bombs—fragmentation, incendiary, and delayed-action—literally rained down, cutting across hangars, workshops, and runways. Rochester, like Eastchurch, was not a Fighter Command station—but it was the home of aircraft factories, among them the important Short Brothers works. It was here that the first of the four-engined heavy bombers, the Stirling, was being built. The destruc-

tion to the facility delayed the heavy-bomber timetable several months. It was a crucial blow to the
long-range plans of the British.

The British fighters attacked the Germans savagely, but outnumbered, nine Hurricanes and Spitfires were lost. The Germans lost only four planes
in the fighting. Still, not all of the British pilots
were lost. Flying Officer John Gibson, a New Zealander of No. 501 Squadron, contemplated his sad
condition. He had made a pass at a German plane
and found himself the victim of the enemy. Over
Folkstone, at the edge of the sea, he gingerly sat
in his blazing Hurricane planning his next action.

Gibson did not want the burning aircraft to crash
on land with the possibility of striking a town, a
village, or a farm cottage. He pointed the blistering
nose of the Hurricane toward the Channel. Then
he had another thought. Gibson wore, as was the
wont of many an RAF pilot, new beautiful, hand-
made boots. The thought of what the sea would do
to such fine craftsmanship gave him pause. Gibson
worked off the shoes and tossed them over the side,
watched them drop for a second toward the earth
below. Once over the water and down now to about
a thousand feet, he flipped the Hurricane over and
dropped out himself. His chute opened and, shoe-
less, Gibson wafted down into the waters of the
English Channel. The blazing Hurricane dived smoldering into the sea.

For his action John Gibson was awarded the Distinguished Flying Cross. More: a Kentish native,
upon finding the handsome boots, mailed them off
to a nearby airfield and soon after Gibson was as
dashingly booted as before his encounter with a
Messerschmitt. It had been an action-packed hour.

Then, inexplicably, at the height of the battle
there came a pause. Having, to a great extent,
thrown Fighter Command off balance by its massive raids, feints, and fighter sweeps, the Luftwaffe
permitted the English nearly two hours in which to
refuel and rearm. The activity, up to this point, had
fallen primarily upon Kesselring's Luftflotte 2. As
soon as his forces had completed their missions,
Sperrle's Luftflotte 3 should have taken over. Such
timing is not always possible under actual operating
conditions. Only in retrospect, in the warm security
of their armchairs and with the even greater security of time (and the warranty of history), can
those who were never there sit in judgment of What

*German pilots recounting their experiences during the
Battle of Britain. Hauptmann Georg-Peter Eder of
Jagdgeschwader 26 (right) carries signal flare cartridges
in his flight boots.* (H. J. NOWARRA)

*Pilots of Jagdgeschwader 27 prepare to take off on an
escort mission to England.* (H. J. NOWARRA)

Might Have Been. At any rate, the British were granted a breathing spell instead of having to contend with Sperrle's bombers and fighters immediately following Kesselring's quite effective attacks. It should also be remembered that even as these attacks were in progress both Kesselring and Sperrle were at Karinhall listening to their intrepid leader, no mean armchair strategist himself, on how to win the Battle of Britain in just a few days.

By five in the afternoon the radar screens again picked up large formations of German aircraft, perhaps two hundred or more, moving from Luftflotte 3 bases in northwestern France. As the fighter escorts, Me-109s, milled around waiting for the bombers and consuming fuel, No. 10 and No. 11 Groups prepared for the attack. The bombers, Ju-88s, were twenty minutes late: this not only gave the British time to prepare but also limited the time the Me-109s might afford protection for the bombers over England. Also in the German formations were Stukas and Me-110s. Even before the first group of German planes crossed the south coast (roughly in the area of the Isle of Wight) eight fighter squadrons—Hurricanes and Spitfires—were air-borne and waiting.

The evening sky erupted with battling aircraft. The Ju-88s of Hauptmann Jochen Helbig's 4th Staffel (of Lehrgeschwader 1) came under severe attack by swarms of Spitfires which had dropped down out of the setting sun. In seconds Helbig's bomber was punched full of holes by the swift British planes—the Spitfire was nearly a hundred miles an hour faster than the Ju-88. The eight guns of the Spitfire converged upon the German bomber with smashing force. Helbig's gunner managed to wing one of the attackers, which fell smoking out of the fight.

Helbig himself sought the safety of lower altitudes, where the Spitfires could not torment him in diving attacks. With his plane in poor condition he could only continue south for home—the Orléans field in France. But of his seven planes, only two returned. It had been a disaster for Helbig's Staffel.

The fighting at this point was a great confusion of tumbling aircraft, of hammering noise, of planes shedding fragments, of silent guns and dead gunners, of great burning veins across the sky—of screaming plunges and the abrupt, bursting crashes of a stricken aircraft. Their scorched, obscene resting places were marked by great scars in the earth. Small cottages burst open to admit precipitate, uninvited death. Orchards were left a burning waste —a village street a litter of scorching brick, glass, wood, and innocent, twisted dead. These were all reminders that the war in the air must finally come to earth.

In the melee of the attack which had decimated Helbig's Staffel, although many of the Ju-88s jettisoned their bombs, two formations fought through the British fighters. Three Junkers succeeded in bombing the naval air station at Worthy Down at Southampton. Another formation of a dozen Ju-88s pressed on farther to the north and struck the important sector station of Fighter Command at Middle Wallop. Even as the bombs shattered across the airfield, striking two hangars and runways, Spitfires of No. 609 Squadron were taking off. The German survivors of this attack reported they had hit Andover airfield (not a fighter base), not realizing the importance of Middle Wallop as a sector station which housed the radar equipment for operational control of the fighters in that sector.

A total of twenty-five German aircraft were lost in this phase of the day's fighting: eight Ju-88s, four Stukas, and thirteen Me-110s. This was at a cost of sixteen Hurricanes and Spitfires.

The scarred, crippled, smoking remnants of the once massive formations had hardly dashed for Cherbourg when another formation was plotted forming over Calais. This was an attack on the left flank after the attack on the south. Sixty or seventy aircraft were coming in over the Straits of Dover and many of No. 11 Group's planes were in need of fuel and landing. No. 501 Squadron's Hurricanes were still air-borne, although after two encounters they were low on fuel and ammunition. Air Vice-Marshal Park could do nothing else but dispatch the Hurricanes to Dover. He quickly added an additional four squadrons from Kent and, later, four and a half others.

At six-thirty Test Group 210, which had bombed the airfield at Martlesham Heath earlier in the day, was returning to bomb two sector stations, one at Kenley and the other at Biggin Hill. Hauptmann Walter Rübensdörffer's test group had enjoyed unusual success: it had also put out the Ventnor radar station on the Isle of Wight three days earlier— and its morning had been fruitful. Now it was returning in freshly bombed-up Messerschmitts (both 109s and 110s) as well as Dornier 17s. Jagdgeschwader 52 was to furnish the escort of Me-109s.

Leading his formation of twenty-three aircraft, Rübensdörffer wondered where the fighter escort was. His bomb-laden Messerschmitts, his fighter-bombers, would not be effective bombers until they had reached their targets and dropped the bombs. Another formation of his test group, twenty-seven Dornier 17s, made up the rest of the attacking force. But where were the fighters?

If he had lost the fighters in the darkening sky, now misting up in the early evening, Rübensdörffer had also lost his way. The Dorniers which were assigned Biggin Hill as their target bombed West Malling instead. Although no sector station, West Malling was put out of operation for several days.

Rübensdörffer made an even more serious error. On descending through the mist he spotted an airfield which he believed to be Kenley. He was only four miles off target, but the field he saw was Croydon, ten miles from London. Hitler's standing order was that Greater London, London itself, was not to be bombed. He still hoped for a negotiated peace and to keep the English reprisal bombers away from German cities.

It was almost seven o'clock in the evening when the Me-110s began dropping bombs on Croydon from an altitude of two thousand feet. The Hurricanes of No. 111 Squadron, patrolling at ten thousand feet, plunged down to the attack. The alarming sudden appearance of the Hurricanes resulted in an almost random spilling of bombs. Although the airfield was struck, causing much destruction to hangars, workshops, and runways, bombs fell haphazardly across the Croydon area. Small war production factories were hit, but so was the Bourjois perfume factory. Sixty-two people died as a result of the bombardment, more than a hundred were injured, many seriously. Once again Rübensdörffer's unit had proved effective, even if in error.

But he himself was in trouble. As he tried to get away from the scene of the attack, a Hurricane caught up with his Messerschmitt. Try as he might he could not shake the British fighter, flown by pilot J. M. Thompson of No. 111 Squadron, as he attempted to speed over Kent and return to France. The Me-110 burst into flame, and still the Hurricane harried them.

Alan Christopher Deere, the indestructible New Zealander who, though shot down more than a half-dozen times, survived the war with a victory score of twenty-two. (IMPERIAL WAR MUSEUM, LONDON)

They had to land. He sought for a likely place in the fields of Kent. He jerked the plane over a small cottage that suddenly came into view, then over a gentle hill and toward a valley beyond. The Messerschmitt trailed sheets of flame and molten metal dripped in its path. And then it was finished for the commander of Erprobungsgruppe 210 as his blazing aircraft struck the earth. Five other Me-110s had also not returned after No. 111 Squadron's Hurricanes attacked them over Croydon. An Me-109 also was lost. The other aircraft of Test Group 210 raced for Calais.

In the twilight moments of the day's battles the smaller skirmishes scattered across the skies of Kent. On his second patrol of the day Flight Lieutenant Alan Deere in a Spitfire (No. 54 Squadron) had in headlong frustration pursued an Me-109 all the way across the English Channel to the Calais-Marck nest of the German fighters. When he sud-

A Spitfire, victim of an Me-109, goes down burning.
(H. J. NOWARRA)

denly realized what he had done, he was himself being stalked by Messerschmitts. Faster than the Spitfire, the German fighters swept into range.

"Bullets seemed to be coming from everywhere and pieces were flying off my aircraft," Deere told the story later. "My instrument panel was shattered, my eye was bleeding from a splinter, my watch had been shot clean off my wrist by an incendiary bullet which left a nice diagonal burn across my wrist and it seemed only a matter of moments before the end."

With his Merlin engine full out Deere raced for England, feeling that never had thirty miles of water seemed so expansive, nor had his Spitfire seemed so slow. But still the hunted, he reached the coast near Folkestone. The German Me-109s, unwilling to repeat his mistake, turned off and returned to Calais-Marck.

Deere was now only eight hundred feet above the ground, and within a minute or so after the enemy planes turned back his straining Merlin engine burst into flame.

"Desperately I tore my straps off, pulled back the hood and prepared to bail out. I was still doing about 300 miles an hour, so I pulled my stick back to get a bit more height. At about 1,500 feet I turned on my back and pushed the stick hard forward. I shot out a few feet and somehow became caught up by the bottom of my parachute. I twisted and turned, but wasn't able to get either in or out. The nose had now dropped below the horizontal and was pointing at the ground which appeared to be rushing up at a terrific speed."

The twisting, plunging Spitfire, now burning fiercely, carried Deere for some minutes when his parachute unsnagged from the seat and the pilot was blown backward along the fuselage. The tail struck his wrist and then he was clear of the plane. He pulled the ripcord.

"None too soon. I hadn't time to breathe a sigh of relief before I landed with a mighty thud in a plantation of thick shrubs." Deere's luck truly held, for his parachute had opened dangerously close to the ground—the shrubs broke the impact of his fall. In a nearby field his Spitfire demolished itself in flame and dust.

After his injuries had been attended to in the hospital, the chief surgeon called Deere's station commander to inform him that the pilot was safe.

In his relief Wing Commander Cecil Bouchier could only say, "Keep him there, he's costing us too many Spitfires!" On that August 15, 1940, Alan Deere—who had shot down his thirteenth German aircraft earlier in the day—had "bent" his fourth Spitfire.

The great air battles of the day ended, a day of very heavy fighting, like a summer storm with the fury spent and small flashes and distant thunder. For the Germans it had been the true Eagle Day, with all three *Luftflotten* taking part in 1786 sorties (to RAF Fighter Command's 974). It was not until much later that the participants realized that August 15, 1940, had been the most active day of the Battle of Britain. It had also been a decisive day. It finished Luftflotte 5 as a daylight threat to England and underscored the vulnerability of the Stuka and the Messerschmitt 110.

The battle had raged over a five-hundred-mile

The remains of an Me-109 brought down on August 15, 1940. Winston Churchill observed the battle in which this fighter participated.

(IMPERIAL WAR MUSEUM, LONDON)

front, from near Tynemouth in the north to Southampton in the southeast. This battle front, however, was three-dimensional and moved inland as well as vertically in a continually shifting pattern. The radar screens, in most instances, were capable of tracing this pattern for the sector stations, from which the sector controller could direct the individual squadrons. It was on this day that Göring ordered the attacks upon the radar stations to stop.

The excited, exhausted pilots of Fighter Command claimed 182 aircraft in the day's fighting. The five massive assaults had come so swiftly that in the confusion of battle several pilots claimed the same plane. The true figure was 89—though not as spectacular it is nonetheless a formidable figure, for many of the aircraft carried multiple crews. The Luftwaffe claimed 82 Spitfires and Hurricanes, plus 5 Curtiss Hawks (which were non-existent in the RAF) and 14 additional aircraft: a total of 101 British planes. The RAF in fact lost 42 fighters (not counting those destroyed on the ground); but 17 pilots, like the indestructible Alan Deere, walked away from their crashed planes.

The bombing of Croydon, so near to central London, infuriated Hitler, who wanted to court-martial the hapless Oberst Paul Deichmann, who had initiated the savage fighting of the day with the Stukas. But this rage was forgotten in the rush of other, bigger matters. Hitler had the Eastern Front on his mind, although he continued discussing Sealion, the invasion of England. Preparations for the invasion must be ready by the end of August; the landings must be made by September 15. At the conference on July 21, 1940, Hitler had pointed out that among the important prerequisites was "complete mastery of the air."

On August 15, only two days after Eagle Day, the Luftwaffe may not have lost the Battle of Britain; but neither could it win it.

7

HELL'S CORNER

For all their vaunted Teutonic efficiency, the Germans were not very well served by their intelligence services, Abteilung 5, under the command of Major Josef Schmid, a non-flying friend of Jeschonnek. Ambitious, hard-working, and convivial, Schmid, who liked being called "Beppo," brought some organization to his not very efficient department with the introduction of new members, most of them men he could trust and who would not menace his position. But he fell into the usual trap of underestimating the British air potential and supplied his superiors with the kind of information they liked to hear. In July 1940 Schmid composed an intelligence paper, "Comparative Survey of Royal Air Force and Luftwaffe Striking Power." The gist of the paper was revealed in the third section, "Conclusion," which opened with the very words Göring wished to see: "The Luftwaffe is clearly superior to the RAF as regards strength, equipment, training, command, and location of bases."

Following the great engagements of August 15, the Luftwaffe High Command estimated, basing this figure on Schmid's reports and upon the reports of fighter "kills," that the Royal Air Force had only three hundred fighters on hand. There were, in fact, more than double that number of operational Hurricanes and Spitfires. As the battle became progressively attritional the Luftwaffe pilots grimly joked about those "last fifty Spitfires." Their High Command had assured them that the RAF was all but depleted, though frequently many more than the last fifty met the German formations near the Channel day after day.

Schmid did not so much as mention the radar system (a subject which wouldn't have interested Göring in any case) and he oversold the German aircraft as compared with the British planes. For example, he noted in his "Comparative Survey," referring to the Hurricane and Spitfire, that "In view of their combat performance and the fact that they are not yet equipped with cannon guns both types are inferior to the Me-109, and particularly the Me-109F, while the individual Me-110 is inferior to *skillfully* handled Spitfires." The emphasis is Schmid's. So is the ignorance of the fact that the Me-109F was not in use by the operational units engaged in the Battle of Britain. The tale of the Stuka came to a sad ending over Britain. This aircraft too was overvalued by the Germans. It was a good close-support plane and capable of precision bombing, but was a deathtrap in aerial combat.

On Sunday, August 18, following a relatively quiet day, the pressure upon Fighter Command was resumed in the morning with heavy attacks upon airfields and some strikes upon radar stations. Kenley and Biggin Hill were severely hit with considerable damage especially at the former. Its being knocked out of operations for two days crippled Fighter Command in the Kenley sector.

In the afternoon there was a concentration of

attacks upon Coastal Command and Fleet Air Arm Stations off the south coast at Gosport, Thorney Island, and Ford. The formations were from Luftflotte 3, consisting of Ju-88s, Ju-87s, and great swarms of Me-109s. The Stukas dive-bombed Thorney Island. At the same time, to the northwest nearby Poling, with its radar installations, was attacked by Stukas of Stuka Geschwader 77. The radar station was knocked out for the rest of the month—and the Stuka was knocked out of the Battle of Britain. Tangling with Spitfires of No. 152 Squadron and Hurricanes of No. 43 Squadron, the Stukas paid for their success. Twelve of the twenty-eight Ju-87s dispatched by *StG* 77's first *Staffel* were destroyed, some falling to earth and others

into the sea. Of the sixteen that managed to return to France, six were so badly shot up that they were of little further use. Another thirty were either lost or so severely damaged that they had to be junked. Over a period of just a few days the losses in Stukas all but wiped out an entire *Gruppe*. Richthofen withdrew his *Fliegerkorps* VIII from Cherbourg to the Pas de Calais area, awaiting the day when Sealion would be launched and there would no longer be an RAF. The Stukas could then be employed against the Royal Navy in the forthcoming invasion. Except for an aborted flurry at the end of the month, the Stuka appeared for the last time over England on August 18, 1940. Its legend was dead.

Mercifully bad flying weather closed in on the next day and for nearly a week only sporadic activity was possible. Both camps had time to consider their positions. The most serious problem confronting Air Chief Marshal Dowding was the shortage of experienced pilots. He was reluctantly given some from Bomber Command by the Air Ministry and the training period for new pilots was continued at two weeks instead of the customary four. It had been hoped that the four weeks' course would be reinstated, but the cost of the battle canceled that. Pilots were posted to front-line squadrons with merely ten or at best twenty hours of solo flying.

The strain on experienced pilots took its toll also and replacements were hard to find. For example, in the period from August 8–18 Fighter Command lost 154 pilots, either killed or wounded seriously enough to be out of action. In the same ten-day period only 63 new fighter pilots were graduated from the training schools. And it was Fighter Command that Göring had selected as the primary target of the Luftwaffe.

On the day following the Stuka slaughter the German Air Force High Command again assembled at Karinhall on August 19. Göring's temper had not improved since the last conference. His four-day timetable for the destruction of the defenses of south England was definitely off. Obviously someone was at fault; losses were too high. He listened to the complaints of the bomber commanders—the fighters, they argued, did not fly close enough to the bombers to give proper protection. By the time they arrived upon the scene, the British had swooped in and shot up the bomber formations.

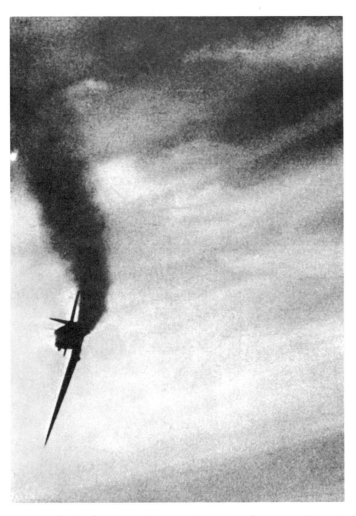

A Spitfire goes down under Luftwaffe guns; although the plane was replaceable, the pilot, if injured or killed, was not. The Battle of Britain reached a critical phase during the daylight raids because of pilot shortage.
(NATIONAL ARCHIVES)

The fighter commanders argued for the "free hunt" technique, which placed the fighters high above and around the bombers. This made it possible for them to achieve flexibility, important to a fighter, and not be chained to the slower bombers. This close-support tactic, it was argued by the German fighter commanders, sacrificed both fuel and the fighter's ability to move about the sky to trouble points.

But the bombers had been suffering terribly under Spitfire and Hurricane attacks. The fighter protection must be doubled, tripled, Göring insisted.

"We have reached the decisive period of the air war against England," Göring told them. "Our first aim is the destruction of the enemy's fighters. If they no longer take the air, we shall force them into battle by directing bomber attacks against targets within range of our fighters." The lesson of Luftflotte 5's misadventure had not been lost on Göring and the ravaged Stuka *Gruppen* of the day before had impressed him also.

"At the same time," Göring decreed further, "and on a growing scale, we must continue our activities against the ground organization of the enemy bomber units. Surprise attacks on the enemy aircraft industry must be made by day and by night. Once the enemy air force has been annihilated, our attacks will be directed as ordered against other vital targets."

This was a passing reference to Sealion, in which Göring had scant interest—and, though they would not have cared to inform him, in which his Luftwaffe High Command had little hope. Time was running out for Sealion, for the autumn days were fast approaching and the Channel would be impossible to cross even without RAF interference. The Royal Navy, still intact, would chop the invaders to bits—those who survived the treacherous Channel waters.

Coincidentally, on that same August 19, 1940, from his No. 11 Group headquarters at Uxbridge, Kent, Air Vice-Marshal Keith Park also issued orders. Having noted that the German attacks had been moving closer inland and with greater concentration upon airfields, Park instructed his controllers in the sector stations upon several points. The main gist was the preservation of pilots.

"Despatch fighters to engage large enemy formations over land or within gliding distance of the coast," Park emphasized. "During the next two or three weeks we cannot afford to lose pilots through forced landings in the sea." The enemy bombers were the major threat. Little was gained by clashing with the Me-109s. "Against mass attacks coming inland despatch a minimum number of squadrons to engage enemy fighters. Our main object is to engage enemy bombers, particularly those approaching under the lowest cloud layer." These, of course, were frequently missed by radar and bombed with devastating accuracy.

When the weather finally cleared enough for full-scale operations on August 24, and continuing through September 6 (when Göring or Hitler issued another fatal decision), the airfields of No. 11 Group came under concentrated attack. The full

Air Vice-Marshal Sir Keith Park, commanding officer of No. 11 Group, whose squadrons were stationed in Kent, in southeast England, and over which most of the fierce fighting of the Battle of Britain occurred.
(IMPERIAL WAR MUSEUM, LONDON)

impact and ferocity of it almost succeeded in realizing Göring's dream of destroying Dowding's shaken Fighter Command.

Kentish skies became an expansive battleground, the setting for desperate encounters between the RAF and the Luftwaffe. In accordance with Park's order to keep the British pilots inland, whenever possible, the fighting occurred over the hop fields and apple orchards of Kent, which to the Germans in this period became known as "Hell's Corner." If the contending pilots suffered in the vicious battles, so did the people below upon whom the de-

Kentish skies became an expansive battleground: *a formation of He-111s approach their bomb run.*
(H. J. NOWARRA)

tritus of battle fell—shell casings, spent bullets, burning pieces of aircraft: the aircraft themselves and jettisoned bombs.

The Luftwaffe's primary targets for the next two weeks were Park's airfields, with emphasis upon the inner fields ringing London. Under Park's command were seven sector stations—Tangmere, Debden, Kenley, Biggin Hill, Hornchurch, North Weald, and Northolt—in southeast England. Twenty-one fighter squadrons* were based on these airfields and the Hurricanes, the Spitfires, and the few Blenheims were flown by about four hundred pilots. Although in a pinch Park could request help from the other groups, it would have to be a tight pinch. Dowding did not want to leave his other sectors open to attack while their fighters were engaged in "Hell's Corner." Although the main blow was struck at

No. 11 Group, the Germans at the same time confused the picture by diversionary feints, attacks upon ports, minelaying, as well as night raids upon various industrial targets. Nor were No. 11 Group's airfields the only ones attacked during the period August 24–September 6. They were, however, the worst hit. And its stations lay within range of the Messerschmitt 109s escorting the bombers.

That there was a new tactic was obvious to the British pilots when they met the German formations head on. The Me-109s outnumbered the German bombers about three to one—and the fighters all but clung to their charges. Breaking through such defenses was costly for the Hurricane and Spitfire pilots, if not impossible. Sheer courage was not enough and despite nearly superhuman effort and sacrifice, the bombers frequently managed to get through.

Of the sector stations, Biggin Hill, just to the south of London, sustained the worst attacks. The sector station had been hit heavily on Friday, August 30—which opened what became known as "the Bad Weekend" at Biggin Hill. The new German tactics of mass formations—few bombers and many fighters—of feints along a broad front, confused the tracking of the radar stations as well as the ground observers. It was difficult to determine, once the plots began coming in, just where the main effort would be.

It was around this time that Park instituted the now famed "Tally Ho!" procedure, which he hoped might clarify the situation. Formation leaders were to sing out this cry upon spotting German formations, along with the approximate number and type of aircraft, the altitude, course, and position of the formation when sighted. This actual visual information would help to prevent the dispatch of a single squadron of twelve Spitfires to intercept a hundred enemy aircraft, most of them fighters.

In the battles with such formations, the point of attrition became critical for Dowding. This was aggravated by the onslaught on the fighter bases and especially so in the case of the sector stations. Biggin Hill's Bad Weekend illustrates what might have been had the attacks continued systematically. Friday's raid was followed by an even heavier one on Saturday. Late in the afternoon low-flying Dorniers—only eight in number, but carrying thousand-pound bombs—slipped by the Observer Corps, radar, and the "Tally Ho!" Biggin Hill, which lay on the route to London, was attacked from the north, an approach which misled the defenses, which generally looked for the German planes to come from either the south or the east. The Dorniers flew up the Thames toward London, then turned sharply to approach Biggin Hill, still under repair from the previous day's attack as well as the morning's raid.

This afternoon raid was devastatingly effective. The bombs from the Dorniers cut across the main part of the installation, cutting power lines and gas and water mains, demolishing workshops, gutting hangars and storage facilities. The worst was a direct hit upon the crowded Operations Room; the projectile ripped through the hutment's roof, struck a steel safe, and deflected into the adjoining room before shattering with fulminating shock.

The building plunged into darkness and the air filled with debris, pulverized plaster and shards of eviscerating glass and steel. Instinctively, perhaps, Group Captain Richard Grice had ordered everyone in the Operations Room to get under tables as soon as he heard the approaching whistle of the bomb. Otherwise casualties would have been higher. As

An RAF Operations Room, from which fighters in the air could be controlled from the ground by radar and *radio. WAAFs (Women's Auxiliary Air Force) keep track of oncoming German raiders on the mapboard.*
(IMPERIAL WAR MUSEUM, LONDON)

it was, more than sixty died or were seriously wounded in the attack. The women of the WAAF inside the Operations Room acquitted themselves admirably, without panic and with a good deal of courage. They continued to carry on with their duties even though services were seriously curtailed. Sergeant Helen Turner and Corporal Elspeth Henderson remained at their phones despite the damage of the direct hit.

Other sector stations were hit on the same day— Duxford of No. 12 Group and two others of Park's No. 11 Group: Debden and Hornchurch. During the raid on the latter Alan Deere experienced another of his incredible adventures. Around the same time that Biggin Hill was being attacked, more Dorniers swung in over Hornchurch. All the aircraft had been hastily scrambled when it became clear that the sector station would be the target. Just as the Dorniers appeared over the field, No. 54 Squadron was taking off. Two sections raced into the air before the bombs began falling. The last section of three planes, led by Alan Deere, was not so fortunate.

The three Spitfires were under way when the first detonations ripped the runway. With the shouting of the controller in their ears and the sound of bomb bursts around them the Spitfires swung into the wind. Deere had the nose of his plane pointed in the right direction, only to find that one of the planes in his section blocked his way.

"Get the hell out of the way, Red Two," he shouted and gunned the engine. Red Two jinked aside and he too had his tail up and the engine roaring. Then all three Spitfires sprinted into the wind: they were air-borne. In seconds they were off the ground and their wheels began retracting into the aircraft. It was at this moment that the bomb hit.

"One moment they were about twenty feet up in close formation," wrote pilot Richard Hillary, who saw the incident, "the next catapulted apart as though on elastic." A bomb had erupted directly under the three planes. Deere's aircraft was thrown up and over on its back before crashing to earth upside down. For a hundred yards the Spitfire crunched and screeched along the runway before jolting to a stop, reeking of highly flammable fuel.

The number three man, Pilot Officer Eric Edsall, had fallen to earth right side up, but with such

force that leg injuries made it impossible for him to walk. He crawled toward Deere's Spitfire, which showed no sign of life. The number two man of Red Section, Sergeant J. Davies, was simply blown out of the airfield, across the boundary fence, where he landed without injury although the Spitfire's tail snapped off. He was missing for a long time that day, for in order to get back onto the airfield he had to walk for miles along the fence.

When Edsall reached Deere's overturned Spitfire he was amazed to find his flight leader still alive,

Prime Minister Winston Churchill on a visit to the Vauxhall Motors plant in Luton, Bedfordshire. Appropriately, the tank was known as the "Churchill."
(HOME COUNTIES NEWSPAPERS, LTD.)

although trapped inside the plane. Deere's most serious injury—which looked worse than it was— was a badly gouged head and the loss of some hair. With Deere pushing from inside and the crippled Edsall pulling from outside, they succeeded in forcing the cockpit door of the Spitfire. Fearing fire, they got away from the plane as quickly as they could hobble. Deere helped Edsall to Station Sick

Quarters. By the next day all three pilots were ready for action again.

The long day came to a close with a night bombing of Liverpool. The technique of night fighting (with the use of radar) was but a primitive idea and there was little that could be done at night, except with searchlight and antiaircraft guns. It was yet another pressure upon Fighter Command. August ended with the heaviest losses for Fighter Command on any single day of the Battle of Britain: thirty-nine fighter planes were destroyed by the Luft-

Luton after a visit from the Luftwaffe; although an aircraft factory had been the target, bombs fell on the city itself and upon the Vauxhall factory, setting some oil barrels aflame.

(HOME COUNTIES NEWSPAPERS, LTD.)

waffe. Fourteen pilots were killed, in addition to those injured or killed in the bombings themselves. The cost to the Luftwaffe, night and day, was forty-one aircraft. The loss ratios were less disproportionate, however than in July, a bad sign for Dowding's Fighter Command. Within days a serious crisis must develop, the tired Air Chief Marshal realized. The "few" were becoming too few.

II

There were no front lines in the sense that they had existed in France. And despite the aerial aspects of the Battle of Britain, the fighting and bombing took their toll on the ground also. On the day that the Bad Weekend at Biggin Hill began, Friday, August 30, 1940, the German raiders pushed through the interceptors and reached the city of Luton, some thirty miles northwest of London. Although some of the bombers jettisoned their bombs while under British fighter attack, the others found Luton at around four in the afternoon.

Luton was a manufacturing town, its main staple being the hat industry. It was also the site of Vauxhall Motors, Ltd., which turned out trucks and the so-called "Churchill" tank. Percival Aircraft, Ltd., manufactured training aircraft (the Oxford and the Proctor) as well as the de Havilland Mosquito. Also located in Luton were the Skefko Ball Bearing Company and Hayward-Tyler & Co., Ltd., which built engines for Admiralty barges.

War had come to Luton on the first day of the war when the city was designated a reception area (defined as "not immune to danger but an improbable target") for evacuees, mainly children, expectant mothers, and the blind from London. Besides the refugees from London (who eventually became homesick and returned) other signs of the war were seen in the narrow streets of Luton. These were smoke screen generators in which sawdust and tar blocks were burned to obscure Luton from possible German bombers. The generators succeeded primarily in coating the hills and homes of Luton with a black oily deposit. Later oil burners were installed for the purpose and were not as dirt-depositing.

But except for such inconveniences, and the alarums of the air raid alarms for raids that never materialized, Luton remained out of the front line until August 30.

Sometimes after, a German communiqué was issued which read: "A squadron of our bombers in daylight on August 23 [sic] raided a plane parts factory in Luton, northwest of London. The first aircraft initiated a great fire, and subsequent aircraft were thus guided to the target, which they completely destroyed."

This is not quite what happened. The bombs fell

A lone German bomber swooped down and dropped its bomb upon a factory in Luton—a factory devoted *to Luton's major industry, the manufacturing of women's hats.* (HOME COUNTIES NEWSPAPERS, LTD.)

first upon the airport, but did not focus there. The explosions ripped across Vauxhall, moving ever closer into the city itself; the bus depot was struck, killing one employee, and a double-decker bus was flung up into the roof of the garage, where it dangled over the rubble. The string of bombs "walked across" Luton, making shambles of the little brick dwellings (most of them belonging to the poor). Bombs even fell upon Vauxhall's cricket ground; the duds gave the bomb disposal crews much work to do.

It was a shocking new experience for everyone. A six-year-old boy ran into his grandmother's house

to tell her of his adventure. The very earth had opened up and lifted him right into the air! When he took her to show her the place, another boy was found there dead. In all, 53 people were killed in Luton that day and 140 injured.

Vauxhall, not a plane parts factory, as the German communiqué claimed, was worst hit. As for the "great fire," while it served admirably as a guide, it was merely some oil barrels at Vauxhall. It did little damage, nor was it a great loss. The damage to the truck assembly factory was more serious, but within a short time even this was cleared away.

Throughout the rest of the war Luton was treated

A not unusual pastoral scene in Kent during the summer of 1940. A Spitfire has just destroyed a German plane, which has come to rest in a sheep meadow.
(SYNDICATION INTERNATIONAL)

to such harsh though not very decisive raids (including some with V-2 bombs toward the close of the war). On October 15, 1940, as the Battle of Britain itself was coming to an end (at least in its intensive phases), the Luton sirens sounded. Shortly after, a lone German bomber appeared high in the sky and dropped a bomb. What its target could have been must remain one of the mysteries of the Second World War. The bomb struck a factory, true, but it was the W. O. Scales and Co., Ltd., a hat factory.

The sportive face of war is no less tragic than its grimmer visage. The explosion of the bomb blasted sewing machines in every direction: some sharp fragments even went into the factory adjoining and killed a young bride who had just come to work that morning. Ribbons, hats, brick, wood, and mortar intermingled in a colorful outburst of swirling death. New Bedford Road brightened when its trees were

suddenly festooned with gaily colored ribbons. But out of this ludicrous gaiety came thirteen dead, most of these dead being young women or girls employed by Scales. There were in addition thirty-five wounded. It took two and a half hours to dig young Tommy Walker out of the debris. The fourteen-year-old boy kept up the spirits of his rescuers by singing all the while.

But Luton was not in Hell's Corner and the people of Kent, who were subjected to much more of such accidental bombings, crashes, and shootings, remained generally in good spirits also. The continual air raid warnings took their toll in loss of sleep as well as loss of production. Watching dogfights even became an interesting pastime, once the initial fears were overcome. This came to be known as "goofing," that is, instead of taking shelter, you goofed.

Few people who watched the fight contrails realized that the spent shells, the lead that went astray, and parts of aircraft came down around them. This was one of the reasons for the tin hats issued to civilians. Jettisoned bombs or out-of-control aircraft, German or British, caused the most frightful, because of its unexpectedness, havoc. Death literally, and senselessly, dropped out of the skies.

But the nature of war had changed so much in a few months and if the sky over your home became a battleground, then your back garden became a graveyard. There was always the chance of a sudden, haphazard, violent end. There were also thousands of close calls which filled the papers with human interest stories. For example, the mother at 4 Hardy Street, Maidstone, Kent, almost every day put her baby out into the garden behind the house to get the sun. On this one Thursday morning she just hadn't gotten around to it. Meanwhile the air had begun to boil over Hell's Corner. The German raiders were heading for Croydon, Biggin Hill, and Eastchurch, among other airfields. It was over Kent that most were intercepted.

Maidstone, where the main office of the *Kent Messenger* is located, afforded many a fine view of the battles. Members of the paper's staff watched from the rooftop of their building. A Spitfire had got onto the tail of a Messerschmitt 110. The battle began high and gyrated and twisted until it was barely a thousand feet over the ground. The Messerschmitt spurted smoke and fire. It lurched and,

War souvenirs in your back yard. These natives of Kent examine what remained of a German bomber after it *came to earth. The "thumbs up" sign was as characteristic as Churchill's V (for Victory) sign.*

obviously in serious trouble, began to fall. As the Spitfire pulled away, a single parachute blossomed under the burning German plane. It was then only about four hundred feet up. The German landed on a rooftop in Hope Street, breaking both legs.

The burning plane continued on to Hardy Street, crashed against the corner of the house at number 4, taking a gable of one room with it, and then smashed into the garden. The baby was not there but in the kitchen and escaped injury. Many staff members of the *Messenger* ran to the scene of the crash to find the Me-110 burning fiercely in the garden. But there was an additional danger: the heat of the flames caused the machine-gun bullets still in the plane to explode, spewing them in all directions. Despite this the fire department was soon on the job to put out the fire.

III

Meanwhile, as German invasion barges began to accumulate along the coast, Fighter Command was in a seriously depleted state. And it was Park's No. 11 Group in Kent which had taken the brunt of the German attack.

"I was worried daily from July to September by a chronic shortage of trained fighter pilots and it was not until the battle was nearly lost that the Air Staff of the Air Ministry assisted by borrowing pilots from Bomber Command and from the Royal Navy," Park later recalled, not without some bitterness.

The Air Ministry, Park felt, was not attuned to the demands of a full-scale war in the air. Later, when he was relieved of his command in the post-Battle of Britain shake-up, Park learned that the

The fortunes of air war; an Me-110 has crashed into Hardy Street, Kent, after a losing battle with a Spitfire. (KENT MESSENGER)

training schools were operating only at two thirds of capacity and "following peace-time routines, being quite unaware of the grave shortage of pilots in Fighter Command." Why this should have been true is difficult to determine today. The Air Ministry viewed the Battle of Britain in long-range terms and may have been inclined to see the problems of Dowding and Park as merely parts of the total problem. It was, too, guided by political considerations which would hardly have interested the hard-pressed Park. It was not a simple situation and was crosscut by personalities and the desperation of the times.

Park recalled another difficulty: ". . . when the German Air Force concentrated on bombing my fighter aerodromes, I could get such little help from Air Ministry to repair the bomb damage that I had to borrow some thousands of troops from the British Army to fill in the bomb craters to keep the aerodromes serviceable. For doing so I was severely criticised by the Air Ministry at the time for accepting Army assistance. Had my fighter aerodromes been put out of action, the German Air Force would have won the battle by the 15th September 1940."

The pressures upon Park mounted daily—and each day, several times a day, he was summoned from his office to No. 11 Group's Operations Room

Cottages in a Kentish village after a German bombing raid. This frequently occurred when Luftwaffe crews jettisoned their bombs to escape RAF fighters.
(KENT MESSENGER)

as soon as unidentified aircraft were detected assembling over France.

"On entering the underground operations room," Park relates, "I would examine the plotting table which showed [the] enemy dispositions and [British] fighter squadrons dispatched. Before dispatching further squadrons I would have to decide whether the German aircraft were on a training flight or a reconnaissance flight or gathering for a feint attack by fighter sweep to draw my squadrons into the air and away from the direction of a coming bomb attack.

"Having decided that the radar indicated the beginning of a bomb attack I would dispatch more squadrons and bring others to a high state of readiness in preparation for takeoff." The standard daily

state of readiness was: five squadrons (of No. 11 Group) were at "Stand-by," meaning that their planes could be air-borne within two minutes; ten squadrons were in "Readiness" (takeoff time five minutes); five squadrons were ready for takeoff in from ten to fifteen minutes and declared "Available." Another five squadrons were "Released," free for the day to rest the pilots and carry on maintenance on the aircraft.

As for the battle itself: "My plan was to make 'Forward Interception' as near as possible to the coast. My aim was always to intercept the German main attack with the maximum number of fighter squadrons that were available. My Spitfire squadrons were directed against the German fighter escort and the Hurricane squadrons were directed against the enemy bombers."

But Park encountered yet another trial, a theoretical disagreement as well as, perhaps, a personality clash. This was with the commander of No. 12

Air Vice-Marshal Trafford Leigh-Mallory, commander of No. 12 Group, which shared the defense of Kent and London with Park's No. 11 Group.
(IMPERIAL WAR MUSEUM, LONDON)

Group, Air Vice-Marshal Trafford Leigh-Mallory, whose command lay to the north of Park's. "Number 12 Group," Park has written, ". . . was frequently called upon to cover my fighter aerodromes around London which were quite defenceless when I had sent all my squadrons to intercept near the coast. Number 12 Group, however, always delayed dispatching its reinforcements in order to assemble wings of four to six squadrons which went off on roving sweeps from the South East of England, and on several occasions allowed my fighter aerodromes to be heavily bombed."

This disagreement between Park and Leigh-Mallory was to have its repercussions after the height of the Battle had passed. Dowding characteristically remained aloof from the argument, feeling that each group leader must be permitted to act without interference from him. Members of the Air Staff, however, upon visiting some of the fighter stations, listened to the pilots and junior officers of No. 12 Group complaining about not being permitted to take part in the battles over Kent because they were not given sufficient time in which to form. Park saw no point in calling upon No. 12

Group (although he did, of course) only to have it form into wings—"Balbos" they were called, after Italo Balbo, the Italian aviator who had led a mass flight from Italy to Chicago in 1933. By the time the wing had formed up the enemy had attacked and left. But when one of the wings, especially the Duxford wing led by Douglas Bader, did succeed in engaging the German formations, Park admitted (although not without a small barb), "that had already been attacked by 11 Group forward squadrons, they were successful." But there was a sentiment in the Air Ministry that the fighter operations over Kent were not efficiently co-ordinated (rather humanly impossible at the time) and that something must be done as soon as it was politic. The result was that in November Dowding was shunted off to an innocuous job as a British representative visiting aircraft factories in the United States. His position at the helm of Fighter Command was taken over by Sholto Douglas, who had served as a fighter pilot in the First World War and was, during the Battle of Britain, deputy Chief of the Air Staff.

Park, after only eight months, was "posted" to Flying Training Command and command of No. 11 Group was taken over by Leigh-Mallory. Evidently the latter's "big wing" theories had impressed Douglas and Archibald Sinclair, Secretary of State for Air. These changes, of which very little was made at the time, did not come about until late in November 1940. Few Britons realized that Dowding and Park had in fact won them the Battle of Britain.

IV

Sealion could not take place unless air superiority over the Channel was secured, and that was possible only by the destruction of the Royal Air Force—and by early September that seemed feasible. Not, however, to the Germans, who, though noting the claims of the Luftwaffe, were puzzled by the appearance of Spitfires and Hurricanes supposedly no longer existent according to the intelligence of Beppo Schmid. On September 3 German Intelligence Chief Schmid estimated, under pressure from Kesselring and Sperrle, that perhaps Fighter Command had only 100 fighters left—or maybe they had 350. Meanwhile hundreds of invasion barges lay in

Kent was "Hell's Corner" as much for the Luftwaffe as for the RAF. A Do-17 burns on the beach in Kent, *like the Luftwaffe its back broken in an attempt to destroy the RAF.* (FOX PHOTOS, LTD.)

French and Belgian ports in readiness for Sealion— and these were suffering under the attacks of British Bomber Command. The earliest date for the sailing of the invasion fleet, Hitler had informed them on the same day, "has been fixed for September 20, and that of the landing for September 21." The German High Command was also informed that the launching of the attack upon the British Isles (through Kent) would occur "on D-Day minus 10," presumably therefore on September 11.

But the Luftwaffe was faced with eliminating the RAF, which theoretically should have been all but wiped out. Schmid did not know that the attacks upon the forward airfields had done extensive damage to five of them and knocked out two, Manston and Lympne, so effectively that they were unusable by fighter aircraft for several days. Six out of Park's seven sector stations had also been hit, with Biggin Hill forced to evacuate two of its three squadrons. In the period from August 24 through September 6 Fighter Command had lost 295 Spitfires and Hurricanes, with 171 severely damaged. In the same period replacements (new and repaired aircraft) numbered 269. But the most serious factor was the loss of pilots: in this same two-week period 103 pilots were dead or missing and 128 were wounded

seriously enough to be taken out of the Battle. At this rate of loss—an average of 120 pilots a week— Dowding would shortly have no Fighter Command.

Inexperienced pilots were too often lost on their first patrols; veteran pilots were exhausted, jumpy, and vulnerable. The gay young fighter pilot was no more. They were raw-nerved, gray-faced, listless, filled with that hatred that Bader described: "We hated those aeroplanes with their iron crosses and their crooked swastikas flying into our English sky. . . ." Only now it was goaded by desperation. The younger pilots were shocked upon seeing their seniors shooting at Germans in parachutes. This was considered a "Hunnish trick" and not cricket. But it was done.

For all their fatigue, despite the shortage of pilots, Fighter Command continued to intercept the German formations—much to the Luftwaffe's consternation. They were being assured that there was no RAF left. They had no idea, however, how close Schmid was to the truth.

The Luftwaffe High Command then on September 3, 1940, in their conference at The Hague, came to a grand decision. They were certain it would wipe out Fighter Command completely. And as with so many of the Nazi Grand Decisions, it saved the enemy.

8

"THE GREATEST DAY"

On September 4, 1940, the day following Göring's meeting with his High Command at The Hague when he had resolved upon a change in Luftwaffe tactics, Hitler spoke on the occasion of the opening of the *Winterhilfe* ("Winter Relief") campaign at the Sportpalast. The majority of his audience consisted of nurses and social workers concerned with *Winterhilfe*.

Hitler was in a rare sardonic, threatening mood—and his audience, including the angels of mercy, responded accordingly to his outbursts.

"In England," he told them, "they're filled with curiosity and keep asking, 'Why doesn't he come?'

"Be calm," Hitler confided, mockery in his voice; the audience tittered. "He's coming! He's coming!"

Hitler's audience responded thrillingly, encouraging him to speak with his customary mastery bordering on hysteria. When his listeners, most of them women, became quiet again Hitler waxed solemn. Winston Churchill, "that noted war correspondent," was "demonstrating his new brain child, the night air raid. Mr. Churchill is carrying out these raids not because they promise to be highly effective, but because his Air Force cannot fly over Germany in daylight."

German planes flew over England every day, Hitler told them. "Whenever the Englishman sees a light, he drops a bomb . . . on residential districts, farms, and villages."

The very air was charged in the Sportpalast as Hitler came to the point of his speech. "When the British Air Force drops two or three or four thousand kilograms of bombs, then we will in one night drop a hundred and fifty, two hundred and thirty, two hundred, or four hundred thousand kilograms—"

Great waves of applause interrupted Hitler at this point.

"When they declare," he shrieked, "that they will increase their attacks on our cities, then we will raze their cities to the ground!"

The audience rose to its feet, screaming, applauding. Their dedication to mankind did not include the British, the French, the Dutch, the Poles.

"The hour will come," Hitler promised in conclusion, "when one of us will break—and it will not be National Socialist Germany!"

"Never! Never!" screamed the nurses, leaping to their feet again, shouting, nearly hysterical, approving and adoring.

Hitler was in his own way approving of the Luftwaffe's decision of the previous day. The major target of the German Air Force would be London. The fiction of "only purely military targets" was ended. The war between the soldiers was over, it would now become a war between peoples. The civilian no longer enjoyed bystander status: modern war had "officially" taken on a new, deadly posture. Perhaps it had always been there but finally no one pretended. The simple "art of war" was revealed for what it was—and is—the technology of slaughter. This great truth may very well be Hitler's contribution to mankind; he had little else to offer.

II

The fateful decision to bomb London came about by accident. On the night of August 24 (this was the day on which the British airfields first came under heavy attack also) German aircraft dispatched to bomb an aircraft factory at Rochester and oil storage tanks at Thames Haven made a slight error in navigation. As a result bombs fell upon London for the first time since 1918, when the Gotha bombers had flown over the city. Great fires were kindled in London Wall and Fore Street; other sections of the city and its outskirts received isolated bombs. In Bethnal Green about a hundred dwellings were destroyed. Militarily practically nothing was accomplished, except that the old warrior, Churchill, demanded a reprisal raid on Berlin.

Bomber Command did not view this request with equanimity. The Luftwaffe could reach London from just across the Channel, but it was a six-hundred-mile trip—one way—to Berlin. Except for psychological effect, Bomber Command saw little of value in striking the German capital. The long distance precluded heavy bomb loads, for a good deal of the weight carried by the bombers would have to include fuel. But Churchill persisted—as did public sentiment—and on the night of August 25/26 eighty-one British bombers took off for Berlin. These were the Wellingtons, Whitleys, and Hampdens of Nos. 3, 4, and 5 Groups respectively. Of these, twenty-nine aircraft (of Nos. 44, 49, 50, 58, 61, 83, and 99 Squadrons) claimed to have bombed Berlin. The operation was greatly hampered by a thick cloud down to two thousand feet. Twenty-seven other aircraft reached Berlin but, unable to identify their targets, did not bomb; of these, twenty-one returned to England with their bombs and six jettisoned them into the sea. Eighteen bombers struck at alternative targets. Seven were forced to turn back because of mechanical troubles. Five aircraft were lost—three of which were ditched in the sea and their crews rescued.

According to German sources only ten bombers actually dropped bombs in what might have been considered industrial target areas. The rest of the bombs scattered through the city. If it had proved a not very successful mission, this first attack on the German capital came as a distinct shock to Berliners. They had been promised by Göring himself that no British aircraft would ever appear over Germany. The effect was minimal, but the implications were appalling.

Three nights later the British bombers came again and for the first time in history German civilians were killed in Berlin. Ten were dead and twenty-nine injured in the very heart of the Reich. The headlines of Berlin's newspapers read: COWARDLY BRITISH ATTACK! A popular epithet for the crews of Bomber Command was "British Air Pirates." It was a curiously unrealistic reaction to the facts of war—as if Germany could rightfully anticipate half a war.

So it was with these bombings of the very heart of the Reich in mind that Hitler promised, threatened, and exhorted. When he pledged, "He's coming!" Hitler alluded to Sealion, for even as he spoke the barges and other invasion craft converged upon ports along the coast from the Netherlands to northern France.

The stimuli for the Luftwaffe's shift from the airfields to London were not simple. It would be an overstatement to say that the plain and simple motive was Hitler's mad desire (though he was capable of it) to retaliate to Churchill's retaliation. Even Hitler from time to time harkened to professional military counsel. It was goading to have the British bombers over the Reich, but they were in truth doing little real damage to the war machine. Göring believed that with Fighter Command all but finished an attack upon London and all it symbolized to the British would bring out the few remaining fighters which he was assured Dowding had pulled back out of Kent. With London just within range of the Me-109s it would be possible to lure the last Spitfires and Hurricanes into the battle and finish them off. Göring was reasonably certain—and Beppo Schmid had concurred—that most of the airfields of Kent were finished. They required no further attention.

This was the first of two misconceptions. True, Park's No. 11 Group was in poor shape, but it was still deployed throughout Kent. Another two weeks of the kind of pounding it had taken might very well have finished it off. But when the decision was made to make London the major target of the Luftwaffe Park still had his squadrons—they were under strength, they were at nerves' end, they were battle-wearied, but they were there.

The other misconception concerned the Londoners themselves. If the attack were mounted upon the densely populated capital and if it were razed, as Hitler had promised the nurses in the Sportpalast, then the "warmonger" Churchill would be forced

had ordered Paris stripped of all its finest statuary. Among these was an especially fine one of Moses which he had placed in his home. One day, so the tale went, Hitler was found on his knees before the statue of Moses saying, "Oh, Moses, tell me, tell me how you got your people over that little bit of water."

The British had no illusions—they knew that if Hitler could possibly cross, he would. Grim preparations were under way, including a fiendish de-

Lockheed Hudsons on patrol over the English Channel. The first American aircraft to go into RAF service, the Hudson was a versatile plane of all work: photography and reconnaissance plane, fighter and bomber. British crews called it "Old Boomerang."

(IMPERIAL WAR MUSEUM, LONDON)

by his own people to sue for a *Pax Germanica*. There would be no need for Sealion, a roseate, though nagging, consideration that Hitler nurtured. It was an idea which Admiral Raeder greatly admired. He had come to detest that English Channel, as did the pilots of the Luftwaffe, who referred to it as the *Shite Kanal*. The concept of a large-scale amphibious operation was regarded with suspicion by the landlocked Germans.

It was around this time that a revealing story was making the rounds of the English pubs, where the natives gathered to enjoy their bitters and bore each other with their bomb stories. This story, however, had to do with Hitler and his problem. He

vice which Churchill found good. Along the southern coast of England, from Beachy Head to Weymouth —the finest landing grounds—a method had been devised to pump oil and petrol into the water. As the first wave of German invasion barges approached this area a single Blackburn Skua dive bomber, piloted by one "Nobby" Clarke, was to flash over the treated waters and drop incendiaries. The invading Germans would be met by a wall of flame. Smaller aircraft, including de Havilland Tiger Moths (ordinarily used as primary trainers), would further harass the invaders with anti-personnel bombs.

It was a grand, if rather horrifying, conception

although never actually put to use—except in one practice session and in various rumors. There were other arrangements awaiting the invaders. The sea approaches were mined, the beaches bristled with barbed wire, the Home Guard was armed with everything from breech-loading rifles of First World War vintage sent by the United States to simple clubs. The doughty Islanders awaited Hitler's coming. Churchill had even prepared a slogan which, like the burning seas device, was never implemented: "You can always take one with you."

For weeks the Photographic Reconnaissance Unit, using the American-built Lockheed Hudson as well as Spitfires, kept a wary camera eye on the Channel coast. The count of invasion barges rose from day to day; to these were added motorboats and other vessels moving from the North Sea toward the Channel ports. At Ostend, for example, there were eighteen barges on August 31. By September 6 the photographs revealed no less than two hundred. The Combined Intelligence Committee in London, after assessing the portents, issued an invasion alert. GHQ, Home Forces alerted its units with the code word "Cromwell," indicating that invasion was expected imminently. In some parts of England Home Guard commanders summoned their members by ringing church bells, thus giving rise to the rumors that parachutists had begun descending upon Britain and that German invasion boats were already approaching the English coast.

That was the mood on Saturday, September 7, 1940, in Britain: some confusion but all in readiness. To Park in No. 11 Group headquarters it promised to be a day like all of the others, with his afflicted airfields heavily attacked and his pilots further taxed. Across the Channel—though Park did not know this until it was released via a radio news broadcast—Göring had arrived at the Pas de Calais. Setting up his headquarters at Cap Blanc-Nez he announced that he had "taken over personal command of the Luftwaffe in its war against England." In his private train Göring brought his personal cooks, a stock of wines, his doctor, his valet, and his nurse.

As Park braced himself for the next round of blows at his sector stations, a massive raid began forming up over Calais. But it was London which was the target and it caught Fighter Command off guard. The first full-scale bombing attack on London

began shortly after five in the afternoon: more than three hundred bombers (Ju-88s, He-111s, and Do-17s), escorted by six hundred fighters (Me-109s and 110s), almost a thousand aircraft, converged on the city.

Although there were interceptions, the change in target did confuse the controllers and the heavy fighter protection interfered with the British attack on the bombers. London's inadequate antiaircraft guns could not stop the bombers either, flying as

An He-111 hovers over the Thames, London, September 7, 1940—the day the Luftwaffe diverted its attentions from the RAF fighter stations to London.
(IMPERIAL WAR MUSEUM, LONDON)

they were at altitudes between seventeen thousand and twenty thousand feet. Tons of bombs rained down upon London—the docks, the Woolwich arsenal, the oil tanks, and other military targets were hit and raged into flame. Bombs fell also on the streets of East End, with its clutter of dwellings —now hardly better than slums—dating from the early Victorian period. The heavily populated streets filled with pitiable rubble, dazed refugees, and the dead.

The fires ignited in the first attack blazed well into the night, lighting the way for the night bombers. While the fire brigades, comprised of great numbers of auxiliaries who had never fought a fire, attempted to contend with the out-of-control conflagrations, the German bombers returned to drop additional bombs into the burning areas.

By midnight London was ablaze with nine "hundred-pump" fires (a thirty-pump fire was considered a very big fire). In the Surrey Docks there were two large fires (one 300- and the other 130-pump); there were a half-dozen hundred-pump fires at Bishopsgate Goods Yard and other points along the docks. The heat from the Quebec Yard of the Surrey Docks became so intense it set the wooden

London burns after a Luftwaffe bombing.
(NATIONAL ARCHIVES)

blocks in the roadways ablaze. Paint blistered off the fireboats three hundred yards distant in the Thames.

At the Woolwich arsenal (200-pump) the firemen fought the fires among boxes of ammunition and crates of nitroglycerin. But the docks storing more conventional stock gave the most trouble. Tea, it was soon learned, produced a blaze which was "sweet, sickly and intense"; one fireman thought it ludicrous to be pouring *cold* water on *hot* tea. Liquefied sugar burned fiercely on the surface of the water. Burning rubber released dense black smoke and asphyxiated the firemen. Cans of paint burst, spraying white-hot flame into the air, coating the fire pumps with varnish—which took weeks to clean off. From a spice storage dock fires carried

pepper into the air, making it almost impossible to breathe. To the firemen, inhaling the peppered air was almost like breathing flame itself. And great stores of rum too created difficulties: the casks themselves burst with bomblike intensity and blazing streams of grog poured out of the warehouses into the streets. Grain warehouses burned violently and filled the air with swarms of black flies; hundreds of rats ran in the street. The burned wheat left a residue—"a sticky mess that pulls your boots off."

"The fire was so huge," one of the fire fighters later recalled, "that we could do little more than make a feeble attempt to put it out. The whole of that warehouse was a raging inferno, against which were silhouetted groups of pigmy firemen directing their futile jets at the wall of flame. . . ."

A stretcher-bearer stationed at the Redriff School in the dock area (portions of which were poor residential sections) thought "it looked one flaming mass and the flames were terrifically high. To us it seemed a remarkable thing that people could get out of that area, and when we saw—when we saw the people come streaming down from dockland we were absolutely amazed. They seemed to come like an army marching and running from the area. The people coming from down town [Bermondsey, an inhabited strip between the Surrey Docks and the Thames River] looked in a very, very bad condition, they were dirty, dishevelled and hurrying to get away."

Not all got away, however, and in the attacks of September 7/8 about three hundred Londoners died and over a thousand were seriously injured. But these impressive figures, and the even more impressive fires in eastern London, were not acquired without cost to the Luftwaffe. Although Dowding's Fighter Command had been prepared for a continuation of the attacks on the airfields, it had sent fighters to intercept the mass German formations. Among the most effective was the hard-fighting No. 303 Squadron (Polish), which ripped into the German swarms with cavalrylike ferocity to get at the Dorniers. Corporal S. Wojtowicz, although he succeeded in shooting down a Dornier, found little to exult over. "I turned back from the chase but I was returning with a heavy heart, in spite of my victories, for the whole eastern suburb of London seemed to be burning." It recalled his homeland to Wojtowicz when he had left it a year before.

The switch to London brought a greater burden of responsibility to the German fighters. They were expected to furnish close escort for the bombers, but the RAF pilots avoided the German fighters to slaughter the bombers. Here the Me-109s are readied for the trip across the Channel: arming up, strapping the pilot's boots, and, finally, closing the canopy and pulling the chock from under the wheel. The "arched cat" insignia belonged to 8/JG 51. (H. J. NOWARRA)

*General Wladislaw Sikorski, head of the Polish govern-
ment-in-exile, visiting No. 303 Squadron (Polish).
Greeting him is Squadron Commander Witold Urbanowicz, highest-scoring Polish ace of the RAF (seventeen*
*victories); Urbanowicz later served in the U. S. Four-
teenth Air Force, brought his score up to twenty when
(1944) he destroyed three Zeros.*
(EMBASSY OF THE POLISH PEOPLE'S REPUBLIC)

Douglas Bader's Duxford wing also intercepted a
large formation of Dorniers with Me-110 and Me-
109 escort to the east of London. Bader's No. 242
Squadron succeeded in mixing with the Germans
and, though his own plane was damaged, Bader
accounted for two enemy fighters. The other two
squadrons of Bader's Duxford wing, Nos. 19 and
310, had not caught up with the Germans in time.
They had been too low when the order to attack
had come. Fighter Command lost forty-two aircraft on September 7, 1940, and fourteen pilots.

All during the day and into the night the German
radio reported the progress of the battle to the
Reich. In the evening a triumphant, vaunting
Göring spoke of the "heavy sacrifices" of the Luftwaffe, but he crowed, "This is the historic hour
when for the first time our Air Force delivered its
thrust right into the enemy's heart!" The thrust had
cost fifty-three aircraft, most of them fighters. It
was a heavy toll, but, Göring reasoned, worth it.
Even so seasoned a leader as Major Hannes Traut-

loft, of Kampfgeschwader 54, noted that they had
been met only by single British fighters "which
could do nothing. . . ." Perhaps Fighter Command
was down to its last Spitfires.

But in turning to London the Germans afforded
Fighter Command the time to put its stations back
into efficient operational status. Repairs could be
made to the ground installations; communications
systems could be restored to normal. The Germans
had, by their switch to London, unwittingly granted
Fighter Command a sorely needed period of grace.
The question was: Could London take it—or would
London go the way of Guernica, Warsaw, and
Rotterdam? Hitler and Göring were confident it
would—with twinges of perplexing doubt which
found expression in the vacillation with respect to
Sealion.

The canny Dowding, however, had no such qualifications. In June, when he knew that the Luftwaffe
had moved into the forward bases in the Low
Countries and France, Dowding said, "The nearness

Arming up a Spitfire for the next round with the Luftwaffe. The advantage of fighting over one's own grounds was that during the lull in the battle, or if ammunition was expended, it was possible to land and rearm quickly. (IMPERIAL WAR MUSEUM, LONDON)

The strain of battle fatigued pilots. Sergeant G. B. Booth catches a few moments of that precious commodity sleep while awaiting the call to intercept. Booth was killed during the Battle of Britain.

(KENT MESSENGER)

of London to German airfields will lose them the war." Not that the German shift in target concentration took all the weight off Dowding's shoulders. The daylight attacks continued, some even striking at the airfields and the radar installations. As for the night bombings, they went nearly unchallenged, for the night fighters were not yet operating with radar and had missed the German planes in the dark. The antiaircraft guns did little more than fill the air with projectiles and succeeded only in annoying the bombers a little.

On September 8, the day following the first large-scale daylight bombing of London, only minor raids ensued. On the ninth, however, Fighter Command was ready for the raids which developed in force late in the afternoon. But of the two hundred bombers dispatched against London, only ninety managed to break through the fighters sent up by Park as well as fighters from Nos. 10 and 12 Groups. Perhaps seventy bombers were diverted from their main objective and bombed secondary targets while nearly sixty German bombers were turned back and did not bomb at all or jettisoned their bombs. Some of the latter fell upon Canterbury in Kent. Thirty-seven German planes crashed to earth or into the sea and an additional seven were lost either during the Channel crossing or in landing in France. Fighter Command lost nineteen aircraft and fourteen pilots.

The fighting of September 9 gave the Luftwaffe pause. Yet there remained the hope that a few more days of heavy fighting would wipe out Fighter Command once and for all. By September 13 Hitler wistfully implied that if all went as they hoped he might never have to give the order for the launching of Sealion. He had, on September 11, postponed it once again and promised another, perhaps on the fourteenth: this would set the actual invasion date for September 24. This depended upon air superiority over southeast England and the internal collapse of England hopefully because of the London bombings. On September 14, with disconcerting regularity, Hitler postponed Sealion once again, setting the new warning date for September 17 (and D-Day, as planned, for ten days after, September 27). The unco-ordinated interceptions by Fighter Command on that day all but confirmed the German hopes. The critical moment was at hand: the moment for the Luftwaffe's *coup de grâce* to Fighter Command.

Some of Churchill's "few": a handful of pilots who took part in the Battle of Britain—Pilot Officer John L. Allen, Flight Lieutenant Robert S. Tuck (No. 92 Squadron), Flight Lieutenant Alan C. Deere, Flight Lieutenant Adolf G. Malan (No. 74 Squadron), and Squadron Leader James A. Leathart—and a bugler. Allen, Deere, and Leathart were all members of No. 54 Squadron (of which the latter was commanding officer) and frequently flew together as a section. Allen died during the Battle. This quintet scored nearly a hundred victories against the Luftwaffe during the course of the war. (IMPERIAL WAR MUSEUM, LONDON)

III

On the morning of Sunday, September 15, 1940, Winston Churchill, accompanied by his wife, Clementine, drove from his home at Chequers (the official country seat of Prime Ministers) to nearby Uxbridge. It was but another in Churchill's countless visits to the scenes of action. Here, at the headquarters of No. 11 Group, Churchill and his wife were taken by Keith Park down into the Operations Room, about fifty feet below ground beneath Hillingdon Golf Course. "The Group Operations Room was like a small theater," Churchill has written, "about sixty feet across, and with two storeys. We took our seats in the dress circle. Below

Spitfires in attack formation.
(IMPERIAL WAR MUSEUM, LONDON)

us was the large-scale map-table, around which perhaps twenty highly trained young men and women,
with their telephone assistants, were assembled."

Opposite the Churchills, Park, and others essential
to the operations was a giant blackboard covering
an entire wall. This was the "tote board" on which,
in a glance, Park was able to ascertain the status
of each squadron in each sector of No. 11 Group.
This was graphically depicted by vertical subdivisions
on the tote board; colored lights indicated the state
of readiness of each squadron. Those squadrons
in action were indicated by red lights. Correlated
with the board was a great map spread across the
room, over which the plotters worked, showing the
disposition of the squadrons and the plots of the
incoming Germans. Officers slightly offstage, so to

speak, in a glass enclosure kept track of British
antiaircraft guns. Thus the tote board reduced the
three-dimensional battle in the skies to little more
than a two-dimensional graph.

The atmosphere was charged with tension, although Park, drawn and tired, said to the Churchills,
"I don't know whether anything will happen today."

Through the previous night the ground crews had
worked on the Hurricanes and Spitfires, patching
those which had been damaged in the day's action.
Fourteen British fighters had been lost; the Germans
too had lost fourteen aircraft, but some of them
had been bombers.

By dawn of Sunday the airdromes of Kent reverberated to the sound of Merlin engines catching
and the roar of their warming up. Armorers threaded

ammunition belts into the wings of the fighters and petrol bowsers darted here and there among the poised aircraft, fueling them up. The tension increased with the coming light—it promised to be a fine day with some cloud patches possible.

The Churchills had barely settled themselves into "the Hole" at Uxbridge when the radar posts along the Channel reported German aircraft activity forming up over Dieppe. "Forty plus," was the estimate; the bulbs along the bottom of the tote board flashed on and Park's squadrons came to "Stand-by" status. It was now eleven o'clock in the morning and as the minutes ticked by the radar stations reported more and more enemy aircraft building up: "Forty plus, sixty plus, eighty plus . . ." Within moments Park ordered eleven of his squadrons into the air; a single squadron from No. 10 Group was requested to cover 11 Group's western boundary. To the north the five squadrons comprising the so-called Duxford wing of No. 12 Group led by Douglas Bader leaped into the air.

Park's Spitfires and Hurricanes intercepted the bomber formations—over two hundred strong with hundreds of fighters escorting—over eastern Kent. The odds, except in numbers, lay with the defenders. For a half hour the radar operators had plotted the massing of the German formations and Park, with uncanny certainty, judged the target to be London. He knew where to place his squadrons for effect. Churchill's cigar had gone dead as he concentrated upon the action unfolding before him.

The Spitfires of No. 72 and No. 92 Squadrons, meeting the Germans over Canterbury, knifed through the formations with guns hammering. It was the first blood of the day. Engines of Dorniers flickered and smoked; some fell from the formation, others broke and turned for the coast. The Me-109s whipped into the melee to protect the bombers. The battle, moving westward across Kent, swarmed in clusters and darting individual combats toward London, leaving in its wake burning aircraft, parachutes drifting through the smoke, and the dead.

The Dorniers of Kampfgeschwader 3, now decimated and with dead men at some of the gun positions, pressed on to London. The shaken crews, who had taken off certain that Fighter Command no longer existed, bombed with no accuracy. Very little of military value was hit: a number of dwellings, a couple of bridges, a suburban electrical plant; a sin-

gle bomb even fell into the grounds of Buckingham Palace, although it proved to be a dud. Sergeant Ray T. Holmes, Hurricane pilot of No. 504 Squadron, which had met the Dorniers on the outskirts of London, was certain he had brought down the plane which had bombed the palace.

Holmes was acting as rear guard for the squadron on patrol; his job was to weave around behind and above the other planes keeping an eye out for German fighters. The squadron had just met the Dornier formation and had broken it up with an attack. "By then," Holmes relates, "the Dornier formation had become ragged and was turning for home, and 504 had broken away to reform and I spotted three Dorniers blazing a lone trail toward London. No one seemed to have noticed them, so I decided to give them a little attention."

Throttling the Hurricane to speed, Holmes overtook the three German planes and then attacked from the flank. The first Dornier spurted oil just as Holmes passed underneath, blotting out his vision when the windscreen was covered. The slipstream cleared the oil away in time for Holmes to get a quick glimpse of the Dornier's tail, just inches from his Hurricane's nose. One of the German's propellers had stopped. Holmes came up from under the plane to attack the other flanking Dornier. The root of the wing caught fire and a parachute ejected from the Dornier. For a few moments the hapless German chutist draped across the wing of Holmes's Hurricane. He then was dragged off into nothingness by the twisted parachute.

Holmes then turned to the lead plane, attacking it from behind. This had little effect and Holmes found himself with only fifteen seconds of firing time left. "I thought a head-on attack might cool his ardor, and climbed up past him to his left from my last breakaway." As he readied for this attack, Holmes noted that his engine sounded rough and that oil (his own) had begun to bubble into his cockpit. As he tore in head-on, eight guns firing, Holmes ran out of ammunition. Frustrated, he simply kept going over the Dornier and "clipped one side of his fragile-looking twin tail with my port wing." The only sensation was a slight bump, and Holmes was certain that little harm could have come to his Hurricane. Then his wing dropped—the tip had been torn off—the nose dropped too, and the controls would not respond. The Hurricane snapped

Douglas Bader (center) with two members of his No. 242 Squadron, George Eric Ball (left) and William L. McKnight. Active through the Battle and the blitz,

Ball and McKnight were killed during fighter sweeps after the RAF went over to the offensive.
(IMPERIAL WAR MUSEUM, LONDON)

into a vertical spin. Holmes fought his way out of the plane and joined his opponents in floating down toward London.

He had afforded Londoners with quite an exciting spectacle, for the German bomber crashed spectacularly into Victoria Station. The surviving German crewmen landed across the Thames in the Kennington cricket oval. Holmes fared not so well: after bouncing off a rooftop in the Chelsea section of London, he came to rest in a Londoner's back-yard trash can.

Although they continued their thrust to London, the tormented German bomber crews wondered where all the Spitfires and Hurricanes had come from. The German fighters—those not tied closely to the bombers—swept in to clear the way, but not all of the British planes could be stopped. These careened through and chopped up the formations.

Adolf Galland, leading his Jagdgeschwader 26 on a forward free hunt, charged into the attacking British fighters but without, even after ten minutes of savage fighting, stopping them. Twisting in his cockpit he saw, nearly two thousand feet below him, a pair of Hurricanes. He flipped into a dive and sent one flaming into the Thames. But after the time spent in France forming up, crossing the Channel, fighting across Kent, and a few minutes of combat, it was time for Galland to streak for home unless he wanted to end up in the *Shite Kanal*.

It was over London on this Sunday, September 15, 1940, that the German bomber formations, having dropped their bombs, and after having traversed miles of smoking sky to do it, received a further shock. Where had all the Spitfires and Hurricanes— which Beppo Schmid had claimed had dwindled to the last fifty—where had they all come from? And

A Spitfire makes a fighter pass on an He-111 over the Channel. In these (probably in a staged action with a captured Spitfire) photographs the British fighter

then from the north, like a biblical plague, screamed a full sixty fresh fighters led by Douglas Bader. He had led his squadrons—his own No. 224, the Czech No. 310, and the Polish No. 302 (all in Hurricanes), and the two Spitfire squadrons, Nos. 19 and 611—as high as possible to get above the Germans and into the sun. When he saw the Germans—forty or more Ju-88s and Dorniers—Bader swiftly studied the air around them for a glimpse of the escort. Then alerting the others to the telltale specks in the distance, Bader nosed into the German bomber formation, shouting, "Break 'em up!"

With his eight guns firing Bader swept into the vanguard of the German planes. He kicked the Hurricane around, pulled up and onto the tail of a Dornier. The guns shook the Hurricane as holes and sparks appeared behind the Dornier's right engine. Then a flash, black smoke—and Bader had to jerk the stick to avoid ramming the stricken German bomber. As he pulled off he saw another Dornier slipping into a cloud bank for sanctuary. Above it a lone Spitfire dived into the same cloud. The British pilot had not seen the German bomber. There was a billow of orange flame, black smoke, and with the wings of the Dornier twisted around the Spitfire, the two aircraft fell churning through the air into London.

Bader, twisting his neck, sought more targets and saw only one other plane, a Do-17 spinning and burning. A crewman managed to get out of the gyrating plane, but opened his chute too soon. The silk brushed through the flame and seared away into the clouds. The hapless German, trailing useless shrouds, plummeted straight down. Bitterly, almost without pity, Bader thought, "Now you've got a little time to think about it and there isn't any answer."

And now, except for wisps of black smoke, the curls of evaporating tracers, the sky was empty. Emotionally tired, his fuel low, Bader turned the Hurricane for Duxford.

By twelve-thirty peace had come again to the Sunday skies of England. But the day was only half

has come under the tail and the starboard wing, flashes by the nose gunner's position, and begins to turn for another attack. (H. J. NOWARRA) over. The second, and heavier, round of Luftwaffe attacks began just before two-thirty in the afternoon. There had been less time to scramble the Fighter Command squadrons than in the morning. Bader, again leading the Duxford wing, was critical of this short notice, feeling that his unit could have done much better had it been given ample time to assemble and to meet the Germans head on before they reached London. When they finally met the Germans Bader's aircraft intercepted them from below—not an advantage at all. The Me-109s could bounce them before they got at the bombers.

The Germans came over in three large formations, crossing the English coast between Dungeness and Dover. Park had dispatched twelve of his squadrons in pairs to meet the Germans as they came in over Kent; soon another seven and a half squadrons took to the air. The leading German formation was intercepted over Canterbury by two squadrons from the Hornchurch sector station; soon these were joined by more Hurricanes which had been patrolling over Maidstone. The heavens, as they had two hours earlier, were racked with the sound of guns, the trail of battle and defeat: the reek of cordite and burning metal.

The radios crackled in the Operations Rooms as the controllers sent the fighters to meet the attackers. The Churchills listened as the tension mounted even more at Uxbridge. The language did not always make sense to the layman, but the urgency in the young voices conveyed the drama of the battle.

"Bullfinch patrol Maidstone, Angels twenty," the controller ordered. "Bullfinch" was the day's code name for one of the squadrons; "angels" was an altitude indication: angels twenty was twenty thousand feet.

Then the radio might come to life as the fighter pilots closed with the enemy (these are authentic transcriptions):

"109s at four o'clock above."

"Keep in, Blue 2" (elements in the squadrons were coded by color and number. Blue 2 was the second plane in blue section; Blue 1 led this section; a third plane completed the section.)

"Watch your tail, Red 3!"

"Break right, Red 3, break right!"

The people in No. 11 Group's Operations Room could hear but not see any of this, of course.

"Got the bastard!" the radio crackled. A squadron mate had come to the aid of Red 3.

"Typan [the code name for a controller] to Ferret leader. Fifty plus near Gravesend. One hundred plus approaching you from southeast. One hundred and twenty plus. Angels eighteen. North of Base 2."

"Ferret leader to Typan. Don't tell me any more, you're making me nervous."

A bomber formation is seen and the "Tally Ho!" is given.

"Black 2 to Black leader. Dorniers at twelve o'clock, just below."

"OK. Head-on attack. Break right and left, I'll break upward."

A brief silence, and an unknown voice crackles, "God, that was dangerous!"

It was dangerous for the Germans too. Again, as in the morning's confused terror, the gnawing question was: What was the source, seemingly inexhaustible, of all those British fighters? How confidently, even disdainfully, had they checked off the British airfields, the aircraft factories, as destroyed in the weeks before. That Park had committed all of his squadrons to the battle, as well as the great Duxford wing and a single squadron from No. 10 Group, might not have assured the harried Germans. To them it seemed that the British fighters materialized out of nowhere.

At the battle's climax Churchill, his eye upon the line of lighted electric bulbs on the tote board, asked, "What other reserves have we?"

"There are none," Park told him. All the squadrons of No. 11 Group were in the air and Park had drawn upon the neighboring Groups for reinforcements. Complications arose when, during the great air battles over London and its suburbs, a small bomber and fighter force slipped across the Channel in the south to bomb shipping at Portland—and perhaps to draw off some of the British fighters from the main attack upon London. A single British fighter squadron, of a possible five of the Middle Wallop sector, intercepted—but only after the German bombs had dropped. Even so, the bombing was inaccurate and little harm was done to Portland.

The day's last attack, again in the south, came shortly after six o'clock when about twenty bomb-laden Me-110s came in over the Hampshire coast.

Shot down while on a raid against London, a German crew is taken prisoner while, in the background, their Heinkel burns. (FOX PHOTOS, LTD.)

The target of Test Group 210 was the Supermarine (Spitfire) factory at Woolston. With only twenty minutes' warning, it was almost impossible for Park to get the squadrons up in time, but he did send some of his and some from No. 10 Group to intercept. Again the British fighters did not find the enemy aircraft until after they had dropped their bombs. Once again the bombing was inaccurate, thanks in this attack to the Southampton antiaircraft guns, which trained on the Me-110s on their bombing run, upsetting the aim of the bombardiers and the flying of the pilots. The bombs missed the Spitfire factory but fell into residential areas. Thus ended the last flicker, a whimper, of the daylight battles.

Churchill by this time had returned to Chequers for his afternoon nap. He had been fatigued by the strain in the Operations Room at Uxbridge. It had been a close one. Just one more sizable German attacking force and they would have had nothing with which to meet it. Having slept Churchill immediately called his secretary, John Martin, to learn the very latest news. Martin had a little good to report from Italy or the Atlantic. "However," he concluded, "all is redeemed by the air. We have shot down a hundred and eighty-three for a loss of under forty."

The evening's BBC broadcast, and the newspapers, added a couple more and proclaimed to a jubilant Britain that 185 German aircraft had been destroyed. The official Air Ministry account called it "the Greatest Day." Churchill dispatched a congratulatory message to Dowding on Monday. "Yesterday eclipsed all previous records of Fighter Command," he wrote. "Aided by squadrons of their

Battle's end: a Hurricane pilot of No. 85 Squadron wearily leaves his cockpit as the sun sets after a hard day of combat. (IMPERIAL WAR MUSEUM, LONDON)

Czech and Polish comrades, using only a small proportion of their total strength [not true, but this message was for public consumption] and under cloud conditions of some difficulty, they cut to rags and tatters three separate waves of murderous assaults upon the civil population of their native land. . . . These results exceeded all expectations and give just and sober confidence in the approaching struggle."

But in the light of postwar truth was September 15, 1940, actually "the Greatest Day"? Not if its greatness is measured by the number of enemy aircraft destroyed. The British lost 35 planes that day and 11 pilots. The Luftwaffe lost 30 Do-17s, 15 He-111s, 3 Ju-88s, 3 Me-110s, and 23 Me-109s, plus four others, a total of 78—not 185—aircraft. But of this total the greater number was bombers—fully one quarter of the total sent against England on September 15 during the daylight attacks (a force of 181 bombers came in over London that night). These were lost despite the heavy fighter protection of nearly five fighters for every bomber. But the order which tied most of the fighters tightly to the bombers, excepting the free-hunt units which generally preceded the bomber streams, crippled their fighting abilities.

The tired airmen on both sides of the Channel, hollow-eyed, nerves tingling, muscles tight, were unimpressed with "the Greatest Day" designation. They were too depleted to care. The RAF crews, however, could delight in the news of a great victory despite their exhaustion. The Luftwaffe pilots were shaken and demoralized: their High Command had, in fact, failed them. First, it had misinformed them about the strength of Fighter Command, and second, it had further handicapped the fighters with unrealistic tactics. Even so, the Luftwaffe did not consider the Battle decided, let alone lost.

Nor, in truth, did the RAF High Command, whose members were more realistic than their German counterparts, consider the Battle won. The Battle was won, however, though neither side was aware of it at the time.

The effort of RAF's Fighter Command on "the Greatest Day" contributed heavily to a decision revealed in an entry in the war diary of the German Naval Staff dated September 17, 1940:

The enemy Air Force is still by no means defeated; on the contrary, it shows increasing activity. The weather situation on the whole does not permit us to expect a period of calm. The Führer therefore decides to postpone Sealion indefinitely.

He was not coming after all; he would never come.

9

THE BLITZ

THE REPULSE of the Luftwaffe—which Göring promptly blamed on the fighters—on "the Greatest Day" neither closed the Battle of Britain nor ended the planning, however dispirited, for Sealion, despite the Führer's deferment. To remove the vessels and troops from the various ports would be an admission of defeat—and that would not do. This was neatly side-stepped by the propaganda machine. On September 18 the German-controlled Paris Radio informed the British, and the world, that "the legend of British self-control and phlegm is being destroyed. All reports from London concur in stating that the population is seized by fear—hair-raising fear. The seven million Londoners have completely lost their self-control. They run aimlessly about in the streets and are victims of bombs and bursting shells."

London, indeed, had become the target—but after the fighting of September 15 the daylight attacks dwindled significantly. On the eighteenth there was a large flurry—about seventy German bombers appeared over London and were fought off ferociously. The final weeks of September were devoted to relatively minor daylight raids upon aircraft factories. Göring's High Command recognized the urgency of denying the RAF a supply of aircraft. The end of October was characterized by a decided lack of mass raids and the introduction of wider use of fighter-bombers (Me-109s carrying thousand-pound bombs). Although these high-flying aircraft could evade the British fighters and made positive identi-

fication difficult—radar and direct observation could not discern whether the Messerschmitts were merely fighters and therefore not worth scrambling after or fighters carrying bombs—they accomplished little.

In short, though he was unaware of it at the time, Dowding had won the Battle of Britain.

But then began a new terror. For fifty-seven nights, from September 7 through November 2, not a night went by without the drone of German bombers overhead, the crash of bombs and fire in the streets of London. "None of it seems real," wrote Anthony Guthrie to Vivien Leigh and Laurence Olivier. "One can't believe that one isn't living in some highly superior Wagnerian production. The night of the big fires was utterly amazing. . . . We came out [of Sadler's Wells Theatre, London] to find the entire sky crimson from the reflected glare of the fires—you could easily read small print in the street—and on every window reflected back the dancing, terrifying glare."

It was unreal, but the rubble, the burned-out streets, and the dead and injured were undeniable fact. So were the barrage balloons which swayed dumpily over London Bridge; Londoners called these balloons, which were not especially effective except against low-flying aircraft, "our dumb friends." Although not of much use, their floating presence was comforting. The air raid warning signals—"sireens" or "Wailing Winnies"—cried out nightly for those fifty-seven nights. The average

Luftwaffe target map. The circled A locates a South-
wark power station on the south bank of the Thames.

Almost directly north, across the river, may be seen
St. Paul's Cathedral.

(IMPERIAL WAR MUSEUM, LONDON)

nightly raiding party consisted of about 160 bombers during this period—ranging from 7 on the night of October 6, when bad weather interfered, to more than 400 on October 15. There was little the defenses could do to counter these attacks. The night fighter, equipped with radar, was but a crude idea in the early days of the blitz; antiaircraft defenses were weak and inaccurate. Like the dumb friends

the sound and flash of the guns were more inspiring than effectual. By September 10 the number of heavy antiaircraft guns protecting central London was increased from 92 to 199; restrictions forbidding gunners from firing at aircraft they could see or which were officially detected led to a massive barrage over London when next the Germans came. This, while rarely if ever accounting for downed

He-111s cross the English Channel during the winter of the blitz. (IMPERIAL WAR MUSEUM, LONDON)

An incendiary bomb burns in a London street; once burning an incendiary was difficult to control and was most responsible for the damage to London during the blitz. (IMPERIAL WAR MUSEUM, LONDON)

A German bomber after a raid on England, lucky to have made the return trip. The pilot, slightly dazed, sits atop the fuselage while others (including cameraman) study what appears to be antiaircraft shell hole behind the port engine. (H. J. NOWARRA)

German bombers, was disconcerting and did force the Luftwaffe formations to fly higher—and it did make a joyful noise for the beleaguered Londoner.

Although the Luftwaffe's objectives were primarily the docks, the railways, public utilities, as well as governmental and financial centers, the chief victims were the ordinary Londoners, generally of the poorer classes. They lost sleep, were improperly fed, lost their pitiable possessions, their homes, and their loved ones. The panic predicted by the Germans, however, did not occur. Instead a grim resolution set in, a tough, bitter humor, a deep sense of fellowship (as class lines, temporarily at least, broke down), and a determination not to be defeated by "'Itler." But they died by the hundreds on each of the fifty-seven nights as well as other nights throughout the remainder of the Second World War.

On the big night of October 15, when 410 bombers dropped 528 tons of high explosives and 177 canisters of incendiaries, 400 civilians died and 900 were seriously injured. Rail traffic between London and the cities to the north and south was disrupted or stopped. Where once fifty trains ran per day, only four were running after the raid. Hundreds of fires broke out and water mains burst, some filling the underground tube stations. While all of this was disrupting, damaging to property, and took a heavy toll of life (although never as high as had been predicted before the war), little of military import was

achieved. Neither did the railroads, docks, factories, or utilities close down, nor did the Londoner petition his government for an early armistice.

There was reason enough for fear and panic. The Germans sowed vicious fires with their incendiaries, more destructive than the high-explosive bombs. They also dropped delayed-action bombs, thus rendering streets and buildings hazardous until the bomb exploded or was dealt with by the UXB (Unexploded Bomb) Disposal Squads. Churchill, in his memoirs, recalled one of these remarkable groups, "the Holy Trinity," consisting of the Earl of Suffolk, his lady private secretary, and "his rather aged chauffeur." This unique, gallant trinity, working at a trade for which none of their previous experience had prepared them, had actually learned how to disarm the UXBs. This was a most delicate operation, calling for courage as well as skill. All the proper mechanisms inside the bomb had to be taken apart without disturbing the detonation device. "Thirty-four unexploded bombs did they tackle with urbane and smiling efficiency," Churchill reported. "But the thirty-fifth claimed its forfeit. Up went the Earl of Suffolk in his Holy Trinity. But we may be sure that, as for Greatheart [a character in *Pilgrim's Progress*], 'all the trumpets sounded for them on the other side.'"

Churchill admired such eccentric valour and while he appeared to make light of their tragic end he mordantly expressed the mood of the time, of people he termed "the grim and the gay," the unbeatable British courage which "'Itler" found so unfathomable.

II

By December 8, 1940, London was no longer the prime target of the Luftwaffe night war. On November 14 Göring had decided, since the bombing of London seemed to accomplish so little, that attention should be given the smaller industrial cities. These presented less sprawling targets than London, if more difficult to find. But with Kampfgeschwader 100 leading the way with incendiaries which were planted with the help of an electronic navigation device they called *X-Gerät* ("X-Device"), there was no problem finding the target for the 450 bombers that night. *X-Gerät* was operated on a complex aircraft over Schweinfurt; Curtiss P-40B Tomahawk in the markings of the American Volunteer Group of the Chinese Air Force better known as "The Flying Tigers;" Douglas SBD *Dauntless* of VS-2 from the *Lexington* which participated in the Battle of the Coral Sea, the prelude to Midway; Avro *Lancaster* B.III of No. 617 ("Dam Busters") Squadron, flown by leader Guy Gibson; North American B-25B *Mitchell* flown by Lieutenant Colonel James H. Doolittle on the Tokyo Raid from "Shangri-La."

Joseph A. Phelan

Various aircraft that participated in "victories" of dubious consequence but of remarkable valor. Counterclockwise, beginning from top left: Vickers *Wellington* III of No. 419 Squadron (RCAF) which participated in the Thousand Bomber Raid; Nakajima "Kate," in the markings of Commander Mitsuo Fuchida who led the air attack on Pearl Harbor; Consolidated B-24-D *Liberator*, "Hail Columbia" of the 98th Bomb Group flown by Major John R. Kane to and from Ploesti; Boeing B-17F *Flying Fortress* of the 305th Bomb Group which lost thirteen (of sixteen)

system of radio beams, a main beam plus beams which intersected it.

A Luton *News* historian noted that on November 14, "just after tea German bombers flew over Luton for hour after hour on the way to the Midland city of Coventry." The Luton hat factories were spared that night, but for about ten hours wave after wave of Heinkels and Junkers dropped five hundred tons of high explosives and about nine hundred incendiaries upon the old cathedral town, which had achieved notoriety with the legend of Lady Godiva and Peeping Tom, dating from the eleventh century.

Coventry housed, besides the legend and a beautiful medieval cathedral, factories devoted to the manufacture of machine tools and parts for aircraft industries. The main target was the facilities of the Standard Motor Company; in short, Coventry, according to the "civilized rules of warfare," was a "legitimate" military target. When the last German bomber left at around six-thirty in the morning Coventry, its cathedral included, was a flaming ruin. By 3:30 A.M. at least two hundred major fires were reported in the center of the city, but hydrants were buried under the debris and many water mains were destroyed. The main railroads were blocked so that rescue teams coming from other towns could come only to Coventry's outskirts and then were forced to make their way through the rubble, flame, and danger of unexploded bombs. The once maligned Civil

Target map, Coventry. Dark areas A and B mark the two factory objectives.

(IMPERIAL WAR MUSEUM, LONDON)

No. 23 Victoria Street, London, falls to earth after a German bombing raid.

(IMPERIAL WAR MUSEUM, LONDON)

Defence workers, who had become unpopular because of their insistence upon no lights showing and who seemed to spend most of their time, with nothing to do, in the local pubs, came into their own. These anonymous heroes, who went about their work quietly and matter-of-factly, saved the lives of countless men, women, and children at the risk and at times the cost of their own lives. Ordinary citizens transformed by emergency dashed into blazing, crumbling buildings to save a life. Or they worked for hours to rescue someone trapped in the wreckage of what was once a home.

The Germans boasted later of what they had done to Coventry; they even coined a word to describe what would happen to other towns devoted to the making of arms: "Coventrated." But because of the widespread havoc, impossible to confine to the purely military targets, Coventry joined Guernica, Warsaw, and Rotterdam as a symbol of German frightfulness and thoroughness.

No less than five hundred shops in the city's shopping center were put out of business; only the spire of the cathedral remained standing; twenty-one factories essential to the aircraft industry were hit. The destroyed water and gas mains halted work in other factories not as severely hit. The death toll reached at least 554 and 865 people were seriously wounded. But despite the shattering damage and the casualties there was no panic and comparatively

London burning following a bad night blitz.
(NATIONAL ARCHIVES)

minimal work stoppage. The fires were under control by the evening of November 15. Three days later all the rail lines, except one which took an additional three days, were cleared and running.

Work was resumed at the Standard Motor Company on November 16 by half of its usual staff. Factories which suffered more severe destruction were longer in resuming production, but despite Coventration, Coventry was not knocked out of the war as Göring presumed. Other "arms towns" including Birmingham, Sheffield, Manchester, and Bristol were treated to the same near-saturation bombing during the winter weeks of November and December. So were the ports, Liverpool, Portsmouth, Southampton, but with the same inconclusive results. There were the same casualties, the same fires and rubble, and the same stiffening of the British spirit.

"Have you ever spent the night in a hole in the garden?" asked a young woman schoolteacher from Norwich. "Well, you're too damn tired to bother about the bombs. Luckily our soil is gravel so it's not as bad as it might be but dirt is dirty and full of ants . . . lift up your tin hat, as you grovel in the entrails of the earth, and see the Milky Way above you and the searchlights finding the bomber which you can hear, directly above you. Would you think you'd be scared or wonder what was going to happen—I should have thought so—but you simply try to see if you can see it and it never enters your head that you might be here, there, and everywhere in about two seconds."

In Clydebank (a shipbuilding center in Scotland) a woman made a comment that deserves preservation. She had just finished sweeping debris from her walk when she said to her neighbor, "Well, there's one thing about these raids, they do make you forget about the war."

Be grim and be gay, Churchill had asked of them. They could be practical too, as witness the statement of a lord mayor of one of the port cities which had been noted for its slums. "At least we can say that the Luftwaffe did for us in twenty seconds what we have been trying to do for twenty years," he said. "It removed the slum dwellings. . . ."

The switch to the arms towns and the ports did not mean that London had ceased to be a target completely. In fact, on the night after the Coventry attack London was the major target and Coventry received only a token visit. Had it been reversed the rapid recovery of Coventry might have been seriously cut short. But Göring was certain he had finished it. So the raids continued on through November and December, weather permitting—for the season of rain, snow, ice, and fog came to interfere with German operations. During December Britain enjoyed fifteen bomb-free nights, thanks to the weather.

On December 29, 1940, a Sunday evening at the end of Christmas week, just before seven o'clock the bombers came. They were led to their objective by ten Heinkels of the pathfinder Kampfgeschwader 100, which, in turn, was turned into the *X-Gerät* beam which was laid directly across London. It was a dark night and the winds, from the west and southwest, ranged to as high as fifty miles an hour at an altitude of six thousand feet. So it was that the incendiaries sown by the ten Heinkels drifted slightly eastward from the beam into the section of London known as The City, London's financial center, as well as Westminster, site of Buckingham Palace, No. 10 Downing Street, and other government buildings. In the center of all this stood St. Paul's Cathedral, the masterpiece of Sir Christopher Wren, which had been built 1675–1710.

The attacking force was not very large: 136 bombers, but they dropped 127 tons of high explosives and more than 600 canisters of incendiar-

ies. The HE, with some scattering, fell mainly into the riverside boroughs of London. The incendiaries, which scattered also, very quickly ignited nearly fifteen hundred fires. Six were classified as "conflagrations," twenty-eight were "major," and fifty-two were "serious." Because it was a Sunday evening many of the buildings, even the churches, were locked, making it impossible to deal with the incendiaries which fell onto the roofs. Also, on this night the Thames was at its lowest ebb, a problem further complicated when bombs ruptured an emergency main pipe used in fighting fires. Hose pressures waxed and waned throughout the blazing nightmare.

For about three hours the German aircraft droned over London and then returned to France to reload. But luckily the bases had become weathered-in and the bombers did not return, affording the hard-pressed Londoners the time to try to save their city undisturbed by further bombing. Some fires even by then were so out of control that nothing could be done. Water evaporated in mid-air even before reaching the flames. Sections of The City were merely abandoned and cordoned off to burn out.

"For miles around the sky was a bright orange-red," one Londoner recalled; "the balloons in the barrage stood as clearly as on a sunny day. St. Paul's Cathedral was the pivot of the main fire. All around it the flames were leaping up into the sky. And there the Cathedral stood, magnificently firm, untouched in the very center of all this destruction."

Not quite untouched, for at least two dozen incendiaries struck the dome and only some bounced off into the street. The men of the St. Paul's Cathedral Watch and volunteers (many of them architects) joined forces to fight the fires. Although the water supply failed early, emergency containers of reserve water placed around the cathedral by the leaders of the watch were put to use. Those incendiaries which blazed against the structure threatening to incinerate the old, dry beams were put out with minimal damage.

But one incendiary had struck the dome and had become lodged in the outer lead shell. It protruded hundreds of feet off the ground, sputtering, melting the lead of the outer dome. Fearfully the men of the watch observed helplessly as the single in-

A Hurricane I night fighter takes off to engage the Luftwaffe during the blitz. In this period the single- *engined fighters did not prove very effective against the German bomber forces.*

cendiary seemed about to fall inside the inner dome into the dry timbers. "We knew," the dean of the cathedral said, "that once the fire got hold of the Dome timbers it would, at that high altitude, quickly be fanned into a roaring furnace."

Across London, a woman in Bethnal Green, wearing her tin hat, stood with some firemen on a roof and gazed toward The City. "And I've always remembered how I was choked," she said; "I think I was crying a little. I could see St. Paul's standing there, and the fire all around, and I just said: 'Please God, don't let it go!'"

The incendiary in the dome, now burning fiercely, moved as the lead flowed in the intense heat. Then the bomb fell away from the dome—no one knows quite how—and into the stone gallery of the cathedral, where the relieved men of the watch disposed of it.

St. Paul's was saved and became the symbol of British strength during the Battle of Britain. But other historic buildings did not escape what became known as the Second London Fire. The first, in 1666, resulted in the rebuilding of the city

Not all raids on England during the blitz were made at night. This Me-109 had made a day sortie over the London area, attacked two British trainers, misjudged their speed, and came to grief in Windsor Great Park.

by Christopher Wren. Eight of Wren's churches were consumed in the Second London Fire; so were the Guildhall, the County Hall, and portions of the Tower of London. Nine hospitals, although not targets, were hit; so were five railway stations and sixteen underground stations. The dead numbered 163 with more than 500 seriously injured. Sixteen firemen died, some of them in the crew which had successfully fought off the flames threatening the house of Dr. Samuel Johnson, just off Fleet Street, not far from St. Paul's. The small crew had just left the historic house and had lost their way in the narrow, smoke-filled streets. They had just emerged near a burning building when a member of the pump crew fighting that fire saw them.

"I thought when I saw them that they were too near," he said. "Just at that moment a wall, which looked as if it was bulging dangerously, crashed down on them. As we looked around all we could see was a heap of debris with a hose leading towards it."

Although the Sunday night raid was the last of the year, it was not the last of the fire raids of the blitz. Bad weather interfered with operations during the first two months of 1941, London and several port cities received major attacks. By March, with the coming of somewhat better weather, the raids were resumed with greater ferocity if not in number. In April some of the German bomber strength had been drawn off to assist in the Balkans. Then an even more critical withdrawal came in May as Hitler prepared for his Russian offensive.

Despite the wholesale withdrawals of the Luftwaffe, or perhaps because of them, the effort of the remaining forces was intensified. The effort devolved upon Sperrle's Luftflotte 3, which had to cover for the units which had slipped away. Between the first great fire raid in December and those later in the winter of 1941 much had been learned, at no little cost, about dealing with the night bombers. Roof watchers were stationed throughout London (and other target cities) to keep an eye out for incendiaries, and techniques were developed to deal with them most efficiently. Also, means had been developed to confute the *X-Gerät* beam, as, for example, on the night of May 8/9, when the target was the Rolls-Royce factory at Derby. The beam was detected early and deflected electronically so that the great German bomber force dropped most of its bombs in the moors northeast of Derby. At the same time "Starfish" were lighted —these were decoy fires which appeared to be pathfinder markers. On this same night Starfish beckoned the German bombers away from Nottingham, which the German pilots mistook for a burning Derby. Consequently, the bomber stream "corrected" and bombed the Vale of Belvoir (mistaking it for Nottingham) with high explosives, an oil bomb, and incendiaries. This effort netted them a casualty toll of two cows and two chickens.

London was easier to find and during the second half of April it received two of its worst raids, so memorable that Londoners ever after referred to them by name, "the Wednesday" (April 16/17) and "the Saturday" (April 19/20). On the first 890 tons of high explosives and 4200 canisters of incendiary bombs fell; on the Saturday the weight increased: 1026 tons of HE and 4252 canisters of incendiaries rained on London.

Then on May 10/11 came another heavy blow, the last of the night offensive. On that same night deputy Führer Rudolf Hess, having stolen a Messerschmitt, flew alone from Germany and parachuted to earth near Glasgow. He was looking for Lord Steward, the Duke of Hamilton, whom Hess had met at the Olympics in Germany in 1936. Hess insisted that he had come on a peace mission; he was certain that he could convince the British with Lord Steward's help of the Führer's kindly intentions toward Britain and bring the war to an end.

Meanwhile London burned. More than 400,000 civilians were to die in the blitz, and 46,000 suffered serious injuries. A million homes were destroyed. The average Londoner was thoroughly familiar with Hitler's intentions. Out of the ruins of one of the buildings a woman emerged covered with blood and powdered brick and plaster. Her eyes were dull, her face drawn, she said nothing to her rescuers except the phrase she repeated, like a litany, over and over again: "Man's inhumanity

---

The main shelter during the blitz was the London Underground, the subway. Deep under the streets of the city, Londoners sought refuge from Hitler's bombers and proved, in the phrase at the time, "London can take it." (IMPERIAL WAR MUSEUM, LONDON)

to man, man's inhumanity to man, man's inhumanity to man . . ."

By the late spring of 1941 the blitz was over. So in fact was all planning for Sealion. But the future of the Third Reich, and its leaders, its cities, its people—innocent and guilty—was assured.

"Man's inhumanity to man . . ."

On that December night when St. Paul's stood out of the smoke and flame with an almost human British show of defiance and dignity, the newly appointed Deputy Chief of the Air Staff stood on the roof of the Air Ministry building watching the fulminating desolation. He was Arthur Harris. Moved by the fiery spectacle, he spoke to the old sentry on the roof, reminding the man that they were looking directly upon history. The old man, however, who called himself "an observer of nature," seemed more interested in the sex life of the cats on the rooftops of Whitehall.

"The last time London was burnt," Harris tried again, "if my history is right, was in 1666." But the sentry was not impressed. The conflagration was to Harris such a "fantastic sight" that he went downstairs and brought up his chief, Air Chief Marshal Sir Charles Portal, from his office to see it.

The two airmen, one of whom would in time be Chief of Bomber Command, watched the sea of flame in bitter silence. As they turned away from the awesome sight, so unreal in its magnitude, Harris said to Portal, "Well, they are sowing the wind."

For they have sown the wind, and they shall reap the whirlwind.

"Man's inhumanity to man . . ."

10

"GIVE IT 'EM BACK!"

THE pattern of modern war was unmistakably defined: Everyman had become a legitimate military target. The war of the peoples had begun.

The Germans were ill advised to expect the Londoners to panic in the street. Instead, there was fear, dread, grief, and loss, but no panic. And there was a hard mood of retribution. During the blitz the King and Churchill made visits to the hard-hit areas; the King, for example, visited Coventry immediately after its devastating attack. Churchill recalled one of his experiences at the site in the south of London where a large land mine had exploded. He was terribly moved, walking through the ruins of what had been two dozen homes of the poor in the district. As if in defiance of the Germans, the people had stuck tiny British flags in the ruins. The people crowded around the old warrior, cheering, happy just to touch him, and saw tears in Churchill's eyes.

They showed him a great crater, perhaps twenty feet deep and forty yards across, at the edge of which teetered an Anderson shelter. (This was the uncomfortable and not always effective government-issued air raid shelter widely used by the poor.) Still alive, though dazed by the miracle of their escape, were the inhabitants, a young man, his wife, and their three children. All were smiling, enjoying their celebrity. As Churchill turned to go, he sensed "a harsher mood" which animated the tattered crowd, then someone shouted, "Give it 'em back!"

"Let *them* have it too!" another shouted, and the cries followed Churchill as he left the scene. "Give it 'em back!" became a battle cry of the non-combatants who suffered under the new mode of the "art of war." And Churchill did all he could to comply with the mood of his people. "Certainly the enemy got it all back," he wrote later, "in good measure, pressed down and running over. Alas for poor humanity!"

II

The members of the Air Staff, viewing the situation more professionally, did not regard the principle of "Give it 'em back!" as militarily sound. With London as a target, it followed in popular logic that Berlin must also be a target. When the towns and cities suffered, then it was expected that the lesser German cities and towns should suffer also. Berlin, especially, as far as the average Londoner—and Winston Churchill—was concerned was a most enticing objective. Bomber Command would have preferred targets of more strategic value. In the long months of the Battle of France, the Battle of Britain, and the blitz, during which the Luftwaffe pretty much dictated the turn of events, Bomber Command operated defensively as much as offensively. Instead of concentrating upon the oil installations in Germany, as it would have wished, Bomber Command had to contend with invasion

A Coastal Command B-17 coming in over an English cottage after an over-water patrol.
(IMPERIAL WAR MUSEUM, LONDON)

barges on the coast of the North Sea and across their own Channel.

When it became reasonably obvious that the Germans had abandoned their daylight attacks and postponed their Sealion plans—toward the end of September 1940—Bomber Command hoped to resume strategic operations upon German industry crucial to the supply of the war machine. But the blitz, with its heavy London toll, plus the temper of London's population (as well as of others with even greater political influence) split the effort. Under pressure it was resolved by Bomber Command to resume the strategic offensive against the industrial complex in the Ruhr and to "Give it 'em back" in Berlin. The German capital was one of a dozen German cities (originally twenty or more) which could be attacked "to affect the morale of the German people." Among the other "morale" targets were Hamburg, Cologne, Munich, Leipzig, Essen, Dresden, Breslau, Frankfurt, Düsseldorf, and Stuttgart.

The primary objectives, now that the invasion threat had receded, were to be oil and morale. The desired emphasis would be upon the oil targets, but with the rather hazy "morale" now accepted as an objective, purely military definition of targets became academic.

Reports from inside Germany encouraged the "area bombings," that is, attacks not aimed at precise military pin points but at the general vicinity of known targets. Fire would do the rest, as successive waves of bombers disrupted the work of the fire fighters. Neutral visitors in Berlin reported that German morale had indeed suffered under the unexpected bombings of their city. Germans were shaken, but like the Londoner, the Berliner proved he could take it. In truth, the effect upon morale never approached the effect expected.

The concession to area attacks upon populated areas was not an admission of wanton British brutality. It was a recognition of a fact: not all bomber crews were so skilled that they were able to find the target area, let alone bomb it. Weather, flak, poor navigation, fear: all interfered with the performance of air crews. There were great distances to cover— the flight to Berlin traversed nearly six hundred miles, part of it over the North Sea and the rest over Germany itself. And then, there was the return trip.

Meanwhile, the Battle of the Atlantic also shunted Bomber Command from strategic targets. As it had during the First World War, the U-boat danger became critical, menacing the food supply and essential war materials, the bulk of which Britain had to import. Also there were the German battle cruisers, particularly the *Scharnhorst* and the *Gneisenau,* which aircrews readily nicknamed the "Salmon" and the "Gluckstein." The *Bismarck,* the great German battleship which had taken a terrible toll of British shipping, was sunk in a combined sea and air battle late in May 1941. But Hitler continued to promise

RAF Coastal Command "Fortress I" (the B-17C) over a British Atlantic convoy on watch for German submarines. (IMPERIAL WAR MUSEUM, LONDON)

to starve the British in their island and to cut off war supplies by sinking their ships from under the sea, on the surface, and from the air.

To fight this Battle the aircraft of both Bomber Command and Coastal Command were confronted with an area of roughly ten and a half million square miles of sea. Not only the U-boat and the battleship must be found in this great expanse but also the Luftwaffe reconnaissance planes and bombers. The British employed not only their own aircraft, such as the Short Sunderland, a giant flying boat, but also American-made Lockheed Hudsons and Consolidated Catalinas. In time, by 1942, the Boeing B-17 Flying Fortress, which Bomber Command had not been able to use effectively for various reasons, was employed by Coastal Command in sea reconnaissance and long-range convoy patrol. Later another heavy American bomber, the Consolidated

The U-boat's friend, the Focke-Wulf Condor, the Luftwaffe's only long-range four-engined aircraft during the Battle of the Atlantic.

(IMPERIAL WAR MUSEUM, LONDON)

The U-boat's chief enemy: the Short "Sunderland." This wide-ranging flying boat was capable of long over-water flights on antisubmarine patrols. The "Flying

Porcupine," as it was called because of its armament (eight guns in various positions) by German pilots, also took part in sea rescues.

(IMPERIAL WAR MUSEUM, LONDON)

B-24 Liberator, joined the B-17 as a reconnaissance aircraft.

Long over-water flights, beset by sudden Atlantic squalls, fog, and the perils of icing, were as hazardous as they were boring, with an occasional spurt of action to relieve the monotony. The quarry was the U-boat or German aircraft which were capable of bombing British convoys or spying them out and radioing their positions to U-boat packs. Thanks to the Luftwaffe's dedication to the close-support concept, no long-range heavy bomber was available for such missions. Pressed into service was the Focke-Wulf 200 Condor, a four-engined transport, late of Lufthansa. Modified, the Condor, despite an impressive range, was still not a true bomber; even the addition of guns—a 20-mm. cannon in a top turret, plus twin machine guns in a forward firing position and another covering the tail—did not complete the conversion. The added weight and protuberances served to decrease the speed of the Condor, rendering it vulnerable to fighter attack. With all its deficiencies as a battle plane, the Condor was the best the Luftwaffe could muster in the Battle of the Atlantic.

With its range of nearly fourteen hundred miles (remaining air-borne for sixteen hours) the Condors, mainly of Gruppe I of Kampfgeschwader 40, harassed the Atlantic convoy routes from bases near Bordeaux in France and Trondheim in central Norway. The old war horses, the Ju-88s and He-111s, were assigned the shorter flights closer in to the British Isles and, from northern Norway, to the run to Murmansk over which the Allies supplied Russia after Hitler chose to abandon Sealion, lessen the air pressure on Britain, and attack his ally, Soviet Russia, in June of 1941.

It was during the winter and spring months of 1940–41 that the Battle of the Atlantic raged most critically; shipping losses to U-boats and German bombers rose alarmingly. In March of 1941 532,000 tons of shipping sank to the bottom of the Atlantic; in April the losses rose to 644,000 tons (of which 296,000 tons was accounted for by the Ju-88s, He-111s, and Condors).

The solution to the problem lay in increasing the efforts of Coastal Command over the Atlantic, stepping up Bomber Command's bombing of U-boat bases and construction yards, and stiffening the antisubmarine convoys which accompanied the mer-

chant ships beyond the range of protecting aircraft. The greater part of the fighting was a matter of ship against U-boat, or U-boat against aircraft—rarely did the classic dogfight occur over the Atlantic. The larger reconnaissance-bomber aircraft were not suited to such actions—and fighter aircraft did not have the range to venture far out to sea.

The work was monotonous and grueling for both German and British crews, what with the erratic weather and the tedium. The pilot of a Lockheed Hudson, one Pilot Officer Down, described how he and his crew longed "for some real liveliness" following a typical escort patrol.

"We did our usual stuff over them for more than a couple of hours, circling round and round in wide sweeps looking for possible danger. There wasn't a sign of anything in the air or on the sea. . . ."

Knowing that his relief was flying out and that his fuel was getting low, Down signaled "Goodbye and good luck" to the convoys and turned for home. But just for good measure he decided to make another circuit of the convoy. Half through the maneuver, Down spotted one of the escort ships signaling "Suspicious aircraft to starboard."

Down was all but certain that the plane was in fact a Coastal Command Wellington also on convoy patrol. "I flew over to have a look at her, pulling up my front gun sights just for practice. In fact, I was just remarking to Ernie [Ernest Corken, co-pilot and navigator] that we were in a lovely position, and that I had the Wellington beautifully in the sights, when he suddenly let out a wild Irish oath—Ernie is from Ulster—and shouted, 'It's a Condor!'"

The two planes, the large Condor and the smaller Hudson, began exchanging gunfire. The faster, more maneuverable Hudson overtook the Condor, pumped shots into it, then swept away. Down came back alongside the big transport until it looked "like the side of a house." From a range of forty feet the Hudson crew again poured machine-gun fire into the Condor. The German plane turned away, exposing its underside, into which the profane Ernie and the Hudson's rear gunner streamed bullets. "There was a wisp of smoke, a sudden belching of smoke, and then flames shot out from beneath his two port engines."

Slowly the Condor, close to the water, seemed to be pulling away. But with distance the big air-

A German U-boat under attack by a Sunderland in the Atlantic. (IMPERIAL WAR MUSEUM, LONDON)

craft also lost altitude until Down and his crew saw the German plane splash into the sea. As he flew over the Condor, Down saw that "its wing tips were just awash—and Ernie photographed [it]. Four of the crew were in the water, hanging on to their rubber dinghy. . . . A fifth man was scrambling along the fuselage. We learned afterwards that a Met. man [weather observer] who had been aboard had been shot through the heart. The others were all right."

II

Sinking a submarine or shooting down a German plane was gratifying to air crews, but it was not quite giving it 'em back. Keeping the supply lines open was essential, but that could be left to the convoys themselves with their depth charges and massive antiaircraft gun concentrations. But striking at Germany and at the Luftwaffe: that, it was believed, should be the main concern of the Royal Air Force and especially Bomber Command.

Gradually, as the force of Bomber Command increased and as its units were released from the Battle of the Atlantic, it could be brought to bear di-

Night attack on a German submarine by a Coastal Command plane. Three flares illuminate the scene as a depth bomb explodes to the right of the U-boat.

(U. S. AIR FORCE)

*A Condor down in the Atlantic after an encounter
with a Coastal Command Hudson.*

rectly upon Germany. But with a difference, for as
had been learned during the Battle of Britain by
the Luftwaffe and by Bomber Command in its initial
operations, bombing heavily defended targets by
day was suicidal. Bomber Command would bring
the war to Germany and to the occupied countries
primarily at night. The concept of pin-point precision upon absolute military targets, subsequently,
diminished in favor of "area" attacks.

By the summer of 1941 a change came into the
policy of Bomber Command. Bombing accuracy had
not been good (after the war it was learned that
of the total number of bombs dropped on south-
western Germany from May 1940 to May 1941
nearly half fell in open country). Hitting factories
in the Ruhr, heavily ringed with flak, was extremely
difficult and costly. On July 9, 1941, Air Marshal
Sir Richard Peirse, Commander in Chief, Bomber
Command, was instructed by the Air Staff to "direct
the main effort of the bomber force, until further
instructions, towards dislocating the German transportation system, and to destroying the morale of
the civil population as a whole, and of the industrial
workers in particular."

In effect, this was a concession to the "Give it
'em back" advocates, but it was also an admission
of the failure of the daylight missions and the night
missions against small targets, such as factories or

oil installations. It was, at the same time, a turn
in the direction of taking the offensive; it boded ill
for the German civilian.

Nor was it "a piece of cake" (or what the Americans were to call "milk runs") for bomber crews.
Missions were long and tiring, formations were small
—so were bomb loads consequently—as individual
aircraft carried their lonely crews to the target and,
if lucky, back. The same determination, courage,
and defiant invincibility that characterized the civilian of the blitz was exhibited by the bomber crews.
Weather made the flights to and from the German
targets a nightmare of navigation, and flak, if not
always accurate, did fill the night sky with bursting
shells. And there was always the chance that on
the return home, as light began to break, German
fighters based in France might intercept the strays
and the crippled.

This occurred in the early morning of July 7,
1941, in the early phase of the "area bombings,"
when a Wellington bomber of No. 75 (New Zealand) Squadron was intercepted by a Me-110. The
Wellington had just successfully dropped its bombs
on Münster, a comparatively small city but an important traffic junction in the Ruhr. Except for the
distraction of searchlights and light flak over the
city, the Wellington ran into no trouble until after
it had left Germany and headed for home over the
Zuider Zee in Holland.

Before it could be driven off by the Wellington's
tail gunner, Sergeant A. J. R. Box, the Messerschmitt had succeeded in hitting the British bomber
with cannon fire and incendiaries. The pilot, Squadron Leader R. P. Widdowson, nosed the Wellington
into a dive in an attempt to elude the attacker. As
the Messerschmitt dropped out of the fight, apparently hit by Box's guns, Sergeant James Ward, ex-
schoolmaster and the plane's copilot, was thrust into
the cockpit by the Wellington's dive. Ward had been
in the astrodome on lookout for German interceptors, and after seeing the Me-110, learned that radio
communications inside the plane were out. As he
approached the cockpit to inform Widdowson of
the problem, Ward was thrown forward by the dive.

The two men, relieved to see the Messerschmitt
leave, soon found much to concern them. Ward
peered out of the cockpit toward the right wing.
"The starboard engine had been hit and the hydraulic system had been put out of action, with the

Wellingtons of No. 75 Squadron (New Zealand) setting out on mission to Germany.
(IMPERIAL WAR MUSEUM, LONDON)

result that the undercarriage fell half down, which meant, of course, that it would be useless for landing. . . . The bomb doors fell open, too, the wireless sets were not working and the front gunner was wounded in the foot.

"Worst of all, fire was burning up through the upper surface of the starboard wing where the petrol feed pipe had been split open."

Attempts to reach the fire with fire extinguishers, even coffee from flasks, were useless, for the flame was too far from the fuselage. The prospect of taking to their parachutes seemed equally hopeless.

The burning Wellington approached the Dutch coast. Before attempting to cross the North Sea Widdowson flew parallel with the shore while he and the crew discussed their next move. "I think," he said, "we'd prefer a night in the dinghy in the North Sea to ending up in a German prison camp." All agreed—they should attempt to get as close to England as possible. The flame was now steady on the wing and did not seem to be spreading. The lattice-like structure of the aircraft (technically known as geodetic) stood out in skeletal relief where the fabric had been burned away. The geodetic method of structure of the Wellington, a kind of loose basket weave, afforded it great strength without adding weight. But to copilot Ward it suggested a kind of askew ladder. It was his idea to get out of the

Sergeant James Allen Ward, V.C.
(IMPERIAL WAR MUSEUM, LONDON)

plane through the astrodome, crawl along the wing (wearing a parachute, of course, and tied to the Wellington by a rope), and put out the fire.

To Ward it seemed to be a better alternative to the possibility of freezing in the North Sea. After a brief argument the crew agreed to participate in the attempt. As the fire grew hotter, the crazy scheme of Ward's seemed less impossible. Widdowson throttled down the Wellington as much as possible and still keep it air-borne, so that the rush of air against Ward would be at a minimum. Ward then crawled through the astrodome. "Then I reached out with one foot and kicked a hole in the fabric so that I could get my foot into the framework of the plane, and then I punched another hole through the fabric in front of me to get a hand-hold, after which I made further holes and went down the side of the fuselage on to the wing. Joe [the navigator] was holding on to the rope so that I wouldn't sort of drop straight off."

Inching along, Ward moved along the wing, on which he gouged and kicked holes for his hands and feet. "Once I could not get enough hold and the wind lifted me partly off the wing and sent me against the fuselage again . . . it was like a terrific gale, only worse than any gale I've ever known."

Ward persisted until he reached the burning area. He had brought along a canvas cockpit cover to stuff into the hole, hoping to smother the fire with it. The cockpit cover, catching the wind, nearly took Ward with it. But he continued to stuff it into the wing—and, before the cover blew into the slipstream, the fire went out. Ward had cut off the supply of fuel long enough to extinguish the flames. It flared up again after Ward returned to the plane so exhausted that he could not remember how he got back. Seeing the flames he could only think, "This is pretty hard, after having got as far as this."

But it was a mere flare-up of fuel which had collected in the fabric and had been ignited by the heat of the exhaust. The fire went out and Widdowson brought the Wellington down "beautifully," as Ward described it, after the crew pumped the wheels down by hand. The only mishap was that the Wellington ended up in a barbed-wire entanglement. "Fortunately nobody was hurt though, and that was the end of the trip."

For his exploit over the North Sea Ward was given the Victoria Cross; Widdowson received the Distinguished Flying Cross and rear gunner Box the Distinguished Flying Medal. Ward died in action within two months of receiving his decoration.

If the British could bomb Germany by night, so could the Germans bomb Britain. Early attempts to deal with the German night raiders were not very successful. Defiants and Blenheims, which were no match for German fighters, were pressed into service as night fighters. Spitfires and Hurricanes were also

The Boulton Paul "Defiant," showing its rear gun turret, which deceived the Luftwaffe briefly (mistaking it for a Hurricane), but which proved to be inferior as a fighter. Mauled during the Battle of Britain, it was converted to a night fighter by the end of the summer of 1940. (U. S. AIR FORCE)

The Bristol "Beaufighter," deadliest of the two-man night fighters introduced into the blitz in the winter of 1940. (U. S. AIR FORCE)

used, but pilots were not properly trained for night fighting nor were fighter bases equipped for night flights. And air-borne radar was crude and inefficient. Consequently, interceptions by British night fighters were rare; claims for enemy aircraft destroyed were even rarer.

By late 1940, as the blitz diminished, certain advances were made in technology and aircraft. The former was the Mark IV AI (Air Interception) set and the latter the twin-engined Bristol Beaufighter. The plane was the first designed which was capable of carrying the added weight of the radar equipment without sacrifice of performance and firepower. With a two-man crew (one to operate the AI set) and generally in co-operation with a ground-controlled radar (GCI, Ground Controlled Interception), the Beaufighter proved a scourge to German night bombers.

The Mark IV AI had a range of about four miles so that the Beaufighter was guided to an enemy plane by ground control. The set also cut off at six hundred feet; by the time the Beaufighter was within that range, the enemy aircraft was generally under visual observation by the pilot. With the enemy plane in his sights, the Beaufighter pilot

One of Britain's outstanding night fighter teams: Wing Commander John Cunningham (left) and Flight Lieu- *tenant C. F. Rawnsley; the former was the Beaufighter pilot and gunner, the latter radar operator.*
(IMPERIAL WAR MUSEUM, LONDON)

was capable of bringing it under massive fire: four 20-mm. cannons were mounted in the nose and six .30-caliber machine guns were set in the leading edges of the wings.

The first squadrons began receiving the Mark IV-equipped Beaufighters in September of 1940. One of these was No. 29 Squadron, to which a young Bomber Command pilot, Guy Gibson, had been assigned as a flight commander. This assignment was regarded as a rest tour at the time, the action in night fighter units till then having proved rather tepid. While "resting" with No. 29 Squadron, however, young Gibson accounted for three enemy aircraft. Obviously the new system worked.

Number 604 Squadron was issued its first Beaufighter in October. Originally flying Blenheims in convoy protection and escort patrols, the squadron's pilots complained of never seeing one enemy aircraft. And then, with the switch to night fighting it was, apparently, more of the same: they rarely saw the German raiders and, if they did, the slow Blenheims were unable to overtake them.

Then came the Beaufighter; within a month No. 604 Squadron had scored its first victory. This had been accomplished by ex-test pilot John Cunningham and radar operator Warrant Officer J. R. Phillipson. By war's end Cunningham was the second highest-scoring night fighter pilot, with twenty victories. (Bransome Burbridge, a conscientious objector when the war began, had the highest score, twenty-one.)

In April 1941 Cunningham formed a deadly partnership with Sergeant C. F. "Jimmy" Rawnsley (as radar operator). One of their early missions, that of the night of April 12, 1941, is typical of a night fighter action. Already air-borne in their Beaufighter they were ordered by GCI to intercept a northbound raid at thirteen thousand feet. Cunningham throttled the Beaufighter to "buster" (full speed), flying due north into the dark night. Rawnsley was ordered after a short while to "flash" his AI set, but he did not pick up the enemy plane.

Ground control then suggested that Cunningham bring the plane down 2000 feet on a course of 350 degrees. During the descent Rawnsley flashed again, picked up a "blip" on the set. Whatever it was was four miles away. With Rawnsley guiding, Cunningham closed in on the blip source. Suddenly out of the misty night, above and about 2500 feet away,

Cunningham recognized the familiar outline of an He-111. Apparently unaware of the approaching Beaufighter, the pilot of the German plane continued in steady flight.

Cunningham brought the Beaufighter within eighty yards of the German bomber before opening fire. "Immediately there was a big white flash in the fuselage centre section and black pieces flew off the fuselage," Cunningham wrote in his report. "E/A went into a vertical dive to the right and about half a minute later the sky all around me was lit up by an enormous orange flash and glow. Bits of E/A were seen to be burning on the ground."

Three nights later, Cunningham and Rawnsley destroyed three Heinkels—the first time a night fighter team had scored a triple victory. (The entire night fighter toll for the month of the previous January had totaled three.) Obviously the Beaufighter and Mark IV, plus the pilot-radar operator teams (Cunningham and Rawnsley, Burbridge and F. S. Skelton, J. R. D. Braham and W. J. Gregory, and others), had proved most formidable against the German night bombers; when the Beaufighter was joined by the de Havilland Mosquito night-bombing became an extremely hazardous undertaking for the Luftwaffe.

Not all effective night fighters were teams. An extraordinary pilot was Richard Playne Stevens, who had been a civil pilot before the war. Stevens enlisted in the RAF at a rather "advanced" age—thirty-two, the maximum limit for enlistment. Stevens, who had not participated in the Battle of Britain, enlisted in the RAF with an especially poignant compulsion to give it 'em back. His wife and children had been killed in a German night raid on Manchester.

Stevens was an exceptionally well-equipped pilot with hundreds of hours of night flying (between London and Paris) to his credit. Using a non-radar-equipped Hurricane Stevens flew with a legendary abandon. Some even hinted that when he attacked a German bomber formation he screamed like a man gone mad. Without ground radar control Stevens found the enemy aircraft by flying into British antiaircraft bursts. He was certain he would find his quarry there.

During the year in which he was active Stevens shot down fourteen German bombers. His score for some time exceeded that of the two-man, radar-

Opponents in the phase of the war that followed the blitz when the RAF turned to offensive "sweeps": the *Me-109E (top left), the newer 109F (top right), the Hurricane Mark II-B (armed with bombs), and the Spitfire Mark V-B.* (H. J. NOWARRA/U. S. AIR FORCE)

equipped Beaufighters. Finally, one night in December 1941, Stevens took off to harass an enemy airfield across the Channel in France and never returned. The demon which had driven him had ultimately brought him peace.

III

Stevens had been killed while on an early intruder mission—sudden night attacks on enemy air-

fields. The tide was changing by the end of 1940: even Fighter Command was operating offensively. Intruder missions and their daytime counterpart, the fighter sweep, were designed to keep the Luftwaffe busy in the west, thus affecting the campaigns in the east, to which Hitler had ordered the bulk of the air forces for his Russian gamble. To contend with the growing RAF forces, the Germans mustered only two *Geschwader,* JG 2 and JG 26, consisting of about two hundred fighters, most of them

RAF armorers belting ammunition in preparation for a Spitfire fighter sweep.

(IMPERIAL WAR MUSEUM, LONDON)

Me-109Es with a sprinkling of the newer Me-109Fs. The Spitfire Mark V was a decided match for the Messerschmitt.

The secondary objective of the sweeps and intrusions was to destroy enemy equipment, aircraft, and installations. The initial "rhubarb," as the smaller (generally two aircraft) fighter assaults were called, occurred on December 20, 1940. Two pilots, G. P. Christie and C. A. Brodie of No. 66 Squadron, took off from Biggin Hill and, after crossing the French coast at Dieppe, pounced upon a German field at Le Touquet, strafed it, and returned to England without opposition.

About two weeks later, weather permitting, two formations of fighters—five squadrons in all—crossed the Channel and wheeled over the German-occupied coast of France. As before, there was no challenge from the Luftwaffe. The next day, January 10, 1941, the first "circus" took place: this was a large aggregation of aircraft, a squadron of Blen-

Spitfire Vs of No. 122 Squadron in various stages of multiple takeoff. Formed after the Battle of Britain, the squadron was very active during the fighter sweep phase. (IMPERIAL WAR MUSEUM, LONDON)

Group Captain Adolf Gysbert "Sailor" Malan of Wellington, South Africa. An exceptional commander, Malan's final victory score totaled thirty-five. He survived the war but died of sclerosis in 1964.
(IMPERIAL WAR MUSEUM, LONDON)

Merchant Navy before he enlisted in the RAF in 1935. Malan's nickname, "Sailor," was a reminder of his nautical days. At Dunkirk Malan scored his first two victories and by the time the evacuation was over was unofficially an ace.

At thirty Malan was just about a decade older than the average fighter pilot. He seemed aloof to the younger men, matter-of-fact, blunt in speech, and not given over to the usual boyish high jinks. In the air Malan was methodical and ruthless. Killing in the air to Malan was simply that: killing and not a sport. He was the author of the RAF's *Ten Rules for Air Fighting,* in which he expounded his

Wing Commander Douglas Bader. Bader best summed up the mood of the British fighter pilot during the Battle of Britain when he said, "We hated those aeroplanes with their iron crosses and their crooked swastikas flying into our English sky and dropping bombs indiscriminately on our English towns."
(IMPERIAL WAR MUSEUM, LONDON)

heims with a six-squadron escort of fighters. The objective was a Luftwaffe airfield near Calais. This time there was a flurry of opposition, costing Fighter Command a Hurricane and two Spitfires, the latter two crashing while landing in England. One pilot died in one of the crashes.

The rhubarbs and circuses were not in fact very decisive as far as "getting on with the war" went, but were good for the morale of pilots, who had for so long been on the defensive. The sweeps were also good preparation for operating in large formations (for future escort missions when the air war would become predominantly a matter of heavy bombardment); at the same time great leaders to lead such formations were developed.

Perhaps the greatest of these new leaders, some of them survivors of "the Battle," was Adolf Gysbert Malan, a South African who had served in the method of survival for the benefit of others. Malan survived the war, a living exemplification of his own theories, ending his combat tour with a score of thirty-two (some sources credit him with thirty-five), before being taken out of battle to instruct and command.

Malan was a superb commander, fearing neither friend nor foe. During the height of the Battle of Britain Churchill visited No. 74 Squadron, then commanded by Malan. The inquiring Churchill asked Malan what might be done to improve operations.

"Send me more bloody petrol bowsers," Malan blurted. These were the little trucks which darted across airdromes to refuel fighters during combat. It is said that within the hour Malan had his bowsers. Churchill greatly admired Malan for his directness and ability and later became the godfather of Malan's son.

By May of 1941 Malan was commander of the Biggin Hill wing. To the north, based at Tangmere, was another wing commander, Douglas Bader, who also led his squadrons over the Channel on sweeps. The long-time advocate of the "big wing" tactic, so controversial during the Battle of Britain, had also evolved another technique, which was called "finger four" formation. The larger formation broke up into units of four planes, rather loosely formed (like the fingertips of one's hand, thus the name). This supplanted the old World War I "vic" or V-formation which had proved so ineffective in the early months of the war. The loose finger four formation permitted the mutual protection of the vulnerable tails of one's squadron mates. The day of the "Hun in the sun" was just about finished.

Wing commanders, almost by virtue of their administrative position, did not always accumulate spectacular victory scores. By the summer of 1941 Bader had taken a toll of more than twenty German aircraft when his colorful fighting career came to an end. Leading a large formation in a sweep over France, Bader, in company with three other Spitfires, bounced a formation of Messerschmitt 109s. In the melee, after accounting for two 109s, Bader collided with another enemy plane. The collision tore the aft half of the Spitfire's fuselage away. Pinned into the wreckage by centrifugal force, Bader fell twenty thousand feet before he was able to tear himself out of the cockpit. And he nearly did

Pilot Officers Eugene Tobin, Vernon Keogh, and Andrew Mamedoff, three of the seven Americans who took part in the Battle of Britain. Following the Battle they transferred into the all-American "Eagle" squadron, No. 71. (IMPERIAL WAR MUSEUM, LONDON)

not make that, for as he attempted to jump from the plane his artificial leg caught in the cockpit.

All but resigned to death, Bader continued to struggle half in and half out of the cockpit when a strong lunge snapped the leg away and he fell free of the shattered Spitfire. As Bader floated earthward an Me-109 approached head on. Whether the German had intended to fire upon the British pilot dangling helplessly under his parachute or not, Bader could never say. The plane loomed closer as Bader stared, wondering what would happen. Then the German pilot flipped away and was soon out of sight. It must have been unnerving to see a fellow airman—even an enemy—falling out of the sky with only one leg.

No. 71 Squadron, February 1941 (from left): William Nichols, Ed Bateman, Stanley Kolendorski (Polish), W. E. G. Taylor, Andrew Mamedoff, Eugene Tobin, Nat Maranz, Luke Allen, Peter Provenzano, K. S. Taylor, R. Tongue (British), Gregory Daymond, and Samuel Muriello. By the time this photograph was taken Keogh had been killed in an accident; Mamedoff and Tobin, also of the original Battle of Britain trio, were later killed in action.

(IMPERIAL WAR MUSEUM, LONDON)

Flight Lieutenant Chesley Peterson and Flight Officer Gregory Augustus Daymond, Americans who served with distinction in No. 71 "Eagle" Squadron.

(IMPERIAL WAR MUSEUM, LONDON)

Eagle Squadron (No. 71) Hurricanes "beat up" the field in traditional RAF style.

(IMPERIAL WAR MUSEUM, LONDON)

Genesis of a "sweep": pilots of No. 340 Squadron ("Ile de France"), composed of Free French personnel, leave an RAF briefing (upper left), study their maps—of their own homeland generally—while waiting for the

order to take off (upper right). The word comes through to man their Spitfires in cockpit readiness (lower left); and finally, "En l'air!"

(FRENCH EMBASSY)

Bader was taken prisoner, treated with respect by Adolf Galland, who also arranged for the delivery by the British for a replacement of the broken artificial limb. (The British complied although to the Germans the delivery lacked somewhat in sportsmanship: a box containing the artificial leg was dropped immediately after a regular bombing raid.) Meanwhile, also, the leg which had been abandoned in the Spitfire was recovered and carefully repaired by the Germans and presented to Bader. From then on he never gave his captors a moment's peace, for true to form Bader spent the rest of the war attempting to escape. He became so difficult that he was finally shipped to the practically escapeproof prison at Colditz Castle, from which he was freed after the end of the war.

Better known in the United States than even the redoubtable Bader during those days of the sweeps were the so-called "Eagle Squadrons," whose members consisted of Americans. These were, initially, No. 71 Squadron, followed by No. 133 Squadron and finally by No. 121 Squadron.

The Eagle Squadrons were the brain children of a soldier of fortune, Charles Sweeny, who originally had hoped to form a kind of Lafayette Escadrille to fight the Russians in Finland. Among Sweeny's first recruits were Eugene Tobin, Andrew Mamedoff, and Vernon Keogh (who eventually ended up in the RAF and participated in the Battle of Britain). Sweeny had about thirty young men willing to fight in the air, but the fall of Finland closed that avenue of adventure. Sweeny then got them into France, from which they were driven by the victorious Germans. Most of the pilots landed in England, where for various reasons—the most important of which was the pilot shortage—they were permitted, along with other aliens, to enlist in the RAF.

Another American, artist Clayton Knight, assisted in enlisting Americans for the RAF, although he was not associated with Sweeny. In time enough Americans had gathered in England, despite official American declarations of neutrality, to warrant the formation of an all-American unit. Thus did Tobin, Mamedoff, and Keogh transfer from No. 609 Squadron to No. 71 Squadron in September 1940.

The Yanks did not get off to a very good beginning. The squadron by the following spring, although in constant training, had seen no action. The Americans did not take too gracefully to the British conception of discipline; Sholto Douglas complained to Henry Arnold that No. 71 Squadron in his opinion suffered from "too many prima donnas." Two months later, when No. 71 Squadron participated in one of its first sweeps over Calais (May 15, 1941), Section Leader John Alexander shot up the Hurricane of his wingman while attempting to get a Messerschmitt which had jumped the wingman. With disconcerting impartiality Alexander fired into both aircraft and succeeded in driving off the Messerschmitt. His wingman barely made it back to England.

In the nine months of the squadron's existence its only score was one scrapped Hurricane. In addition, it had lost pilots in training accidents, among them the veteran Keogh. And when No. 121 Squadron was formed, the day after the shooting up of Alexander's wingman, the situation worsened because of the rivalry between the two units and jealousy over publicity.

It appeared that the Eagle Squadrons were more trouble than they were worth, but again, leadership made the difference. Under the command of Walter Churchill (not related to the Prime Minister) and later H. de C. A. Woodhouse the American units became fine combat units. From among their own members too came such outstanding pilot-leaders as Gregory Augustus Daymond, late of Hollywood and only twenty when he became a full-fledged fighter pilot; another great Eagle leader was Chesley Peterson, who had been rejected by the U. S. Army Air Force because of an "inherent lack of flying ability." Both men in time won the Distinguished Flying Cross and in turn commanded No. 71 Squadron.

The Eagles proved themselves during the period of the fighter sweeps and received credit for destroying more than seventy German aircraft—enough planes to outfit six German squadrons. Besides the sweeps, the Eagles participated in less exciting, but no less essential, convoy patrols—this duty generally fell to No. 133 Squadron.

With the entry of the United States into the war the survivors of all three Eagle Squadrons were absorbed into the U. S. Air Force as the 4th Fighter Group. They would be heard from again.

Brenden "Paddy" Finucane, Irish poet of the air, leader of fighter sweeps, whose final words when he fell into the Channel were, "This is it, chaps."
(IMPERIAL WAR MUSEUM, LONDON)

IV

But until England could depend upon massive aid from America the Channel sweeps continued. No longer did anyone speak of the Battle of Britain, nor even the blitz; the fight was being taken back to the enemy, by the bombers at night and the fighters by day. A new spirit of hope had begun to glimmer. The mood was once again more gay than grim.

This was expressed by Brenden Finucane, better known as "Paddy," an outstanding pilot and wing commander by the summer of 1942. "It's a grand life," he said, "and I know I'm lucky to be among the squadrons that are carrying out the sweeps."

Finucane loved flying and the sky. "Sure," he once said, "the queen of heaven tonight has more stars than she knows what to do with. Often and often I'm put to it not to collide with the stars up there, and me dodging in and out the clouds. Stars now, have a great hold over me."

It was Finucane's dream that he might destroy twenty-one enemy aircraft by October 14, 1941, his twenty-first birthday. Poet he may have been, and a dreamer, but by that date he had shot down two dozen German planes and had been awarded the Distinguished Service Order. Finucane had one great hatred—the English Channel, which he called "demented."

The Channel persisted as a formidable ditch and mercilessly swallowed up Bomber Command planes returning from German raids and fighter pilots after sweeps, despite the brilliant rescue work of the RAF's Sea Rescue launches and planes.

The frightful Channel weather was greatly responsible for the success of the famous Channel Dash (February 11–13, 1942), when the battle cruisers *Scharnhorst* and *Gneisenau,* plus the cruiser *Prinz Eugen,* broke out of the French port of Brest, slipped through the English Channel, and returned to ports in the fatherland. The success of the operation was also due to unusually close cooperation between German naval and air forces. Adolf Galland's units, some flying the new Focke-Wulf 190 fighters, participated in the action. Despite heroic attempts by British fighters and bombers under poor weather conditions the German ships actually made it through "their" Channel to the shocked dismay of England.

That the German ships had had to flee French waters was an indication of the turn of battle, the true and conclusive end of the Battle of Britain.

It was in the summer of 1942, long after the German ships had fled, that Paddy Finucane took his last flight. Having completed a sweep, Finucane, accompanied by his wingman, a Canadian, Pilot Officer Alan Aikman, had swooped down for some strafing on the way home. Hidden among the sand dunes near Le Touquet was a machine-gun nest which opened fire on the lead Spitfire as it passed over. Finucane's plane shuddered momentarily and then continued toward England. Aikman, meanwhile, dropped down, strafed the gun position, then swung out over the Channel to overtake Finucane.

Pulling up alongside the Spitfire, Aikman radioed, "You've had it, sir, in your radiator."

"I thought so," Finucane replied; "my engine's running a temperature. I shall have to get out of this." The Spitfire had lost altitude and was too low for Finucane to parachute; he would have to ditch in the "demented" Channel. As his plane splashed into the water Finucane said, "This is it, chaps." The Spitfire fell tail first and sank immediately. Aikman circled the spot in vain, for Finucane never came to the surface. The twenty-two-year-old wing commander drowned in the waters he never loved.

The ascendancy of such leaders as Malan, Bader, and Finucane marked the official close of the Battle of Britain, of the transition from the dogfighting, exciting days of the Battle to the more deadly, businesslike making of war. Although Britain was hard pressed by a lack of supplies and men, this lack was inadvertently to be provided for by a handful of warlike men in Tokyo.

TRAGIC
VICTORIES

Contents

Preface

THE previous volume closed with the coming of the inconclusive, but destructive, blitz upon the cities and towns of England after it was realized in Nazi Germany that the Battle of Britain had not been what they had hoped for; nor would an invasion of England be attempted. This was the major outcome of the Battle of Britain.

When Japan attacked Pearl Harbor on December 7, 1941, legend has it that Hitler was unhappy, that he liked to call the grand strategic shots. But this is unlikely. When the Japanese struck, the Germans were not doing too well. The Russians had begun a counteroffensive and the British were about to stop Rommel's Afrika Korps to relieve Tobruk. There were later temporary victories, but Moscow and Tobruk did not look well on the record of the invincible Wehrmacht and Luftwaffe.

The Japanese assault upon Pearl Harbor, one in which aircraft played the major role, is generally regarded as a magnificent victory—and, in a way, it was. But in another it failed, for its major function in time proved to be to draw the United States into the war. It was carried out with remarkable tactical precision, destroyed ships, killed men, but did not eliminate the United States from the war. It was a great victory, but it decided nothing in the victor's favor. In time, it would cost him everything.

In the early, confused months of the war it might have appeared as if Japan had, indeed, achieved a decisive master stroke. Americans became desperate for a triumph of their own. For a time only a small band of flyers of fortune, known popularly as the Flying Tigers and based in China, appeared to provide any ray of hope. But their quasivictories, magnified in the press, were bought at great cost to them in misery, privation, frustration, and for some, at the cost of their lives. They did prove that the mysterious Zero fighter was not invincible and that the Japanese was not some form of superpilot. But they were also the victims of corruption, waste, neglect, and cynical masters: the Chinese leaders for whom they fought. When it was possible to get away, most did and then served in the U. S. Air Force.

The most exciting non-victory of the early months of the war was Doolittle's daring raid on Tokyo. Militarily it accomplished nothing, cost a number of lives, and lost all the aircraft involved in the attack. Still, it was a victory of courage, imagination, and sheer flying skill; but these do not really win wars.

The Battle of Midway, a concatenation of tragedies and loss, was a true turning point. But its details, those details which lie way below grand strategies and tactics, could—and should—make strong men weep. The sacrifice and pain on both warring sides, if viewed in retrospect, make one wonder why it was not decided to stop it all then and there. Instead, each became more grimly determined to press on "at all costs," to the rhythm of recurring tragic victories.

In Europe, until the Allies could cross the English Channel, the only way of reaching the industrial heart of Germany was by air, by bomber. While individual combats afforded glamour and excitement for the magazines and newspapers, the daily and nightly (in the case of RAF's Bomber Command) grind was a monotony of dread. Otherwise it was waiting, briefings, waiting, bombing-up, waiting, taking off, forming (another form of waiting), and flying to the target—the deadliest wait of all. The key to impact lay in concentration. The bigger the bomber formations, the greater the destruction to the target— and environs (inevitably hit by spillage and inevitably inhabited by the "innocent," women, children, and the old).

The early history of the heavy bombing campaigns against Germany is a recitation of great deeds and small accomplishment. Great plans were devised, carried out with incredible valor, and then it was discovered that it hadn't quite worked out as planned. What were the right targets to hit? How hard? And how often—at what cost in men and planes? These were the somber questions that could only be answered after the dismal fact.

The great Thousand Bomber Raid on Cologne, the raid of Gibson's Dam Busters, the American forces that fought in the affrighted skies over Ploesti and Schweinfurt are such tales of human performance that they should never be forgotten; nor should the men who participated. Their perseverance, sacrifice, gallantry, and the terror and pain they had to suffer are beyond imagination.

Nor should it be forgotten that despite their effort, and loss, the outcome too soon after was almost as if the effort and the loss had never occurred. Such deeds must be justified—not rationalized long, and safely, after that event, but understood within the context of the war and the limitations of the men who fought it. When the Ruhr dams burst it was expected that the ravages of their waters would cripple Germany's arms industries—and for a time they did. But for a disappointingly short time. The oil fields of Ploesti were not knocked out long enough to have justified the loss of the crews of sixty aircraft. But no one (except the enemy) expected, or hoped for, the loss of those men and planes. And it was the same with Schweinfurt.

These were all great victories for the human spirit if not for the military "art." But the human spirit might be better devoted to more creative pursuits. Besides, inside each victory is a hard core of tragedy for both the vanquished and conqueror. It is one of the fortunes—and facts—of war.

EDWARD JABLONSKI

TRAGIC
VICTORIES

BOOK I
Greater East Asia Co-Prosperity Sphere

If it is necessary to fight, in the first six months to a year of war against the United States and England I will run wild. I will show you an uninterrupted succession of victories. But I must also tell you that if the war be prolonged for two or three years I have no confidence in our ultimate victory.

—ADMIRAL ISOROKU YAMAMOTO

I

"HARK! THE VOICE OF
THE MOMENT OF DEATH"

The huge aircraft carrier pitched in the dark, heavy sea and great lashing waves saturated the small groups of men struggling on the vast, perilous deck. Ropes had been strung between open spaces to give them something to which to cling. Alongside, dangerously close, a fuel tanker bobbed and tossed, threatening to snap the hoses coupling it to the carrier. The howling wind drowned out all communication, even shouting, so that refueling the carrier was dependent upon hand signals. Their previous training for such a contingency had not prepared the men for this. Even the massive carrier seemed an insignificant cork in the turbulent seas.

The two ships pitched eccentrically, a hose ripped apart, whiplashing across the carrier deck. Seamen were swept overboard screaming into the icy Pacific. Their shipmates stared in helpless stupefaction, but only for a moment, for their officers, prodding and gesticulating, made it clear that the refueling must continue. No attempt was made to recover the men from the water. There was too little time and time was more precious than life in their grand enterprise. Certainly it was more precious than the lives of a few nameless seamen, perhaps even more precious than the life of the admiral himself. He stood on the upper bridge, a squat, heavy old man,

his face a wet, impassive mask. He had been opposed to this operation from the beginning.

The date was November 28, 1941; and he was Vice-Admiral Chuichi Nagumo. Aristocratic, conservative, a samurai, he was, with misgivings, leading a massive Japanese task force upon the "Hawaii Operation." Nagumo's flagship, the *Akagi,* originally designed as a cruiser, had been converted into a heavy carrier to subvert the restrictions upon battleships as result of the Washington Conference (1921–22). Under Nagumo's command were no less than six carriers: besides the *Akagi* there were the other heavy carriers *Kaga, Soryu,* and *Hiryu* and two light carriers, *Zuikaku* and *Shokaku.* To these had been added two battleships and two heavy cruisers in the support force (under Vice-Admiral Gunichi Mikawa); the scouting force, under Rear Admiral Sentaro Omori, consisted of a light cruiser and nine destroyers. Three submarines patrolled in advance and along the flanks of the armada. A supply force of eight tankers would attend to the necessary, and hazardous, chore of refueling the task force in its three-thousand-mile passage from Tankan Bay in the Kurile Islands to a point in the Pacific Ocean about two hundred miles north of Oahu, Hawaiian Islands.

Vice-Admiral Chuichi Nagumo, Japanese Imperial Navy, who commanded the Japanese Task Force in the Hawaii Operation. A traditionalist, Nagumo had little faith in aircraft in a sea war. (U. S. NAVY)

Hideki Tojo, a general in the Japanese Army, whose rise to political power culminated in his appointment as premier of Japan in October 1941, and led to war with the United States and Great Britain.

(NATIONAL ARCHIVES)

Despite the imposing forces at his command, Nagumo was tormented by doubts. He was, after all, a traditionalist, a torpedo expert, and the heavy reliance upon aircraft for the success of the operation impressed him very little. Sea battles were decided by the great battleships trading volleys, not by a few flimsy aircraft.

The Hawaii Operation had been the brain child of Admiral Isoroku Yamamoto, Commander in Chief of the Combined Japanese Fleet. Called "the father of Japanese naval aviation," the fifty-six-year-old Yamamoto possessed the sharpest mind in the Japanese Navy. Harvard-educated, he had served

in Washington in the Japanese embassy during 1925–27. Yamamoto liked Americans and their ways and had become a devoted baseball fan, an excellent bridge player, and quite deadly at poker. It was during his stay at Harvard, where he majored in the study of the oil industry, that Yamamoto became interested in aviation. This was around the close of the First World War. Japan, allied in that war with Great Britain, France, and the United States, though not very active, was rewarded after the war with the German possessions in the Pacific north of the equator: the Marshall and Caroline islands and the Marianas (excepting Guam, which was a possession of the United States). These islands, little known to Americans in the twenties, would become household terms in the forties.

Yamamoto, like most of the leaders of the Imperial Japanese Navy, did not want to go to war with the United States. However, the United States had traditionally been the major, if hypothetical, adversary of the Japanese Navy in the Pacific. The Japanese Army regarded Russia as its foe, although China was its earliest real victim. For his stand against war with the United States Yamamoto had risked assassination by the zealots promulgating the "Greater East Asia Co-Prosperity Sphere." Among these were General Hideki Tojo, who in October 1941 became Premier of Japan—a triumph for the Japanese war party.

Tojo, a veteran of Japanese aggression in China, in progress since 1931, was head of the Kodo (Army) party. He had served as commander of police security forces in Manchuria (established as the puppet state Manchukuo in 1932). Tough, aggressive, authoritarian, Tojo was an admirer of Hitler and his methods. The concept of the Greater East Asia Co-Prosperity Sphere was an Army inspiration that originated with General Hachiro Arita while he served as Minister of Foreign Affairs. He had also engineered a pact with the Axis powers against Russia.

Arita's Greater East Asia Co-Prosperity Sphere called for recognition of the economic and political interdependence of the Japanese Empire and the so-called Southern Regions—the raw-material-laden East Indies, Malaya, the Philippines, Java, Sumatra, Thailand, and Burma. On the surface, the scheme appeared to be a plea of "Asia for Asians" (the Chinese, apparently, excepted), but its ultimate and true aim was the acquisition of oil, primarily, for the Army and Navy of Japan. Tojo and his followers in the cabinet realized that such a course would inevitably lead to dealing with Russia on land and with Britain, the Dutch, and the United States on the sea.

However, with both Russia and Britain embroiled with Germany and with Holland under domination, only the United States remained as the major obstacle to the dream of a Japanese Empire in the East. By September 1940 Japan had signed a Tripartite Pact with Italy and Germany, stipulating that the signatories would assist each other should any one of them be attacked by a nation not then at war when the pact was signed. Obviously this could have been only the United States. A year later, at an Imperial Conference, Japan resolved to go to war with the United States "when necessary."

Yamamoto opposed the pact with the Axis; so did Premier Prince Fumimaro Konoye. But the war party was gaining power rapidly and Japanese expansion in the Pacific had begun to arouse the British, Dutch, and Americans. Steps were taken to curb Japanese designs. President Franklin D. Roosevelt placed an embargo on scrap iron and steel "to all nations outside the Western Hemisphere except Britain." On October 8, 1940, the Japanese Ambassador to the United States, Admiral Kichisaburo Nomura, referred to the embargo as "an unfriendly act."

In Tokyo the Army party was less euphemistic and Premier Konoye, fearing a collision course in international relations leading to war with the United States, summoned Yamamoto. The Prince anxiously inquired about the chances of victory in the event of war. Yamamoto's reply was characteristically outspoken and terse. "I can raise havoc with them," he said, referring to the United States, "for one year or at most eighteen months. After that I can give no one any guarantees."

Yamamoto, as usual, spoke from facts with which he was completely familiar. He knew the status of the Japanese fleet and the naval air forces; he realized at the same time how long the limited supply of oil would hold out in the event of war, "when necessary."

Prince Konoye, weak, vacillating, but hoping for peace, tried to curb Tojo, then serving as Minister of War. The Army and the industrial trusts, the Zaibatsu controlling factories, mines, trading firms, banks, and newspapers, had too firm a grip on the government. Even the exalted Emperor could not restrain the jingoistic surge to war.

The Konoye cabinet fell on October 18, 1941; Tojo then became Premier and formed a new cabinet around his war party. War was now inevitable. The implement would be the plan, conceived by Yamamoto in May 1940, called "the Hawaii Operation." If war they must, Yamamoto contended, then the United States fleet must be eliminated from that war at the outset. While the stunned Americans picked up the pieces from this single, sharp blow, the Japanese would be free to swoop down upon

Target of the Hawaii Operation: Pearl Harbor; Ford Island lies inside the harbor, most of its area devoted to airstrips. Pearl City is to the right; above left:

U. S. Navy Yard. This photograph was taken some weeks before the attack; the ships are not situated as they were on December 7, 1941.

(NAVY DEPT., NATIONAL ARCHIVES)

the rich islands to the south. A defense perimeter running from Japan through the Pacific around the Marshalls and Gilberts, New Guinea, and the East Indies up into Burma would be established. The military forces, it was assumed, of Britain and the United States would then be battered against the strong perimeter until they cried for a negotiated peace.

But all depended upon the Hawaii Operation, Yamamoto said. For all its audacity and now admired brilliance, it was not an original idea. As early as 1909 the American Homer Lea, who had served as a general in the Chinese Army, had

warned of such an attack. This he put forward in his book *Valor of Ignorance*. But this was theory. In 1938, however, it was proved in practice by Admiral H. E. Yarnell, U. S. Navy. This occurred during a naval practice maneuver, Fleet Problem XIX, in which Yarnell led what he called a "task force" (a new term at the time) from the carrier *Saratoga*. Yarnell staged a successful surprise attack upon Pearl Harbor by launching aircraft just before dawn on a Sunday. No aircraft rose to meet the "attackers," which executed mock bombings upon the Ford Island Naval Air Station, the Army's Hickam and Wheeler fields, and the Wailupe radio station. All "enemy" aircraft returned to the *Saratoga* after theoretically sinking the ships in Pearl Harbor. The portent of Fleet Problem XIX was lost neither upon Admiral Yarnell, who failed to get a sympathetic ear, nor upon Admiral Yamamoto, who did not lack for bellicose ears in Tokyo.

All minds, however, were not attuned to Yamamoto's. When it became obvious that there would be war with the United States, Yamamoto set in motion studies predicated upon an attack on the U. S. Pacific Fleet, then based as a deterrent to Japanese expansion, at Pearl Harbor. It had been there since April 1940; Yamamoto began considering his Hawaii Operation the following month. By the beginning of the next year the secret explorations for Hawaii Operation had begun in earnest.

Yamamoto's chief of staff, Admiral Shigeru Fukudome, first learned of the plan when he was ordered to find an air officer "whose past career has not influenced him in favor of conventional operations." Fukudome was expected to accomplish this quietly, without admitting even other members of the Naval High Command into the planning.

His choice was Rear Admiral Takijuro Ohnishi, then serving as chief of staff to the commander of the Imperial Navy's land-based air force. One of Ohnishi's major problems was to devise a means of launching aerial torpedoes into the shallow waters of Pearl Harbor. This was critical, for either the torpedoes, as now used, would bury themselves into the mud in the harbor bottom, or else they would bounce over the decks of ships without result. To assist him, Ohnishi called in another naval aviator, Commander Minoru Genda. Only recently returned from London, Genda was quite excited over a recent feat of Britain's Fleet Air Arm. His own intelligence reports had revealed how in November 1940 torpedo-laden Fairey Swordfish bombers took off from the carrier *Illustrious* on a nighttime mission against the Italian fleet based at Taranto and succeeded in sinking three of Italy's six battleships. A mere eleven torpedoes launched from the obsolescent Swordfish had, in a single attack, completely transformed the naval situation in the central Mediterranean. Italy's battleship strength had been cut in half, leaving the remaining half at the mercy of the Royal Navy. Both Genda and Yamamoto had noted this exploit with considerable interest, especially since the depth of the Taranto harbor was about eighty feet (Pearl Harbor was just a bit more than half that). The torpedoes had been specially prepared by the British with the simple addition of wooden fins. If the British had succeeded, why not the Japanese? It was a matter of devising a torpedo which could work in a depth of about forty feet.

But Genda and Yamamoto were not alone in recognizing the fuller significance of the Taranto attack. American Secretary of the Navy Frank Knox informed Secretary of War Henry L. Stimson in a memorandum that the "success of the British aerial torpedo attack against ships at anchor suggests that precautionary measures be taken immediately to protect Pearl Harbor against a surprise attack in the event of war between the United States and Japan. The greatest danger will come from the aerial torpedo. . . ."

Stimson agreed and so informed the Hawaiian Command. But Admiral Husband E. Kimmel, Commander in Chief, Pacific Fleet, objected to the placement of torpedo nets in the harbor because of the resulting interference with the movement of ships in so confined an area. He was, of course, right in his judgment, but it would prove to be an exorbitant rectitude. It was all but unthinkable that Japan, though launched on a campaign of conquest, would venture so far from home waters. Then too there was the problem of the torpedoes. True, the British had cut the required depth for launching in half; nothing pointed to the possibility of Japanese technicians cutting it in half again. Besides, it was widely known that the Japanese had inferior aircraft and that their equally inferior pilots would never master the technique of dive-bombing. It was an audacious conceit indeed.

After completing preliminary studies Ohnishi estimated a 60 per cent chance of success for the Hawaii Operation, provided absolute secrecy was maintained—and along with it complete surprise. His superior, Fukudome, was less optimistic; he gave the plan about a 40 per cent possibility. Yamamoto, however, upon analyzing Ohnishi's conclusions, was more than ever convinced that the plan could succeed. Though still opposed to war with the United States, Yamamoto firmly believed that if his government wanted war his Hawaii Operation was the only assurance of short-range success.

The General Staff of the Imperial Japanese Navy, which was responsible for operations, did not con-

Frank Knox (center), although opposed to Roosevelt's New Deal, was appointed by him as Secretary of the Navy (1940–44). Roosevelt hoped that this appointment would contribute to national unity in a time of crisis. It did and Knox would, before his death, become secretary of one of the world's largest navies. To his right is William Halsey; on his left is Chester Nimitz. Both of these men were to play important roles in the rebuilding of American naval power in the Pacific following the Pearl Harbor disaster.

(NAVY DEPT., NATIONAL ARCHIVES)

Husband E. Kimmel, commander of the U. S. Pacific Fleet at the time of the attack on Pearl Harbor. Relieved of his command subsequently for "errors of judgment," Kimmel believed to the end of his life that Roosevelt was responsible for Pearl Harbor.

(NAVY DEPT., NATIONAL ARCHIVES)

Roosevelt's Secretary of War Henry L. Stimson (left) in conversation with Major General James Doolittle (this photograph was taken somewhat later in the war, after Doolittle's famous raid on Tokyo).

(NATIONAL ARCHIVES)

cur. The consensus was that it was too risky. When war games were held in Tokyo during August the General Staff was further convinced of the risks when, on paper, two carriers were lost when the plan was tried out. While they argued, the Imperial Conference on September 6, 1941, decided that, "when necessary," Japan would go to war with the United States.

This did not settle the arguments between the General Staff and Yamamoto, but it did precipitate the need for definite planning. Some members of the Naval General Staff believed that Japan should strike to the south and attack America only in self-defense should the American fleet venture out of Pearl Harbor—which, of course, it would do as soon as Japan attempted to move into the Philippines.

In the face of opposition Yamamoto stood adamantly. Upon receiving a detailed paper from the General Staff in which five major objections to the Hawaii Operation were enumerated (the major one being that any loss of surprise would prove costly in casualties), Yamamoto sent a blunt message to the Staff. Unless his plan was accepted Yamamoto "must resign from his position and retire into civilian life." The date was now November 3, 1941—and this was quite a blow. The crisis was resolved quickly. Rather than lose their respected commander in chief, all argument over the feasibility of his plan ended. The Hawaii Operation was on.

Within two days Yamamoto issued Operation Order Number 1, of which the critical sentences were: "In the East the American fleet will be destroyed. The American lines of operation and supply lines to the Orient will be cut. Enemy forces will be intercepted and annihilated. Victories will be exploited to break the enemy's will to fight." This was followed shortly by Yamamoto's setting "X-Day" for Sunday, December 7, 1941. This day was selected because of the well-known American propensity for relaxing on weekends; it was likely, too, that a good proportion of the fleet would be in Pearl Harbor, in keeping with that propensity.

The fervid Army war party was anxious to open the war on December 1, but Yamamoto held out for the additional week in order to have a little more time for preparations. The Army Command, which was to lead a simultaneous attack southward into the Philippines and Malaya, acceded. On this same date, exactly one month before X-Day, Yamamoto appointed Admiral Nagumo, head of the First Air Fleet, commander of the Pearl Harbor striking force.

Surreptitiously, in twos and threes and singly, the carriers and ships of the striking force slipped out of their various ports and made for the assembly area, Tankan Bay in the cold and fog-enshrouded Kurile Islands to the north of Japan. By November 22 the thirty-one-ship armada, including the three screening submarines, had anchored in Tankan Bay for refueling and final orders. Only then did the pilots of the six carriers learn the reason for the many weeks they had spent in practicing shallow-water torpedo bombardment. The news that they were to attack the United States fleet was received with exultant acclamation. Healthy young men excitedly screeched out their banzais ("Ten thousand years!") to the Emperor and to Japan. Their joy was tinctured by their realization of the great risk of their mission and of the possibility that they would all die in such a venture. To die for the Emperor in glorious battle was the dearest wish of every pilot in the striking force.

They were to be led by Commander Mitsuo Fuchida, an experienced naval aviator of some twenty-five years' service, who had trained them for their "divine mission." Fuchida had, aboard the 6 carriers, 423 aircraft, of which 353 were to be used in the attack; the rest of the planes were held in reserve or patrolled over the ships of the striking force. Fuchida's planes were the Nakajima B5N (later named "Kate" by the Americans), the Aichi D3A ("Val"), and the Mitsubishi A6M ("Zero"). The Kates had a dual function: some would operate as high-altitude level bombers and others as low-level torpedo bombers. The Val, with its fixed landing gear, obviously German-inspired, was to function as a dive bomber. The Zero was a fighter aircraft, completely unknown in the West, and would serve as escort for the bombardment aircraft. The Zero was superior to any fighter planes the Americans then had in the Pacific.

While Nagumo contemplated the wretchedness of his lot and Fuchida's young pilots glorified theirs, hundreds of miles to the south of the main task force the advance force of twenty-seven submarines refueled at Kwajalein in the Marshalls and bore down upon Hawaii. Five of the submarines were

Zero fighters on a carrier deck ready to take off for Pearl Harbor. (NAVY DEPT., NATIONAL ARCHIVES)

assigned to the "Special Attack Unit" and carried midget, two-man submarines on their decks in a large tube. The conventional submarines were to encircle Oahu to sink any American warships that might escape Nagumo's planes and cut off any reinforcements and supplies that might be sent to Hawaii from the American mainland. The midget submarines were expected to penetrate into Pearl Harbor itself, after the aerial attack had begun, to contribute to the havoc. The air leaders, and Yamamoto himself, did not approve of the submarines' participation in the attack, but were overruled. The submarine service wished to take part in the divine mission also. The men in the midget submarines, certain they were going to death, gloried in the sentimentality of such lovely doom. Most, as it eventuated, found that very destiny.

That not one of Nagumo's thirty-odd ships was

Map of Pearl Harbor carried by Japanese pilot indicating positions of ships (not always accurate) and depth markings. (NAVY DEPT., NATIONAL ARCHIVES)

spotted during the eleven-day voyage from Tankan Bay to the point about two hundred miles north of Oahu where the planes were to be launched, must be one of history's most curious accidents. Nor were the submarines discovered until early in the morning of December 7, about five hours before the actual air attack had begun. Absolute radio silence was maintained by all ships. To cover up this blackout, ships remaining in the home waters supplied the missing signals of the absent ships.

The course of Nagumo's armada lay pretty much out of the usual shipping lanes, which is one good reason he was not discovered. If he had been discovered before December 5 the whole operation would have been canceled. The weather, too, proved an ally, although costing the lives of a few crewman. As the striking force veered southward on December 4, it approached improved if not ideal weather conditions. No word had come, as Nagumo hoped, to call off the attack. Instead, on December 2 Yamamoto radioed from his flagship *Nagato,* anchored in Hiroshima Bay, *Niitaka Yama nabore* ("Climb Mount Niitaka"), which philosophically meant "Climb the highest mountain." Niitaka is the highest peak in Formosa. This was the order to carry out the Hawaii Operation.

The ships with the beautiful names, "Flying Crane," "Haze," "Summer Cloud," "Wind on the River," "Blue Dragon," proceeded as planned. On December 6 the course shaped due south. In an emotion-packed ceremony the tattered, history-imbued flag flown by the immortal Admiral Heihachiro Togo at the Battle of Tsushima Strait (where he wiped out the Russian fleet in 1905) was run up the mast of the *Akagi*. All hands who could be spared were permitted on deck, where they joined in singing the national anthem. Impassioned cries of banzai pierced the night air and ascended to a cloud-dimmed moon. The ships in Nagumo's task force surged ahead at twenty-four knots, leaving the tankers behind.

There was one frustrating note that night. Reporting from Honolulu, Ensign Takeo Yoshikawa, posing as "Vice-Consul Morimura" in the Japanese embassy while keeping an expert eye on the American fleet in Pearl Harbor since August (1941), reported that as of 1800 (6 P.M.), December 7 (actually December 6 in Hawaii), Pearl Harbor, although a paradise of targets (more than ninety ships), harbored not one American carrier.

This was bitter news for Yamamoto, who hoped to cripple the American's chances of retaliation from the air. To Nagumo the absence of the carriers made little difference. Yoshikawa had reported nine battleships in the harbor (actually there were eight); this was target enough. Still Nagumo was made additionally uneasy when he considered that the American carrier planes could wreak havoc with the carefully laid plans of the Hawaii Operation if they caught the task force at the launching point.

Unknown to the Japanese only two of the expected four carriers were in the Pacific. The *Hornet* and the *Yorktown* had been transferred to the Atlantic; the *Saratoga*, it was known, had left long before for the West Coast for general overhaul. That left the *Enterprise* and the *Lexington*. Where were they? Yamamoto, aboard the *Nagato* three thousand miles away, was concerned. Aboard the *Akagi*, Admiral Nagumo did not sleep.

The elusive American carriers had, in fact, slipped out of Pearl Harbor days before. On November 28, just two days after the Nagumo task force left Tankan Bay—in fact, on the day that Nagumo had lost seamen during the first refueling—the *Enterprise,* under Rear Admiral William F. Halsey, had set out for Wake Island accompanied by three cruisers and nine destroyers. Aboard the *Enterprise* were the men and planes of Marine Fighter Squadron 211 (VMF-211), led by Major Paul A. Putnam. The squadron took off from the flight deck of the *Enterprise* in their dozen Grumman F4F-3s (Wildcats) on December 4 to bolster the garrison at Wake. On December 7 Halsey was well on his way back to Oahu—about two hundred miles to the west—when the attack came.

As for the *Lexington,* it too had left Pearl Harbor, under Rear Admiral J. H. Newton, in the company of three heavy cruisers and five destroyers. The *Lexington* was bound for Midway Island to deliver there Major C. J. Chappell, Jr.'s VMSB-231 (a scout-bomber squadron) and eighteen Vought SB2U-3s (Vindicators). Newton had not arrived at Midway on December 7, and when he learned of the attack, he turned around and returned, with the Vindicators, on December 10.

On Sunday morning, December 7 (December 8 in Tokyo, across the International Date Line), at six o'clock, Nagumo reached latitude 26° north, longitude 158° west—about 275 miles due north of Pearl Harbor. This was the launching point. Already two float planes, one each from the heavy cruisers *Tone* and *Chikuma,* had been catapulted into the dawn's darkness to scout ahead and for one final look at Pearl Harbor for signs of unusual activity.

The flight decks of the Japanese carriers erupted into feverish preparation. Planes were manhandled and pushed around, engines snarled, figures darted here and there. In the pilots' briefing room Fuchida reviewed the plan of attack. He would lead the first wave in one of the high-altitude Kates. If certain that surprise had been achieved, he would fire a single flare, in which case the attack was to open with the torpedo attacks upon the ships in the harbor by the Kates. This would be followed by the other Kates with conventional bombing after which the dive-bombing Vals would swoop down. The Zeros would contend with any American attempt at defense and could strafe the installations also.

Pearl Harbor bound: December 7, 1941. The Americans are about to be introduced to the Mitsubishi "Zero," an aircraft superior to any then in the Pacific.
(NAVY DEPT., NATIONAL ARCHIVES)

The spearhead of the Japanese attack on Pearl Harbor: the Nakajima "Kate" (Type 97) attack bomber/torpedo bomber. These Kates are armed with torpedoes.
(NAVY DEPT., NATIONAL ARCHIVES)

If surprise had been lost, Fuchida would fire two flares. The attack then would begin with the Vals, dive-bombing to create confusion to enable the Kates above to concentrate on their bomb runs, particularly on the harbor defenses. Then the torpedo bombers could deal with the ships.

As he spoke Fuchida referred to a blackboard on which the disposition of the American fleet in Pearl Harbor was chalked. Pilots made last-minute notations. Fuchida then left the briefing room and hurried up to the bridge, saluted, and told Nagumo, "I am ready to carry out my mission."

The old man replied, "I have confidence in you." It was a solemn moment, grim, simple, and gloriously infused with ineffable *amor patriae*. Neither man realized, in the exhilaration of the moment, the fuller implications of what they were about to do. Only Yamamoto, tense though impassive in

Hiroshima Bay, understood—for he had grasped the significance of the absence of the American carriers. Neither Yamamoto nor Nagumo was to live to see the devastation the Hawaii Operation would bring upon their beloved Japan. The seed of tragedy, as Yamamoto knew, was implanted in the blossom of victory.

Aircraft engines throbbed, then roared, on the pitching carriers whipped with salt spray. The early morning darkness was alleviated only by two parallel lines of soft blue lights along the flight deck, designating the runway. The carriers almost in unison turned into the wind—northward, opposite to the direction in which they had been moving—so that the planes could take off into the wind. In the uneasy seas the aircraft would need all the lift possible.

Fuchida sprinted to his waiting Kate. He wore a

white silk *hashimaki* (the traditional warrior's head-band, symbol of his willingness to die), a gift from the maintenance crews. The ends of the band fluttered in the slipstream as Fuchida clambered into the cockpit. At the opposite end of the flight deck a faint green light described a circle in the murky darkness; the pilot throttled the engine into full power. The Kate bounded along the wet deck, which lurched in the swelling sea. Blue lights winked past each wingtip as the Kate thundered down the flight deck. When it had almost reached the end, the carrier itself seemed to heave the Kate into the air. Cries of banzai celebrated the airmanship of the take-off.

While Fuchida circled above, the other planes of the first attack wave rose from the carriers to join him—183 aircraft in all, and all were air-borne without an accident. Fuchida had taken off the *Akagi* at 6 A.M. By six-fifteen all planes were ready to form up for the flight south. Cloud layers had formed from about three thousand feet to ten thousand. Leading his formation, Fuchida climbed into the clear air above the clouds. From that height he could not see the ocean, and no one on the ocean could see him. Fuchida's Kate was followed by forty-eight others—the level bombers. To his right, and slightly below, Lieutenant Commander Shigeharu Murata, of the *Akagi*, led forty torpedo-bearing Kates; to Fuchida's left, and above, Lieutenant Commander Kakuichi Takahashi of the *Shokaku* spearheaded the Vals, fifty-one in all, to serve as dive bombers. Lieutenant Commander Shigeru Itaya's forty-three Zeros appeared to dart nervously over the bomber formations, ready to pounce at the first sign of enemy activity.

But there was no activity. An Army radar station on the northern tip of Oahu, manned by two privates, George Elliot and Joseph Lockard, had earlier picked up the blip of one of the float planes scouting ahead of the attack force. They noted it, but because it was a Sunday they could assume that it was a private pilot out for an early morning flight. It was a fine morning for it. If the weather just north of Hawaii was a bit murky, it was fine over the islands: the clouds had begun to break, a dazzling sun came through. It promised to be a glorious day.

When Elliot and Lockard reported their plot, nothing was made of it. One officer, perhaps not

An Aichi "Val" dive bomber, its dive brakes down, plunges on "Battleship Row," Pearl Harbor.

(NAVY DEPT., NATIONAL ARCHIVES)

quite recovered from Saturday night's festivities, cracked, "Hell, it's probably just a pigeon with a metal band around its leg."

A couple of minutes after seven o'clock the two men were startled to see one of the most massive blips they had ever seen on the radar screen. Had the green Elliot caused the set to go haywire? Lockard checked it over and it seemed all right; sure enough, there was a big plot about 140 miles to the north and just about 3 degrees east. They immediately reported this—for they had never seen such a plot before—to the plotting center at Fort Shafter near Honolulu. They failed to arouse any official reaction. The duty officer, Lieutenant Kermit Tyler, was quite certain that they had spotted the Boeing B-17s due in that morning from California; or else the *Enterprise,* returning from Wake, had launched some planes.

The Japanese planes had been air-borne for an hour and a half; the sun had begun to break through the cloud which had hidden the formations from observation from below. Fuchida "strained [his] eyes for the first sight of land. Suddenly a long white line of breaking surf appeared directly beneath [his] plane. It was the northern shore of Oahu."

The Kate banked to the left, swinging toward the western shore of Oahu as the great formation followed. The sky over Pearl Harbor appeared to be clear—of cloud as well as aircraft. "I peered through my binoculars at the ships riding peacefully at anchor. One by one I counted them. Yes, the battleships were there all right, eight of them! But our last lingering hope of finding any carriers present was now gone. Not one was to be seen." But "below me lay the whole U. S. Pacific Fleet in a formation I would not have dared to dream of in my most optimistic dreams."

As his radio operator sent the signal to attack, "To . . . to . . . to . . . ," Fuchida fired the flare. In the Sunday-sleepy harbor below it was obvious that they had carried off the surprise. The dive bombers climbed out of harm's way to fifteen thousand feet as the level bombers swooped down to about three thousand and the torpedo bombers knifed down to sea level. They would initiate the attack. But something was obviously wrong. The Zeros had not taken their "Surprise Achieved" positions. Fuchida, realizing that the fighters may not have seen the signal, fired another flare. As far as

the bombers were concerned, surprise had been lost, and the plan became confused. The dive bombers, along with the now alerted Zeros, plunged into action. Worse, the torpedo planes too were screaming in upon Pearl Harbor from the sea. Fuchida looked at his watch: seven forty-nine, Pearl Harbor time.

Despite the last-minute blunder with the two signal flares, Fuchida was certain that they had caught the Americans completely off guard. More off guard than he imagined, for the delivery of the official ultimatum in Washington, delayed while the lengthy message was being decoded in the Japanese embassy, was delivered an hour and twenty minutes after the attack had begun. Instead of giving the Americans a half hour advance notice, as Yamamoto had anticipated, the other blunders of the day had plunged Japan into a Pacific war with a "sneak attack."

"Tora . . . tora . . . tora . . ." ("Tiger, tiger, tiger"), Fuchida's radio operator signaled to the anxious Nagumo on the *Akagi,* informing him that the surprise attack was successful. Because of some freakishness in the atmospheric conditions, the message was distinctly picked up in distant Tokyo and by Yamamoto's flagship in Hiroshima Bay.

The Army's Wheeler Field, a fighter base, was the first objective. Neat rows of Curtiss P-40s were lined, wingtip to wingtip—as a precaution against sabotage—on the field. Twenty-five Vals, led by Lieutenant Akira Sakamoto, proceeded to erase all fighter opposition they might have expected from Wheeler Field. At the same time Lieutenant Commander Takahashi, who led the dive bomber units, pounced with twenty-six Vals upon Hickam Field, the Army bomber base, just south of Pearl Harbor. The formation diverged as some of the Vals broke off to attack the various installations on Ford Island, in the center of Pearl Harbor. It was around the island that most of the important ships, singly and in pairs, were berthed.

The languid Sunday tranquillity was shattered by the scream of diving aircraft, the whine of falling bombs, explosions—followed by the characteristic blossom of thick, black smoke of flaming metal. This same smoke, as he feared, complicated the mission of Lieutenant Commander Murata's Kates, which were to torpedo the ships grouped around Ford Island.

A Japanese photograph records the first strikes around Ford Island. Outer row of ships are (left to right): Vestal, West Virginia, *and* Oklahoma; *inner row:* Nevada, Tennessee, *and* Maryland. *Of these the Okla-* homa *was sunk, the* West Virginia *sunk but later repaired, the repair ship* Vestal *and battleships* Nevada, Tennessee, *and* Maryland *damaged and later repaired.*

(NAVY DEPT., NATIONAL ARCHIVES)

A Val *has just dropped a bomb near the* Oklahoma *and* Maryland *on the far side of Ford Island. On the near side, the* Utah *(a target ship the Japanese thought was the carrier* Saratoga)—*the third ship from the* left—*lists to port. In the upper right of the photograph another* Val *sweeps over the Navy Yard.*

(NAVY DEPT., NATIONAL ARCHIVES)

One of Murata's pilots, his second-in-command, Lieutenant Inichi Goto, was infuriated when, just as he was leveling off for the run on the battleships at anchor, the Vals flashed by him. Goto was then flying in the vanguard of one column of Kates, while Murata led the other. Not realizing that Fuchida had fired the second flare which precipitated the attack by the Vals, Goto was angrily certain that the dive bombers had jumped the gun to steal the glory of making the first attack on the Americans.

There was nothing else to do but proceed, despite the confusion and now the smoke. Goto concentrated on his run: speed, height, and then the correct release point. The battleship—the *Arizona*—grew larger in his sight; there seemed to be no one on the decks of any of the ships. Oblivious to everything else, Goto timed the moment of release, and the torpedo, with its odd wooden fins, dropped from the Kate's belly. The weight gone, the Kate vaulted as Goto pulled back on the stick and kicked the rudder bar to get up and away. For a fleet moment he twisted his head to see over the tail: a foaming white wake churned the water, leaving a momentary track which terminated at the side of the *Arizona*.

Antiaircraft fire from American ships, once the impact of the surprise attack had worn off, begins to seek out Japanese Vals. (NAVY DEPT., NATIONAL ARCHIVES)

Panorama of Pearl Harbor minutes after the opening of the attack: ships burn in the harbor and the sky fills with antiaircraft bursts.

(NAVY DEPT., NATIONAL ARCHIVES)

Struck by the heavy concentration of fire from the American ships, a Val begins a fiery plunge into Pearl Harbor. (NAVY DEPT., NATIONAL ARCHIVES)

A broiling geyser of flame, smoke, and water shot high into the air.

"We hit her!" Goto shouted and circled round to view the damage.

But the "Americans were better prepared and reacted much faster after the shock than I would ever have thought possible." Machine-gun tracers were fanning and curving up at the Kate; Goto decided to pull away from the heated air over Ford Island. It was true, within minutes after the first bombs fell some of the men on some of the ships had begun firing at the Japanese planes. But the sudden impact of the realization that there were real aircraft, with orange-red circles on their wings, dropping real bombs and shooting real bullets created uncertainty and confusion on the ships as well as ashore. Army personnel were sure that some crazy Navy pilots were having sport with them—and vice versa. That this could be real war took time to penetrate. Men who once regarded themselves as professionally military wandered about not quite knowing what to do.

Those who might have gone into immediate action were handicapped for other reasons: many guns were simply not ready to be fired, or there was no ammunition available—and if it was, perhaps it was

locked away and no one seemed to have the key. For many there were simply no weapons at all. One sailor, in impotent despair, threw wrenches and other handy objects at the low-flying Japanese planes. Adult males burst into blubbering tears of helpless frustration. The abrupt reality of what was happening was difficult to grasp: one minute it had been a typical, peaceful Sunday; the next it had become an incredible concatenation of hundreds of swirling, flashing airplanes, explosions, acrid smoke, shouting, the sound of bugles, alarms, waterspouts, and little, moving, parallel scallopings of water caused by the twinkling guns in the planes strafing them. Suddenly someone you had known for years was inexplicably dead. Or the ship on which you had served for a decade had become a shattered, smoking hulk sinking into the mud of Pearl Harbor.

The battleships clustered around Ford Island were sumptuous objectives. The Kates hammered them from the side in torpedo attacks and from above with level attacks. Within minutes, so-called Battleship Row and American naval power in the Pacific were a shambles. Simultaneously the same destiny was allotted to the Naval Air Station at Kaneohe, on the eastern side of Oahu, where twenty-seven of thirty-six Consolidated PBYs (Catalinas) were destroyed. The Marine Corps Air Base at Ewa, ten miles west of Pearl Harbor, lost almost all of its fighter planes (forty-seven out of forty-eight), belonging to Marine Aircraft Group 21 (MAG-21), to strafing Zeros.

At Hickam Field, just south of Pearl, gouts of oily smoke ascended from mangled old Douglas B-18s, as well as from the more recent Douglas A-20s (Havocs) and Boeing B-17s. Several of the factory-fresh, unarmed B-17s, just flown in from California, were caught up in the attack as they came in to land. Many of them were shot up by Zeros as they attempted to land and if they landed, were strafed along with their hapless crews. As at Wheeler, the Army fighters at Bellows Field, almost directly east of Honolulu, were rent and flared where they rested on the ground. Very few American fighters, in fact, got off the ground.

Several pilots of the 47th Pursuit Squadron succeeded in reaching Haleiwa, a small, relatively insignificant training field in northwestern Oahu, by automobile. The field had not been as diligently worked over by the Zeros as the major airfields and

U. S. Naval Air Station, Pearl Harbor. The Chance Vought OS2U "Kingfisher" has been hit by a bomb. *It is one of eighty U. S. Navy aircraft destroyed in the attack.* (U. S. NAVY)

A rescue party searches for survivors from the burning West Virginia. One seaman is being assisted out of the *water; two more may be seen on the bridge.* (NAVY DEPT., NATIONAL ARCHIVES)

Hickam Field, the Army Air Force bomber base near Pearl Harbor; more than twenty bombers were destroyed at Hickam. (U. S. AIR FORCE)

As the Pearl Harbor attack opened, twelve new B-17s were approaching Hickam Field after a flight from the United States. Early radar detection of the Japanese attack were mistaken for the approaching B-17s, many of which arrived over Pearl Harbor during the attack. This was one of the new B-17s. Piloted by Captain Raymond Swenson, it was attacked by Zeros. A bullet ignited flares in the radio compartment and upon landing the burning plane broke in half. All of the occupants escaped except Flight Surgeon William Schick, who was killed by a strafing Zero as he ran from the wreck. (NAVY DEPT., NATIONAL ARCHIVES)

a few of its planes were still flyable. Taking off, without orders, by the way, a fact which would have later consequences, in P-40s as well as obsolescent P-36s, they attempted to intercept the attackers. Neither of the American planes was any match for the Zero. Even so, Lieutenant George S. Welch claimed four enemy planes before the Japanese finished with Pearl Harbor; although Welch received the Distinguished Flying Cross for his actions that day, a request that he be awarded the Congressional Medal of Honor was turned down because he had taken off without orders. Other pilots who managed to take off were Lieutenants John J. Webster, Harry M. Brown, Kenneth A. Taylor, and John L. Dains. On his third time up the last-named was shot down over the Army's Schofield Barracks by antiaircraft fire. Other pilots of the 44th and 46th Pursuit Squadrons attempting to get into the battle were shot down by the fast, amazingly adroit Zeros; many American pilots were killed on the ground as they ran for their planes.

Ten thousand feet above the writhing shambles, Fuchida prepared for the run by the level bombers upon the battleships moored around Ford Island. A few, berthed inland and adjacent to another ship, were difficult for the torpedoes to hit. Antiaircraft bursts from both the ships and the land batteries burst around the Kate formation. Fuchida's Kate recoiled as the firing became uncomfortably accurate. The plane bounced from a close one which punctured the fuselage and damaged a rudder control wire. But the plane remained in flight so Fuchida, with his eye on the lead plane, continued on the bomb run. Just then they flew into cloud, missing the release point—they would have to do it again. The air around the Kates was pocked with the gray-black puffs of shellbursts.

Fuchida's pilot banked the Kate, circled around Honolulu, and returned to Battleship Row. Other planes, meanwhile, had succeeded in dropping their bombs. Just as he was about to make a second attempt, Fuchida witnessed a "colossal explosion in Battleship Row," the violence of which tossed the Kate about seven miles away from Ford Island. The battleship *Arizona,* anchored at the northeastern tip of the island, adjacent to the repair ship *Vestal,* had gone up in one massive explosion. Bomb hits from above (for the ship was moored inland from the *Vestal* and was barely hit by torpe-

does) on the powder magazines and boilers tore the old battleship apart. A fireball shot five hundred feet into the air, a shock wave flared out, blowing men off the decks of nearby ships into the oily waters of Pearl Harbor. A complete loss, the *Arizona* sank into the offshore mud, taking 1103 lives with it of the total of 1400 men aboard. Among those lost were Captain Franklin Van Falkenburgh and Rear Admiral Isaac C. Kidd, who died instantly as they stood on the bridge of the *Arizona.*

Antiaircraft smudges continued to harass Fuchida but he proceeded with the bomb run. This time the lead plane dropped its bombs and the other Kates dropped in unison. Fuchida then fell to the floor where he lay, eye to peephole, to observe the results. The size of the bombs diminished as they plunged downward. He saw concentric ripples in the water where some missed, but as he watched two of them fell directly to the left of two ships moored side by side. The *Maryland* and *Oklahoma* shuddered under the detonations.

Upon completing their runs, the bombers fled to the north and the safety of the carriers. No attempt was made to screen the direction—there wasn't enough fuel left for that. By 8:30 A.M. almost all aircraft of the first attack wave, excepting Fuchida's Kate and a few strays, had left for the carriers. An unreal quiet suffused the air over Pearl Harbor, seemingly clear of Japanese aircraft. But the harbor itself and the area around it were choked with the effluvium of flaming ships, aircraft, harbor installations, and men. The living, now wrathful, made preparations for what might come next. Makeshift gun installations of wreckage and debris were erected; guns were ripped off ruined planes and set up in odd places. Guns were even issued to the weaponless (some, it is true, without firing pins and many without ammunition). Rescue operations were under way immediately in Pearl Harbor itself.

The second wave came in around 8:54 A.M. Lieutenant Commander Shegekazu Shimazaki of the *Zuikaku* led the formation of 170 planes. Shimazaki personally led the 54 Kates assigned the level bombing; Lieutenant Commander Takashige Egusa (*Soryu*) led the 80 Val dive bombers and Lieutenant Saburo Shindo (*Akagi*) commanded the 36 Zero fighter covers.

Fuchida, as over-all commander of the aerial attack, had remained behind to observe and direct

One of the spectacular explosions witnessed by Mitsuo Fuchida as he lay in the belly of a Kate: the Shaw *blowing up in a dry dock in the Navy Yard.*

the second wave. As, he watched, the Zeros darted in to strafe Battleship Row and the airfields. The Vals hurtled in from the east to maul further the ships at and around Ford Island. Most of the level bombers concentrated on Hickam Field as others bombed Ford Island and the Kaneohe Naval Air Station. Smoke and flame of the early attack interfered with bombing accuracy—and antiaircraft was fiercely thick, Despite this not one bomber of the second wave was lost, although several were holed by gunfire. Six Zeros and fourteen Vals of the second wave did not return to the carriers. The first wave had lost only three Zeroes, one Val, and five Kates. The total losses of both waves were twenty-nine aircraft and their crews (fifty-five men).

In terms of "the values of war" it was a small price to pay. In roughly two hours at a "reasonable" expenditure of a handful of men and a few planes (plus one submarine and all five of the midget submarines), the Japanese had achieved precisely that which Yamamoto had promised them with the Hawaii Operation. The nearly total crippling of the American Pacific Fleet at Pearl Harbor cleared the way for the conquest of the Philippines, Malaya —and for the other objectives of the Southern Operation.

American losses were appalling: 2403 killed, 1178 wounded. Of the 68 civilian dead, many died in or near military installations. Those killed in Honolulu were undoubtedly the victims of American shells incorrectly fused in the chaos of activity. At Pearl Harbor, of the battleships, the *Arizona* and *Oklahoma* were destroyed beyond recovery; the *California* and *West Virginia,* also sunk, were

Seamen salvage a Kate from the waters of Pearl Harbor; only five were lost in the attack.

eventually put back into service; the *Maryland, Tennessee, Pennsylvania,* and *Nevada* had all suffered damage but could—given time—be salvaged. Of the cruisers, the *Helena, Raleigh,* and *Honolulu* were damaged but repairable. Destroyers *Cassin* and *Downs* were lost; the *Shaw,* though hit and spectacularly exploded, was later restored to service. Both the *Utah,* a radio-controlled target ship, and the *Oglala,* a minelayer, were completely out of action. The repair ship *Vestal,* which had been next to the *Arizona,* was restored to service. So was the seaplane tender *Curtiss,* which lay smoldering under the wreckage of Lieutenant Mimori Suzuki's Zero, which had crashed into the deck during the attack.

Not a single battleship which lay in Pearl Harbor that day escaped the attack, which had been most thoroughly planned and efficiently executed. Although the damage was not absolute, it would be a long time before the salvageable ships would be ready for action.

Almost half of all the aircraft—Army, Navy, Marine—on Oahu were destroyed, a total of 188 of the pre-attack strength of 394, not all of which were truly operational. But the carriers had been spared and so had the repair shops at Pearl Harbor. And so had the fuel depots, rich with oil. Instead, the Japanese had bombed a baseball diamond in the belief that it was a cleverly camouflaged fuel tank farm.

Upon reporting to Nagumo aboard the *Akagi,* Fuchida—as well as other air commanders—suggested an additional strike at Pearl to deal with targets that might have been obscured by smoke

The first Zero to go down under American guns: it is the aircraft of pilot Takeshi Hirano of the Akagi's *first wave.* (U. S. NAVY)

or simply overlooked in the excitement of the moment. Besides, he hoped it might give them the opportunity to deal with the still untouched carriers, wherever they might be. But Nagumo, with his chief of staff, Rear Admiral Ryunosuke Kusaka, concurring, maintained that the attack had accomplished its strategic objective—excepting those hauntingly missing carriers. The task force, therefore, before the Americans completely recovered, would set course north-northwest and withdraw. No amount of respectful debate could force Nagumo to change his mind. At one-thirty that vivid Sunday afternoon the *Akagi* raised a signal flag: all ships were to head for home waters. Swiftly and silently the ships slipped into the heavy mist.

Back at Pearl Harbor frenetic preparations were under way for the invasion which seemed the inevitable next phase in Japanese operations. Wild rumors swept Oahu; nervous sentries became a greater menace than the new enemy. The least unexpected noise or light ignited a chain of frenzied shooting.

Everything that flew was fair game. The planes of the *Enterprise* suffered from friend and foe alike. Early in the morning Commander Howard L. Young with Lieutenant Commander Bromfield B. Nichol as his passenger took off from the carrier and headed for Pearl Harbor. Nichol was a member of

Admiral Halsey's staff and was being sent ahead to report the delivery of the men and planes to Wake Island; the information was considered highly secret and therefore could not be sent by radio, even in code. The two men were accompanied by another plane, also a Douglas SBD (the Dauntless). Other SBDs were launched later to scout the seas. The *Enterprise*'s crew was envious, for the planes would be in Oahu within two hours—the carrier would require an additional six.

But by the time Young arrived over Ford Island, conditions of the island prompted him to think that all safety precautions were being violated by the Army. Then one of the "Army" planes pulled away from the island and hurtled at them. Nichol was rather surprised to note that "a lot of burning cigarette butts" came flashing by. Some, flicking against the wing, ripped pieces of aluminum into the slipstream. Then the plane turned and the red-orange circles became visible.

Young and his wingman dived their Dauntlesses for Ford Island, escaping the Japanese planes but running into shattering fire from "friendly" guns on the ground. As Young braked the Dauntless, a sailor stood up with a machine gun; he hated all aircraft. He was prevented from firing at Young's Dauntless by a pilot who recognized the plane—but this only by threatening the sailor with a tremendous rock.

The other planes from the *Enterprise* were not so fortunate, especially those of Scouting Squadron 6. Swarms of Zeros pounced on them as they came in for landings. The death of one young pilot was heard at the *Enterprise,* which then learned that Pearl Harbor was under attack. Ensign Manuel Gonzales was heard over the radio, "Do not attack me! This is 6-Baker-3, an American plane!"

Then Gonzales' voice again, "We're on fire. Bail out!"

Soon after, flags were run up the yardarm of the *Enterprise.* There was something unreal about their message: *Prepare for battle.* Scout planes, torpedo planes, and fighters were launched to search for the attackers. Grumman Wildcats hovered overhead on combat air patrol (CAP). The Wildcats also escorted the torpedo-carrying Devastators, but although there were many alarums, there were no enemy carriers or planes about. That night the Devastators returned to the *Enterprise,* but the Wildcats because of less fuel capacity were ordered to

A homemade propaganda leaflet dropped by a Japanese pilot over Pearl Harbor. Japanese inscription on left reads: "Hark! The Voice of the Moment of Death. Wake up, you fools." Japanese wishful thinking is evident in the bursting aircraft carrier, not one of which was in Pearl Harbor the Sunday of the attack. That the carriers escaped would have its later effect in the Pacific war; but "the fools" had been rudely awakened that morning. (NAVY DEPT., NATIONAL ARCHIVES)

return to Pearl Harbor. The six planes with landing lights full on and with wheels down wheeled in over Ford Island after clearing with the tower. A single machine gun opened up on them across the channel from Ford Island, another joined in, then others, and all of Ford Island flashed as tracers converged on the Wildcats. One merely continued its glide across the channel into Pearl City, where it crashed and burned, killing pilot Herbert Menge. Two others were shot down, one crashing and burning in a cane field. Three of the pilots flicked off their lights and jammed their throttles and headed out to sea until things quieted down. Two managed to land, but pilot David Flynn's engine gave out and he was forced to parachute. It had proved a costly and fruitless search for the Japanese carriers.

But they had vanished into the spacious Pacific. Yamamoto had proved that the airplane was more than a match for the immobile battleship, but it was an infamous victory.

2

AMERICAN RENEGADES

Mei-ling Soong, exquisite, formal, and hard as nails, best known to the world as Madame Chiang Kai-shek of China, referred to a small band of American youngsters as her "angels—with or without wings." It was a neatly turned phrase, much used during the early months of the Pacific war, even if few could explain its precise meaning. Another winsome phrase, also widely quoted, was "the Lady and the Tigers," with all its curious ambiguity. Not to the "angels," however. If the genteel Madame had to make the choice, for all her endearing phrases, they would be angels indeed. There was no sacrifice too great, in terms of the lives of others, for her beloved China.

Within weeks after Japan went to war in the Pacific, Madame Chiang's "angels" were renowned as the "Flying Tigers"; no one knows the derivation of the name. The Japanese preferred calling them "American renegades," partly because they had become, as the American Volunteer Group, members of the Chinese Air Force and partly because of their unorthodox fighting style. In fact, during those grim early months of the Pacific war, only the Flying Tigers spoiled the succession of Japanese aerial victories—and this while flying inferior aircraft.

Credit for the Flying Tigers' tactics and for their ability to meet the Japanese in battle with a type of aircraft which, in other areas, the Japanese destroyed readily, must go to the man who led them, an ex-U. S. Army Air Corps captain, Claire Lee Chennault. Hard-bitten, tough, and self-sufficient, Chennault had been in China since 1937, when he was retired from the Air Corps because of chronic bronchitis and partial deafness. He had been hired by Generalissimo Chiang Kai-shek to serve as his adviser in military aviation; Madame Chiang, it might be noted, was the National Secretary of Aviation. Chennault, then forty-seven, was given the rank of colonel in the Chinese Air Force.

He found, however, that he had little effective air force to command. The Japanese were well established in Manchuria and bombing Chinese cities at will. The Chinese armies, those under Chiang's command, fell back before the better-equipped and disciplined Japanese. The Generalissimo abandoned Nanking, then Hankow, until the seat of his Kuomintang government was temporarily established inland at Chungking. The Japanese, however, were not Chiang's only foes. He was either at odds or made deals with various provincial governors, war lords and the Communists under Mao Tse-tung. Consequently during the war in China there were in fact several wars as these factions fought together and then fought each other.

Into this typical oriental political situation descended Claire Chennault, who was fated to an extraordinary education in duplicity, graft, cupidity, nepotism, equivocation, and the old-fashioned double cross. While these themes are not directly germane to the development of the air weapon, they were to vex Chennault considerably during his service in China. The cost in goods, time, money, and lives would not be trivial.

Chennault's was not the first attempt at patterning the Chinese Air Force along foreign lines. As

early as 1932 an "unofficial" air mission led by Colonel John H. Jouett gave it a try. Bringing nine American pilots—including one Harvey Greenlaw, who would in time become Chennault's chief of staff—Jouett found the Chinese Air Force ineffectually graft-ridden. With Chiang Kai-shek's blessing Jouett generally shook up the organization, set up a proper training school, and arranged for the purchase of modern foreign planes. But diplomatic pressures from Japan, as well as differences with Chiang, forced Jouett out of China in 1934. In desperation Chiang turned to other nations for assistance in building a modern air force; he found the Russians and the Italians most willing. However, the occidental soldier-of-fortune *laissez faire* outlook (this was especially true of the Italians) did little to improve the efficiency of Chiang's air force. Very soon the planes Jouett had purchased piled up around the Chinese countryside.

Madame Chiang attempted to remedy the woeful situation by hiring a couple of ex-U. S. Army Air Corps stunt fliers, William C. McDonald and John H. Williamson, to organize a flying school in 1936. The two men had been members of a trio known as "Three Men on a Flying Trapeze," which had thrilled the crowds at air shows and races. Their most celebrated stunt was flying through complex aerobatics while their planes were attached, wing to wing, by a twenty-foot length of rope. The leader and third member of the group was Claire Lee Chennault. McDonald and Williamson suggested that Madame Chiang approach Chennault to do something about the hapless Chinese Air Force. Chennault, by then retired, was known for his textbook *The Role of Defensive Pursuit,* the doctrine of which had made a deeper impression upon the younger pilots than Chennault's superiors.

Chennault's first exposure to the internationally manned air force was disheartening. Many an aircraft was wiped out merely in the process of landing; half of his small force of American and British fighters (eleven out of twenty-two) was destroyed in this way; likewise four out of five Martin bombers. The last bomber was lost during a surprise Japanese air raid. The polyglot air force took off in every possible direction, crashing into the bomber on the ground and further erasing fifteen fighters from the operational inventory.

One of Chennault's first moves was to institute

Madame and Generalissimo Chiang Kai-shek and Chinese dignitaries at the inauguration of Chiang as president of China, October 1943.

(U. S. OFFICE OF WAR INFORMATION)

Claire Lee Chennault, master tactician and pilot who created the "Flying Tigers." This photograph was taken *after the Flying Tiger phase—when Chennault commanded the Fourteenth Air Force later in the war.*
(U. S. AIR FORCE)

Back door to China: the Burma Road, more than seven hundred miles of hazardous driving—and corrupt Chinese officials. (U. S. OFFICE OF WAR INFORMATION)

was an almost insuperable effort. The Russians, who had been supplying the Chinese with money, planes, guns, and even aircrews, had, by the summer of 1941, a Nazi invasion to contend with—which closed that avenue of aid. The Japanese controlled the eastern seaports of China, as well as Indo-China (thanks to Vichy France), leaving the one major life line into China via the port of Rangoon, Burma. Materials delivered to Rangoon were sent by rail to Lashio, in the north; this was the western terminus of the Burma Road, a curling ribbon of more than seven hundred miles, a tortuous drive by truck, which had been all but clawed out of the mountains by hand during 1937–38. At the eastern end of the road lay Kunming, China.

By March of 1941 the United States, awakening to the Japanese threat in the Pacific, was committed to full lend-lease aid to China. The Burma Road thus became more crucial than ever. Only two obstacles intervened in the full exploitation of the Burma Road: the Japanese bombers based at Hanoi and the Chinese officials responsible for the Burma Road. Graft, featherbedding, and sheer inefficiency prevented the delivery to China of much of the materials that arrived in Rangoon. Even despite the official commitment to China and the widespread sympathy in the United States for the Chinese, there was no overwhelming aid on the way, in fact. Both military and government officials in the United

an early warning system with lookout stations, linked by radio, strewn across China. Whenever the Japanese bombers left their base at Hanoi, Indo-China (after the fall of France), it took but a few minutes before Chennault knew about it in Kunming. In the beginning (before the Flying Tiger era) the main job was to get the few surviving Chinese aircraft dispersed or evacuated to escape bomb damage. Later, of course, the early warning system could be employed for interception. Proof of Chennault's capabilities as a teacher was demonstrated late in the summer of 1937. Chinese pilots, taught by Chennault, intercepted Japanese bombers over the battered city of Nanking and shot them out of the skies.

But the teaching of tactical potency was Chennault's minor problem. He required more men and more aircraft. Merely getting materials into China

Curtiss P-40 "Tomahawk" with Flying Tiger shark's mouth, Rangoon. (U. S. AIR FORCE)

States, with wary eyes upon Europe and recent developments in north Africa, viewed Hitler and not Tojo as the major threat.

Prompted by the seriousness of the China situation, Chennault returned to the United States in the spring of 1941 accompanied by General P. T. Mow of the Chinese Air Force. Chennault by this time was a brigadier general. With the co-operation of T. V. Soong, Chinese Foreign Minister and brother of Madame Chiang, Chennault eventually reached the sympathetic ear of President Roosevelt. Basing his plea for aid to China on the importance of keeping the Burma Road open, Chennault asked for aircraft—and a voluntary force of experienced American pilots to fly them. This was a delicate proposition politically, for such open aid would be in violation of American-Japanese neutrality, such as that was. Besides, Hitler continued to engage American attention.

The aircraft were forthcoming, thanks to the intervention of Secretary of the Treasury Henry Morgenthau, Jr., who had Roosevelt's backing. Although all first-class aircraft were high-priority items for the burgeoning U.S. national defense program, or for shipment to Britain and Russia, Chennault was able to obtain the release of a hundred Curtiss Wright P-40Bs ("Tomahawk"), originally allocated to Sweden—and which had already been rejected by the RAF as obsolescent. Despite this rejection, the P-40s were better planes than those Chennault already had. And the RAF continued to use them until the later D and E models ("Kittyhawk") appeared.

Assured of his aircraft, Chennault broached the subject of trained pilots. Predicting a general outbreak of war in the Pacific, he succeeded in arousing the sentiments of Roosevelt as well as officials in the War and State departments. So it was that from May through July of 1941, various Army and Navy air bases were visited by Chennault or by Captain Harry C. Claiborne, C. B. Adair (both ex-U. S. Army Air Corps men), and Richard T. Aldworth, a former World War I pilot and a vice-president in an organization known as CAMCO, Central Aircraft Manufacturing Corporation.

This was an interesting firm. It was, in fact, the contracting agent between the American volunteers and the Chinese government. According to the contract signed by the pilots and ground crew volunteers, they were to serve for one year in China "to manufacture, service and operate aircraft" as members of the American Volunteer Group. There was no mention, not even in fine print, of fighting the Japanese. Minimum salary for flying personnel was $600 per month in American money (lend-lease, of course). Flight leaders received $675 and squadron commanders $750. A bonus of $500 was promised for every confirmed Japanese plane destroyed— this point was verbal and also not included in the CAMCO contract. Ground crew salaries ranged from $150 to $350 a month; for this time—the summer of 1941—these could be regarded as very good salaries.

The attractive fiscal promises were not the sole reasons for volunteering. Some pilots, in training for years, longed for a little action. Others sensed that, in time, the United States would have to go to war and hoped to gain combat experience (this was especially true of the Navy pilots). Some volunteers were driven by the simple spirit of adventure and others by a dedication to the cause of China. This was before they learned that the cause of China and the cause of the Chiang Kaisheks were not necessarily identical. Others admitted that they were out for the money—so there was a complexity of reasons for the forming of the American Volunteer Group. Some may even have succumbed to the rather exaggerated blandishments of the recruiting staff—who were rewarded for their efforts in bounty, so much per head. As Gregory Boyington, an ex-Marine pilot who had volunteered to escape serious financial problems, observed, "The two ingredients necessary to accomplish this human sale were greedy pilots and a few idealists."

Whatever their motivations, 90 pilots (over half of whom came from the ranks of the Navy and Marines) and 150 non-flying personnel assembled in July in San Francisco. Among the ground people were radio operators, mechanics—even a flight surgeon and two nurses. Supplies, too, had been purchased with lend-lease funds by Soong and Chennault, who had gone on ahead to arrange for a training base in Burma. The first contingent of the American Volunteer Group slipped out of San Francisco aboard a Dutch ship on July 11, 1941, more or less secretly. The furtiveness encompassed some quite blatant passport falsification. When he left on a subsequent ship, Boyington was, according to his passport, "a member of the clergy." It could hardly be considered inventive typecasting.

It was September, after a meandering voyage of many stops, before the first of the American Volunteer Group arrived at Rangoon, some twenty miles up the Rangoon River from the Gulf of Martaban. A subsequent trip by rail took them deeper into the jungle to an RAF base at Toungoo, where they were to receive their schooling from Chennault. Burma, it turned out, was not quite the tropical paradise painted by the recruitment staff. Getting off the toy train at Toungoo, many a young pilot felt foolishly country-clubbish as he carried tennis rackets and a set of golf clubs. There were no golf courses or tennis courts at the Kyedaw airdrome, about ten miles out of Toungoo. There were only moldering troop barracks, oppressive heat, an incredible proliferation of insect life, giant rats, poor food.

Some of the P-40s, however, had arrived at Rangoon, and were assembled and flown up to Toungoo. "The runway," Chennault wrote in describing the place, "was surrounded by quagmire and pestilential jungle. Matted masses of rotting vegetation carpeted the jungle and filled the air with a sour, sickening smell." Even before training got under way, Chennault was handed the resignations of five pilots who "were eager to return to the United States and air-line jobs."

Chennault drew upon his past experiences with the Japanese and as a teacher, "ranging from the one-room schools of rural Louisiana to director of one of the largest Air Corps schools," to prepare the new pilots for what would come. He stressed the excellent flying qualities of the Japanese pilots, although emphasizing their tendency to fly mechanically and employ a set tactical routine. Chennault also introduced the Americans to the Zero fighter, indicating its strong points as compared with the P-40: higher ceiling, superior maneuverability, and better climbing ability. But, Chennault also pointed out, the P-40 was a more rugged aircraft, could take more punishment, and, thanks to the self-sealing fuel tank, was not so readily combustible. The P-40 was also equipped with armor plate, which the Zero lacked, thanks to the Japanese pilots' insistence on high maneuverability. Also, the heavier P-40 could outdive (that is to say, outrun) the Zero. "Use your speed and diving power to make a pass, shoot and break away," Chennault told them.

Another dictum: "Fight in pairs." These tactics were quite unorthodox to pilots who had been trained along the romantic dogfight concepts of the First World War. The "hit and run" principle was particularly upsetting (but exceptionally wise, as they would learn). When this idea filtered around, the RAF issued an order that any British pilot seen diving away from a combat would be subject to court-martial. The Chinese Air Force had a more direct solution: a firing squad.

But Chennault prevailed, although his lecture on the Zero seems to have led to a few more pilot resignations. Those who remained then had to contend with the P-40, for which few had little regard. Many longed to use the Brewster Buffalo, which the RAF had, instead. Chennault, no admirer of the P-40 himself and particularly not of its liquid-cooled Allison engine, realized that for all its imperfections, the P-40 could be used to beat the Japanese, if properly handled.

The transition to the P-40 by pilots who had been trained in other aircraft (some had even piloted B-17s) was not simple. The narrow-tread landing gear of the P-40 made landing upon hard, earthen runways a hazard. Even experienced pilots washed out precious planes. And there were other accidents. Former Navy pilot John D. Armstrong (Hutchinson, Kansas) collided in a mock dogfight in mid-air with Fighter Leader John G. Bright. The latter managed to take to his chute, but Armstrong did not and died in the crash. A few days later Maax Hammer (Cairo, Illinois), caught in a sudden monsoon, crashed while attempting to land and was killed. On another training flight, Peter W. Atkinson (Martinsburg, West Virginia) suffered a malfunction of his propeller governor; the propeller ran wild and the P-40 all but fell apart in a screaming power dive, taking Atkinson with it.

There being no spare parts for the P-40s, the wrecks were salvaged for replacement parts. There were no replacements for the men. As training progressed, both men and aircraft, especially the latter, were consumed. The military grapevine began to transmit the libelous rumor that Chennault's volunteers would not, as worded in a wire from T. V. Soong, "be ready before February 1942 and will not last two weeks in combat. Your comment requested."

Chennault's printable comment was that the group

would be ready by November 1941. He was correct, although by this time he had only forty-three operational P-40s and eighty-four pilots. Of these "survivors," Erikson E. Shilling (who doubled also as Group Photo Officer) conceived the idea of decorating the remaining P-40s with a blood-red mouth, shark teeth, and an evil eye in the radiator area. The Japanese, Shilling was certain, would be superstitious about the shark and the evil eye. This was not original with Shilling, of course, for the British had so decorated their P-40s and the Germans had used similar designs on their Ju-87 Stuka and the Me-110. At the same time someone with Hollywood connections had approached the Walt Disney studios for an idea of an identifying insignia. A Disney artist came up with a cunning leaping tiger, with tiny wings, jumping through a V, the V for Victory sign popularized by Churchill. It was from this insignia that the popular name Flying Tiger came into currency, although the group was already called that before the design had been drawn, possibly because of the tiger shark connotation.

Chennault divided the remaining men and planes into three squadrons. The first, called "Adam and Eve," was commanded by Robert J. Sandell, an ex-Army pilot from San Antonio, Texas; the second, "Panda Bear," was led by John Van Kuren Newkirk, formerly of the Navy and Scarsdale, New York; "Hell's Angels" was the popular name of the third squadron, which was under the leadership of Arvid Olson, a Californian and onetime Army pilot.

Despite this paper readiness, the Flying Tigers had not yet tangled with the Japanese in November, as Chennault had predicted; nor, for that matter, did they join in battle immediately after the Pearl Harbor attack. Wisely, Chennault did not wish to send his pilots into combat until they had the fullest possible preparation. There were other considerations: a promised delivery of supplies had not materialized in November and there was an acute shortage of aircraft, ammunition, and parts.

II

Curiously, the popular belief continues that the Flying Tigers fought against the Japanese before the Pearl Harbor debacle. In fact, nearly two weeks passed—during which the Americans who fought back, especially in the Philippines, suffered badly—before the Flying Tigers encountered Japanese planes for the first time.

On December 10 Chennault initiated the evacuation of the Kyedaw airdrome. Arvid Olson led the Hell's Angels (i.e., the 3rd Squadron), consisting of twenty-four pilots and twenty-one Tomahawks, south to Mingaladon, near Rangoon, to co-operate with the RAF in protecting the port from Japanese aerial attacks. This handful of men and planes were added to another handful in No. 67 Squadron, a British fighter squadron equipped mainly with the Brewster Buffalo (later they were to receive Hurricanes). The remaining two AVG squadrons left for the main base at Kunming, China, on December 18, some flying their operational aircraft and others, mainly ground personnel, taking to the Burma Road in trucks and other vehicles. "The departing travelers," observed Russell Whelan in his story of the group, "shed no tears as they looked their last on Toungoo, that suburb of Gehenna."

Kunming was no Garden of Eden either, although the AVG base had been rather sumptuously appointed with fine living quarters, a library, a good hospital, tennis courts, and a baseball diamond (Chennault was an ardent proponent of physical conditioning). But Kunming, capital of the Yunnan province, had been bombed by the Japanese just prior to the arrival of the Americans. With a population of more than 500,000, Kunming was an enticing target for Japanese Army air units based in French Indo-China. From former French air bases formations of Kates, escorted either by Claudes or Zeros, came over to bomb Kunming, and like most oriental cities, it burned with a lovely light, or so it appeared to those flying safely above the shambles. It was this destruction, rather than a quaint Chinese city, that the Flying Tigers first saw when they came to the Yunnan province.

The following day, December 19, 1941, was uneventful while the 1st Squadron waited impatiently in the ready shack. The next morning the Adam and Eves took the morning patrol—five P-40s and Squadron Leader Robert Sandell in his plane. But the sky remained clear of the enemy. The six men, tense, almost disgusted by the inaction, landed to refuel. It was then that the radio crackled and word came through that a formation of Mitsubishis (Sallys) appeared to be headed for Kunming and were then about sixty miles away. Chennault immediately ordered Newkirk and three others of his Panda Bear squadron up to protect the field. As soon as Newkirk sighted the enemy formation, he radioed Chennault, who then dispatched Sandell and thirteen others to intercept.

Within moments the Flying Tigers and the Japanese met in battle for the first time. The bombers, confident after so many uncontested months, had no fighter escort. The Tigers approached the Sallys from above—the Japanese planes unconcernedly flying in a beautiful flat-V formation. Sandell had spotted "ten enemy two-engined bombers, single tail, aluminum construction—and that red sun on the wing tips." The Tigers, as per Chennault's teaching, attacked in pairs, leaving a "weaver" above to look out for the unexpected appearance of fighters.

At Sandell's signal the dozen P-40s pounced upon the neat Japanese formation. Fritz E. Wolf (Shawano, Wisconsin) "attacked the outside bomber of the V. Diving down below him, I came up underneath, guns ready for the minute I could get in range. At 500 yards I let go with a quick burst from all my guns [four .30 caliber in the wings and two .50s in the upper nose]. I could see my bullets rip into the rear gunner. My plane bore in closer. At 100 yards I let go with a burst into the bomber's gas tanks and engine. A wing folded and a motor tore loose. Then the bomber exploded. I yanked back on the stick to get out of the way and went upstairs. . . ."

Selecting another bomber, Wolf dived down again. Pulling up behind he watched the Japanese rear gunner frantically firing, but felt no hits. He closed in to within fifty yards before letting loose with his full battery of guns, concentrating on one of the Mitsubishi's engines. Flame and smoke wisped into the slipstream, followed by a blossom of fire, and the Japanese bomber was ripped to pieces in a violent orange-red explosion. Wolf kicked rudder and dived away from the massive zone of flame and debris.

The Tigers swooped into the bomber formation from all directions, confusing the gunners but not disrupting the symmetry of the formation itself. Chennault had been right, the Japanese flew almost mechanically. When a bomber fell burning, another plane gracefully moved in to tighten the formation. In an attack on the formation Edward Rector

Edward Rector of Marshall, North Carolina (in a post-Flying Tiger portrait), flight leader of the 2nd ("Panda Bears") Pursuit Squadron. Rector remained with the Flying Tigers even after it was officially disbanded in 1942.

(U. S. OFFICE OF WAR INFORMATION)

(Marshall, North Carolina) sliced under the Mitsubishis, got one, and took a burst of fire himself. His smoking Tomahawk was last seen by other Tigers under control; obviously Rector was seeking an emergency landing place. There were few of these in the thick jungle below.

Finally, after perhaps twenty minutes or so, with ammunition gone, or guns jammed, the Tigers, excepting Rector, returned to the Kunming base. They had lost one, but the Japanese had lost six, and even some of the remaining four Mitsubishis limped back toward Hanoi trailing smoke. It was a very good score, but Chennault's laconic comment was, "It was a good job . . . next time get them all."

A search party went out to look for Rector but had to return empty-handed when darkness enveloped the jungle. The next morning Rector himself phoned from a nearby town. He had crash-landed the P-40 in the jungle, had somehow managed to

Arvid E. Olson, Jr., Los Angeles, California, squadron leader of the 3rd ("Hell's Angels") Pursuit Squadron, AVG. (U. S. OFFICE OF WAR INFORMATION)

find his way to the town, and was on his way back to Kunming with only minor injuries. The first Tiger encounter with the Japanese had proved an almost total victory. But Chennault cautioned them; the next time there would be fighter escort. But they had learned, too, of the Japanese aircraft's susceptibility to fire because of the lack of self-sealing fuel tanks.

Meanwhile, a thousand miles away in Rangoon, the men of the Hell's Angels fretted, anxious about the presence of the Japanese. Certainly Burma lay in the path of the conquering juggernaut of Japan. The victories at Kunming only galled them more. Finally, on the morning of December 23, 1941, the not very efficient air raid sirens of Rangoon sounded, but after the exciting scramble no bombers appeared in the sky. Before noon the sirens wailed again. Antiaircraft fire was seen bursting irregularly in the sky over Rangoon, and the distant *chunk* of bombs bursting on the ground signaled that the Japanese planes had truly arrived.

At Mingaladon airdrome the Tigers and the RAF roared into action: about twenty-seven Allied aircraft, P-40s and Buffalos, swept up to meet the bombers. The first wave consisted of eighteen bombers and the second of about thirty. The latter was escorted by a large swarm of twenty Zeros.

The Tigers leaped upon the second formation, concentrating upon the bombers, hoping to disrupt their formations before they could release their bomb loads. The British pilots, in their Buffalos, gallantly went for the Zeros. First blood of the bomber formation went to Kenneth Jernstedt (Yamhill, Oregon), who destroyed one of the bombers in his first diving attack. His wingman was Henry Gilbert (Lovell, Wyoming), at twenty-one the youngest of the Flying Tigers. As he dived Gilbert shot out bursts at a couple of bombers, striking them but without hitting vital spots. In the attack, his P-40 was hit by a cannon shell and screamed out of the battle to crash into the jungle below. There had been no parachute and Henry Gilbert was the first Flying Tiger to die in combat.

The second fatality came soon after. Charles Older (Los Angeles) had flared one of the bombers, which burst into an inferno of detonating ammunition and bombs. Neil Martin's (Texarkana, Arkansas) P-40 flew into the spewing mass and followed the wreckage of the bomber to the ground.

Older by then had whirled about to shoot another bomber out of the air, which had become turbulent, fiery, and confused as fighter attacked bomber and fighter attacked fighter. The Zeros joined in the tumbling and soon Tiger Paul Greene (Glendale, California) found himself beset by Zeros. The nimble craft danced around him, firing into the P-40 until the plane took fire. Greene swooped the P-40 onto its back and dropped out of the cockpit. But once his chute had opened, one of the Zeros had flipped around to deal with Greene, dangling helplessly in the chute. Frantically grabbing at the chute risers, Greene managed to avoid the bullets, but the chute itself was holed. As a result Greene landed so forcefully that he injured his spine.

Greene's plane, of course, was lost, as were those of Gilbert and Martin. Another, piloted by George McMillan, was wiped out when he came in for a landing, although he escaped injury. The Tigers, therefore, had lost two men and four aircraft in their first air battle over Rangoon. Five RAF Buffalos, with pilots, had fallen to Japanese guns. The Japanese lost six bombers (probably with five-man crews) and four fighters. It was, then, a victory for the Tigers and the RAF. But Rangoon had been heavily bombed by the first wave of bombers. Fires raged and the toll was high—at least two thousand killed. The looting of corpses and sacking of dwellings in the bombed-out sections of the city somehow seemed more horrifying than the merciless bombing itself. The Burmese harbored little fidelity to the English and loved the Indians and Chinese only a little more.

Two days later, Christmas Day 1941, the Japanese returned. There was scant advance warning, for the single radar unit then operating in Burma was hardly sufficient (to say the least) and was further burdened by out-of-date equipment and an inefficient telephone service.

To circumvent this handicap, Squadron Leader Arvid Olson had put up a trio of P-40s for aerial reconnaissance. George McMillan, who had lost a plane in the battle two days before, sighted a large bomber force approaching Rangoon. About sixty miles from the city, there were about eighty bombers and twenty fighters. McMillan immediately radioed the base; at about the same moment the RAF received its report.

Thirteen P-40s and fifteen Buffalos were rushed aloft in an attempt to gain altitude before the bombers reached the city. About ten miles from Rangoon, the Japanese force divided—about half proceeding on to Rangoon and the rest heading for Mingaladon airdrome. The Tigers dived at the stream heading for the city, leaving the RAF's Buffalos the thirty or so bombers aiming for Mingaladon.

The Tigers, employing Chennault's hit-and-run technique, knifed through the bomber formation at top speed, snapping bursts into the Japanese aircraft and avoiding entanglement with the Zeros as much as possible. Within minutes of their first assault, five Japanese bombers blazed into the rice paddies below. But almost immediately another formation hove into view, this time twenty bombers with eight fighters. There was no lack of targets: a total of 28 Allied planes opposed 108 Japanese bombers and fighters.

Robert Smith (Los Angeles), having dived through the initial formation, had no time to gain altitude, so he attacked the new wave from below. The Nakajima practically blew up in Smith's face, pockmarking his P-40 with bits of engine. The Tomahawk staggered momentarily but Smith got it under control and dived into the battle again. Edmund Overend (Coronado, California) was not as fortunate. Although he had succeeded in ripping the

wing off one of the bombers, he had run into gunfire which jammed his controls and interfered with his maneuverability. A Zero darted onto his tail and Overend had good reason to be grateful for the armor plating which lined the back of the cockpit. Exploiting this safety factor, plus the P-40's diving speed, he left his attacker behind. But then he realized he did not have enough fuel for the return flight to Mingaladon. Rather than abandon the plane, Overend set the P-40, wheels up, into a swamp. Within hours he was back at the airdrome to learn of the battle's outcome.

Of the thirteen Tomahawks which had taken off, eleven had returned to Mingaladon, including one piloted by Parker Dupouy (Farmingdale, New York) with four feet of wing gone. When his guns jammed, Dupouy had a Zero on his tail. Kicking the P-40 around abruptly, Dupouy rid himself of the harassing fighter by colliding with it. The Zero collapsed and fell, but Dupouy made it back to the base.

Like Overend, George McMillan had been knocked out of the battle but had crashed into the jungle and returned on the following day, nursing an injured ankle, in an oxcart. In exchange for the two P-40s, the Tigers were officially credited with destroying thirteen bombers and ten fighters. Other Japanese aircraft had also been destroyed but fell into the Gulf of Martaban and could not be confirmed. The RAF pilots were credited with six bombers and the thwarting of serious damage to the base. The cost to No. 67 Squadron was five pilots and their Buffalos. The total Japanese loss was at least twenty-nine aircraft, most of them bombers, or about a third of the attacking force. It was a most disproportionate exchange.

However, the Christmas Day bombing of Rangoon proved even more vicious than that of December 23, the casualty toll reaching as high as five thousand dead. But Japanese losses impressed the enemy and large bomber formations stayed away from Rangoon for a while. During this uneasy period thousands fled the city, causing near paralysis of its functions and vital services—including the movement of supplies up to the Burma Road. But in time a local paper could announce a return to near normality with: "Daylight robberies have started again."

During the lull Olson's 3rd Squadron was relieved

Pilots race for their P-40s. (These are not, of course, Flying Tigers, but the base is in China and re-creates the action of a Tiger interception.) (U. S. AIR FORCE)

by Newkirk's 2nd (Panda Bear) Squadron, which arrived at Mingaladon by December 29, 1941. The Japanese bombers and fighters came back in force on the same day. Again a handful of Tigers in their P-40s and the British in their lumbering Buffalos rose to meet the formations, which as on Christmas Day split in two to strike at both Rangoon and Mingaladon. The bombers this trip, however, succeeded in getting to the air base in addition to contributing to the panic and waste in Rangoon. But again the losses for the Japanese were off balance, the Tigers claiming eighteen and the British seven. One P-40 flown by Allen Christman (Fort Collins, Colorado) was lost in the encounter, but Christman parachuted to safety. The RAF lost six pilots with their planes. By this time the Americans had begun to appreciate the ruggedness of the P-40s and no longer envied the British in their Buffalos.

Burma had become an aerial thorn in the side to the Japanese. All other aerial battlefields—over the Philippines, Malaya, Hong Kong—were dominated by Japanese bombers and the superb Zero fighters. Only the "American renegades" and a squadron of the RAF Buffalos (rapidly depleting) seemed capable of spoiling the succession of Japanese victories.

The Japanese closed the year with a change in tactics. First a small formation came over to lure off the Tigers and the RAF, and then a larger formation would follow at about the time the defenders would have to return to the ground to refuel and rearm. There was more concentration also on Mingaladon. On the first attempt seventeen Allied planes were dispatched to fend off about sixty Japanese attackers. Fifteen of these, officially, did not return to their base at Hanoi.

By January 1, 1942, the Flying Tigers had sixty confirmed victories to their credit. It prompted a tribute to them, and to Chennault, via Radio Tokyo: "We warn the American aviators at Rangoon that they must cease their unorthodox tactics immediately, or they will be treated like guerrillas and shown no mercy whatsoever." Radio Tokyo also inflated the forces of the AVG—man and planes; the victory claims over them, if true, would have wiped out Chennault's small band three or four times over.

But they were not supermen. At besieged Rangoon hunger was added to their other discomforts, among which were fatigue and illness. And they contributed further to their fame as "no angels" in the bars of Rangoon, which seemed more impervious to the ill fortunes of war than most other businesses. It became a tiresome war, almost without purpose and without hope of victory. To the men in Burma it seemed obvious that their fate was but a secondary consideration in the larger strategies. Supplies, tools, materials of all kinds only trickled in. Their P-40s before long had become a patchwork of scraps. Engines, rejects to begin with, wheezed and smoked and maintenance became a heroic epic in itself.

The truth was that the China-Burma-India theater of operations did rank low on the priorities lists. Churchill and Roosevelt had met and resolved that the major enemy was Nazi Germany and that first considerations in terms of strategic thinking, men, and supplies would be devoted to that philosophy. The Pacific, meanwhile, was subsidiary, with the beleaguered China-Burma-India area at the bottom of the list. Even those supplies that were eked out for delivery on the Burma Road often were intercepted en route and "requisitioned" by other services and areas.

It was then with a feeling of being neglected stepchildren that the Flying Tigers took to the air day after day to fight overwhelming numbers of Japanese. Though they fought remarkably, miraculously well, the end, so far as Burma was concerned, was inevitable. Unknown to the Tigers, the political situation would affect them. Churchill had hoped to reinforce the British garrisons in Burma but to his

David L. "Tex" Hill of Hunt, Texas, squadron leader of the "Panda Bears" (2nd). Hill's score was more than a dozen Japanese aircraft.
(U. S. OFFICE OF WAR INFORMATION)

bitterness he was refused an Australian division which he had wanted to send to Burma. This left a Burmese army to confront the surging Japanese.

Late in December, Chiang Kai-shek, realizing what a Japanese invasion of Burma would mean to the Burma Road, offered to send Chinese troops to help in its defense. But Sir Archibald Wavell, the commander in Burma, demurred. He had no love for Chiang and little confidence in Chinese troops. He had other complexities, for the Burmese resented and detested the British as well as the Chinese, believing that such allies were a greater threat than the bringers of the Greater East Asia Co-Prosperity Sphere.

The Tigers, too, with the New Year, changed their tactics: they went over to the offensive. On January 3, 1942, John Newkirk led Noel Bacon (Randalia, Iowa) and David Hill (Hunt, Texas; Hill was, naturally, called "Tex") on a strafing mission. Leaving Mingaladon while it was still dark, the three Tigers swept in upon the Japanese base at Tak, Thailand (about two hundred miles east and slightly north of Rangoon). But as Newkirk gunned the Japanese planes parked along the runways, about a half-dozen enemy fighters, already air-borne, tumbled out of the clouds upon the attacking Tigers. One of the Japanese fighters attached itself to Newkirk's tail as he, unaware of it, hammered at the grounded aircraft. Bacon came to his leader's aid and began shooting at the plane shooting at Newkirk. In turn, Bacon was attacked and Tex Hill swooped in to his aid. Another Japanese fighter joined the train as Newkirk, leading a formation of shooting aircraft, gave his full attention to strafing the men and planes on the ground. So intent was he on his "work" that he was still unconscious of the drama unfolding in his wake. Bacon shot the fighter off Newkirk's tail and Hill cleared Bacon's tail and whipped around to destroy another Japanese fighter. Hill, however, had his share of problems, for a fuel tank had been punctured in such a manner that it did not seal and he was losing gas; in addition he was out of ammunition. Hill had to streak for home while Newkirk and Bacon continued strafing Tak. Soon they too pulled away and flew westward.

Upon landing at Mingaladon, they were greeted by Hill, who congratulated Newkirk upon his flying skill, which had so frustrated the Japanese fighter

James H. Howard, St. Louis, Missouri, squadron leader at one time of the "Panda Bears"; Howard later transferred to the Ninth Air Force in Europe (when this photograph was taken). (U. S. AIR FORCE)

on his tail over Tak. Newkirk found this unbelievable until he checked the tail section of the Tomahawk and found more than twenty bullet punctures in it.

While the three Tigers had been strafing Tak, others had intercepted a large formation of Japanese fighters near Rangoon. Two had gone down in an early attack, but five of them concentrated on Allen Christman's P-40. The deadly cross fire shredded the plane's rudder and ripped out an aileron. The plane lurched out of control so that Christman was for the second time forced to jump. But the Japanese, who so heartily condemned the "unorthodox tactics of the American renegades," were not finished with Christman. They bore down on him as he floated under his chute, gunning him as they flashed by. Seeing this, George Paxton (Abilene, Texas) rushed in to aid the helpless Christman. Although he succeeded in driving off the Japanese fighter, in the encounter Paxton was wounded in the arms and legs and had to leave for the base.

The other Tigers, infuriated by the attack upon Christman, attacked the remaining Japanese so ferociously that they drove them off. But this was only a temporary reprieve for Christman. Twenty days later—January 23, 1942—he was once again forced to leave his seriously damaged Tomahawk during an air battle and was later discovered dead in a rice paddy. He and his parachute were riddled.

Early in January, probably because of the mauling their formations took, the Japanese introduced another innovation: night bombing. None of the aircraft at Mingaladon were equipped for night flying, so the Japanese bombers came over, took careful aim, enjoyed a fine bomb run, and generally ranged over Rangoon unmolested. The only antiaircraft fire of any consequence came from the warships in the river—and these guns were of little use above three thousand feet. On January 8 an attempt was made to intercept the bombers, but it was a vain attempt. Also, in trying to land in the dark, Peter Wright, blinded by gushing hydraulic fluid from a damaged landing gear, lost control of the Tomahawk. The plane veered off the runway and skidded into a parked car. Wright was not seriously injured but Kenneth Merritt, who had been asleep in the vehicle, died in the flaming wreckage.

It was the day's second loss, for during a strafing attack upon Meshot airdrome, Charles Mott's Tomahawk, evidently hit by ground fire, streaked flame. Mott parachuted to safety—and imprisonment for the duration.

The next day's strafe proved more successful. Newkirk and four other Tigers, accompanied by six RAF Buffalos, paid a return visit to Tak. When all planes pulled away safely they left behind at least two dozen burned Japanese aircraft, three burned-out trucks, and a pocked, windowless administration building.

In mid-January Chennault sent reinforcements from Kunming. Robert Sandell flew down with five others of the 1st Squadron; among these was Gregory Boyington. Shortly after, an additional eight men flew in to bring relief to the exhausted men of 2nd Squadron.

Boyington was happy to be away from Kunming, where he had not endeared himself to Chennault's second-in-command, Harvey Greenlaw. Greenlaw's experiences in China, begun in 1932 with the arrival of the unofficial Jouett air mission, no doubt

*P-40s over the unfriendly, mountainous terrain of China,
the "theater of operations" of the Flying Tigers.*
(U. S. AIR FORCE)

made him useful to Chennault. Greenlaw's wife,
Olga, was listed on the AVG roster as "War Diary
Statistician." According to Boyington, her husband
was not very popular with the pilots. He had acquired the rank of lieutenant colonel, in the Chinese
Air Force, and had a penchant for threatening one
and all with immediate court-martial for minor as
well as major breaches in discipline. The Flying
Tigers found discipline, except in the air, a most
unimportant commodity in their forgotten theater
of operations. Boyington could not bring himself to
take Greenlaw and his threats seriously either. From
time to time he found himself snarling at Greenlaw,
"Get lost, Greenlaw, or I'll bend your teeth."

That there were personality problems among the
Flying Tigers was of course normal, if not in keeping with the legend of dedication and self-sacrifice to
the Cause as propounded in the semifictional newspaper accounts of the time. Considering their living
and fighting conditions, it is surprising that they managed to fight at all—let alone not clash from time
to time with one another. The Flying Tigers, they
themselves would have conceded, had more than

their fair share of mavericks—it was the very nature
of the unit. They even, though rarely, had a coward
or two. Boyington must be included among the more
colorful mavericks.

In his first encounter with the enemy, however,
Boyington came away profoundly disappointed with
himself. He had taken off as part of a ten-plane formation. Two of the planes, led by veteran Louis
Hoffman (San Diego, California), at forty-three the
oldest member of the Flying Tigers, served as top
cover. The other eight, presumably led by another
veteran, were to deal with any Japanese planes.
It was too late when Boyington realized they were
being led into combat for the first time by one of
their own inexperienced number. They then stum-
bled upon a large formation, perhaps forty or fifty
Japanese fighters with fixed landing gears (either
Nates or Claudes), within minutes after taking off.

Their formation "leader" blindly led them directly beneath the Japanese planes flying about two
thousand feet above them. Between the misled Tigers and the Japanese flew Hoffman and the other
pilot, both oblivious to the danger overhead, assuming that the "leader" knew what he was doing.

Boyington, twisting his head, looked up in time
to see the Japanese planes begin to peel off to dive

A helping hand: Chinese warn American pilots of the presence of Japanese aircraft in the vicinity. An elaborate if primitive but most effective warning system was devised by Chennault. If he received desultory co-operation from Chinese officials, Chennault was graciously treated by the Chinese people.

(U. S. AIR FORCE)

upon the P-40s. Hoffman's plane took a heavy pounding and fell straight down. The remaining Tigers scattered in all directions, like startled minnows. Suddenly Boyington found himself all alone in a wide, empty sky—except for Japanese fighter planes determined to shoot him out of it. Smarting under the ignominy of it, Boyington put the P-40's diving ability to full use: he ran for his life. Then he relearned something he forgot in the confusion of the moment: never try to outturn a lighter aircraft, or attempt to dogfight with a more maneuverable aircraft. Also, that day Boyington learned something they were not telling the folks back home. The Japanese were very skilled pilots who obviously did not suffer from myopia and could shoot.

Boyington fired at the darting little planes, but did not succeed in knocking one down. The rattle of return fire sounded ominously funereal. The P-40

tossed under the strike of an incendiary shell which came into the cockpit, pinking Boyington's arm—although he was not aware of it at the time. When he landed the shell stuck into his sleeve and had burned his arm slightly. Boyington was so upset by his performance that he hardly found the wound worth mentioning.

Hoffman had crashed near the field and was buried the next day; he had left a wife and two children. The day after that, January 28, 1942, Boyington, having been introduced to the facts of war, went into battle again. He was a member of the same formation, excepting Hoffman of course, that had been in the earlier battle. But this time he came in from above. Still terribly affected by the death of Hoffman, the Tigers fought savagely. Boyington destroyed two planes himself. During the battle he heard a voice over his radio shouting, "This is for

Cokey [Hoffman], you son of a bitch!" Sixteen Japanese aircraft never left the vicinity of Rangoon on that day.

To the residents of Rangoon, particularly the English colony, it was, as Boyington put it bitterly, "a bloody good show." But they lived in a vacuum and on borrowed time. Certain that the Empire would win the last round as it had always, according to tradition, they merely waited for that final day. They were unaware, or seemed to be, that the only battle being won was the small one in the air over Rangoon. On the ground the invading Japanese approached inexorably.

The last bastion of the Burra Sahib was the Mingaladon Golf Club, but even that fell to the invasion of boisterous young pilots, British and American. This was most disturbing, for the youngsters laughed loudly, shouted vulgarly, drank the whisky, and bought up the cigarettes. The managing member was approached by a delegation ordering him to see that the sale of cold beer and cigarettes to "the young roughnecks" be stopped. After all, he was reminded, "the members' needs must be considered first. If we sell our stocks to all these young fellows there'll be nothing left for the members."

The members were in fact running out of everything, including time.

On January 20, 1942, two divisions of the Japanese Fifteenth Army had crossed the Thai frontier at Moulmein; within ten days they had flanked the Indian division defending the area and had taken the city. The Japanese now had a firm foothold in Burma. The handwriting was on the clubhouse wall and the roof about to fall in.

Not until mid-February was it deemed crucial enough to accept Generalissimo Chiang Kai-shek's offer of aid, which took the form of two crack units, the Chinese Fifth and Sixth Armies. But it was already too late, even as they moved southward toward Rangoon. Also arriving too late was Lieutenant General Joseph W. Stilwell, who had been appointed chief of staff to Chiang Kai-shek. The outspoken, fifty-nine-year-old, gruff Stilwell, an expert in Chinese affairs (he spoke and wrote the language), was descending into a political-military miasma. There was little love lost between Chiang Kai-shek (and of course the Madame) and the British, who were, in fact, doing most of the fighting in the theater.

III

High-level decisions also spelled trouble for Chennault. Plans had already been made to establish a Tenth U. S. Air Force in the China-Burma-India theater with Brigadier General Clayton Bissell in command. The Flying Tigers would, it was proposed, be absorbed into this command as the 23rd Fighter Group. Chennault would then be subordinate to Bissell. Neither Chennault nor Chiang found this ideal. Quickly a feud between Bissell and Chennault developed. Stilwell, soon enough, found himself entangled in it besides developing an antipathy to Chiang and feuding, in turn, with Chennault also.

On February 14, 1942, Stilwell left the United States for this prickly assignment. There being yet no efficient Air Transport Command, his long voyage was confused, miserable, and meandering. On the day his plane took off from Miami for Africa, Singapore, the impregnable, fell to the Japanese. In his diary Stilwell had written, "Events are forcing all concerned to see the vital importance of Burma." By the time Stilwell landed in India, on February 25, the fall of Rangoon—and of Burma—was only days away. Perhaps Burma was of vital importance, but Stilwell had neglected to consider other elements besides Japanese terrorism—namely a crumbling colonialism, feudalism, and the infinite capacity for pettiness among the great.

The state of the tattered Flying Tigers at Rangoon was low too. "Where, oh where is the U. S. Army?" one Tiger noted in his diary. "Where, oh where is General Wavell? Does the First Squadron of the A.V.G. and a few R.A.F. kids have to handle the whole Japanese invasion?" Men as well as machines had begun to wear dangerously. Robert J. Sandell, commander of the 1st Squadron, was killed testing his newly repaired Tomahawk. Robert H. Neale (Seattle, Washington) succeeded Sandell as leader of the Adam and Eves, and now commanded the AVG effort in Burma. His command, in late February, consisted of ten weary pilots, nine overworked ground crew men, and seven wearier P-40s. The British had three Buffalos, four P-40s, and twenty Hurricanes.

The evacuation of Rangoon began in earnest around February 20, 1942, although it had initiated with the first bombings. Now the road to the north and the river were choked with refugees and every description of vehicle. The dacoits (professional thieves) preyed upon the refugees, Burmese as well as British, killing them for their few possessions and money. Rangoon itself was shambles.

O. D. Gallagher described the final blistering days: "With few exceptions the normal civilian population had gone, including the fire-brigade and all municipal employees. The empty streets were patrolled by troops carrying tommy-guns and rifles. The only other inhabitants were criminals, criminal lunatics and lepers."

One civil service officer, having misread his instructions pertaining to the evacuation of Rangoon, had inadvertently released five thousand convicts upon the already afflicted city. "At night," Gallagher recalled, "they made Rangoon a city of the damned. They prowled the deserted streets in search of loot. When they were seen looting they were shot by the soldiers." As for the diseased— "Lepers and lunatics wandered about aimlessly in search of food some sharing pickings of the refuse-heaps with the many mongrel dogs." Fires, set by looters or by the owners of property themselves who did not want the Japanese to take over their homes, raged through the city. Military demolition contributed to the holocaust. Ammunition, fuel, and other supplies which might be put to use by the Japanese went up in smoke. Looters destroyed medical supplies on the docks. It seemed to them there was no possible use for the small bottles except to throw them against walls of buildings. The more volatile liquids exploded and burned wastefully, chokingly, to the gleeful laughter of the now maddened Burmese.

This was the final deranged scene that the few remaining Tigers, the last defenders of Rangoon— for the British had pulled out three days before —witnessed before they scrambled away to a new base at Magwe, farther north. Neale led a formation of the few operational Tomahawks; the rest, pilots and ground crew under crew chief Harry Fox, piled themselves and their equipment into whatever trucks they could commandeer and took to the north road. In one of the last air battles over Rangoon Edward J. Liebolt's plane had been shot up so that he had to take to his parachute. He floated down into captivity, for by then Japanese troops had all but encircled Rangoon.

Rangoon fell on March 7, 1942; at Magwe the Tigers and the RAF dug in. The remnants of the

Burma Army escaped up the Irrawaddy River toward Prome. The Chinese armies coming south were still of no help. Chiang and Stilwell had an early disagreement over the disposition of these troops: Chiang believed they should attempt to hold Mandalay; Stilwell thought it would be better to reinforce the British farther south and to keep, if possible, the Japanese from ever getting to Mandalay.

By March 20 reconnaissance planes reported that Japanese planes were already based at Mingaladon. The British quickly dispatched ten old Hurricanes and nine Blenheims to bomb their former base. Arriving unexpectedly the small force succeeded in destroying sixteen planes on the ground and, in the ensuing air battle, a further eleven in the air. Of these, two were knocked down by the Blenheims. It was a blow in the face to the conquering Japanese.

Retaliation came the following day and continued into the next. On the morning of March 21, with but little advance warning, the first wave of ten Japanese bombers, with an escort of twenty fighters, came over Magwe. Five planes rose to meet them, three Tigers (William Reed, Kenneth Jernstedt, and Parker Dupouy) and two Hurricanes. Even as their engines labored to get the five aircraft high enough to meet the attackers, more enemy bombers and fighters came in from the northeast. Bomb bursts erupted on the airdrome as the Tigers dived into the Japanese formations.

Dupouy, on his first pass, slashed a Zero out of a seven-plane formation, only to find himself besieged by the remaining six. These whirred and darted about his P-40 until Dupouy himself was struck. He dived for Magwe. Reed had already suffered the same fate and had returned to the field also. Jernstedt careened into a formation of ten bombers, the guns of which focused on his plane and rapidly sieved it, wounding the pilot. Jernstedt too was forced to return to the doubtful "safety" of besieged Magwe.

Soon, also, one of the Hurricanes came scurrying in, attempted to set down on the bomb-pocked runway, struck a hole, overturned, and came to a grinding crash near a slit trench occupied by some of the Tigers. Frank N. Swartz (Dunmore, Pennsylvania), John Fauth (Red Lion, Pennsylvania), and a ground crew man, William Seiple, scrambled from the trench to pull the British pilot out of the Hurricane. As they ran a bomb explosion caught them and all three went down. Dr. Lewis Richards, surgeon of the Tigers, left the trench to administer to Swartz, who appeared to be injured most seriously. Richards then had Fauth and Seiple pulled into the trench and he, despite the bursting bombs and strafing Zeros, placed Swartz into a jeep and raced to the base hospital. Fauth died the next morning and Swartz and Seiple were evacuated to Calcutta, but Swartz later died of his wounds. Magwe itself was a ruin—besides damage to the buildings and runways, six P-40s, eight Hurricanes and three Blenheims had gone up in smoke.

The next day brought more of the same; remaining at Magwe was pointless. Some of the Tigers flew their flyable aircraft farther north to Loiwing. The RAF remained longer in a vain attempt to hold off the Japanese but they too were quickly overwhelmed. More planes were damaged and five of the surviving P-40s had to be evacuated to Loiwing by truck. The British fled to the west, to Akyab on the Bay of Bengal and eventually to India, out of harm's way, to attempt a recovery. Except for the few impoverished Tigers at Loiwing, it was the end of air power in Burma.

Driven out of Burma, the RAF flew to India and the Tigers returned to Kunming. Chennault then planned a surprise raid on the major Japanese air base at Chiengmai in central Thailand. To accomplish this, Chennault mustered a handful of men and aircraft of the 1st Squadron, led by Robert Neale, and the 2nd Squadron, led by John Van Kuren Newkirk: a total of ten P-40s.

Chiengmai lay beyond the range of the P-40 so the Tigers flew to a nearly deserted advance field at Nam Sang on March 23, and slept that night under the wings of their planes. They had gassed up for a long flight and took off in two sections before daybreak of the twenty-fourth. The plan was to rendezvous near Chiengmai (rather than approach it en masse, which would alert the Japanese) and then swoop down upon the base while it was still dark. The ground would be discernible from the air, though the Tigers' P-40s would be difficult to see from the ground.

For some reason the two groups missed the rendezvous. Neale's small unit of six planes arrived first, but there was no sign of Newkirk and his men. They were unable to wait: both the covering dark-

ness and surprise would be lost. Neale ordered William D. McGarry and Edward Rector up to twenty thousand feet to provide high cover and then, leading Boyington, William Bartling, and Charles Bond, dived on a fine concentration of Japanese aircraft below.

At twelve thousand feet they were met with vicious antiaircraft fire. Plunging through, luckily unhit, the four P-40s, their engines howling and guns chattering, spread fire among the planes and running figures. Flames shot up in their wake as they pulled up, banked, and came in for another pass. Now the field was alight with the fire of burning planes and they could better see their targets. But with more light also came more intense ground fire. Rifle and machine-gun slugs nicked and ripped at the Tomahawks.

To McGarry and Rector, observing the inferno from above, the excitement was too much to ignore. When the original quartet dived in for a third pass, the top-cover men plummeted down to contribute also. With all six guns hammering, the two extra Tomahawks intensified the flaming havoc as they ran the gamut of heavy ground fire. At least twenty fires were burning on the field and Neale knew it was time to get away. As they did the sky puffed with random bursts of antiaircraft.

McGarry obviously was in trouble, for his P-40 trailed smoke as they left Chiengmai. Though he tried desperately to keep the plane in flight, McGarry realized that with rapidly failing oil pressure he had no chance. But they were still fifty miles from the Salween River, inside Thailand. On the other side of the river lay the safety of the Chinese troops, but the oil pressure went completely and McGarry inverted the plane and parachuted into the jungle. (He was captured by the Siamese and turned over to the Japanese and remained a prisoner until the war ended.)

Meanwhile Newkirk, realizing that he and the Panda Bears had missed the rendezvous with the Adam and Eves, decided that they could attack another, nearby field while the 1st Squadron attended to Chiengmai. But they found no aircraft on the satellite airdrome so Newkirk pulled away and headed for Chiengmai also. On the way they strafed a railroad station, setting some warehouses afire. Newkirk then spotted two armored cars on a road. They were tempting targets and so, followed by Henry Geselbracht and Frank Lawlor, Newkirk dived upon the cars with all guns shuddering the P-40. As he shot over the cars, Newkirk's plane suddenly gushed flame. The stricken Tomahawk hurtled into the ground at full speed, trailing fire and molten metal, scorching a trail through the jungle before it came to rest, a blazing mass of crumpled metal. His wingmen found it hard to accept the death of "Scarsdale Jack" Newkirk, who had led the 2nd Squadron from the inception of the Flying Tigers. For miles, as they returned to China, they could see his black funeral pyre curling out of the green jungle of Thailand.

Newkirk's successor as commander of the 2nd

Kweilin, China, the last—and best—major base of the Flying Tigers. It had a mile-long runway, revetments for the protection of parked aircraft, and caves in the hills for men and machines. (U. S. AIR FORCE)

Somewhere in China: Lieutenant General Henry H. Arnold, Brigadier General Claire Chennault, his antagonist Lieutenant General Joseph Stilwell, British Field Marshal Sir John Dill, and Brigadier General Clayton L. Bissell. The latter's position in the China-Burma-India theater was a delicate one since he was placed in command over the veteran, and favorite of Chiang Kai-shek, Chennault. Bissell's careful attention to details in his planning earned him the nickname of "Old Woman" among the Chinese, accustomed to Chennault's more hell-for-leather approach. (U. S. AIR FORCE)

Squadron was James H. Howard (St. Louis, Missouri), an ex-Navy pilot of remarkable courage. Soft-spoken, undemonstrative, Howard had made an early impression upon the RAF pilots one day when he singlehandedly plowed into a large formation of Japanese fighters. Howard took his service in the Flying Tigers seriously; he had been born in China.

But they were locked obviously in a losing battle and, despite the Tiger victories, still remarkably disproportionate, the battle had come to seem so aimless. For every Japanese plane destroyed, another ten appeared to take its place. But there were no replacements for the Tigers—and new planes were hard to come by. A few P-40Es (Kittyhawks) had trickled in, but that was all. Exhausted, ill, or depressed, or just simply sickened by conditions, pilots and ground crew men resigned or were "dismissed."

Boyington was one of those who had his fill of fighting for Madame Chiang's China. A six-victory ace, he decided to get out and to have his commission in the Marine Corps reinstated—as had been secretly agreed upon when he signed up for the AVG. Chennault did not take an enlightened view of Boyington's wish to return to his old branch of the service. Boyington left, nonetheless, and worked his way homeward. He found, upon arriving at Karachi, India, requesting transportation by air, that Chennault, instead of authorizing air travel to the United States for Boyington, suggested that the black sheep be drafted into the Tenth Air Force as a second lieutenant. Boyington, steaming, booked passage on a ship bound for New York. His subsequent career in the Marine Corps speaks for itself, though he may have gone on the rolls of the Flying Tigers as a "deserter."

Chennault had other, more serious burdens as

well. The Burma Road was closed (necessitating the flying of supplies over "the Hump" of the Himalaya Mountains between India and China); Chiang Kai-shek and Stilwell detested each other; Madame Chiang demanded more help from the United States, broadly hinting from time to time of making a separate peace with Japan; and then there was Bissell, who would command the Tenth Air Force and Chennault along with it.

Bissell had appeared at Kunming to give a recruiting lecture which proved ill-timed and badly worded. Resentful, morale at low ebb, some of the Tigers trained a young Chinese boy to greet the ever growing number of Air Corps planes carrying brass with the phrase "Piss on Bissell, piss on Bissell." It did not impress Very Important Persons on the arriving aircraft with the state of American military discipline in China.

Chennault and Stilwell too had their disagreements, partly a question of rank (Stilwell being Chennault's superior), as well as the traditional hostility between the ground-oriented soldier and the air expert. Chennault had certainly proved himself, but Stilwell had little faith in the piecemeal air force at his disposal in Burma and China. Crusty and stubborn, he even refused to be evacuated by air from Burma with the Japanese hard on his trail. "The Air Force didn't bring me here," he declared, "and it doesn't have to fly me out. I'll walk." And he did.

"It's the ground soldier," he snapped at Chennault one day, "slogging through the mud and fighting in the trenches who will win the war!"

"But God damn it, Stilwell," Chennault rasped in cogent reply, "there aren't any men in the trenches!"

The men of the Flying Tigers, also, found conditions more and more difficult to take. Dispirited, wearied, repelled by Chinese corruption and indifference to loss of life, they became more disgruntled and found their sacrifices difficult to reconcile with their achievements.

Their relationship with Chennault even deteriorated and at one point, in a disagreement with an order from Chennault (to make a flight over Chinese troops to improve their morale), twenty-eight out of thirty-four Tigers resigned. Whereupon Chennault threatened to have anyone who attempted to leave Loiwing shot. Chennault later reconsidered and the

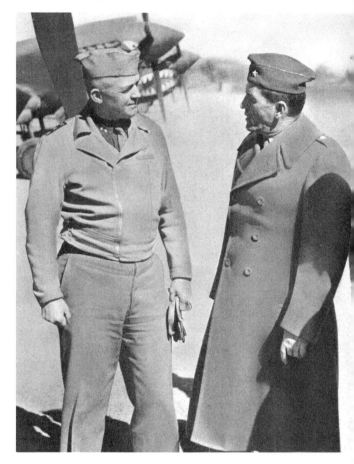

U. S. Air Force General Henry Arnold visits Chennault in China, shortly after the Flying Tigers had been disbanded. (U. S. AIR FORCE)

resignations were withdrawn, but the mood of the Tigers remained dismal.

It was the irascible Stilwell who summed up the Burma experience: "I claim we got a hell of a beating. We got run out of Burma and it was humiliating as hell. I think we ought to find out what caused it, go back and retake it."

The Tigers, withdrawn to Kunming, existed in military limbo. Their planes were barely operational and some pilots refused to fly them. They speculated upon their future—if any, in the Tenth Air Force. Many only wanted to return to their homes for a while before considering their military future. By May 1942 it seemed that they could contribute so little, with their few planes and exhausted men, to the war in China.

Meanwhile, U. S. Army Air Force brass had also invaded China. Some, men newly from civilian ranks, assumed that the "famous" Flying Tigers were bound to be a "bunch of prima donnas." As the day of contract expirations approached pressure was applied on both pilots and ground crews to transfer over to the U.S. air forces. One particularly arrogant recruitment speech, the gist of which was roughly: "join up now or be drafted a private as soon as your contracts expire," caused a small incident. Many Tigers simply got up and walked out on the high ranker with his mouth open. Such men, fresh from the States, eager to avenge Pearl Harbor, anxious to get on with the war, and undoubtedly a bit envious of the reputation and the actual achievements of the Flying Tigers, could not comprehend the weariness of the Tigers, or their anxiety to get home just once again before "getting on with the war," to recover from nagging illnesses caused by overwork, various tropical diseases, and malnutrition. When disbandment time came they simply wanted to go home for a while.

Radio Tokyo jubilated over the approaching end of the Tigers. A quick dispatch of their replacements in the green Tenth Air Force was joyously predicted by Tokyo Rose. But a transition had been in progress for a long time and the interim would not prove to be as vulnerable a period as Tokyo believed. Chennault was to remain in command of what would be called the China Air Task Force (under Bissell's Tenth Air Force), which would consist of the 23rd Fighter Group and the 11th Bombardment Squadron (M). Chennault had already selected his commander for the 23rd Fighter Group: Colonel Robert Scott. Scott, a Transport Command pilot who had been stranded in China and who had attached himself to the Tigers. Although at thirty-four he was considered overaged for a fighter pilot, Scott had proved himself in fact a "one-man air force" while on missions with the Tigers and on solo hunts.

The bomber squadron was equipped with North American B-25s, the famed Mitchells of the Doolittle Tokyo raid. (Eventually, in March 1943, though not without acrimony and torment, the China Air Task Force evolved into the Fourteenth Air Force, Major General Claire Lee Chennault commanding; the Tenth Air Force then confined its responsibilities to Burma and India.)

The official day of deactivation of the American Volunteer Group was July 4, 1942. By this time it was known that very few of the original Tigers had decided to remain in the China Air Task Force —just five pilots, David Hill, Edward Rector, Charles Sawyer, John G. Bright, and Frank Schiel, Jr., plus a few of the ground crew—that was all. Several pilots, rather than transfer into the U. S. Army, found jobs in China with China National Airways and with aviation industries. Others returned to their homes to rest and then, if they passed their physicals—which many did not—returned to their old branch of service.

Twenty pilots, to confute Radio Tokyo, offered to remain on duty with the 23rd Fighter Group under Scott during the transitional period. During this time one of the veteran pilots, John E. Petach (Perth Amboy, New Jersey), was killed in a dive-bombing attack upon gunboats in a lake near Nanchang. Petach had married Emma Jane Foster (State College, Pennsylvania), who had served, along with Josephine Stewart (Dallas, Texas), as a nurse in the American Volunteer Group.

The 23rd Fighter Group, known also as the Flying Tigers, continued in the tradition of their predecessors in defense of the air route over the Hump (as once the original Tigers had defended the Burma

Robert Scott, ex-transport pilot turned Flying Tiger. During the final days of the AVG Scott roamed the skies with the Tigers or alone and left a pile of Japanese planes in his wake. Scott remained with Chennault to command the 23rd Fighter Group.

(U. S. AIR FORCE)

Men of the 23rd Fighter Group, heirs to the traditions of the Flying Tigers: Colonel C. D. Vincent, Major Albert J. Baumler, Colonel H. E. Strickland, and

Brigadier General Claire L. Chennault, commander of the China Air Task Force (later to form the nucleus of the Fourteenth Air Force). (U. S. AIR FORCE)

Road) and chopped away at Japanese air strength in the China-Burma-India theater. After Scott left for other duties other commanders took over, among them Colonel David Hill, and later, Colonel Edward Rector, of the original AVG.

In the brief span of its operational existence, officially from December 18, 1941, to July 4, 1942, the Flying Tigers had destroyed 286 (confirmed) Japanese aircraft. The true toll would probably be closer to double that number, for many "kills" were not officially accepted when enemy aircraft plunged into thick jungle or water and could not be found. But even the officially accepted figure represents a great loss in terms of planes and men—for most were bombers with multiple crews. The cost to the

AVG was nine pilots (not counting Petach, who was lost after the dissolution of the AVG) and less than fifty P-40s. An additional nine pilots were killed in flying accidents and four were listed as missing in action.

The major contribution of the Flying Tigers, besides proving Chennault's tactical genius, was in the revelation that Japanese aerial invincibility was an illusion. During the early months of the Pacific war, while British and American defenses crumbled, the Flying Tigers, outnumbered, ill equipped, even ill used, but resilient, fought the Japanese and won. That they had done this may have been, in time, even more important than their accredited 286 Japanese aircraft at $500 per head.

3

FIRST SPECIAL AVIATION PROJECT

MAN'S CAPACITY for "the bold undertaking" is infinite; the romanticism, not the risk, is all. The challenge of unfavorable odds merely increases incentive and, once initiated, the venture is confronted as if success must be the only possible outcome. Risk, motivation, questioning uncertainty—all are submerged in what appears to be the logic of preparation.

So it was with the unique Doolittle raid on Tokyo and other Japanese cities in the spring of 1942, a dismal spring in the wake of a series of Japanese victories in the Pacific. As an expression of human ingenuity, courage, audacity, and daring the Doolittle mission was an immortal feat; as military strategy it was evanescent—but of extensive impact.

Lieutenant Colonel James H. Doolittle, however, on the day after the raid sat dejectedly in the wreckage of the plane that he had had to abandon, certain he would be tried by a military court. All sixteen aircraft which had participated in the attack had been lost; of the eighty men he had led, Doolittle could account for only five. And one of them was himself.

II

To strike back at Japan was all but an obsession in high governmental and military circles in the weeks and months following the Pearl Harbor attack. President Franklin D. Roosevelt rarely missed an opportunity to bring it up during his sessions with the Chiefs of Staff. It was, however, simpler to dwell upon than to execute. There were no land-based bombers near enough to Japan to bomb it. Carriers could not venture near enough to the Japanese home islands to launch their fighters and scout bombers without risking the loss of carriers—as well as the aircraft. However alluring the conception, it appeared to remain impracticable until bases could be established in China, or even Russia. Obviously the Philippines were already lost.

But with all the talk of vengeance in the air, someone was bound to offer some kind of suggestion. This came from the U. S. Navy's Captain Francis S. Low, an operations officer on the staff of Admiral Ernest J. King, Chief of Naval Operations. Low's

Architect of the "First Special Aviation Project," Captain Francis S. Low, operations officer on the staff of Admiral Ernest J. King. Low was the first to offer practical suggestions for activating an idea which a nation shared after the attack on Pearl Harbor: a bombing raid on Tokyo.

(NAVY DEPT., NATIONAL ARCHIVES)

Implementer of the Low concept: Captain Donald W. Duncan, Admiral King's air officer. Duncan proved, on paper and within certain limitations, it was possible to send bombers to bomb Japan.

(NAVY DEPT., NATIONAL ARCHIVES)

idea hinged upon the possibility of finding a long-range medium Army bomber which could take off from the deck of a carrier. Thus could a striking force be launched beyond the danger zone around Japan, keeping the vulnerable carrier out of the reach of bombers. This was an impetuous, perhaps quixotic, but appealing conception—even to the hardheaded King. He sent Low to see his air officer, Captain Donald W. Duncan, on the following day, a Sunday, to explore the probabilities further. King also cautioned Low to speak to no one else of the idea.

The two men met on January 11, 1942. Duncan immediately rejected one aspect of the idea. No bomber, not even a medium, could possibly land on a carrier deck. They required a long runway

and did not come equipped with arrester hooks for carrier landings. But it was possible that such a bomber, fueled and bombed-up, could take off from a carrier, complete its mission, and (thanks to its range) continue on to bases on land.

The plane Duncan had in mind was the North American B-25 (Mitchell), and the carrier, the recently commissioned *Hornet*. He would, however, need to work out the details before offering any real suggestions. Five days later Duncan emerged with thirty handwritten pages (the subject matter being too sensitive to entrust to a secretary for typing) of closely reasoned computations. Weather, winds, range, bomb loads, fuel, number of aircraft, minimum take-off run, and a dozen other complexities had been carefully worked out by Duncan.

Admiral King, who was not easily impressed, *was* impressed with Duncan's work. He then ordered Low and Duncan to approach Lieutenant General Henry H. Arnold, Commanding General of the Army Air Forces, with the idea. He saw them on the next day, January 17, and the subject of their visit must have proved a bit startling to Arnold. On January 4, 1942, for example, he had composed a memorandum upon returning from a White House meeting, part of which read: "We will have to try bomber take-offs from carriers. It has never been done before but we must try out and check on how long it takes." (This was relative to the coming invasion of north Africa and not to an attack upon Japan, however.) The memo went to the War Plans Division of the Army Air Forces for study, but before Arnold had heard from his staff, here were two Navy men confronting him with the idea and assuring him it could be done.

Arnold was most enthusiastic over the idea and promptly called King to settle the division of responsibility and to get things under way. King selected Captain Duncan as the Navy co-ordinator and Arnold agreed to provide a man to undertake the Air Force's end of the project. This was not difficult —the one man who had the flying skill, the technical background, and a love of derring-do was James H. Doolittle of Arnold's staff. One of the great aviation pioneers, Doolittle combined aerial swashbuckling with scholarship. He had received several trophies for breaking records in speed flights, for aerobatics, and for more scientific contributions such as taking off, flying, and landing a plane without ever seeing out of the plane's cockpit. He had served in the Army Air Corps and had a Doctor of Science degree from the Massachusetts Institute of Technology. Resigning from the Air Corps in 1930 (he had enlisted in 1917), Doolittle became manager of the aviation department of the Shell Oil Company. He was recalled to active duty, with the commission of major, in July 1940. Doolittle's job was to work with the auto industries then converting to defense industries. Early in 1942 he was called to Washington to serve on Arnold's staff as a special trouble shooter. One of his first problems was the myth of the "Widow Maker," the pilot's name for the Martin B-26 (Marauder). Doolittle proved that this fast, effective medium bomber was no killer and that pilots properly trained could handle it. He had just about completed this assignment when Arnold called him into his office to ask an odd question.

"Just what airplane," he began, "have we got that will get off in five hundred feet with a two thousand bomb load and fly two thousand miles?"

No maker of snap judgments, Doolittle informed his chief he would have to give the problem some consideration. Upon returning the following day he told Arnold that either one of two planes just might do it. The Douglas B-23 or the North American B-25 with modifications seemed the most likely.

Arnold offered one more condition. "The plane must take off from a narrow area not more than seventy-five feet wide."

"Well," Doolittle told him, "then the only answer is the B-25. It has a sixty-seven-foot wing span."

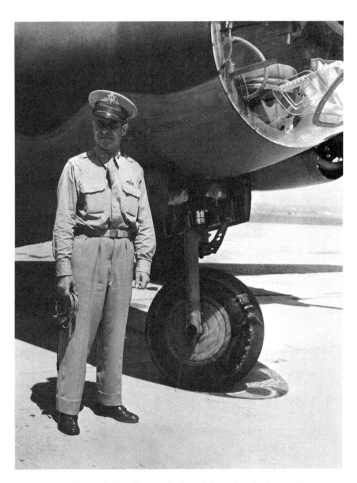

The man selected by General Arnold to lead the raid on Tokyo: James H. Doolittle, here standing beneath the nose of a Martin "Marauder," which he had proved was an outstanding aircraft. (U. S. AIR FORCE)

The span of the B-23 spread to ninety-three feet, much too wide for a carrier deck.

Only then did Arnold tell Doolittle what it was all about. He and King had agreed that a Navy task force would move out with the bombers around the first of April. Doolittle was to train the crews and supervise whatever modifications might be required which could enable the B-25s to take off a carrier deck, say within four or five hundred miles off Japan, bomb various military targets, and continue on to land bases in China or Russia.

Doolittle, characteristically, went into immediate action. He flew to Wright Field, near Dayton, Ohio, to confer with Brigadier General George C. Kenney, commander of the Air Corps Experimental Division and Engineering School. Kenney and his staff were given the task of preparing the B-25B aircraft for a mission about which they knew absolutely nothing. However, they too attacked the problem of designing new fuel tanks, bomb shackles, and other innovations for the planes. Soon after Doolittle wrote

a memo to Arnold: "The work of installing the required additional tankage is being done by Mid-Continent Airlines in Minneapolis. All production and installation is progressing according to schedule and the 24 airplanes (6 spares) should be completely converted by March 15th."

At the same time other work progressed. By the end of January Brigadier General Carl Spaatz, then serving as Arnold's deputy for intelligence, had furnished a list of ten likely target cities, among which were Tokyo, Yokohama, Kobe, and Nagoya. As for the Navy's role Captain Duncan had arranged for the *Hornet* to be in San Francisco by April 1. Near Norfolk, on February 2, Duncan had stood with Captain Marc A. Mitscher, commander of the *Hornet,* to observe an experiment. The day before, two Army B-25s were hoisted aboard and after being taken out to sea the two Mitchells, piloted by Lieutenants John E. Fitzgerald and James F. McCarthy, proved that a two-engined medium bomber could indeed be flown off the deck of an aircraft carrier.

Admiral Chester A. Nimitz, Commander in Chief, Pacific Fleet (left), who approved of the Special Avia- *tion Project and assigned Vice-Admiral William Halsey (right) and the carrier* Enterprise *to the mission.*
(NATIONAL ARCHIVES)

Upon accomplishing this epochal feat, the two young pilots, mystified, returned to their landlocked base wondering why they had done what they had done.

Duncan later flew out to Hawaii to meet with Admiral Chester W. Nimitz, Commander in Chief, Pacific Fleet, and to arrange for more hands. Nimitz, who approved of the project, assigned Vice-Admiral William Halsey to it, thus adding a second carrier, the *Enterprise,* to the armada. Before he left for San Francisco to confer with Mitscher (and finally to tell him what it was all about), Duncan wired Arnold: *Tell Jimmy to Get on His Horse.* It was the signal for Doolittle and his crews to head for California.

Doolittle had begun assembling his crews immediately after initiating the modification program on the B-25s. All crews came from the three squadrons of the 17th Bombardment Group and its cognate, the 89th Reconnaissance Squadron. These units were not special, hand-picked combat veterans (although some had had experience with dealing with submarine patrols); they were simply the most experienced with the relatively new Mitchell bomber. In other words, they were not an elite unit, but a typical Air Force assemblage of men. However, upon being informed that volunteers were needed for a very hazardous but most important mission, the response was overwhelming. From these volunteers twenty-four crews were mustered and, under Major John A. Hilger (who was C.O. of the 89th Squadron and selected by Doolittle as his second-in-command), reported in at Eglin Field, Florida, by the first of March.

The B-25s to which these crews were assigned were not the planes they had known before. The fueslage interior looked like a Rube Goldberg invention and was crowded with extra fuel tanks in the bomb bay, in the crawlway between sections of the plane, and later even in the position where a belly turret had been originally installed. This lower turret gave so much trouble that Doolittle remarked, "A man could learn to play the violin good enough for Carnegie Hall before he could learn to fire that thing." The malfunctioning, jamming lower turret was pulled out to make room for a sixty-gallon collapsible rubber fuel tank. The one remaining turret, however, would plague the mission with its vagaries, and the added fuel tanks and fittings with theirs.

To save weight the large radios were removed; with radio silence essential the heavy radios would be of no use. For protective firepower the B-25 now had only the twin .50 machine guns in the upper turret and a single .30 in the nose. There had been no tail guns, an oversight attended to by Captain Charles Ross Greening, the mission's gunnery and bombing officer, who fashioned fake twin .50s from broomsticks, painted black and protruding menacingly from the tail. It was hoped these would be enough to discourage attack from the vulnerable rear.

Greening also contrived an ingenious bombsight. The famed Norden sight would not be of any use at the low altitude at which the attack was to be carried out; besides, the Air Force had little desire to risk so valuable an instrument upon so risky a mission. One at least would have been bound to have fallen into enemy hands. Therefore Greening devised a simple gadget, which he called the "Mark Twain," from about twenty cents worth (in 1942) of metal, which proved to be more accurate at the proposed fifteen-hundred-foot bombing altitude than the Norden.

On March 3 Doolittle arrived at Eglin and to an assembly of puzzled airmen said, "My name is Doolittle. I've been put in charge of the project you men have volunteered for. It's a tough one and it will be the most dangerous thing any of you have ever been on. Any man can drop out and nothing will ever be said about it."

Stressing the need for complete secrecy, Doolittle would not reveal to them the nature of their mission or their targets. They would have to follow him blindly and hope for the best—or drop out, as he had offered.

Then their special training began. This was characterized by another rather curious touch, the crews thought. Lieutenant Henry L. Miller, USN, an instructor from the Pensacola Naval Air Station, had come to teach them how to lift a heavily loaded B-25 off the ground within an impossibly short distance. This would require pulling the B-25 up in a dangerously near-stall attitude after a take-off run of about five hundred feet, about one tenth the distance they had been originally trained to use. But with few exceptions, under Miller's tutelage, they learned. Soon twenty-four pilots could yank the B-25 into the air, its tail wheel all but scraping the

Henry L. Miller, an instructor at Pensacola Naval Air Station who was given the job of teaching U. S. Army Air Force pilots how to take off from a carrier deck with a heavily laden bomber. (U. S. NAVY)

tice bombs, they found that Greening's "Mark Twain" sight worked very well.

About mid-March Doolittle became concerned with his part in the mission. Would Arnold pull him out once he had completed the modifications and the crew training? Having come so far, Doolittle wished to go all the way. He flew to Washington hoping to get Arnold's permission to lead the attack. This might not prove to be easy. Doolittle was forty-five, twice the age of most of the pilots on the mission, and he was an irreplaceable member of Arnold's staff. Still Doolittle, applying what he later called "my sales pitch," gave it a vigorous try. He produced every possible reason for leading the mission, all but swamping Arnold with words. In self-defense, Arnold simply passed the buck.

"OK, Jimmy," he managed to wedge in a word, "it's all right with me provided it is all right with Miff Harmon" (Major General Millard F. Harmon, Arnold's Chief of Staff).

Whereupon Doolittle shot into Harmon's office, where he pulled off an ancient ploy in the repertory of every boy whoever talked his parents into giving him something neither really wanted him to have.

"Miff," Doolittle began as soon as his foot was in the door, "I've just been to see Hap and gave him my report on this project I've been working on. I told him I wanted to lead the mission and he said it was OK with him if it's OK with you." Arnold had, of course, counted upon Harmon to say no. But "Miff was caught flat-footed, which is what I intended," Doolittle recalls. Harmon could only answer, "Sure, Jimmy, whatever is all right with Hap is all right with me. Go ahead."

Doolittle went, pausing only long enough outside Harmon's door to hear him explaining to Arnold why *he* had given Doolittle permission to lead the Tokyo raid. Before Arnold caught him to countermand the consent, Doolittle hurried back to Eglin. Not until the *Hornet* had put out to sea was Doolittle absolutely certain that he would lead the mission.

Shortly after Duncan's suggestion that he get on his horse came through, on March 23 twenty-two B-25s took off the landing strip at Eglin for the last time; two others, training casualties, remained behind. Three days later all aircraft arrived safely at McClellan Field, near Sacramento. It was here that the final inspections and adjustments were to be

ground, some within less than four hundred feet.

While the pilots learned short-run take-offs, other crew members practiced their specialties. It became appallingly obvious that most gunners had never fired a weapon before, nor had any ever operated a power turret. The turrets proved to be consistently troublesome and required so much repair and adjustment that the crews had very little time for actual gunnery practice in flight. Another source of trouble was the auxiliary fuel tanks, which developed leaks. Engines and carburetors were finely adjusted for the most economic fuel consumption— this could mean the difference between landing in the sea or on land.

Simulated bomb runs were practiced over the Florida coast. The B-25s came in from the ocean at low level, skimming housetops, dodging trees, and sweeping under telephone wires. In dropping pracmade before the final fifteen planes would put out to sea aboard the *Hornet*.

Doolittle ran the gamut of annoyances at McClellan. The Sacramento Air Depot employed a number of civilians, along with the Army men, as maintenance personnel. None were aware of the pressures upon Doolittle—nor were the civilians particularly impressed with military demands. Suddenly, literally out of the clear blue sky, they had received twenty-two tampered-with B-25s with a little man in charge demanding immediate attention. The crews made a point of sticking together and remaining aloof from the people on the base (a security measure, though mistaken as snobbishness by base personnel). When it became apparent that things were moving too slowly despite his admonitions, Doolittle called Arnold, who managed to stir up some action from Washington. It did not add to Doolittle's popularity.

New propellers, painted black for protection from salt air and water, were to be installed. The crazy tubing of the auxiliary fuel tanks was to be checked. But, Doolittle cautioned, nothing was to be removed

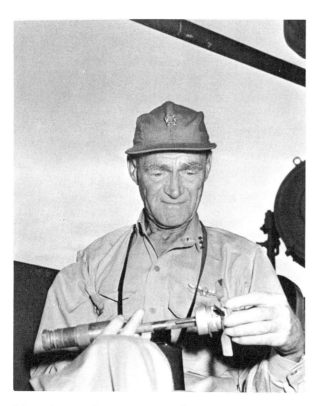

Marc A. Mitscher, captain of the Hornet *and host to Doolittle's Tokyo raiders.*
(U. S. OFFICE OF WAR INFORMATION)

from the planes, nor were any mechanical settings to be changed. In spite of this there was still margin for well-intended error. One day Doolittle caught a mechanic revving up an engine and backfiring it. That was bad enough, but then the mechanic explained that the carburetors had been "checked, found way out of adjustment and fixed up." Some, as those on the plane he was revving up, had even been changed. The hairline adjustments on the engines made at Eglin now amounted to nothing.

Doolittle stormed and raged, but it was too late to begin a new series of adjustments at McClellan. Doolittle had his own crews try to put the engines back into shape. By this time the men of the "First Special Aviation Project" were quite unpopular around McClellan Field, with Doolittle, otherwise a most genial and friendly type, leading the list. The consensus was that they were all a bunch of "jokers," had odd ideas on how a B-25 should be maintained, and were not quite right in the head.

On April 1 Doolittle was ordered to fly the planes to the Alameda Air Station, not far from McClellan Field. As he was about to climb into his plane he was given a form to sign, a typical Army paper necessary to the clearance of his aircraft. The form invited comment upon the work done at McClellan.

Doolittle took the form and wrote a single word across the face of it: "Lousy."

"Just a minute, sir," the base operations officer stammered. "You must fill in a detailed report. This won't do."

"I haven't got time," Doolittle answered, jumped into the plane, and took off.

John Hilger, his executive officer, stood nearby grinning. The disgruntled base officer came over to him saying, "He has no clearance to leave this base and I won't sign it. . . . Who does he think he is? . . . I'll tell you one thing: your colonel is heading for a lot of trouble."

"He sure is," Hilger concurred. Doolittle invariably found trouble.

III

At Alameda the Navy took over the B-25s, attached them to "donkeys," and towed them to the pier to be hoisted by crane to the flight deck of the *Hornet*. Their crews, all of them graduates—including Doolittle himself—of Captain Henry Miller's special training course, had been selected as the top of their class of the twenty-two flight teams. Doolittle took over the plane of Captain Vernon L. Stinzi, who had become sick. Ultimate selection of the crews was left by Doolittle to his staff and to Miller.

All fifteen Mitchells, as had been originally planned, were aboard when Doolittle scanned the deck and thought perhaps there was room for one more. He suggested to Mitscher that an extra bomber be brought aboard. Once they were out to sea it could be flown off and sent back. It seemed a good idea, even if only to demonstrate to the crews that it could be done. None of them, including Doolittle, had actually done it. "It would give them a lot of confidence," Doolittle offered. Mitscher ordered a sixteenth B-25 lifted aboard. Their Navy instructor, Lieutenant Henry Miller, was then all but kidnapped in order to serve as copilot for the extra Mitchell. Besides Miller, there were also seventy officers and sixty-four enlisted men of the Army Air Forces as guests of the Navy. The *Hornet* pulled out of the harbor at ten-eighteen in the morning (in broad daylight) on Thursday, April 2, 1942. Still no one aboard, except Doolittle, Mitscher, and Miller, knew where they were heading.

There was no little uneasiness among the espionage-conscious aircrews as Task Group 16.2 steamed under the Golden Gate and Oakland bridges in full view of motorists above. It would take little military intelligence to gather that something was afoot: a carrier, three cruisers, four destroyers, and a tanker. The carrier was the oddest sight, with a number of large planes (not carrier planes obviously) lashed to the aft end of the flight deck.

Later that afternoon Mitscher announced over the ship's loudspeaker: "This force is bound for Tokyo." At the same instant the word was flashed to the other ships in the group. Great cheers resounded over the waters as the ships plowed ahead. Morale could not have been better, nor could the relationship—co-operative and considerate—which developed between airmen and seamen. To avenge Pearl Harbor, whatever the risks, was exhilarating and above all the most desirable objective of the war at that moment.

Soon after, the deadly business of preparation got under way. Target folders were distributed and vari-

The flight deck of the Hornet *with an unusual cargo, U. S. Army Air Force B-25Bs on the way to bomb Tokyo. Two of the escorting destroyers bring up the rear.* (U. S. AIR FORCE)

ous targets were assigned to the five three-plane elements. It was decided to keep the extra B-25. Doolittle would open the attack with his single plane approaching Tokyo at around dusk to bomb the Shiba Ward, an industrial section, about three hours before the other bombers followed. The fires laid by Doolittle's bombs would serve as beacons for the others. Lieutenant Travis Hoover would follow with the first element to bomb factories, warehouses, and gas and chemical installations in northern Tokyo; Captain David M. Jones's second element would concentrate on oil storage tanks, power stations, and several factories in an area to the north of the Temple of Heaven, the Emperor's palace (which was declared off limits as a target). Captain Edward J. York's element was to hit factories and power stations in the southern Tokyo area bordering on Yokohama. Captain Charles Ross Greening's element was given targets in Yokohama proper, with concentration on the dock areas and the Navy Yard. The fifth element, Major John A. Hilger leading, would fan out over the coast and hit targets assigned in Nagoya, Kobe, and Osaka.

Such a distribution would in a sense diffuse the effectiveness of the attack; they could hardly hope to erase an important industry from Japan's war-making potential. They would do some damage, but

The sixteenth, and last, B-25 with its aft section jutting over the Hornet's *fantail. It was this aircraft's propeller that during the takeoffs injured Navy man Robert Wall.*
(U. S. AIR FORCE)

most of that would be to the morale of the people of Japan, who had been assured that their home islands would never be touched by the enemy.

The task group steamed toward the scheduled rendezvous with Task Group 16.1, Halsey's group with the *Enterprise,* on Sunday, April 12. Halsey's return to Pearl Harbor, however, was held up by storms so that the rendezvous was delayed by one day. The days at sea were devoted to sessions with Doolittle on procedure. The crews checked and rechecked their planes. The Navy furnished an intelligence officer, Lieutenant Commander Stephen Jurika, who lectured the crews on the Orient and Orientals. Commander Apollo Soucek, air officer of the *Hornet,* reviewed the subject of carrier takeoff and carrier operations. Until the actual takeoff, therefore, none of the crews would have ever taken off a carrier, nor would they have ever seen a B-25 lifted off a carrier. This did not seem to worry the crews, particularly the pilots.

Commander Frank Akers found the pilots ". . . a carefree, happy group [who] seemed little concerned as to the danger of their mission or what might happen to them if they were shot down over Japan." They were, Akers found in lecturing them on navigation, quite inattentive. Their major prob-

lem was getting the plane off the deck—the rest of the mission would follow in due course.

The still inexperienced gunners managed to get in some practice from the *Hornet's* deck by shooting at kites, the closest they were to come to shooting at an air-borne target until they would be in combat.

Each plane was to carry four five-hundred-pound bombs, in most cases three demolition and one incendiary. In the discussions on bombing Doolittle told them, "You are to look for and aim at military targets only, such as war industries, shipbuilding facilities, power plants and the like." He stressed again that the Emperor's Imperial Palace was to be untouched and that they should keep their bombs out of residential areas.

There still remained the question of where they would land after they had completed their missions. Doolittle had left the United States believing that this problem had been solved, but in truth it was not; also, because of the strict radio silence, it was not possible to inform him of this hitch. In the early stages of the mission's planning negotiations had got under way with both China and Russia. The reaction from both was not encouraging. Russia, despite the tantalizing offer of fifteen only slightly used B-25s on lend-lease, refused upon learning that they were to bomb Japan first. Still at peace with Japan, Russia did not want to become involved with such a project.

Chiang Kai-shek was hardly more co-operative. He was given the merest gist of the First Special Aviation Project, just the fact that Japan was to be bombed. Nothing about how or when. This was for a very good reason: military information in China, including that of Chiang's staff, became Japanese property with disconcerting speed. Chiang offered two objections, suggesting that the mission be delayed. First, he reasoned that the bases being requested for use for American bombers were too close to Japanese-held territory. Second, he feared reprisals upon the Chinese if Japan were attacked. It was a curious point of view, considering the years of "reprisals" which had already been inflicted upon the Chinese. However, his fears were not without foundation, as the aftermath of the mission would prove.

Unknown to Doolittle and his men, therefore, no actual preparations were being made for their arrival as they pored over their target folders at sea.

Aircrews, Doolittle, and Mitscher (left foreground) assemble on the deck of the Hornet *in mid-Pacific.*
(U. S. NAVY)

The verbiage between Chungking and Washington became increasingly frigid. Chiang strongly believed that the aircraft could be better employed against Japanese bases in Burma. But by this time, Washington informed him, it was too late to cancel the mission. By mid-April, Chiang, after frequent changes of mind, gave halfhearted permission for arrangements to be made to receive the B-25s in China. A number of forward bases would be furnished with radios to send out a beam to guide the planes to land; there they would be refueled and flown deeper into China—to Chungking.

IV

Halsey's delay in returning to Pearl Harbor had no effect upon the mission. He left Hawaii, flying his flag on the *Enterprise,* commanded by Captain George D. Murray, on April 8. Halsey's group consisted of a carrier, two cruisers, four destroyers, and a tanker. In addition, two submarines patrolled the areas in advance of and to the flanks of the two groups, which on April 13 merged as Task Force 16 under the command of Halsey.

By this time the Japanese had been aware of an impending action for five days. They had monitored radio signals between Mitscher, Halsey, and Pearl Harbor and could conjecture that a fairly large-scale operation was in the making. It was even surmised that an attack upon Japan itself would take place, the guess being that it would occur around April 14. The radio silence which then descended upon TF 16 threw off that prediction and the Japanese relaxed somewhat, although never completely.

Combined Fleet Headquarters in Tokyo ordered a concentration of naval aircraft from the 26th Air Flotilla into the Tokyo area. The vast network of picket boats, most of them onetime fishing boats, ringing the eastern approach to Japan were alerted. These picket boats, equipped with radios, operated about 650 to 700 miles offshore, beyond the range of carrier-borne aircraft. They could warn of the approach of enemy carriers long before the planes might be launched. Although expecting some form of early warning system, the Americans were not aware of the extent of this floating picket line. Meanwhile, in Tokyo, certain of its efforts, Combined Fleet Headquarters sensed no need for alarm.

Task Force 16 surged due west at sixteen knots for five days (losing Tuesday, April 14, on crossing the International Date Line) without incident. The *Enterprise* maintained a screen of fighters and scout-bombers on combat air patrol, weather permitting—and the weather turned foul. It was as if the theme of the Pearl Harbor attack had returned. Ships tossed and rolled and refueling became a dangerous essential operation. One man was thrown overboard but was pulled from the sea by one of the destroyers. (To this extent the theme varied from the Nagumo operation.) As the bad weather persisted the hope was that the bombers could be launched within five hundred miles of Japan.

Constant vigil was maintained and tension mounted as the launch date, set for April 19, approached. On the fifteenth an English broadcast was picked up from Tokyo:

Reuter's British News Agency has announced that three American bombers have dropped bombs on Tokyo. This is a most laughable story. They know it is absolutely impossible for enemy bombers to get within five hundred miles of Tokyo. Instead of worrying about such foolish things, the Japanese people are enjoying the fine spring sunshine and the fragrance of cherry blossoms.

This was a stunning bit of news, even if not true. Had the Japanese somehow learned of the First Special Aviation Project? Had they been spotted and was the Japanese fleet, plus its formidable armada of aircraft, waiting for them to finish what had been left undone at Pearl Harbor?

Whatever the individual trepidations the broadcast produced, the preparations on the *Hornet* continued. The air patrols spotted no Japanese activity, which was a good sign. There was more than enough to keep the crews busy, with tricky fuel systems, the power turrets, and small mechanical problems with plugs, generators, and the hydraulic systems.

After the tankers and destroyers left the task force, on April 17, the carriers with four cruisers as escort increased speed to twenty knots. The weather continued to be blustery and winds approached gale force. The B-25s were positioned on the flight deck; Doolittle's, which was first in line for take-off, had but 467 feet of runway. White guidelines were painted on the deck, one for the left wheel and the other for the nosewheel. Lining up on these, the pilot would manage to keep his plane's right wing tip about six feet away from the *Hornet*'s island. The sixteenth plane, assigned to Lieutenant William Farrow, was parked at the stern with its tail section protruding. All, with minor mechanical reservations, was ready for the April 19 launchings.

But then, unexpectedly, the tension was released with the expectation of action. At three in the early morning of April 18, the *Enterprise* reported a radar sighting of two enemy surface craft. "General Quarters" reverberated through the entire task force as all ships veered sharply to avoid the enemy craft and all hands peered into the gloom. For a single instant a light flashed in the distance and then nothing. Forty-one minutes later the "All Clear" was sounded and all who could returned to their bunks and the tension returned intensified.

At dawn, despite the squalls, the *Enterprise* dispatched its search flights and fighter patrols— Douglas SBDs (Dauntlesses) and Grumman F4Fs (Wildcats)—which fanned out in advance of the force. At 5:58 A.M. Lieutenant O. B. Wiseman, in an SBD, sighted a Japanese patrol craft. Ducking into cloud he attempted to hide, but was reasonably sure he had been seen. Returning to the task force,

Mission leader Doolittle affixes Japanese medals (which had, in peaceful times, been awarded to Navy men H. Vornstein, J. B. Laurey, D. J. Quigley, and S. Jurika) to a five-hundred-pound bomb which was then loaded into The Ruptured Duck, *piloted by Major Ted W. Lawson.* (U. S. NAVY)

Wiseman flew low in order to enable his gunner to drop a message on the deck in a "beanbag." Again Halsey ordered a shift in the task force's bearing. But by seven thirty-eight, with winds buffeting and waves sweeping across the decks, it was obvious to Halsey that he must do something about the Army bombers. At this time lookouts on the *Hornet* had spotted a Japanese vessel—it was Patrol Boat No. 23—the *Nitto Maru*. If they saw the little boat in the swelling seas, obviously the Japanese could see a great carrier. This was confirmed moments later when the *Hornet* intercepted a signal which had originated nearby. The picket boat had wired, *"Three enemy aircraft carriers sighted our position 650 nautical miles east of Inubo Saki at 0630 [Tokyo time]."*

Aboard the task force ships it was 7:30 A.M. The *Nitto Maru* had seen both the *Hornet* and *Enterprise* (obviously mistaking one of the cruisers for a third carrier). Halsey ordered the *Nashville* to deal with the *Nitto Maru*.

As for the bombers, Halsey realized, there was nothing to do but get them off. This was a real risk (though a lesser one than exposing the men

Japanese fishing boat sighted by American search planes and which was sunk by a Navy ship. The ap- *pearance of the* Nitto Maru *forced the Tokyo raid to get under way sooner than had been hoped.*

(U. S. AIR FORCE)

and ships of the task force to a full-scale attack) for they were more than six hundred miles offshore —and two hundred miles from a point at which it was hoped they could have launched the bombers. Also, it was a day earlier than Chiang had been informed the attack would occur; perhaps the airfields would not be ready to receive the bombers after the raid. This was assuming they would have enough fuel to reach them. Halsey at this time had no idea that the preparation of Chinese bases had crumbled in a series of disagreements and plane crashes.

At eight o'clock Halsey flashed a message to the *Hornet:*
Launch Planes To Colonel Doolittle and his gallant command Good Luck and God bless you

V

The *Hornet* exploded with activity; signal horns blared and men raced for their action stations. Doolittle, who had been on the bridge with Mitscher, hurtled down the ladder shouting, "This is it! Let's go!" The ship's klaxon boomed, "Now hear this: Army pilots, man your planes!"

The deck swarmed with men rushing about their various businesses. The airmen clambered into their planes, tossing in their baggage, equipment, map folders, and odd personal possessions (one officer carried a small record collection and a wind-up phonograph). The Navy deck-handlers, called "airedales," scurried over the wet, wind-spumed flight deck, taking their positions for the launch. The rough seas would not make the already complex operation any simpler. Soon the deck boomed and roared to the sound of thirty-two engines.

Lieutenant Edgar G. Osborn poised at the end of the tossing bow, checkered flag in hand, eyes on Doolittle's plane, his feet gauging the pitch of the deck and the feel of the sea. The *Hornet* had rolled into a trough and began to rise; Osborne rotated the flag, faster and faster. At the right moment, he hoped, Doolittle would gun the engines, the airedales pull the wheel chocks and drop to the slippery deck. Osborn gave the signal to go. The engines of the B-25, full power on, thundered and the plane moved—all too slowly it seemed. The flaps were down for more lift and the aircraft moved faster and faster, trundling clumsily toward the end of the deck, now being lifted by the swelling sea. The two Wright Cyclones grew louder and the Mitchell picked up speed; even before he ran out of the short span of deck, Doolittle eased the heavily loaded plane off, all but hanging on his propellers, and pulled up and away from the *Hornet,* whose decks resounded with cheers, shouts, whistles, and the merriment of capering men. Doolittle circled, swooped low, and swept over the deck to check his plane's compass—the weeks aboard ship would have undoubtedly thrown the compasses of the B-25s off. Satisfied, Doolittle pointed the aircraft at Tokyo and was quickly enshrouded in the distant mist and out of sight. The next plane, Travis Hoover's, pulled off the deck five minutes later, described the same circle as had Doolittle's, and it too disappeared in the morning haze.

The original plan, of course, had been abandoned; there would now be no three-hour wait for the rest of the planes. The *Nitto Maru* had decided that.

One after the other the B-25s took off from the flight deck, almost without incident. The water spray and unsteady decks, even the powerful gusts of wind, made for anxious moments as men slipped on the deck or staggered dangerously close to the whirling propellers. In the last section of planes, Lieutenant Donald Smith's B-25 nosed into the tail of Hilger's, which preceded his in the take-off line. Smith took off with a gaping hole in the plexiglass nose of his plane.

The last plane (William G. Farrow, pilot) was caught in the roll of the ship and seemed destined for a watery doom. It poised momentarily on the crest of a wave, then began to skid in reverse. Airedales ran to stop its movement, lest it fall into the sea. They succeeded, but as Farrow gunned the plane forward again Seaman Robert W. Wall slipped and fell into the path of one of the propellers. A blade struck him and Wall went down; he lay stunned under the spinning blades for a moment, then oblivious to the danger tried to rise. His crewmates moved in quickly and dragged him away. Farrow, sickened by the implications of the accident, had no recourse but to proceed with the takeoff. (Wall had been struck in the left arm; it was subsequently amputated and he recovered).

The time was 9:20 A.M., exactly one hour from the moment that Doolittle had taken off—Doolittle would have 620 miles to fly to his target, Farrow faced 600 miles of over-water navigation. Now all B-25s were air-borne and bound for Japan. The instant Farrow slipped into the fog, Halsey ordered all ships to turn about and head full speed away from the dangerous waters before they met more potent vessels than picket boats. Like the Nagumo force at Pearl Harbor, Task Force 16 vanished into the Pacific.

Not without some moments of fury. Three Japa-

The order has come from Halsey to "Launch planes," and the deck of the Hornet *becomes alive with the sound of engines. Deck handlers lie on the deck to avoid propeller blades. The day is dark and damp, visibility is poor.* (NAVY DEPT., NATIONAL ARCHIVES)

Doolittle, in the lead Mitchell, begins the take-off run along the wet—and short—deck of the Hornet.
(U. S. AIR FORCE)

Doolittle lifts the B-25 off the Hornet. *White lines painted along left of carrier deck are there to guide the pilots in the alignment of their left undercarriage* *and nosewheels to keep the right wing of the plane from striking the carrier's island.* (U. S. AIR FORCE)

nese patrol boats were sunk, five prisoners were taken, and three American aircraft were lost. The crews of two were rescued, but one, based on the *Hornet*, went down taking its pilots, Lieutenants G. D. Randall and T. A. Gallagher, with it. They were victims of the weather, not enemy gunfire.

Three minutes after Doolittle's plane left the *Hornet*'s deck the *Nashville* succeeded in sinking the *Nitto Maru*. The tiny, bobbing craft proved an elusive target and it required "938 rounds of 6″ ammunition" to sink it. Even dive bombers could not get at it "due to difficulty of hitting the small target with the heavy swells . . ." as the gunnery officer of the *Nashville* later reported. Finally the *Nitto Maru* did sink, and although a search was made, no survivors were found.

It was a small victory, for already Tokyo had put "Tactical Method No. 3 against the United States Fleet" into operation. Vice-Admiral Nobutake Kondo's Second Fleet, just returned from actions in the southern seas, was ordered to confront the U.S. fleet. Kondo's force was to be supported by Vice-Admiral Shiro Takasu's First Fleet out of Hiroshima Bay. Even Vice-Admiral Nagumo's carrier force, at the moment of alarm passing through the Bashi Strait near the southern tip of Formosa upon completion of its operations in the Indian Ocean, was ordered to rush homeward to engage the enemy. More immediately, however, the bombers and fighters from the Kisarazu Air Base near Tokyo were dispatched to begin the search for the American ships.

At Combined Fleet Headquarters in Tokyo, where the bulk of the preparations was under way, all was anxiety and tension. There had been no second message from the *Nitto Maru* to confirm its sighting. The patrol planes had not reported anything (thanks to the covering of bad weather under which Task Force 16 lay). One of the regular patrol planes, however, on its morning patrol had reported seeing a twin-engined landplane about six hundred miles at sea. Such a report could not be taken seriously in Tokyo—no American plane could have reached that point from any American base and, certainly, there were no such carrier-borne aircraft extant. Meanwhile, the weather in the search area deteriorated and the Japanese search planes were forced to return to Kisarazu after a fruitless quest.

If the weather at sea was harsh, the sky over Tokyo was bright and clear. Along the waterfront a few barrage balloons drifted in the brilliant sun. Its rays flashed from the wings of several aircraft also, aloft practicing for a demonstration a week hence celebrating the Emperor's birthday and the dedication of a shrine to the war dead. By coin-cidence that morning at nine o'clock a practice air raid drill took place. The public did not participate, but firemen and air raid wardens did. By noon the drill drew to a close; most of the barrage balloons had been pulled down. The only planes still flying were a few trainers and three Army Defense fighter planes; at this point in the alarums and excursions at Combined Fleet Headquarters the Army was not regarded as particularly essential. The threat to the Empire, as far as the Navy officials were concerned, still lay far out at sea. There was no air of foreboding in Tokyo as its people went about their customary Saturday bustle. It was as if there were no war at all—their great military leaders had assured them of their immunity from enemy attack.

At twelve-thirty that Saturday afternoon the illusion was shattered. The dream drew to an end the moment that James Doolittle raised his B-25 off the deck of the *Hornet*. "Took off at 8:20 A.M. ship time," he was to write in his report later. "Take-off was easy. Night take-off would have been possible and practicable.

"Circled carrier to get exact heading and check compass. Wind was from around 300°.

"About a half hour after take-off, was joined by A/C 40-2292, Lt. Hoover pilot, the second plane to take off. About an hour out passed a Japanese

A Mitchell leaves the Hornet *as the others await their turns. Note the choppiness of the water in the foreground.* (U. S. AIR FORCE)

Yokosuka Naval Base from the right-hand cockpit of No. 40-2247 (Crew No. 13), Lieutenant Edgar E. McElroy, pilot, and Lieutenant Richard A. Knobloch, copilot and photographer. (U. S. AIR FORCE)

camouflaged naval surface vessel of about 6000 tons. Took it to be light cruiser. About two hours out passed a multi-motored land plane headed directly for our flotilla and flying at about 3,000 ft.—2 miles away. Passed and endeavored to avoid various civil and naval craft until landfall was made north of Inubo Shuma.

"Was somewhat north of desired course but decided to take advantage of error and approach from a northerly direction, thus avoiding anticipated strong opposition to the west. Many flying fields and the air full of planes north of Tokyo. Mostly small biplanes apparently primary or basic trainers.

"Encountered nine fighters in three flights of three. This was about ten miles north of the outskirts of Tokyo proper. All this time had been flying as low as terrain would permit. Continued low flying due south over the outskirts of and toward the east center of Tokyo.

"Pulled up to 1,200 ft., changed course to the southwest and incendiary-bombed highly inflammable section. Dropped first bomb at 1:30 (ship time).

[It was twelve-thirty in Tokyo when the first bombs fell.]

"Anti-aircraft very active but only one near hit,"

Having released its bombs, McElroy's Mitchell pulls away from Yokosuka as machine shops burn from a bomb hit. (U. S. AIR FORCE)

Doolittle noted. "Lowered away to housetops and slid over western outskirts into low haze and smoke. Turned south and out to sea. Fewer airports on west side but many army posts. Passed over small aircraft factory with a dozen or more newly completed planes on the line. No bombs left. Decided not to machine gun for reasons of personal security. Had seen five barrage balloons over east central Tokyo and what appeared to be more in the distance.

"Passed on out to sea flying low. Was soon joined by Hoover who followed us to the Chinese coast. Navigator plotted perfect course to pass north of Yaki Shima. Saw three large naval vessels just before passing west end of Japan. One was flatter than the others and may have been converted carrier. Passed innumerable fishing and small patrol boats.

"Made landfall somewhat north of course on China coast. Tried to reach Chuchow on 4495 [kilocycles] but could not raise.

"It had been clear over Tokyo but became overcast before reaching Yaki Shima. Ceiling lowered on coast until low islands and hills were in it at about 600'. Just getting dark and couldn't live under overcast so pulled up to 6000' and then 8000' in it. On instruments from then on though occasionally saw dim lights on ground through almost solid overcast. These lights seemed more often on our right and pulled us still further off course.

"Directed rear gunner to go aft and secure films from camera. [Unfortunately, they were jerked out of his shirt front where he had put them when his chute opened.]

"Decided to abandon ship. Sgt. [Fred A.] Breamer, Lt. [Henry A.] Potter, Sgt. [Paul J.] Leonard and Lt. [Richard E.] Cole jumped in order. Left ship on AFCE (automatic pilot), shut off both gas cocks and I left. Should have put flaps down. This would have slowed down landing speed, reduced impact and shortened glide.

"Left airplane about 9:30 P.M. [ship time] after about 13 hours in the air. Still had enough gas for half hour flight but right front tank was showing empty. Had transferred once as right engine used more fuel. Had covered about 2,250 miles, mostly at low speed which more than doubled the consumption for this time.

"All hands collected and ship located by late afternoon of 19th. Requested General Ho Yang Ling, Director of the Branch Government of Western Chekieng Province to have a lookout kept along seacoast from Hang Chow Bay to Wen Chow Bay and also to have all sampans and junks along the coast to keep a lookout for planes that went down at sea, or just reached shore.

"Early morning of 20th, four planes and crews, in addition to ours, had been located and I wired General Arnold, through the Embassy at Chungking: *Tokyo successfully bombed. Due bad weather on China coast believe all airplanes wrecked. Five crews found safe in China so far.* Wired again on the 27th giving more details.

"Discussed possibility of purchasing three prisoners on the seacoast from Puppet Government and endeavoring to take out the three in lake area by force. Believe this desire was made clear to General Ku Cho-tung (who spoke little English) and know it was made clear to English-speaking members of his staff. This was at Shangjao. They agreed to try to purchase of three [American prisoners] but recommended against . . . due to large Japanese concentration.

"Bad luck:

"(1) Early take-off due to naval contact with surface and air craft.

"(2) Clear over Tokyo.

"(3) Foul over China.

"Good luck:

"(1) A 25 mph tail wind over most of the last 1,200 miles.

"Take-off should have been made three hours before daylight, but we didn't know how easy it would be and the Navy didn't want to light up. Dawn take-off, closer in, would have been better as things turned out. However, due to the bad weather it was questionable if even daylight landing could have been made at Chuchow without radio aid.

"Still feel that original plan of having one plane take off three hours before dusk and others just at dusk was best all-around plan for average conditions."

When he dropped out of the B-25, Doolittle, like the others in the crew, fell into the unknown. There was no certainty that they had been over Chinese-held territory, nor even that they were over inhabited country. Prepared for anything in the deep blackness, Doolittle remembered, once his chute had jerked open, to come down in a knees-up attitude. He had broken both his ankles in a youthful accident and did not want to chance it again. His landing, however, was "soft" in the extreme, for he landed in a rice paddy, up to his neck in fertilizing night soil. Reeking and cold from the dampness, Doolittle set out to find refuge from the night winds. He soon learned that the phrase they had been taught aboard the *Hornet, "Lushu hoo megwa fugi"* ("I am an American"), did not exactly open doors (he later learned that it was the wrong dialect for the section in which he had come down). He found refuge finally in an old water mill, although sleep was an impossibility because of the cold.

In the morning he found a farmer who led him to a military outpost and trouble. The Chinese major in charge, who understood some English, found it difficult to believe Doolittle's story. He had not heard of the mission because the word had not been transmitted because of the breakdown in the preparations. Doolittle then led a group of soldiers to the farmhouse whose door had been bolted to him the night before, and the frightened people inside denied the whole tale. Hoping to furnish his parachute as evidence Doolittle led the major and three soldiers to the rice paddy in which he had come down in the night. It was gone. The soldiers began muttering among themselves and the major looked more doubtful than ever. But at this moment two of the other soldiers emerged from the farmhouse carrying the parachute; the farmer would have willingly exchanged Doolittle's life for such a great quantity of high-grade silk.

Finally convinced, the major smiled, shook Doolittle's hand, ordered food, and sent word back to the outpost to send out search parties for the rest of the crew. All by this time had experienced their own little dramas. Crew chief Paul Leonard had been fired upon by a small patrol and took to the woods; navigator Henry Potter and bombardier Fred A. Breamer were taken prisoner by a band of guerrillas and robbed. They were aided by an

Disheartened, Doolittle sits beside the wing of his B-25 the morning after the Tokyo raid.

(U. S. AIR FORCE)

English-speaking Chinese boy. The guerrilla chieftain returned their valuables and arranged for them to be taken to the outpost. The search went on until all of the crew had been found, all luckily unhurt except for bumps and bruises.

Doolittle, accompanied by Leonard, clambered up the mountain on which the B-25 had crashed. It was a depressing sight, for it was nothing now but a mangled pile of junk. Silently the two men picked through the debris. Doolittle found his oil-soaked Army blouse—someone had already clipped off the brass buttons. It then all caught up with him; dejected, he sat down.

Leonard spoke gently. "What do you think will happen when you go home, Colonel?"

"Well," Doolittle replied, "I guess they'll send me to Leavenworth."

"No, sir," Leonard offered. "I'll tell you what will happen. They're going to make you a general."

Doolittle managed a weak smile at Leonard's obvious attempt to cheer him up. He had lost sixteen planes and at this gray instant, he had no idea where seventy-five men could be.

". . . and," Leonard persisted, "they're going to give you the Congressional Medal of Honor."

Doolittle worked up another smile at the extravagance. Even Leonard recognized that and added, "I know they're going to give you another airplane and when they do, I'd like to be your crew chief."

Tears, a rare Doolittle commodity, filled his eyes. This was the highest tribute of all, from one professional to another. He was never to forget Leonard's request on that mountaintop. (All of Leonard's predictions came true: Doolittle was awarded the Medal of Honor and promoted to brigadier general—skipping a colonelcy—and when he returned to active duty in north Africa flying a Martin B-26, Master Sergeant Paul Leonard served as his crew chief. Leonard was killed on January 5, 1943, during an air raid on an Allied base near Youks les Bains, Algeria.)

Within hours after Doolittle had wired Arnold of the completion of their mission, the news of the bombing of Tokyo and the other cities was flashed across the nation. Affecting an air of mystery President Roosevelt announced that the B-25s had taken off from Shangri-La, a Tibetan never-never land in the popular novel *Lost Horizon* by James Hilton. A full year went by before it was revealed that the Mitchells had been launched from the deck of the *Hornet*. Meanwhile, a wave of jubilant excitement swept the country with a resultant quickening of morale.

Morale in Japan sank, despite the fact that the military damage inflicted by Doolittle's crews was light. The Japanese war leaders had lied to their people about their invulnerability to American attack. This introduced an uneasy air of doubt where once all had been optimistic. Hoping to regain this optimism, the Japanese leaders quickly flooded the media with further deceits.

The official voice of the militarists was the Tokyo

Asahi Shimbun, which, in part, printed of the Doolittle raiders that "While fleeing helter-skelter to avoid the curtain of shells which burst forth from our antiaircraft batteries, the enemy planes chose innocent people and city streets as their targets. They did not go near military installations. They carried out an inhuman, insatiable, indiscriminate bombing attack on the sly, and the fact that they schemed to strafe civilians and non-combatants demonstrates their fiendish behavior."

Radio Tokyo added its permutations: "The cowardly raiders purposefully avoided industrial centers and the important military establishments and blindly dumped their incendiaries in a few suburban districts, especially on schools and hospitals." The motif of the bombardment of schools and hospitals was developed into a major theme in the propaganda following the raid. Claims were also made for nine American planes shot down.

VI

Of the sixteen aircraft participating in the First Special Aviation Project only one made a safe, intact, wheels-down landing, the one piloted by Captain Edward J. York. During their flight to Tokyo York had noted that fuel consumption had been alarmingly high. Upon bombing a factory in the Tokyo area, York asked navigator Lieutenant Nolan A. Herndon for a heading to Russia instead of China. Thanks to the carburetor switch made at Sacramento they could hardly anticipate better than ditching in the sea three hundred miles off the China coast. Russia remained their only chance, even if they had been told (not ordered) to stay away.

After an uneventful flight York brought the B-25 down onto an airfield about forty miles north of Vladivostok in a perfect landing. Perhaps, York hoped, since they and the Russians were allies they might be permitted to refuel and get out of Russia in the morning to rejoin the others in China. Instead, the five men were interned and the plane confiscated. Although the Americans were reasonably well treated, they remained virtual prisoners until they escaped (by arranging bribes) into Iran about a year later.

Eleven crews, including Doolittle's, bailed out and four attempted crash landings. The crews which bailed out generally fared best. Corporal Leland Faktor, engineer-gunner in Lieutenant Robert M. Gray's plane, however, died of injuries sustained when he landed in mountainous country in his parachute. His burial was attended to by an American missionary, the Reverend John M. Birch. Most of the others who bailed out, and who were injured, suffered sprained ankles, leg and back injuries. Faktor was the only fatality.

Lieutenant Dean Hallmark attempted to ditch his plane in the water near Hanchang, on the China coast. The impact threw Hallmark through the windshield and injured the others. Hallmark, however, in company with Robert J. Meder and Chase J. Nielsen, despite their injuries, set out for the beach. Meder turned back when he saw William J. Dieter and Donald Fitzmaurice floundering in the surf. He pulled Fitzmaurice onto shore and, though injured and exhausted, returned to the ocean to look for Dieter. He found the bombardier on the beach, face down in the water. Both Fitzmaurice and Dieter were dead of injuries and possibly drowning. But the three surviving officers were fated for worse: all three fell into the hands of the Japanese.

Ted Lawson also attempted to bring his plane down in the coastal waters and, like Hallmark, was flung through the windshield, along with navigator Charles L. McClure and copilot Dean Davenport. Robert Clever, the bombardier, smashed through the plexiglass and metal nose of the aircraft. Of the five-man crew only engineer-gunner David J. Thatcher was not seriously injured, or rather, was the least injured. Lawson, whose left leg was ripped open terribly, was in the worst state. Limping and in pain himself, Thatcher attended to the injuries of the others. With the aid of Chinese he had the men moved inside a nearby hut (though not without hideous pain to all), for once the news of the Tokyo raid was known and the B-25s came crashing down, Japanese patrol activity became intense.

By various means, ranging from junk to improvised stretcher, the men were spirited into unoccupied China, to a small hospital in the village of Linhai. By this time Lawson was so far gone with infection that he could neither eat nor speak. Thatcher informed Chungking of their state and

The Chinese, civilians as well as soldiers, rallied to the aid of the Tokyo raider crews. Those Chinese who were suspected of helping the Americans suffered terribly at the hands of the Japanese soldiers.

(U. S. AIR FORCE)

was joined in a few days by Lieutenant Thomas R. White.

White was the unique member of the mission; he was not an airman at all but a doctor who had volunteered for the raid. He was permitted to go as a gunner member of the crew of Lieutenant Donald Smith. The latter had crash-landed his plane in the same vicinity, so White, once informed of the fate of Lawson's crew, made his way to Linhai. To keep out of the path of the Japanese, Smith, his crew, and the remarkable Thatcher of Lawson's crew moved on to Chungking. White remained with Lawson, McClure, and Davenport, treating them skillfully with the primitive means at hand. He also doubled as a dentist for the Chinese villagers. In time, White was forced to amputate Lawson's left leg, which saved the pilot's life. When some recovery was made, White had the three men evacuated out of the path of the vindictive Japanese.

Lieutenant William Farrow's crew, of the ill-fated

After the mission: Madame Chiang awards the Tokyo raiders decorations in appreciation for their feat. With her are Doolittle (now a brigadier general; he had been a lieutenant colonel when he took off from the Hornet), *Colonel John A. Hilger (pilot of the fourteenth plane), and Lieutenant Richard E. Cole, who had been Doolittle's copilot.* (U. S. AIR FORCE)

sixteenth plane (the propeller of which had gashed Seaman Wall's arm), bailed out near the China coast at Shipu, in Japanese-occupied territory, and fell into the waiting arms of the Japanese. Along with the survivors of Hallmark's crew these men were "tried," after a long period of hideous treatment, by a Japanese military court. This mockery, held on August 28, 1942, in Shanghai, decreed that all eight prisoners were to be executed because they had "suddenly exhibited cowardice when confronted with opposition in the air and on the ground, and with intent of cowing, killing, and wounding innocent civilians, and wreaking havoc on residences and other living quarters of no military significance whatsoever" and further "did carry out indiscriminate bombing and strafing." The early themes of press and radio were worked up in the "trial" as a full-fledged symphony.

The eight prisoners, who had been tortured and starved and were in poor health (Hallmark, for example, was unable to sit up and attended the proceedings in a cot), had no conception of what it was all about. They were made to sign blank papers which were subsequently filled in in Japanese. They even signed "confessions," also in Japanese, without the slightest conception of content. All men were in a state of befuddlement as well as physically weak.

Ultimately the death sentence was applied to only three of the eight—Hallmark, Farrow (both pilots) and Harold Spatz (engineer-gunner), all three having unwittingly signed their own death warrants; their portions of the "confessions" admitted to bombings of civilians and strafing. The remaining five, George Barr, Robert Hite, Jacob DeShazer (all of Farrow's crew), Nielsen, and Meder, were "spared" through the alleged god-given leniency of the Emperor. Their sentence was life imprisonment as "war criminals."

This meant forty months of solitary confinement for the five men. During this tortuous period Meder died of maltreatment, disease, and sheer neglect. Nielsen, Barr, Hite, and DeShazer were rescued by an American parachute team on August 20, 1945, at Peiping. Of the survivors, DeShazer eventually returned to Japan—as a missionary, an exemplification of compassion in the highest degree.

Substantial, if not definitive, damage was done by the Doolittle mission. Possibly the greatest injury was to the self-esteem of the Japanese Samurai. Although it had not been hit, the very fact that the air over and around the Emperor's Imperial Palace had been violated by enemy aircraft was a gross affront to those who had sworn their very lives to keep this from happening. The militarists, with a keen professional eye, tended to denigrate the raid—English-speaking members referred to it as the "Do Nothing Raid"—but they knew better. It was a harbinger of things to come.

The reaction to the raid was savagery unleashed. The mistreatment of the eight prisoners was reprehensible, but the slaughter of the Chinese which followed the raid was manic barbarism without military justification. Fifty-three battalions of Japanese troops moved inland, ravaging the land, and in about three months they had killed 250,000 Chinese—soldiers as well as civilians—in the rampage. Villages in which the American airmen had hidden or were cared for were all but deracinated. Chinese who had taken small token gifts—coins, gloves, a scarf—or who had taken parts from the planes were tortured and killed. Wang Poo-fang, a village schoolteacher from Ihwang, near which the plane of Lieutenant Harold Watson had crashed, related a single incident which could be multiplied a thousand times over.

"We fed the Americans," Wang said, "and carried them to safety so that they could bomb Tokyo again. Then the dwarf-invaders came. They killed my three sons; they killed my wife, Angsing; they set fire to my school; they burned my books; they drowned my grandchildren in the well." The schoolmaster, too, had been flung into the well, but managed to climb out after the Japanese had moved on. There was little of his village left to him.

All airfields, which might have served as landing spots for possible future raids, were destroyed, ridged with trenches (all work being done by Chinese), and rendered unusable. And then the Japanese troops moved back from a wasteland of twenty thousand square miles.

Another unreasonable means of vengeance was the so-called "balloon bombs," the Japanese equivalent to the German V-weapons of the later months of the European war. The balloon bombs, however, were much less sophisticated though equally senseless. They were constructed of rice paper and potato paste by Japanese civilians in their homes. Carrying

Made in Japan: vengeance balloons released over the Pacific to drift on the winds to the United States. At top left is one of the balloons in flight over the northwest United States. Below it is a close-up demonstrating the workings, theoretically, of the balloon. Balloons did not always work and, in the lower photograph, woodmen chop a tree in which one had become lodged. Others worked, however, and killed several people, haphazardly and senselessly.

(U. S. AIR FORCE)

booby-trap bombs, about ten thousand of these giant balloons were released near Tokyo to be carried across the Pacific at high altitudes by prevailing winds. Many actually completed the voyage—about 280 were found in the American Northwest, Canada, and Alaska. Six picnickers were killed in a forest near Lakeview, Oregon, when they came upon one of these homemade balloon bombs. As late as 1955, a decade after the last of the balloons had been released, one was discovered in Alaska and tested by the Department of Defense, which found the device "still highly explosive and dangerous."

The Doolittle raid had not been, as Imperial General Headquarters in Tokyo implied, a "Do Nothing Raid." Perhaps its most strategic consequence was that it settled a bitter controversy. This argument had been under way for weeks between Combined Fleet and the Imperial Naval General Staff. Yamamoto had been pressing for an early, full-scale, decisive battle with the U. S. Pacific Fleet.

That the carriers had escaped the Pearl Harbor attack never ceased to vex him. The truth was emerging that aircraft, not battleships, would decide the Pacific war, but the Imperial Naval General Staff did not wish to rush into a major fleet engagement.

The coming of Doolittle decided the issue. Yamamoto sensed that the bombers had come from an American carrier—and he reminded his critics that the failure to keep Doolittle from Tokyo was a reflection upon the General Staff as well as Combined Fleet. Consequently by the end of April Yamamoto's controversial plan was completed and approved by the General Staff. On May 5, 1942, Admiral Osami Nagano issued, in the name of the Emperor, Imperial General Headquarters Navy Order No. 18, directing Yamamoto "to carry out the occupation of Midway Island and key points in the western Aleutians in co-operation with the Army."

4

MIDWAY: TRAGIC VICTORY

By the spring of 1942 the virus that came to be called the "Victory Disease" infected the Japanese. Few were immune, from the man in the street on up into the honored and seemingly invincible purlieus of Combined Fleet and the Naval General Staff.

Invincible indeed—from Pearl Harbor through the fall of Wake Island, the destruction of the British ships *Prince of Wales* and *Repulse,* the surrender of Hong Kong and Singapore—the uncoiling of the Greater East Asia Co-Prosperity Sphere into the southern Pacific had gone unchecked for nearly six months. Then came news of the fall of the Philippines with the surrender of Corregidor on May 6, 1942. Yamamoto had truly "run wild." His leadership had been as good as his word, but the question was, in early 1942, what were the long-range plans to be? Even the most optimistic among his admirers had not expected so unremitting a succession of victories.

Should they consolidate their cheaply won holdings, or should they extend their "security perimeter"? In Yamamoto's mind there was little question of the next move. He knew they could not dig in and wait for the American industrial machine to grind into action and take it all away. Several plans had been under consideration by the middle of January. One favored an all-out attack upon Hawaii, another pointed toward India and

Ceylon, and a third advocated an Australian offensive. This last originated from the Naval General Staff, the argument being that Australia must be cut off as a future springboard for an Allied counter-offensive against Japan. The attack upon Hawaii had originated from the Chief of Staff, Combined Fleet, Rear Admiral Matome Ugaki, who based his thinking upon the possibility of such an attack luring the American fleet to its destruction by the Imperial Navy.

The Navy's plan to take Ceylon was rejected by the Army, which did not have the troops to back up the amphibious landings proposed. Ugaki's Hawaii plan was shot full of holes by his own staff because of the impossibility of achieving another surprise attack. Also, there was the formidable job it would pose for carrier-borne aircraft to maintain air superiority over so large an area as the Hawaiian Islands. The Australian plan was scuttled also by the Army High Command, which insisted it would be unable to supply the required ten divisions. However, there was obvious merit in isolating Australia.

Yamamoto, however, favored another plan—related to Ugaki's Hawaii proposal, but not so formidable in terms of area. In early April he introduced his Operation MI, the major point of which appeared to be the occupation of the Midway atoll. In truth, the occupation of the atoll was secondary in

Yamamoto's mind; his wish, his dream, was to lure the American fleet, and especially its carriers, into one massive decisive battle with the Imperial fleet. Once over—with a Japanese victory, inevitably— the reeling Americans must ask for peace before they had properly geared for war.

Yamamoto's proposal set off another round of debate. The Naval General Staff rose in opposition to the plan. One of the most serious objections was: Even if the atoll were taken, how would it be kept supplied, if, for some reason, the U.S. fleet had

Before the storm: flight deck of the U.S.S. Enterprise, *Pacific 1942.* (NAVY DEPT., NATIONAL ARCHIVES)

not been destroyed? Could Midway truly function as an advance base for Japanese air patrols, considering the range (six to seven hundred miles) of patrol planes? Would the United States actually sue for peace merely because Midway had fallen? Finally, Midway was within bombing range of Hawaii; would not the long-range U.S. bombers menace the occupation force as well as attempts to supply it?

But these arguments were beside the point, for Yamamoto's dream, incited by the fever of the Victory Disease, visualized the mass sinking of American carriers. Despite the objections, Yamamoto—as he had before the Hawaii Operation— made it clear what he desired. The Naval General

Staff, bludgeoned, halfheartedly assented to the operation. Arguments, even opposition, continued on into April until the Doolittle raiders appeared over the sacred soil of Nippon. Debate was ended and Operation MI went into active preparation.

II

If the Doolittle raid was a portent, during the planning of the Midway operation another occurred of even greater immediate significance to Yamamoto, the Battle of the Coral Sea. This was the first naval battle in history in which the ships themselves did not exchange a shot. All the fighting was done by aircraft and in this battle, though ostensibly "won" by the Japanese, Japan suffered its first setback of the war.

This crucial engagement was ignited by Japanese operations aimed at the dual-pronged invasions of Tulagi, in the Solomons, and Port Moresby, in strategic proximity to Australia, in southern Papua, New Guinea. From the first of February the American carriers *Enterprise* and *Lexington* had been making hit-and-run raids upon Japanese-held positions in the Marshalls, the Solomons, and northern New Guinea. Yamamoto recognized the importance both of clearing this area of the American carriers and of the establishment of bases for future operations.

What Yamamoto did not know was that, thanks to Army cryptographers, the Japanese codes were no secret to the enemy and his plans, in turn, were no secret to Admiral Nimitz. By mid-April Nimitz was aware of the impending operations; by the twentieth he even knew the date: May 3. Whereupon he sent Task Force 17, built around the *Yorktown* and *Lexington* and under the command of Rear Admiral Frank Jack Fletcher, to counter the Japanese move.

To accomplish this Fletcher had only about half the force that was at the disposal of Vice-Admiral Shigeyoshi Inouye, Commander in Chief, Imperial Fourth Fleet. This massive force was, it is true, divided into three parts, each of which was assigned its special task in the Port Moresby-Tulagi invasions. The Tulagi Invasion Group (twelve assorted ships) was to occupy that base, which was defended by a few Australian troops, and establish an air base there for future operations. The Port Moresby Invasion Group consisted of eleven troop transports covered by several heavy cruisers, light cruisers, and the light carrier *Shoho*. Also covering the two invasions was the main Carrier Striking Force (carriers *Zuikaku, Shokaku*) with its protective heavy cruisers and screen of destroyers. The plan envisioned was that the invasions would bring out the American carriers, which, when they ventured into the Coral Sea, would be destroyed by the Japanese forces.

The already alerted Nimitz was ready with Task Force 17, to which had been added a support group (two heavy cruisers, a light cruiser, and two destroyers) of what was then called "MacArthur's Navy" under Rear Admiral Crace, Royal Navy.

On May 3 the Japanese opened the battle by taking Tulagi; on the following day planes from the *Yorktown* bombed the Japanese positions at Tulagi. This revealed that an American carrier was indeed somewhere in the area. The *Zuikaku* and *Shokaku* were headed south from Rabaul (where they had gone to deliver fighter planes) to engage the enemy task force. Meanwhile, the Port Moresby Invasion Group continued on its course.

Not until dawn of May 7 did search planes make contact—in the Coral Sea. Japanese scouts reported sighting the American task force, specifically "a carrier and a cruiser." Rear Admiral Chuichi Hara, commander of air operations, under orders from Vice-Admiral Takeo Takagi, commander of the Carrier Striking Force, sent out the entire bombing strength of the two Japanese carriers (a total of seventy-eight bombers, torpedo planes, and fighters) to make an all-out attack. The "task force" turned out to be the destroyer *Sims* and the oiler *Neosho*, neither really worth the wholesale effort. Both were sunk, the *Sims* first (almost within minutes); the *Neosho*, which had been spared at Pearl Harbor, was scuttled a few days later, after smoking and drifting helplessly. But the loss of these ships had pulled the Japanese planes away from the *Lexington* and *Yorktown*, whose planes had been launched. While the Americans were off on their own wild-goose chase ("two carriers and four heavy cruisers"—actually two outdated light cruisers, three gunboats, and a seaplane tender) they unexpectedly came upon the light carrier *Shoho*. The *Lexington*'s Scouting Squadron 2 led the assault, followed by a torpedo squadron and a bombing squadron. All

three had scored hits, but the *Shoho* had turned into the wind to launch its planes. The *Yorktown* planes arrived at this moment, catching the *Shoho* in a position where evasive action was impossible, and soon the word went out in the excited voice of Lieutenant Commander Robert Dixon, commander of the *Lexington*'s scout bomber squadron: "Scratch one flattop!"

Within minutes the *Shoho,* a burning shambles, sank into the sea, taking five hundred crewmen to

Below decks of a carrier, the hangar deck, where engineers work on a fighter, the Grumman F4F "Wildcat." (NAVY DEPT., NATIONAL ARCHIVES)

the bottom. This development unnerved Vice-Admiral Inouye so much that he called off the Port Moresby invasion and recalled the transports to Rabaul. Until he was certain the American carriers had been cleared out of the Coral Sea, Inouye felt that he could not expose the invasion forces to aerial attack. This was a decision that later greatly displeased Yamamoto, for Inouye could not exploit the advantages that came his way later in the battle.

On May 8, finally, the Japanese spotted the American carriers and launched another full-scale attack. The Japanese had the advantage of heavy weather cover, but the *Lexington* and *Yorktown*

Prelude to Midway: the Battle of the Coral Sea, the first major sea battle in which surface ships did not exchange a shot. Fought by aircraft in the vicinity of the Solomon Islands, the Coral Sea battle blocked the Japanese in their drive toward Australia and New Zealand. One of the American losses was the carrier Lexington. Wildcats on the flight deck following bomb hits by Japanese planes.

(NAVY DEPT., NATIONAL ARCHIVES)

A destroyer moves in to pick up Lexington crew men after the order to abandon ship has been given. Japanese torpedo planes and dive bombers caused fires and internal explosions; the "Lady Lex" was finally sunk by the American destroyer Phelps.

(NAVY DEPT., NATIONAL ARCHIVES)

lay in bright day. The Americans missed finding the *Zuikaku* but did locate the *Shokaku* and succeeded in hitting it with two bombs. Seventy Japanese aircraft, meanwhile, attacked the American carriers savagely. The *Yorktown,* struck by a single bomb, lost sixty-six men, but the *Lexington,* torpedoed and bombed, was left burning and listing after the encounter. Damage-control parties seemed to bring the three fires which blazed under control, but internal explosions doomed the "Lady Lex." New fires spread as gasoline poured into the flames. Captain Frederick Sherman ordered "Abandon Ship," the wounded were evacuated, and the *Lexington,* rather than be abandoned to the Japanese, was sunk by American destroyers.

Trading the *Lexington* for the *Shoho* was no true victory, but the invasion of Port Moresby was canceled. Also, both the *Shokaku,* which would be out of commission for two months being repaired, and the *Zuikaku,* which had lost many of its pilots, were to be denied to Yamamoto for his Midway operation. This fact did not trouble him, for his pilots had sunk the *Lexington* and claimed to have sunk the *Yorktown.*

Nimitz, however, was concerned over the temporary loss of the *Yorktown* in his planning to counter Yamamoto's Midway assault. It was estimated that three months would be required to return the carrier to fighting trim. However, at the Pearl Harbor dry dock a miracle occurred. An army of workmen swarmed over the carrier, working night and day, and within two days the patched-up, scarred *Yorktown* was ready for action.

Despite his losses, Yamamoto was ready, afflicted as he was by then with singleness of purpose and the Victory Disease. He wanted those other American carriers.

III

Midway atoll lies about 1150 miles to the northwest of Hawaii. Its two major islets, Sand and Eastern, were not impressive land masses—Sand Island, the largest, was barely two miles long. In 1859 one Captain N. C. Brooks claimed the two islands for the United States; Secretary of the Navy Gideon Welles placed it under informal U. S. Navy jurisdiction in 1867. Two years later the Congress author-

ized channel dredging between the two islands. In 1900 the Japanese arrived for the first time to prey on the islands' bird population, killing the terns, gannets, and goonies for their feathers. In 1903, fearing that Japan would claim the atoll, President Theodore Roosevelt again placed it under naval jurisdiction and the Japanese poachers were driven off. Midway became a link in the trans-Pacific cable between the Philippines and Hawaii in the same year.

Americans recalled Midway best before the war as one of the way stations for Pan American Airways' *China Clipper* in 1935. Four years later the Navy's Hepburn Board, along with other recommendations, found that Midway was "second in importance only to Pearl Harbor." By August 18, 1941, Midway was commissioned as a Naval Air Station with a complement of around eight hundred men. Dock facilities and airstrips were built and gun positions installed. Although shelled on December 7, 1941, Midway had escaped serious damage and invasion. The planned air strike was canceled

Frank J. Fletcher, Task Force 17 commander—and victor—in the Battle of Midway.

(NAVY DEPT., NATIONAL ARCHIVES)

because of bad weather. While the Japanese concentrated on Wake Island, which proved no easy objective (although overrun by the Japanese on December 23), Midway was granted a period of grace, except for an occasional shelling by submarine.

The strategic position of Midway, relative to the Hawaiian Islands, would bring out the American fleet, which was Yamamoto's most feverish dream. It was no fantasy, however, for his Hawaii Operation, having put most of the U.S. battleship strength out of consideration, placed the Americans in the position of the underdog. Even though the Coral Sea Battle had "scratched" one light carrier and sent the *Shokaku* and the *Zuikaku* into temporary retirement, Yamamoto was capable of amassing a large number of ships for his Midway Operation— nearly two hundred. Among these were eight carriers (four heavies), eleven battleships, twenty-two cruisers, sixty-five destroyers, and twenty-one submarines. About seven hundred aircraft, dive bombers, torpedo bombers, and fighters, were at Yamamoto's disposal.

Rear Admiral Frank J. Fletcher had to counter this force with 3 carriers (including the hastily repaired *Yorktown*), 7 heavy cruisers and 1 light cruiser, and 15 destroyers. Aboard his carriers, Fletcher carried about 230 aircraft; in addition, there were a number of Midway-based planes, Marine fighters and scout bombers, Navy torpedo bombers and patrol bombers, totaling 98. The Army Seventh Air Force, too, had moved 17 B-17s up from Hawaii and 4 B-26s, converted into torpedo bombers. Although handicapped in terms of sheer weight, Fletcher enjoyed certain advantages: he knew Yamamoto was coming, he knew where Yamamoto would strike and when, so that he could concentrate his meager forces at the point at which they would prove most effective.

Yamamoto, on the other hand, split his forces in a characteristic attempt at a diversionary feint. This took the form of what was called the Northern, or Aleutians, Force under Vice-Admiral Moshiiro Hosogaya, who was to spearhead the Midway Operation by an attack upon American installations at Dutch Harbor and the invasion and occupation of Attu and Kiska. Two carriers, *Ryujo* and *Junyo,* whose air commander was Rear Admiral Kakuji Kakuta, accompanied the Northern Force. It was

hoped that this attack, so close to the American homeland, would bring out the American fleet, send it scurrying off into the northern Pacific, and leave Midway more or less unguarded for the main attack.

If not, Yamamoto planned to meet the American fleet and planes, after Midway itself had been struck, when they came out of Pearl Harbor to meet the surprise Japanese thrust. Yamamoto's forces consisted of the 1st Carrier Force, under command of Admiral Chuichi Nagumo, who had led the Hawaii strike upon Pearl Harbor. Nagumo had, in addition to screening and support groups of battleships, cruisers, and destroyers, four great carriers, *Akagi* (his own flagship), *Kaga, Hiryu,* and *Soryu.* That the temporary loss of the *Shokaku* and *Zuikaku* denied him one third of his air power did not disquiet Nagumo. He was certain, after six months of victory, that he and his carriers were invincible.

Yamamoto, aboard his flagship, the giant battleship *Yamato,* would command all the Midway-Aleutians forces, from what was named the "Main Body of the Main Force." This force, consisting of three large battleships, the light carrier *Hosho,* cruisers, destroyers, and seaplane carriers, would be situated about six hundred miles northwest of Midway, ready to come to the aid of Nagumo and the Midway Invasion Force or the Aleutian Invasion Force, as the course of the battle demanded.

Before the strikes were made various submarines of the Advance Submarine Force were to be dispersed northwest of Hawaii to spot the American ships as soon as they left Pearl Harbor to meet Nagumo's challenge at Midway. That, at least, was the plan—on paper. In practice, it did not work out quite as Yamamoto had expected.

The submarines were to have been in position by June 1, but because of delays in overhauling some of them and poor weather, the sub cordon was not established until June 4. By this time the great armada of Combined Fleet had been steaming toward its several objectives for ten days, ten days of nearly complete ignorance of the movements of the U.S. fleet.

The elaborate preparations required for the Midway-Aleutians Operation filled the airwaves with messages, most of which U. S. Intelligence intercepted, decoded, and flashed to Pearl Harbor. Thus two of the favorite Japanese techniques, surprise and feint, were rendered pointless from the beginning.

Task Force at sea, spring 1942: a view from the aft flight deck of the Enterprise *bearing TBFs; bringing* up the rear are a destroyer, a tanker, and, in the distance, the Hornet and a tanker.

(NAVY DEPT., NATIONAL ARCHIVES)

Not that every step of the proposed operation was lucidly outlined for Nimitz. His guess was that, in view of the massive preparations which were under way, the objective must be Midway. But there was no absolute certainty that the "AF" to which the Japanese referred so frequently in their messages was, indeed, Midway. Admiral King, in fact, was equally certain that it was Oahu, Hawaii.

Naval Intelligence then tricked the Japanese into the identification of AF. Dutifully, as ordered, Midway sent a message in the clear to Pearl Harbor reporting that its water distillation apparatus had broken down. Within days a Japanese radio message was intercepted reporting that AF was low on water. Midway it was!

This was only the first in a series of unanticipated errors which would beset Yamamoto. Another occurred when the submarine squadrons were delayed in taking up their positions to the north and northwest of Hawaii. By the time they had arrived, the

The lost Zero of the Aleutians; Tadayoshi Koga's Reisen *on its back in the tundra of Akutan Island. The Americans now had a nearly intact, once mysterious,* Zero. (NAVY DEPT., NATIONAL ARCHIVES)

two American task forces had already crossed the
assigned cordon lines. When the time came for
opening the Midway-Aleutians Operation, Yamamoto had no idea of the whereabouts of the American fleet, nor of its composition, however disproportionate compared to his.

Even while the several Japanese task forces approached their targets the American task forces lay
in wait at "Point Luck," about 350 miles northeast
of Midway. On May 28, the day the last Japanese
ship left port, Rear Admiral Raymond A. Spruance's
Task Force 16 (the *Enterprise* and *Hornet*) left
Pearl Harbor for Point Luck. Two days later Rear
Admiral Frank J. Fletcher, aboard the expeditiously
rejuvenated *Yorktown,* left for Point Luck to join
forces with Spruance and to take tactical command
of the task forces. Nimitz would oversee the battle
from his headquarters at Pearl Harbor. Thus he
would be able to watch the progress of the battle
from a central point. Yamamoto, on the other hand,
would be aboard the *Yamato,* and thanks to the
need for radio silence, would frequently be completely out of touch with the progress of the battle.

Nimitz was taking one risk in assuming that the
main force was aimed at Midway and not the
Aleutians. He concentrated his main striking force,
therefore, in the vicinity of Midway, leaving the defense of the Aleutians to a small token force, mainly
cruisers, under the command of Rear Admiral Robert A. Theobald. Fortunately for Nimitz his guess
had been right, and although the Japanese succeeded
in landing troops on Attu and Kiska, they neither
gained strategic ground nor succeeded in luring the
main American forces away from Midway. In fact,
they suffered one serious loss in the Aleutians. This
occurred on May 3, 1942, with an inconclusive attack by a formation of Kates, escorted by a half-
dozen Zeros, upon Dutch Harbor. After leaving the
carrier *Ryujo,* the Japanese planes encountered no
opposition but heavy rain and thick fog. Over
Dutch Harbor it was clear enough for the Kates to
bomb and the Zeros to strafe the harbor installations and moored flying boats. There was some return fire from the few Americans based there, but
Dutch Harbor was left a smoking shambles as the
Japanese formation completed its attack and pulled
away to reassemble for the return flight to the
Ryujo.

It was then that Flight Petty Officer Tadayoshi

*The crew of the Navy Catalina that spotted the Japanese
fleet approaching Midway. Back row (left to right):
R. J. Derouin, Francis Musser, Ensign Hardeman,
Jewell H. Reid (pilot), R. A. Swan. Front row: J. F.
Grammell, J. Goovers, and P. A. Fitzpatrick.*
(NAVY DEPT., NATIONAL ARCHIVES)

Koga, flying an A6M2 *Reisen,* noticed that his aircraft trailed fuel in his wake. By radio he informed
the bomber leader, Lieutenant Michio Kobayashi,
that he did not have enough fuel to return to the
Ryujo and would attempt to land at one of the designated emergency landing sites in the area. He
would then await a pickup by Japanese submarine,
according to the plans made for such emergencies.

Koga came in upon Akutan Island, a small island
to the east of Dutch Harbor. Choosing a smooth,
clear area, Koga lowered the wheels, opened his
canopy, and cranked up his seat for the landing
approach. Kobayashi, meanwhile, had scouted the
landing area, which he later described as perfect.
Koga skillfully brought the Zero lower, touched his
wheels down, and with a great splash the Zero
whipped over onto its back. The "flat and clear"
landing spot was actually spongy tundra. Kobayashi
circled over the wrecked Zero and assumed that
Koga was either dead or seriously injured. He also
assumed that, because of the marshy terrain, it
would be impossible, or extremely difficult, to re-
trieve the "heavily damaged" plane. Five weeks

The Enterprise, *with the Douglas TBD-1s ("Devasta-tor") of VT-6 on deck, races from "Point Luck" toward Midway.* (U. S. OFFICE OF WAR INFORMATION)

later, however, after the Zero was spotted by a Navy reconnaissance plane, the U. S. Navy sent a party to Akutan Island. There they found Koga hanging from his seat straps in the cockpit. He had evidently struck his head when the plane turned over and was killed. But the Zero was not as damaged as Koba-yashi had supposed. It was in fact virtually intact, the first Zero to fall into American hands in so good a condition. Koga's plane was salvaged and shipped to the Naval Air Station, North Island, San Diego, and restored to flying condition. Tested by Ameri-can pilots, the Zero revealed all of its secrets, good points as well as bad. It also led to the production of a plane specifically designed to deal with the Zero, the Grumman F6F ("Hellcat"). The loss of the single plane in the Dutch Harbor attack, the hoped-for diversion opening the Battle of Midway, was to cost the Japanese dear and ended the reign of the Zero over the skies in the Pacific.

Assuming that the Aleutian attacks were feints, the Americans awaited the main thrust at Point Luck. From Midway itself scouting planes were sent out to search for the oncoming Japanese fleet. It was around nine in the morning of June 3 that Ensign Jewell H. Reid, pilot of a Midway-based Catalina, flying about seven hundred miles to the

west of Midway, spotted a large number of Japanese ships. He had found the transports of the Midway Invasion Force. Reid tracked the ships, dodging in and out of clouds, counting, checking direction and speed. For nearly two hours Reid and his crew observed what they believed was the main Japa-nese fleet headed for Midway at nineteen knots; the eleven ships were pointed east. As Reid re-ported his find to Midway and Pearl Harbor, Rear Admiral Raizo Tanaka, commanding the transport group, informed Yamamoto that all hopes for sur-prise were over. Yamamoto had counted upon un-leashing an aerial attack upon Midway before the Americans ever realized the battle had begun. The initiative had now fallen into enemy hands. A heavy antiaircraft barrage forced Reid away from the Japa-nese surface force, but he had seen enough.

Midway, so long under the tension of waiting, came alive with preparation. Nine B-17s, led by Lieutenant Colonel Walter Sweeney, took off shortly after noon and reported that "Late in the afternoon, at a distance of 570 miles south of west of Midway, interception of the Japanese force was effected."

Sweeney's reaction upon seeing the vast Japanese fleet was less phlegmatic. "Good God," he said to his copilot Everett Wessman, "look at 'em!" It seemed that as far as the eye could see the waters below were dotted with ships trailing thin white wakes, like skates on a frozen pond. Smaller escort ships circled around the armada describing less regular patterns, like nervous water insects. It was an awe-inspiring sight; Sweeney estimated (erroneously) no less a force than forty-five ships.

The B-17s attacked in elements of three, Sweeney leading the first, dropping his six-hundred-pound bombs at the gyrating ships from an altitude of eight thousand feet. Antiaircraft fire flashed up at them furiously, appearing to one crewman "like a Times Square electric sign gone haywire." The next three Flying Fortresses followed, dropping their bombs from ten thousand feet; the last three dropped theirs from an altitude of twelve thousand feet. All three elements claimed either direct hits or near misses, and as all nine B-17s wheeled away from the antiaircraft fire, Sweeney looked back to see a battleship and a transport, seemingly still in the water, with "huge clouds of dark smoke mushroomed above them."

Although a total of thirty-six bombs were dropped by the B-17s, not one struck the dodging Japanese ships. The claims, plus others to follow, as well as the newspaper headlines attributing great feats to the Air Force bombers, would lead to much wartime feuding between the U. S. Navy and the Air Force.

Vice-Admiral Nagumo, meanwhile, was literally in a fog. His huge carrier striking force lay under a blanket of heavy weather, screening him from enemy search planes. At the same time it rendered navigation hazardous and also prevented Nagumo's search planes from being launched. One nagging question haunted him, one which he blurted out finally to his by now apprehensive staff; "But where is the enemy fleet?"

Some of the fog under which Nagumo proceeded was man-made. Yamamoto's staff, aboard the *Yamato,* had picked up radio transmissions in the Hawaii area which led them to suspect unusual enemy activity and the possibility of an American sortie. But Yamamoto did not inform Nagumo of this activity. He assumed that Nagumo was aware of it, which he was not, because Nagumo's ships were hundreds of miles closer to the enemy. Yamamoto was also all but fanatical upon maintaining radio silence. Meanwhile Nagumo glared into the swirling fog, hoping that the American carriers were still in the vicinity of the Solomon Islands, where Japanese intelligence had last placed them. The 1st Carrier Striking Force plunged through the fog toward Midway. Tomorrow, June 4, would re-

solve all things when Nagumo sent his planes off to bomb Midway.

Admiral Fletcher, in the area of Point Luck, had considered Ensign Reid's report of the sighting of the main force of the Japanese fleet. If Reid was right, then Fletcher's task forces were ill situated to challenge the invasion attempt. But Fletcher, judging from Reid's report of the location of the Japanese ships, concluded that they must be part of the invasion fleet and not the main attack force at all. There had been no carrier detected. And Fletcher's sixth sense told him that the air strike would materialize out of the area of murky weather to the northwest of Midway; further: the Japanese would, according to previous practice, launch their planes at dawn. So far, there was no sighting of Japanese carriers, however. But Fletcher's carriers would be in place, about two hundred miles north and slightly east of Midway, when morning came.

Dawn began to break at around four that morning. Though still under cloud, Nagumo's carriers came into a clearing. Despite the broken clouds and intermittent showers, stars were visible for the first time in days. A light wind blew from the southeast, which would aid the launch of the first attack wave. Nagumo could find some comfort in that. They would be precisely on schedule and Nagumo was aware of Yamamoto's addiction to timetables.

A Dauntless is given the signal to take off on a search mission. (DOUGLAS AIRCRAFT)

At almost the same moment that attack preparations were under way on the Japanese carriers, Midway too resounded to the roar of engines. Eleven Navy Catalinas were about to take off on search missions; streaks of light fanned into the dark eastern sky—it was 4:30 A.M. when the Catalinas, already fifteen minutes air-borne, prodded the western darkness in search of the Japanese ships. The PBYs were followed shortly after by bomb-laden planes from the Seventh Air Force's 5th and 11th Bombardment Groups, ready to attack the oncoming ships of the invasion force, which had been attacked the day before. Obviously, Nagumo was not aware of the attack, for before he ordered the first attack wave launched, he issued an estimate of the situation which revealed an unwonted optimism in Nagumo's generally conservative outlook. Two items, in retrospect, were tragically ironic: "The enemy is not yet aware of our plan, and he has not yet detected our task force," Nagumo had observed. And "There is no evidence of an enemy task force in our vicinity." According to all of the intelligence at his command, Nagumo could send his airmen off to bomb Midway believing that which he hoped was true was, indeed, true.

At a point about 240 miles northwest of Midway the 108 planes of the first attack wave took off from the four Japanese carriers. Thirty-six Zeros served as escort for the 36 Vals (dive bombers) and 36 Kates (torpedo bombers). The first wave was led by Lieutenant Joichi Tomonaga, on his first mission in the Pacific war. By 4:45 A.M. the formation had taken off and headed for Midway. The Vals and Kates flew in V-shaped echelons and the faster Zeros darted here and there over the formations to stay with them. As soon as the first wave was under way, Nagumo ordered the second wave, also 108 aircraft, to be readied. These would attack an enemy task force if it should appear, or if a second strike upon Midway were necessary, they would be ready. Eighteen Zeros circled over the striking force on air combat patrol.

Although not expecting American carriers or warships until after the Midway attack had begun, Nagumo, as an extra precautionary measure, dispatched several search planes to scour the seas to the south and east of his four carriers. Even so, the measure was much less systematic than usual. Of the seven planes, two took off on schedule; one developed engine trouble and returned before completing its search pattern and others returned early upon flying into the squally weather which clung to

Marine SB2Us (Vought-Sikorsky "Vindicator") leave Midway in search of the Japanese fleet, June 4, 1942.
(U. S. NAVY)

Nagumo's ships. The critical planes, as it turned out, those which were to be launched from the cruiser *Tone,* were delayed a half hour because of a malfunctioning catapult. The search pattern of one of the planes would have carried it over the American carriers—had it been launched.

Fletcher, too, was sending off search planes, ten Dauntlesses from the *Yorktown,* but they also missed the enemy carriers, still hidden under heavy weather. But the pilots of PBY Flight 58, Lieutenants Howard Ady and William Chase, churning through patches of clear and cloudy sky, spied a thin feather on the water to the north. It was a ship's wake; then another, another—and more. They dipped down and saw Japanese carriers below. They immediately radioed a maddeningly laconic message to Midway, intercepted by Fletcher waiting in the dark, "Enemy carriers." That was all. This answered very few of the questions racing through Fletcher's mind. Where were the carriers? How many were there?

These questions were not immediately forthcoming, for the Catalina had been spotted and antiaircraft fire rose up from the ships. Zeros, too, began climbing to intercept the American plane. Ady and Chase dipped into a cloud bank and were lost to the Japanese gunners, as well as to the fighter pilots. After some moments, they selected another break in the clouds and circled back for another look. Almost directly below them they saw Tomonaga's bombers and fighters, halfway to Midway. Their radio crackled, "Many planes heading Midway, bearing 320°, distance 150." And then Fletcher began accumulating his answers when a third message came in, "Two carriers and battleship bearing 320°, distance 180, course 135, speed 25." Because he had to wait for the search planes, Fletcher ordered Spruance to "proceed southwesterly and attack enemy carriers when definitely located. I will follow as soon as planes recovered."

At Midway too all hands prepared for action. Shortly after the message "Many planes heading Midway," the radar picked up the Japanese formation. Air raid sirens blared, aircraft lifted into the air, and men rushed to gun positions and shelters. The B-17s headed for the transports were reached by radio and directed to strike at the carriers. The four B-26s armed with torpedoes and six Grumman TBFs ("Avengers"), making their first combat sortie,

The Brewster F2A ("Buffalo"), no match for the Zero, made its single U.S. combat effort at the Battle of Midway and was hopelessly outperformed—to the tragic cost of Marine pilots. (NAVY DEPT., NATIONAL ARCHIVES)

were vectored toward the Japanese carriers. In addition Marine dive bombers, sixteen SBD-2s (Dauntlesses) led by Major Lofton B. Henderson, and eleven SB2U-3s (Vindicators) led by Major Benjamin Morris, all of VMSB-241, were also sent to deal with the carriers.

As for the oncoming Japanese bombers and fighters, within ten minutes of their first sighting Marine fighters of VMF-221 were air-borne for interception. There were twenty-five fighters, nineteen of which unfortunately were the hopelessly inferior Brewster F2A Buffalos; the remaining six were Grumman F4F Wildcats. Major Floyd B. Parks led the first attack upon the Japanese formation with a dozen planes. Thirty miles out at fourteen thousand feet Parks sighted a Japanese formation twenty thousand feet below him. The Zeros, evidently assigned to strafe Midway and not expecting interception, flew beneath the dive bombers. Parks led a diving attack upon the unsuspecting bombers. Within minutes he was joined by Captain Kirk Armistead with the other thirteen Marine fighters and a general melee ensued. The Zeros swarmed over the Buffalos and Wildcats and of the twenty-five which had gone into the battle, only ten Marine fighters returned. In exchange for five or six Japanese planes the Marines lost thirteen Buffalos and two Wildcats,

Midway following the Japanese air attack by Tomonaga's first wave of Vals and Kates. Two of the island's *indigenous inhabitants, gooney birds, nest in the foreground.* (NAVY DEPT., NATIONAL ARCHIVES)

and of the ten planes which returned only two were operational.

Tomonaga pressed on to Midway and at six-thirty the first bomb fell; bombs continued falling, despite the heavy antiaircraft fire, for the next twenty minutes. Hundreds of bombs tumbled down upon both Sand and Eastern islands. Several buildings were left burning on both islands; the powerhouse on Eastern was struck, so was the post exchange; a bomb crashed into the command post of Major William W. Benson, killing him and several other men. Bombs fell along the northeastern edge of Sand also, demolishing barracks, setting a seaplane hangar aflame, and detonating fuel storage tanks. Very little damage was done to the airstrip and, of course, since most of the Midway-based aircraft were out searching for Nagumo's carriers, very few planes went up in smoke. Thirteen Americans lay dead and eighteen were wounded. Although unaware of the small casualty toll, Tomonaga saw that not enough damage had been done to Midway—and that

Midway flag raising. The Japanese attack came simultaneously with the raising of the colors, which proceeded as scheduled despite the "bombs bursting in air." (Note: this was not a posed photograph.)

(U. S. NAVY)

Grumman TBF ("Avenger"), which made its battle debut at Midway. (NAVY DEPT., NATIONAL ARCHIVES)

Of the six new Avengers that had been dispatched from Midway, only one returned; this is it.

(U. S. NAVY)

antiaircraft fire was savagely profuse as he led the formation away from Midway, now marked by curling columns of black smoke and fire. He radioed to Nagumo on the *Akagi,* "There is need for a second attack. Time: 0700."

When this message was received Nagumo was in a state of passive perturbation; the Catalina piloted by Ady and Chase had been seen and clearly it had seen them. The Americans must now be aware of the presence of Japanese carriers. What to do? Should he send another strike against Midway, or should he hold his planes in readiness for a possible attack from enemy carriers, if they were around?

A bugle blared announcing "Air Raid!" At this time the Japanese had no radar system. It was just five minutes after Tomonaga's request for a second Midway attack. A flag whipped up the mast of one of the destroyers: "Enemy planes in sight." Shortly after, a bridge lookout on the *Akagi* shouted, "Six medium land-based planes approaching! Twenty degrees to starboard. On the horizon." Nearly ten miles away were the four Army Marauders, "their bellies cut and sutured to carry torpedoes," a detachment from the 22nd Bombardment Group (Medium) and the 38th Bombardment Group (M). Leading the four B-26s was Captain James F. Collins. As he sighted the Japanese ships he saw also six Navy Avengers, low on the water, swarming with Zeros.

The Avengers were a detachment of Torpedo

Squadron 8, the main body of which was based on the *Hornet* at Point Luck. Caught by the impending battle at Midway en route to join the rest of the squadron, they had to operate from the islands rather than from the *Hornet*. The six TBFs were led into the battle by Lieutenant Langdon K. Fieberling. He and Collins had sighted the Japanese carriers at about the same time.

Leading the attack, Fieberling bore down upon the carriers through a virtual curtain of antiaircraft fire and a trio of Zeros, the pilots of which took the chance of being struck by their own shellfire. Within moments three of the Avengers were aflame and cartwheeled into the water. But the survivors pushed onward, through the all but impenetrable gunfire. By this time the Marauders, too, had joined in the attack, flying through the barrage of gunfire. Even the big guns on the larger ships were depressed to fire into the onrushing planes, raising great waterspouts in their flight paths as dangerous as the fire itself. It was near suicide, as the planes and crews were chopped to bits in the unescorted attempt at the carriers.

When the torpedo bombers came within range only three planes of the original six remained. One of the Marauders was shot down, then another. The last, which had managed to release its torpedo, flashed over the deck of the *Akagi,* burst into flame, and plunged into the sea. When the attack was over, only two B-26s and one TBF returned to Midway. Not one of the torpedoes had hit its target. The ferocity of the Japanese defense had forced the Americans to release the torpedoes from too great a distance, which enabled the ships to maneuver out of their paths. Nagumo watched one of the torpedoes pass harmlessly by the *Akagi* in a curling white wake.

As soon as it was clear that the Americans had either been driven off or had crashed into the sea, Nagumo made his decision. As Tomonaga had suggested, there would be a second attack upon Midway itself. Evidently the land-based torpedo bombers would give them no further trouble.

This decision entailed complications for the deck crews of the *Akagi* and *Kaga,* for the planes then ready on their flight decks were armed with torpedoes in readiness for an attack upon American carriers. But to this moment none had been sighted. So the planes were brought below decks and the torpedoes removed and replaced with conventional bombs. The aircraft of the *Hiryu* and *Soryu* were not affected by Nagumo's decision, for they were already armed for dive-bombing. The torpedo bombers from these carriers were part of Tomonaga's first attack wave; the dive bombers for this wave had come from the *Akagi* and *Kaga.*

As this changeover was being feverishly made, the carriers came under another attack, this time from Sweeney's Flying Fortresses. From the *Akagi* great water geysers could be seen rising around the *Hiryu* and *Soryu* as the fourteen B-17s, untroubled by the Zeros, whose pilots seemed wary of the big bombers, dropped their full load of bombs. Again, upon their safe return to Midway, claims for hits upon the carriers were made, but actually no bomb from the B-17s hit any of the carriers.

Nagumo could take pride in the effective manner in which the men in his force dodged the American missiles or destroyed their planes. But to his surprise, the delayed *Tone* search plane had wired back a report of "Ten ships, apparently enemy. . . ." But what kind of ships? Nagumo wished to know. This was an unexpected turn, for American surface ships, hundreds of miles from Midway, were not anticipated for another day or two. Nagumo sent orders below and to the *Kaga:* Stop rearming the bombers with conventional bombs and begin arming with torpedoes.

There was another interruption in the rapidly developing battle. The Marine Dauntlesses and Vindicators from Midway, led by Henderson and Morris, arrived to make glide-bombing attacks upon the carriers. Henderson led, with his sixteen Dauntlesses, an attack upon the *Hiryu.* Because of his pilots' unfamiliarity with the Dauntless, Henderson decided upon a glide attack rather than a dive-bombing. At eight hundred feet he was met by a swarm of Zeros and within minutes eight of the Dauntlesses, including Henderson's, went down in flames. There were no hits made on any enemy ships.

Major Morris's slower Vindicators came upon the Japanese ships shortly after Henderson but not in a position for an attack on any of the carriers. They attacked battleships instead and although claiming to have hit the *Haruna* or *Kirishima,* may have only succeeded in a near miss. Two of the Vindicators were lost in the attack and a third crashed in the sea five miles from Midway. The pilot was alive,

Enterprise *Wildcats prepare for takeoff to escort the bombers and torpedo planes of the U.S. fleet.*
(NAVY DEPT., NATIONAL ARCHIVES)

but the gunner, Private Henry I. Starks, was dead; he had never fired a machine gun before in his life until the Battle of Midway. Major Morris later took over the command of VMSB-241, upon the loss of Henderson, but was himself lost later in the day during a search flight for "a burning enemy carrier," which was never found.

Once again the Japanese carriers had fought off heroic but ineffectual American attacks, and Nagumo could take some consolation in that. But then the *Tone* search plane wired another report on the American surface fleet it had found: "Enemy ships are five cruisers and five destroyers."

There was a break in the tension on the *Akagi's* bridge.

"Just as I thought," said intelligence officer Lieutenant Commander Ono, expressing everyone's sense of deliverance; "there are no carriers."

Eleven minutes later the *Tone* plane reported, "Enemy force accompanied by what appears to be aircraft carrier bringing up the rear." The imprecision—"what appears to be aircraft carrier"—was hopeful, but maddening. Ten minutes later the plane reported, "Two additional ships, apparently cruis-

ers. . . ." Nagumo realized he must face reality; so great a number of ships must contain at least one carrier. If so, however, where were the carrier aircraft?

Nagumo now decided that he must launch his torpedo-armed aircraft against the American surface fleet, whatever its composition. The Japanese would then however, be without proper fighter escort, for all of the Zeros from the projected second wave had been sent aloft to fight the several waves of attackers which had come from Midway. The Zeros would need to land to refuel. And any moment would bring the return of the first attack wave; Tomonaga's bombers and fighters would need the deck space for landing—and they too would require refueling and rearming. While Nagumo pondered his next move, he received a message from Rear-Admiral Tamon Yamaguchi, whom many regarded as the heir of Yamamoto and who led the 2nd Carrier Division (the *Hiryu* and *Soryu*). "Consider it advisable," Yamaguchi radioed, "to launch attack force immediately." Yamaguchi, having successfully dodged the B-17s, was concerned with the *Tone's* search plane's reports of the American surface fleet and the probable carrier. The enemy task force must be attacked immediately.

But Nagumo continued to vacillate. He was aware of the importance of attacking the American ships, but he could not send off the torpedo planes without escorting Zeros—or with Zeros on the verge of running out of fuel. He had himself witnessed the virtual butchery of the American attackers without escort. Then he made up his mind: they would recover the Midway returnees, rearm, and be ready for the enemy surface fleet. Another order went to the hangar decks below as the readied planes were cleared from the flight decks to receive the incoming aircraft. The bombs were to be changed to torpedoes—again. As this proceeded Nagumo sighted the first of the returning planes. He signaled the *Kaga, Soryu,* and *Hiryu:* "After completing recovery operations, force will temporarily head northward. We plan to contact and destroy enemy task force." He then radioed Yamamoto, hundreds of miles away aboard the *Yamato,* and Vice-Admiral Nobutake Kondo, with his Midway Invasion Force, of his decision. Finally, after nearly forty minutes, all of the first attack wave planes had been recovered

and were being feverishly refueled and rearmed. Nagumo ordered the carrier force to steam away from Midway to a position from which the second attack wave could be sent against the American fleet. Meanwhile, his carriers were in their most vulnerable state: decks and hangar decks crowded with planes, bombs, and fuel hoses. But this nagging thought was overlooked in the excitement of preparing to finish off the American fleet.

Spruance, in the *Enterprise,* with the *Hornet* as company, had steamed toward the Japanese carrier force as soon as word had come of its location. Spruance, like Nagumo, had difficult decisions to make. He had planned to launch planes about a hundred miles from the Japanese carriers, but his chief of staff, Captain Miles Browning, described by Samuel Eliot Morison as "one of the most irascible and unstable officers ever to earn a fourth stripe, but a man with a slide-rule brain," suggested an earlier launch. Browning's thinking told him that Nagumo would attempt to launch a second attack upon Midway. Why not catch him while he was refueling his

John Waldron, dedicated commander of VT-8, "Torpedo 8" of the Hornet, *which was wiped out at Midway; right: Clarence W. McClusky, air group com-*

mander of the Enterprise *who led the attack on the Japanese carrier* Kaga.

(NAVY DEPT., NATIONAL ARCHIVES)

planes? Decisive, brilliant, even enigmatic, Spruance took the advice, and further, he decided to launch a full-scale attack (knowing that Fletcher would follow later with reinforcements from the *Yorktown*).

About 7 A.M. the *Hornet* and *Enterprise* turned into the wind; they were nearly two hundred miles away from the expected position of the enemy carriers, but Spruance believed the risk of the long distance would be worth it, indeed, if Browning were proved correct. At this same moment, Tomonaga's planes had begun their return flight from Midway and Nagumo's carriers had come under the attack of the Army B-26s and the Navy Avengers.

Among the first aircraft off the *Hornet*'s flight deck were the torpedo bombers of the main section of Torpedo 8, fifteen ancient Douglas Devastators. Leading this squadron was a Navy career pilot, tough, aggressive, sharp-eyed, proud of his Sioux Indian forebears, Lieutenant Commander John C. Waldron. A devoted Navy man, Waldron had welded his men into a well-disciplined unit without ever losing their devotion. Along with the Torpedo 8 (VT-8) planes, the *Hornet* launched thirty-five bombers and ten fighters. The total of sixty *Hornet* aircraft were led by the carrier's Air Group Commander, Commander Stanhope C. Ring.

Lieutenant Commander Clarence W. McClusky led an equal number of aircraft (actually thirty-seven bombers, fourteen torpedo bombers, and ten fighters) off the *Enterprise*. The air reverberated to the roar of more than a hundred planes, which formed into units and headed for the expected point of interception with the Japanese carriers. Fletcher too followed these planes up with a dozen torpedo bombers, seventeen dive bombers, and six Wildcats—these last under the leadership of Lieutenant Commander John S. Thatch. The dive bombers were under the command of Lieutenant Commander Maxwell F. Leslie, who suffered an ironic mishap early in the flight. When the planes had climbed to an altitude of ten thousand feet, he signaled the squadron to arm their bombs. Leslie himself pushed the newly installed electrical device and, to his dismay, experienced the unmistakable lurch of a suddenly lightened aircraft. He soon learned through hand signals from his number two man on the left (whose rear gunner joined in the frantic wigwagging) that the squadron commander had lost his thousand-pound bomb. From the right another

Dauntless veered over, pilot and gunner signaling. Obviously a short or some other mechanical quirk had caused the bomb to fall instead of merely arming it. There was nothing for Leslie to do but to lead his squadron into the battle without a bomb. Within minutes, to his further dismay, he learned that three other planes had suffered the same accident. All seventeen planes pushed on, though only thirteen were properly armed. Lieutenant Paul Holmberg, Leslie's number two man, laconically commented, "When this bad news was confirmed, the skipper made many frustrating motions with his hands and lips. . . ."

Meanwhile, the *Hornet* and *Enterprise* planes neared the point of interception. Nagumo's decision to turn north, away from Midway, while his planes refueled actually took the carriers out of the line of interception. Intermittent cloud cover, too, played its role. For as Ring led the *Hornet* planes along the line, he saw none of the Japanese carriers, then hidden under cloud. He continued farther, along the line, followed by the bombers and fighters, until he saw nothing but ocean or clouds. Perhaps Nagumo had turned southward, toward Midway, Ring thought, and turned toward the atoll. But he found nothing there but the smoking reminders of the Japanese bombings. He had made a wrong guess. Although some of his planes managed to return to the *Hornet,* some, dangerously low on fuel, had to put down at Midway; some did not make it and splashed into the waters around Midway.

Waldron, leading Torpedo 8, on the other hand, sensed that Nagumo would change course. To Waldron's left, a few miles to the south, flew Lieutenant Commander Eugene F. Lindsey's fourteen Devastators of Torpedo Squadron 6. Above him, at twenty thousand feet, zigzagged the ten Wildcats led by Lieutenant James S. Gray as fighter escort of the *Enterprise* bombers. The agreement between Gray and Lindsey was that when the torpedo bombers found the Japanese carriers, Lindsey would signal Gray for fighter protection during the attack. However, in flying through cloud Gray's fighters attached themselves inadvertently to Waldron's Devastators. There was no agreed signal, of course, between the *Hornet*'s Waldron and the *Enterprise*'s Gray.

Thus, because of a series of small twists and turns of fate, Waldron's slow-moving Devastators were the first of the carrier planes to find the Japanese car-

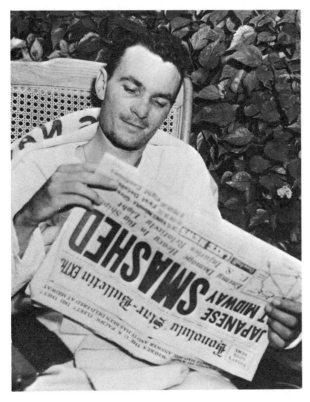

Ensign George H. Gay (recuperating in the U.S. naval hospital at Pearl Harbor), the lone survivor of Waldron's Torpedo 8.

(NAVY DEPT., NATIONAL ARCHIVES)

riers. Certainly one of the reasons was Waldron's mystical determination. When his men received their attack plan that day, attached to it was a letter from Waldron:

Just a word to let you know that I feel we are ready. We have had a very short time to train and we have worked under the most severe difficulties. But we have truly done the best humanly possible. I actually believe that under these conditions we are the best in the world. My greatest hope is that we encounter a favorable tactical situation, but if we don't, and the worst comes to worst, I want each of us to do his utmost to destroy our enemies. If there is only one plane left to make a final run in, I want that man to go in and get a hit. May God be with all of us. Good luck, happy landings and give 'em hell.

Waldron led the Devastators to the point of interception, and when he found nothing, some sixth sense told him to turn north. This brought them around the edge of the large bank of cloud through which they had passed. And there—about eight miles distant, off his starboard wing—lay Nagumo's carrier striking force. Ordering Torpedo 8 into bat-

tle formation, Waldron descended to within a few yards above the Pacific, assigning targets to the various elements, barking commands in a dry, emotionless voice. The fifteen Devastators lined up on their targets, Waldron selecting the nearest carrier.

Fifty Zeros which had been circling over the Japanese fleet dropped down to intercept the intruders. Without fighter protection they should be relatively simple to deal with. The Devastator was slow, underarmed (one .50-caliber and one .30-caliber machine gun: the pilot controlled the forward firing gun and the radio-gunner manned a flexible gun); the Douglas TBD-1 was obsolete by 1942. It could barely manage two hundred miles an hour top speed, and when on its torpedo run, the plane lumbered along, a moving target.

Even before Waldron reached anywhere near a torpedo release point, the swift Zeros thronged around the hapless Devastators. In seconds, the Pacific erupted with the blazing splashes of fiery Devastators. The Zeros closed in from all sides and shot the torpedo bombers literally to pieces. Ensign George Gay, the squadron's navigator, piloted the fifteenth Devastator and watched the decimation of Torpedo 8 with horror. One after the other the burning planes careened into the water, crumbling in the impact, spurting foam, smoke, and flame. Gay saw Waldron still pressing on although both his wingmen had been shot down. A Zero flashed across the Devastator's path, spraying it with machine-gun fire, and Gay saw flame licking from a ruptured fuel tank; then the tank burst into an orange-red blossom. Waldron, evidently trying to get away from the scorching flames, clawed the canopy open and stood up. At full speed, with torpedo still slung under the fuselage, the blazing Devastator slammed into the Pacific.

Gay continued on his run. The skipper was gone, he realized; as he darted his eyes over the water, he realized too everyone was gone but him. His was, in Waldron's tragically prophetic phrase, the "only one plane left." The Zeros whirred in to attack the fifteenth Devastator. Gay tried to ignore them as he centered his sight on a carrier, even then maneuvering out of his line of sight. He sensed the thud of Japanese machine-gun fire striking the plane; there was stinging pain in his left arm. A spent slug had dug into the flesh of the arm; another fragment of steel, possibly a piece of the cockpit torn away, cut his hand. His gunner, Robert Huntington, shouted, "Mr. Gay, I'm hit!" Through the frenzied, unremitting attack of the Zeros, Gay prodded the Devastator toward his target.

The single aircraft became the center of attention of the ship's antiaircraft guns as well as of the converging Zeros. Bits of cockpit burst in around Gay's feet, control cables severed, and he had trouble keeping the Devastator under control. He had to release that final "pickle," as Waldron called the torpedoes. Gay, of the thirty men who had begun the attack, was the only man alive. Huntington sprawled lifelessly in the rear cockpit.

Gay had further trouble with his torpedo release mechanism, undoubtedly shot up by the Zeros. Unable to use his left hand, Gay gripped the control column between his knees and with his right hand pulled the emergency release lever. The torpedo dropped and the lightened plane leaped up into the air and within minutes skimmed barely ten feet over the bow of the carrier. Gay kicked the rudder, turning south, now barely above the waves. It was over for Ensign Gay, so he flattened out the Devastator and stalled into the sea. He splashed in with great force, tearing away the right wing, which bounced along the surface like a flat rock. Gay tore open the canopy as water poured in on him. He glanced again at the rear cockpit. There was nothing to do for Huntington. Quickly Gay swam away from the sinking plane, concerned over what would happen when the Zeros came around to investigate.

Inflating his life jacket, Gay bobbed around the waters strewn with the debris of battle. He found a boat bag, which contained an inflatable rubber raft, holding onto it for future use. It would not be healthy to use it now, with the Zeros whipping over now and then. Then he found a floating cushion which had been knocked free of the Devastator. Placing the cushion over his head, Gay found refuge from the searching Zeros and for the next few hours watched the unfolding drama of the Battle of Midway. (After dark Gay inflated his rubber boat and was found the next day, the sole survivor of Torpedo 8's attack, by a Navy PBY. Upon being taken to Pearl Harbor for medical attention, Gay was asked by a doctor how he had treated his wounds. In his Texas-inflected speech Gay replied that he had soaked his wounds in "salt water for several hours.")

A Dauntless, dive brakes down, drops a bomb.
(DOUGLAS AIRCRAFT)

It was a jubilant Zero leader who could report to Nagumo that all fifteen American torpedo bombers had been sent burning into the sea. Not one torpedo strike had been made. The war gods smiled, indeed, upon Nagumo.

But Nagumo hardly had time for an impassive smile, for a lookout shouted, "Enemy torpedo bombers, thirty degrees to starboard, coming in low!" This was followed by another exclamation, from the opposite lookout, "Enemy torpedo bombers approaching forty degrees to port!" The tempo was accelerating. The starboard attackers were Lindsey's fourteen Devastators of VT-6 (the *Enterprise*), which had flown parallel to Waldron's squadron, but some miles to the south. Like Waldron, Lindsey sensed that the carriers lay to the north instead of closer to Midway, as Ring had thought. Also like Waldron, Lindsey swooped in to attack (his major target being the *Kaga*) without fighter escort. For some reason Lindsey never called Gray, still circling over the the scene of the battle at twenty thousand feet. Instead, he plunged into the attack and was cut to

Dauntlesses at Midway: as a Japanese ship burns following an earlier attack, another wave of SBDs close in for the kill. (NAVY DEPT., NATIONAL ARCHIVES)

ribbons by antiaircraft and the swarms of Zeros. In minutes, ten of Lindsey's fourteen planes (including his own) were sent spinning and flaming into the sea. The four remaining planes released their torpedoes, but again not one struck home.

Almost stimultaneously the *Yorktown*'s VT-3, commanded by Lieutenant Commander Lance E. Massey, a dozen Devastators in all, in company with Thatch's six Wildcats, arrived upon the scene. As they hurtled toward the Japanese carriers, some of the Zeros could be seen landing. Obviously the earlier fighting had depleted the fuel and ammunition of the Japanese fighters. But this did not prevent others from swamping Thatch's little band and also Massey's Devastators on their torpedo run-ins. The air once again filled with puffs of smoke and machine-gun fire crisscrossed above the water, breaking the surface with evenly spaced, vicious geysers. Like Waldron and Lindsey before him, Massey raced headlong into certain devastation. His and six other planes were quickly shot into the sea. The five remaining planes continued on the run-in and

splashed their torpedoes into the churning water. Three planes were flamed by the Zeros just moments after. Of the twelve TBDs Massey took into the attack, only two returned to the *Yorktown*.

In about a half hour, roughly from 9:28, when Waldron's VT-8 had attacked, until 10 A.M., when the last of Massey's torpedoes went astray, Nagumo's carriers had been attacked by forty-one American aircraft and had destroyed thirty-five. Not one torpedo struck any Japanese ship. Now at last the battle-churned skies were free of enemy aircraft and the sea, here and there, emitted rising smoke. But the destroyed planes did not stay afloat long and all that remained was oil-soaked, scorched flotsam. Under one of the insignificant dots floated Ensign Gay.

Now Nagumo could give his full attention to launching the counterstrike. All during the attack by the doomed torpedo bombers preparations had gone on to get the planes ready to strike at the carriers, the source of the thirty-five planes they had just annihilated. Soon after, the planes were bombed-up and ready for take-off. The four carriers turned into the wind. Within five minutes their bombers would be air-borne and racing for the American carriers. The gods continued to smile. At ten-twenty Nagumo gave the order to begin launching the attack.

At ten twenty-four the air officer on the *Akagi* signaled, and a Zero gathered speed and roared off the deck. A lookout screamed, "Hell-divers!"

Plummeting out of a nearly cloudless sky were several Dauntlesses. The men on the deck of the *Akagi* watched this sudden materialization with stunned horror. The dive bombers plunged toward the *Kaga*, almost unopposed except for sporadic machine-gun fire from a few alert crews and some splotches of antiaircraft fire. The Zeros had been pulled down to the water by the attack of the torpedo bombers, whose sacrifices now would begin to assume implications beyond blind heroism.

The Dauntlesses were the *Yorktown* dive bombers led by Maxwell Leslie, whose own bomb had been accidentally dropped into the sea. He and the sixteen others arrived not long after the Japanese carriers had scurried out of the way of Massey's torpedo attack. Leslie had his eye on the nearest two, the *Soryu* and the *Kaga*. The latter, with more than twice the tonnage of the *Soryu*, impressed Leslie as the more tempting target. Signaling his wingmen, he led the bombers into a seventy-degree dive. Although bombless, Leslie contributed to the general destruction by firing his .50-caliber machine gun, beginning at ten thousand feet and pulling out at four thousand because the gun had jammed. On the decks of the *Kaga* he saw many planes apparently ready for take-off.

Leslie was followed by Lieutenant Paul Holmberg, who like his commander aimed the Dauntless at the great red circle painted on the *Kaga*'s flight deck. The wind screamed over the Dauntless as Holmberg dived down to twenty-five hundred feet. He pushed the electric bomb release and, just to make certain, also snatched at the manual release. Holmberg's thousand-pound bomb burst near the *Kaga*'s superstructure, spilling flame, flinging shattered metal, ripping and tearing across the deck, leaving a screaming, red trail of horror in its wake. More planes dived, some achieving only near misses, but three other bombs followed across the flight deck. Planes were flung over the side into the sea by the force of the explosions. Fuel tanks burst and poured flame into the holocaust, fires enveloped the flight deck and poured onto the men and planes below. Within minutes, the *Kaga* was a hopeless flaming pyre, despite the efforts of damage-control crews.

As Leslie and his men attacked the *Kaga* McClusky and his thirty-seven Dauntlesses from the *Enterprise* came upon the scene. McClusky had followed the wake of a destroyer which had left the main carrier group to deal with an American submarine, the *Nautilus,* which had been harassing it. The destroyer, moving at a fast clip would head, McClusky was certain, for the carriers—and he was right. McClusky's planes came in from the southwest, almost at right angles to Leslie's. The *Akagi,* which had been fleeing northwestward, was nearest to McClusky's formation; the giant carrier made a sharp turn to the south. The smaller *Soryu,* which had been passed over by Leslie in favor of the *Kaga,* was also in McClusky's view. The first bomb had already burst on the *Kaga*'s deck, billowing black smoke. McClusky felt certain it would need no further attention. The remaining two carriers (the *Hiryu* was farther to the north and out of sight) had turned into the wind to launch aircraft.

Two minutes after Leslie dropped down upon the *Kaga,* the *Enterprise* Dauntlesses, divided into two formations, dived on the *Soryu* and the *Akagi.* Mc-

Clusky led the *Soryu* attack and Lieutenant Wilmer E. Gallagher led the attack upon the *Akagi,* Nagumo's flagship. Unopposed by the Zeros, the Dauntlesses whipped through the air toward their targets, dropped their bombs, and pulled away. Two direct hits smashed onto the *Akagi*'s deck—neither of which would have normally seriously stopped the carrier. But the detonations flared the fuel in the waiting planes; the intense heat, in turn, detonated the bombs and torpedoes the Japanese planes carried. The air became deadly with metal splinters and flame. Pilots died in their cockpits, or were blown overboard burning into the sea. Deck hands became screaming torches. The helpless wounded were literally roasted to death on the twisted, scorching decks.

Three direct hits transformed the nearby *Soryu* into a similar inferno; within twenty minutes Captain Ryusaku Yanagimoto ordered the carrier abandoned. Men leaped into the water away from the searing heat and explosions. Because of the several order changes of the bombers' bomb loads, many bombs and torpedoes had been left lying about the decks, which added further hazard. The *Soryu* was obviously doomed. His men tried to force Yanagimoto, who was an extremely popular officer, to leave the bridge, but the captain refused. A burly petty officer, a Navy wrestling champion, was sent to take Yanagimoto by force if necessary. He was prevented by the determined look in his captain's eyes—he left without touching the officer. The last known act of Yanagimoto was his singing of *"Kimigayo"* the national anthem, as he remained on the smoke-obscured bridge. Shortly after 7 P.M., following nine hours of drifting and blazing, the *Soryu* sank steaming under the sea. It was the first of the Japanese carriers to be lost.

The *Kaga* followed within twelve minutes—at 7:25 P.M. During its fiery death throes the carrier came under a submarine attack. Three projectiles streaked for the stricken carrier; two missed and one struck a glancing blow. It was a dud which broke in two; the warhead sank harmlessly into the depths but the buoyant rear portion of the torpedo remained afloat to serve as an improvised floatboard for several of the *Kaga*'s crew. But eight hundred others went to the bottom when the burning hulk, torn by severe explosions, sank to the bottom.

Nagumo found the realities difficult to grasp.

Japanese torpedo bombers race through heavy anti-aircraft fire for the American ships. Shrapnel splashes *in the foreground. A cruiser (left) and a destroyer (right) fire at three approaching enemy planes.*
(U. S. NAVY)

From the *Akagi*'s bridge he could see the smoke of the *Kaga* and *Soryu* staining the distant skies. Around him there were confusion, shouting, the acrid stench of burning metal; Rear Admiral Ryunosuke Kusaka, Nagumo's chief of staff, was shouting something to him. In the noise of explosion, the confusion, the smoke, Nagumo stared at him. Kusaka said something about leaving the *Akagi*. Nagumo seemed oblivious to the sense of Kusaka's statement; he nodded and turned away from his chief of staff. The *Akagi*'s deck was a flaming shambles, but Nagumo did not wish to leave.

"Sir," Kusaka pleaded, "most of our ships are still intact. You must command them." The old man, ashen, found it all very difficult to believe: in two minutes a handful of planes had wiped out three quarters of his carrier force. Captain Taijiro Aoki joined the men, added his voice gently to the argument. The *Nagara,* a light cruiser, had pulled up alongside and the two men convinced Nagumo that he should retire to the *Nagara.* Aoki assured Nagumo, "I will take care of the ship. Please, we all implore you, shift your flag to the *Nagara* and resume command of the force."

Aoki also argued that since there were no communications systems working, Nagumo must leave the ship in order to carry on. The old admiral realized the sense of this statement and consented to leave. By this time the fires had spread so heavily that Nagumo could leave the bridge only by sliding down a rope to the deck. He was then led along an outboard passage to the anchor deck, where he stiffly climbed down a rope ladder into a waiting boat, which took him to the *Nagara.*

Yamamoto, who had positioned the ships of the main force too far away from Nagumo's carriers to be of any help to him, found it difficult also to comprehend the meaning of what was happening. When Captain Aoki, still aboard the doomed *Akagi,* wired for permission to sink the carrier after ordering the survivors off, Yamamoto, upon intercepting the message, ordered the scuttling delayed. Aoki then lashed himself to the anchor, on the only fire-free portion of the ship, and waited. Eventually, Yamamoto sensed the inevitable and gave the order to sink the carrier. A rescue party went aboard and convinced Aoki he should not go down with the ship. Rather than permit the ship to fall into enemy hands, even

The ·Yorktown *under attack by torpedo bombers led by Tomonaga, whose plane was destroyed by American* guns *after it had released its torpedo. The* Yorktown *lists, the result of earlier strikes.*

in derelict form, Japanese destroyers sent torpedoes into its sides. At 4:55 A.M. in the morning of June 4, Nagumo's flagship sank bursting into the sea, carrying 263 dead with it. That was the third carrier to go.

Aboard the *Hiryu,* the fourth and last carrier of Nagumo's striking force, Admiral Yamaguchi prepared to attack the American ships. Because of his position to the north of the other three carriers, he had escaped attack from the dive bombers. Gazing around the horizon, Yamaguchi was readily aware of his responsibilities: his planes only could strike at the American fleet.

Just four minutes before a reluctant Nagumo abandoned the *Akagi,* the resolute Yamaguchi launched eighteen dive bombers and six Zeros against the now known position of an American carrier. The small force was led by Lieutenant Michio Kobayashi, a veteran of Pearl Harbor. On the flight Kobayashi lost two of his escorting fighters, whose overzealous pilots darted away to attack a

formation of American Dauntlesses returning from the battle scene. These may have been Leslie's planes triumphantly finished with the *Kaga.* Kobayashi lost further to an American Wildcat attack, so that by the time he came within the vicinity of the carrier, only eight of the original eighteen bombers continued to follow him.

Meanwhile, just before noon of that June 4, the radar aboard the *Yorktown* detected the approach of Japanese aircraft, and all preparations were made to meet an enemy attack: refueling of aircraft was stopped, watertight doors were slammed closed, an auxiliary tank on the stern holding eight hundred gallons of aviation fuel was pushed over the side, fuel lines were drained and filled with carbon dioxide. Fighters were sent out to meet the attack, and returning planes, including Leslie's flight, already low on fuel, were waved off and ordered out of antiaircraft fire zones.

Kobayashi swept in for the attack with his decimated forces; two of the eight planes went down before the guns from the ships and the remaining six swept through the murderous wall of fire. Three bombs struck the *Yorktown,* the second of which caused the most serious damage because it had pierced the side of the carrier and detonated within the ship. A rag stowage compartment burst into flames, sending harsh black smoke out of the *Yorktown.* The other two bombs also caused intense fires, but working quickly and efficiently, the damage-control parties soon checked the most serious blazes. However, by twelve-twenty the *Yorktown* stood dead in the water, the engines stopped. Fletcher knew he would be out of communication with his other ships if he remained aboard the stricken, burning *Yorktown.* He transferred with his staff to the cruiser *Astoria.* Meanwhile, damage-control work continued on the *Yorktown.*

While Kobayashi led the attack upon the *Yorktown,* Yamaguchi finally learned the full measure of the American carrier strength. A *Soryu* scout plane had returned to the Japanese fleet and, finding its home carrier ablaze, landed upon the *Hiryu.* The pilot's radio had gone out on him and he was unable to report that he had seen three carriers, naming them—the *Enterprise,* the *Hornet,* and the *Yorktown!* which was supposed to have been sunk at the Coral Sea.

Only five bombers of the original eighteen and three fighters of six returned to the *Hiryu.* Among the missing was attack leader Kobayashi. From the surviving pilots Yamaguchi ascertained that the elusive *Yorktown* was dead in the water and spouting smoke. With two more carriers in the vicinity Yamaguchi ordered an immediate attack. All available aircraft must seek out and strike the two remaining carriers. It was not a very impressive array of air power: ten bombers (one of them an orphan from the *Akagi,* burning in the distance) and six Zeros (two of them strays from the *Kaga,* also smoldering), sixteen planes altogether to be led by Joichi Tomonaga, who had led the morning's attack upon Midway. In that attack the left-wing fuel tank had been punctured, but Tomonaga ordered his plane readied despite this. When he took off he knew he was on a one-way flight. Even if not struck down by the enemy, he would not have enough fuel in the single intact tank to bring him back to the *Hiryu.*

All sixteen planes had cleared the *Hiryu's* decks by twelve forty-five. During this period between attacks, the fires on the *Yorktown* were brought completely under control. The decks were cleared of wreckage, holes patched up, and four boilers warmed to life. Within two hours, no longer smoking, the *Yorktown* moved under its own steam. The planes circling overhead were signaled to land, although some, with fuel too far gone, splashed into the waters near other ships. Among these were the aircraft flown by Leslie and Holmberg. Their two Dauntlesses stalled into the water near Fletcher's new flagship, the *Astoria,* and the pilots and gunners were taken from the sea.

About an hour later—at 2:42 P.M.—Tomonaga's small force swarmed in upon the *Yorktown* from all sides. The air boomed and cracked to the sound of gunfire, antiaircraft bursts, and the engines of planes. American fighters attempted to intercept the bombers and tangled with the Zeros. Japanese torpedo bombers were blasted out of the air, but some broke through once again. Tomonaga weathered the storm of fire, dropped his torpedo, and disintegrated under a direct hit. The Japanese force was cut precisely in half: of the ten bombers which took off from the *Hiryu* only five returned; of the six Zeros, three returned. But they claimed two hits upon "a carrier of the *Yorktown* class." Having found the newly restored *Yorktown* moving through the Pacific, apparently unharmed, Tomonaga mistook it for another carrier.

But of the five bombers which had survived the attack, two had indeed sunk a torpedo each deep in the port side of the *Yorktown.* Within minutes the great carrier listed dangerously. The power had gone off and counterflooding, to correct the list, was impossible. There was nothing for Captain Elliott Buckmaster to say but "Pass the word along to abandon ship."

Back at the untouched *Hiryu,* Yamaguchi learned that a second carrier—as his by now exhausted pilots believed—lay dead and smoldering in the water. To Yamaguchi it meant that only one more carrier remained; there was still the chance to snatch some fraction of victory out of their frightful losses. He still had five dive bombers, four torpedo bombers, and six Zeros—with these Yamaguchi would launch a twilight attack upon the "last" American carrier.

But the surviving pilots, many of whom had been active since the morning Midway strike, must rest.

Around five o'clock in the afternoon, during a lull, they were served sweet rice balls (for many the first meal since dawn). A search plane was made ready to find the last carrier for the twilight attack.

Fletcher, meanwhile, realizing he was cut off from on-the-scene reports from pilots, placed Spruance in command of the carrier activities. At almost the exact moment that Tomonaga's bombers came in to attack the *Yorktown* for the second time, a *Yorktown* search pilot, Lieutenant Samuel Adams, spotted the *Hiryu*. He radioed its position back to the carriers and Spruance prepared for an attack on Yamaguchi's ship. Twenty-four Dauntlesses warmed up on the *Enterprise;* they were armed with thousand-pound and five-hundred-pound bombs. Some of the aircraft were from the listing *Yorktown;* all were led by Lieutenant Wilmer E. Gallagher, who had taken part in the earlier attack upon the *Akagi* and *Soryu* with McClusky. On the *Hornet* Captain Marc Mitscher watched sixteen Dauntlesses ready to take off in search of the *Hiryu.* The first planes began taking off around three-thirty in the afternoon.

Gallagher's force found the *Hiryu* at five o'clock, just as the weary pilots wolfed down their sweet rice balls. The scout plane was about to leave the deck when the dread cry rang out, "Enemy dive bombers overhead!" Gallagher's Dauntlesses hurtled down upon the carrier. Antiaircraft fire was pumped up at them as the carrier's captain, Tomeo Kaku, ordered full right rudder in an evasive turn. Three bombs fell into the sea, but there were more and four of them crashed explosively along the flight deck. Flame and gouts of smoke heaved into the air. As on the other three carriers, gassed-up and bombed-up planes burst into flame, spreading the fiery, consuming havoc.

When the *Hornet*'s planes arrived they found the *Hiryu* burning and turned to attack the other ships in the area. But their attacks upon the *Haruna, Tone,* and *Chikuma* were fruitless. Likewise, once again, some of the B-17s from Midway arrived and dropped bombs without making any hits. The *Hiryu,* however, was, like all of the other Nagumo carriers—the *Akagi,* the *Kaga,* the *Soryu*—doomed. The entire carrier force was erased from the Pacific. Attempts were made to bring the fires under control, to get into the engine rooms—but to no avail. Before dawn on June 5 Yamaguchi ordered all the survivors—about eight hundred men—to

Raymond A. Spruance, commander of Task Force 16 at Midway. (NAVY DEPT., NATIONAL ARCHIVES)

come on deck. He had decided to order abandonment of the *Hiryu.*

"As commanding officer of this carrier division," he told them, "I am fully and solely responsible for the loss of the *Hiryu* and *Soryu.* I shall remain on board to the end. I command all of you to leave the ship and continue your loyal service to His Majesty the Emperor." Characteristically, his staff pleaded to be allowed to share his fate, but Yamaguchi ordered them to leave the ship also. Captain Kaku, the ship's skipper, was also determined to remain and begged Yamaguchi to leave; it was the captain's place to go down with the ship. But Yamaguchi was firm, saying merely, "The moon is so bright in the sky."

Kaku, taking his place beside Yamaguchi, said, "We shall watch the moon together." Thus, poetically, did they face the end. Yamaguchi had ordered the final scuttling of the *Hiryu*, which occurred around dawn of the next day, June 5, when four torpedoes were shot into the carrier's sides. However, a search plane which Yamamoto had sent off from the carrier *Hosho* (the single light carrier which had been attached to the main force) to find Nagumo's force located the *Hiryu* still afloat an hour and a half later. The pilot also saw several men still alive on the derelict. Immediate orders went off to Nagumo to send a rescue ship, but when it arrived after daylight no trace of the *Hiryu* remained. (The survivors, members of the engine-room crew who had been trapped below decks, were freed when the Japanese torpedoes blasted open a passage for them. When the *Hiryu* sank they floated around in an abandoned lifeboat they had found until rescued by an American ship. None of these men saw either Yamaguchi or Kaku, who may have already committed suicide.) More than four hundred crewmen went down with the *Hiryu,* along with Yamaguchi and Kaku.

The last of Nagumo's impressive carrier force was gone; the few surviving aircraft, those Zeros which had been in the air when the dive bombers struck, fluttered helplessly over the burning ships, unable to land. As the fuel ran out, the planes fell into the sea.

The fate of the *Hiryu,* if it totally depressed Nagumo, did not take the fight out of Yamamoto, miles from the battle arena aboard the *Yamato.* He had no real idea of what ensued hundreds of miles east. Battle reports were all but incoherent, but one fact was clear: Nagumo's carriers were suffering at the hands of the American airmen. Reacting forcefully, Yamamoto, shortly after noon on June 4, ordered the carriers of the Aleutians Force to race down to Midway; he ordered the heavy cruisers, which were to cover the Midway invasion, to close with the American fleet—and he too would move in to engage the enemy in a last-ditch surface battle. Yamamoto hoped that the cruisers of the Kondo force might meet the Americans in a night action.

But the wary Spruance did not wish to press his luck. Instead of pursuing the Japanese fleet, and risking a night engagement, he reversed course. "I did not feel justified," he reported, "in risking a night encounter with possibly superior enemy forces,

but on the other hand, I did not want to be too far away from Midway the next morning [June 5]. I wished to have a position from which either to follow up retreating enemy forces or to break up a landing attack on Midway."

Yamamoto continued to receive grim news from the scene of action. Even after he had heard that the *Hiryu* had been stricken, he transmitted orders of unbelievable optimism:

> (1) *The enemy fleet has been practically destroyed and is retiring eastward.*
>
> (2) *Combined Fleet units in the vicinity are preparing to pursue remnants of the enemy force and, at the same time, to occupy Midway.*

But Nagumo persisted in afflicting him with oppressive information. At each successive report the American forces seemed to increase until Nagumo reported on the evening of June 4 that "Total enemy strength is five carriers, six heavy cruisers, and fifteen destroyers. They are steaming westward. We are retiring to the northwest escorting *Hiryu.* Speed, eighteen knots."

"The Nagumo force," Chief of Staff Rear Admiral Matome Ugaki bitterly and wearily said, "has no stomach for a night engagement!" But Yamamoto, whose stomach literally churned and pained, did and he continued to plan for such an engagement. He relieved Nagumo of his command, except for the still floating but burning *Akagi* and *Hiryu,* and turned the surface fleet command over to Vice-Admiral Nobutake Kondo, who commanded the ships of the Midway Invasion Force (Second Fleet). Kondo managed to instill some of the lost aggressiveness to the fleet and made plans for the night action. But soon, what with Spruance's evasive move to the east, it became obvious that the action could not possibly take place until dawn. Once again in daylight their ships would be at the mercy of the American carrier planes. Various alternative plans were discussed by Yamamoto's staff, each one more impractical than the previous one. One suggestion was that all possible large Japanese ships approach Midway on the following day, June 5, and shell it, a suicidal and therefore attractive solution to the problem of defeat. It would have placed most of the Japanese Navy within the reach of shore-based batteries and shore-based aircraft as well as of the remaining carrier planes. Admiral Ugaki disabused the staff of this idea. He suggested that they wait

The Japanese heavy cruiser Mikuma, *its eight-inch guns useless after attacks by Marine and Navy Vindicators and Dauntlesses, lies helpless in the water. The*

Vindicator of Richard Fleming smolders on the aft turret (right). The Mikuma *was sunk soon after by Navy carrier Dauntlesses.*

(NAVY DEPT., NATIONAL ARCHIVES)

for the Aleutian carriers and then perhaps launch another attack. "But even if this proves impossible," he asserted, "and we must accept defeat in this operation, we will not have lost the war."

There was a gloomy silence following this statement, for Ugaki had voiced the unspeakable. Who among them could face the prospect of defeat? "But how can we apologize to His Majesty for this defeat?" someone inquired.

"Leave that to me," Yamamoto interjected sharply. "I am the only one who must apologize to His Majesty." He recognized the fruitlessness of

attempting to engage the Americans at night. The *Kaga* and *Soryu* were gone; he then had to turn to the scuttling of the *Akagi*. It would be the first time in history that a Japanese warship was scuttled. It was a difficult decision; at 2:50 A.M. on June 5, Yamamoto gave the order. Within five minutes he issued another, the first sentence of which read:

"THE MIDWAY OPERATION IS CAN-CELED."

But the drama was not ended simply because its author so decreed; events and characters had taken on their own dynamisms. Within an hour after Yamamoto had canceled the Midway Operation an American submarine, *Tambor*, under the command of Lieutenant Commander John W. Murphy, Jr., patrolling about ninety miles west of Midway, spotted several Japanese ships. They appeared to be heading away from Midway at high speed; they were, in fact, four heavy cruisers, in company with two destroyers, which had been dispatched to carry out a night bombardment upon Midway. When the cancellation order came, the ships, under the command of Rear Admiral Takeo Kurita, turned around and steamed northwest. Upon sighting them, Murphy, still uncertain of the ships' nationality, began to stalk them. In the dark, it was all but impossible to identify the cruisers, so Murphy stalked them until dawn. He then identified the ships as Japanese, but almost simultaneously the Japanese spotted the *Tambor* and the alarm went out. Murphy ordered a dive and the Japanese ships began emergency maneuvers. The first two cruisers, the *Kumano* and *Suzuya*, turned hard to port as ordered. So did the *Mikuma*, next in line, but the *Mogami*, the last ship in line failed to read the emergency turn signal and plowed into the *Mikuma*. The *Mogami*, in ramming into the *Mikuma*, suffered a serious slicing away of a portion of the bow and was forced to stop. The *Mikuma*, although not as seriously damaged, left a telltale trail of oil in its wake. Eventually both ships continued under way, but at reduced speed.

When the morning's searches began on June 5, the oil slick of the *Mikuma* was picked up by Midway-based dive bombers of Marine Aircraft Group 22, six Dauntlesses under Captain Marshall A. Tyler and six Vindicators under Captain Richard E. Fleming. Tyler led the Dauntlesses in a diving attack upon the *Mogami*, but scored only near misses. Almost simultaneously B-17s dropped bombs from high altitudes but without success.

Fleming brought his flight in upon the *Mikuma* in a glide attack. As he headed for the target his Vindicator burst into flame from heavy antiaircraft fire. Fleming managed to drop his bomb, but could not pull away, for the old plane was blazing furiously. It crashed at full speed into a turret just aft of the bridge. Flames from the fiery wreck were sucked into an air-intake system and detonated fumes in the starboard engine room, killing all the men inside. Fleming's crash, mistaken for a suicide attack by the Japanese, caused more damage to the

Mikuma than the near misses (two men were killed on the *Mogami*) and its collision with the *Mogami*. Now both cruisers limped away from the fury of the avenging Americans.

At dawn the following day, June 6, Spruance dispatched the last air strikes of the Battle of Midway. Around eight in the morning Mitscher's *Hornet* dispatched twenty-six dive bombers with fighter escort; at ten forty-five the *Enterprise* sent off thirty-one dive bombers, three torpedo bombers, and a dozen escorting Wildcats. The final sortie was launched at one-thirty, after some of the earlier planes had returned to relate the successes of the initial strikes. The *Hornet*'s twenty-six dive bombers, upon returning to the scene of battle, found little to do. The first wave from the *Hornet* attacked both cripples, with the heaviest casualties being suffered by the bow-less *Mogami*. The *Hornet* and *Enterprise* Dauntlesses finished off the *Mikuma* with five direct hits. Spreading fires set off internal explosions, which sent the ship to the ocean bottom. The *Mogami*, despite its rent bow and the six hits which rendered it a floating vessel of anguish, eventually reached Truk, although it was to be out of operation for a year. The *Mikuma* (discounting the four lost carriers) was the heaviest warship lost by Japan since the war's opening. In addition, there were many dead and wounded aboard the destroyers, the *Arashio* and *Asashio*, assigned by Yamamoto to stand by the damaged cruisers. These too came under bombing and fighter attacks. With no Zeros to oppose them the Wildcats strafed at will.

The *Yorktown*, which the Japanese had claimed three times to have destroyed, had not sunk after being abandoned on June 4. Fletcher directed that the *Hughes*, a destroyer captained by Lieutenant Commander Donald J. Ramsey, "stand by *Yorktown*. Do not permit anyone to board her. Sink her if necessary to prevent capture or if serious fire develops."

By the morning of the fifth Ramsey saw that the *Yorktown* was not sinking; the list was stabilized at twenty-five degrees. He suggested that salvage operations be attempted and several ships were dispatched to assist. A burst of machine-gun fire from the tilting deck of the *Yorktown* revealed that two crewmen, left for dead, had recovered slightly from their wounds; they were taken off the *Yorktown*. A further search revealed that in the abandon-

The Yorktown *in distress at Midway with destroyer* Hughes *at "Stand by." Although badly hit, the York-* town *seemed capable of being saved and taken under tow.* (NAVY DEPT., NATIONAL ARCHIVES)

Men of the Yorktown *walk the slanting deck of their carrier; Japanese torpedoes from submarine I-168* ended all hope of saving the Yorktown.
(NAVY DEPT., NATIONAL ARCHIVES)

Hit in the same torpedo attack as the Yorktown, *the* Hammann *sinks into the Pacific.* (U. S. NAVY)

Midway secured; it belongs again to the goonies, the Marines, the Navy, and the Seventh Air Force, whose B-24 approaches for a landing. (U. S. AIR FORCE)

ment a number of secret papers and decoding devices had been left aboard. The minesweeper *Vireo* arrived around noon and took the *Yorktown* in tow. It was a great burden for the little ship and little speed was made, but the wounded ship moved slowly toward Pearl Harbor.

Buckmaster, the *Yorktown*'s skipper, asked for a volunteer salvage crew to board the carrier. Soon, with 141 enlisted men and 29 officers, he boarded the destroyer *Hammann,* which in company with destroyers *Benham* and *Balch,* pushed off for the crippled *Yorktown.* They arrived at daybreak on June 6 and immediately began working according to the plan drafted by Buckmaster. The various parties were hard at work; cooks prepared lunches, gunners were on duty at their antiaircraft guns, a medical group attended to the identification and assembling of the dead. Electrical power was drawn off the *Hammann,* directly alongside, to run the pumps to drain the flooded engine rooms. Water was pumped aboard to quench the fire in the rag-stowage room. By midafternoon the list had decreased by two degrees. Destroyers circled around the *Yorktown* and *Hammann.*

Suddenly a hoarse cry went out: "Torpedoes!"

Men aboard the *Hammann* opened up with their

Isoroku Yamamoto, who, as he had promised, "ran wild" in the Pacific "the first six months" after the initiation of the Hawaii Operation. His time began running out at Midway and ended over the jungles of the Solomon Islands. (U. S. NAVY)

guns on the four white streaks in the water rapidly closing from the starboard side. One streak missed completely and continued on harmlessly, but one detonated into the side of the *Hammann* and the other two, passing underneath the destroyer, smashed violently into the *Yorktown.*

The torpedoes had come from the Japanese submarine I-168, commanded by Lieutenant Commander Yahachi Tanabe. Originally sent by Yamamoto to "shell and destroy enemy air base on Eastern Island" in the vain attempt to deal with Midway with surface ships, Tanabe had attempted that but with little success. Later, when the drifting *Yorktown* was found by a float plane, Yamamoto ordered Tanabe to attack the carrier. Having found it, Tanabe delivered his torpedo attack. The I-168 soon came under attack also, but despite the heavy depth charging (Tanabe counted sixty near misses),

the submarine escaped. His was the only decisive Japanese naval action of the Battle of Midway.

Within five minutes the *Hammann,* all but broken in half, sank to the bottom. The *Yorktown,* which had been listing to port, lost a good deal of the list because of the hits in the starboard side, but the carrier now lay deep in the water. Buckmaster continued to hope to salvage the ship, but during the night the *Yorktown* again listed to port. At dawn, June 7, 1942, it could be seen that the *Yorktown* was finally doomed. The ships flew their colors at half-mast; men, many in tears, removed their hats. The death rattle from the *Yorktown*— the sound of loose gear that slipped along the decks, the other equipment and furniture below—echoed over the still waters. The flight deck rolled under the oil-slicked waters, then the gallant *Yorktown,* heaving and shuddering, vanished into the Pacific.

The Battle of Midway was over.

EPILOGUE

A great mantle of secrecy descended upon the outcome of the Battle of Midway in Japan. Only the mildly successful, though inconsequential, Aleutian Operation was mentioned in the newspapers. Nothing was said of the Midway encounter itself and all references to it were deleted from diaries and official reports. The wounded were even held incommunicado and brought into naval hospitals after nightfall. Captain Mitsuo Fuchida, who had led the aerial attack upon Pearl Harbor and was prevented from leading the attack upon Midway by illness, was taken wounded from the *Akagi,* and tells of his stealthy evacuation from a hospital ship ". . . after dark . . . on a covered stretcher and carried through the rear entrance [of the hospital at the Yokosuka Naval Base]. My room was in complete isolation. No nurses or medical corps men were allowed in and I could not communicate with the world outside. All the wounded from Midway were treated like this. It was like being a prisoner of war among your own people."

Yamamoto too went into isolation. He had led the Imperial fleet of Japan into its first major naval defeat in three hundred years. Four of Japan's finest carriers had been sent to the bottom of the Pacific —3500 Japanese seamen (among them about 100 first-line, irreplaceable pilots) died, ten times the number (307) of Americans lost. More than 300 aircraft were lost (the total number based on the carriers, plus some which were being ferried to be based on Midway as soon as it was under Japanese domination); American aircraft losses numbered 147. The course of the Pacific war was completely changed at Midway.

As the Japanese fleet sped out of the range of Spruance's planes, the latter called for a halt of the pursuit. After several days of intense fighting he knew the pilots must be near nervous and physical exhaustion; his ships were running dangerously low on fuel and they were approaching dangerous waters. They had destroyed about half of Japan's carrier strength, but little of the remainder of the surface fleet. Wisely Spruance ordered a return to port.

Yamamoto, ill with severe stomach cramps, remained in his cabin unable to eat anything except gruel for several days. In the wake of the retreating *Yamato*, the *Nagara* too sped toward safer waters. Aboard the cruiser was Admiral Nagumo, dispirited, broken, a man without a ship—the man who had led the Pearl Harbor attack had failed at Midway. Though he returned to sea, Nagumo was a depleted man and did not find peace until July 6, 1944, when he committed suicide on an island named Saipan. His body was never found.

Yamamoto recovered from his mysterious illness and regained his powers sufficiently to press for the occupation of Guadalcanal in the Solomon Islands. This was Japan's southernmost conquest. After hard and painful fighting it was taken back by the Americans—the Greater East Asia Co-Prosperity Sphere was gradually, and bloodily, shrinking. But despite these setbacks, the Japanese continued to revere Yamamoto and to respect his leadership. The very presence of the man in a distant outpost —and no matter how primitive the outpost, the man was invariably immaculate, composed, dedicated— inspired all who saw him.

So it was that following the fall of Guadalcanal Yamamoto planned to fly to Rabaul, New Britain, headquarters of the Seventeenth Army—which had fought at Guadalcanal—and then to proceed eastward to inspect naval bases near Bougainville in the Solomon Islands. Bougainville was the northernmost of the Solomon group and still held by the Japanese; Guadalcanal, the southernmost island, lay about four hundred miles away. According to the planned schedule, Yamamoto, in company with several officers including his chief of staff, Vice-Admiral Matome Ugaki, would leave the main naval base at Truk, spend an evening at Rabaul, and then leave for Kahili airdrome, on the southern tip of Bougainville, arriving at precisely 9:45 A.M.

As before, all preparations for this "secret" move were known by American cryptologists within hours after the coded messages were sent to the Japanese forward bases alerting them of Yamamoto's impending inspection. Word was flashed to Washington; Secretary of the Navy Frank Knox immediately issued orders to intercept Yamamoto's party and "destroy it at all costs." The loss of Yamamoto would tell heavily upon the Japanese and upon the future development of the war. Along with the order arrived a most meticulous itinerary indicating Yamamoto's exact position during his entire tour. Admiral William Halsey, commanding the southern Pacific, assigned the mission to Rear Admiral Marc A. Mitscher, COMAIRSOLS (Commander Air Solomons), who turned it over to Major John W. Mitchell of the Air Force's 339th Fighter Squadron.

A total of eighteen Lockheed P-38s (Lightnings) were to take part in the mission. Mitchell would lead the sixteen-plane cover section and Captain Thomas G. Lanphier the four-plane attack unit. It was decided that the best means of carrying out the mission was to intercept Yamamoto as he came into the Kahili airdrome. It was not without hazards, for the Kahili-Buin area swarmed with Zeros (or Zekes, as the newer models were called). Only the P-38 had the range—a round trip of nearly a thousand miles—taking into consideration the circuitous route which would be necessary to escape detection. Navigational as well as flying skill was essential to the mission.

Mitchell's timetable was carefully geared into that of the punctual Yamamoto's. At exactly seven twenty-five in the morning of April 18, 1943, Mitchell led his planes off the runway of Henderson Field, Guadalcanal. The field was named for Major Lofton R. Henderson, who had died in the Battle of Midway. Two of the eighteen P-38s were forced to turn back almost immediately; one had malfunctioning auxiliary fuel tanks and the other blew a tire during the take-off run. These two planes cut Lanphier's attack section in half, leaving himself and Lieutenant Rex T. Barber (of the 70th Fighter Squadron) to carry out the attack. Mitchell then assigned Captain Besby Holmes and Lieutenant Raymond Hine to join the attack section.

The sixteen P-38s flew for two hours and nine minutes, about 30 feet above the Pacific, a distance of 435 miles, dodging small islands which might be harboring enemy coast watchers. At 9:35 A.M., if all had gone well, they would meet Yamamoto about 35 miles west of Kahili. All through the flight absolute radio silence was observed; Mitchell's navigation was superlative. As the time drew near

the hazy mountains of Bougainville appeared out of the sea. The P-38s swung inland. It was nine thirty-three.

Suddenly the silence was broken by the voice of Captain Douglas S. Canning in the cover section. "Bogey. Ten o'clock high!" About five miles distant Lanphier made out a flight of two Mitsubishi (Betty) bombers, escorted by six Zekes. This was one hitch: they had hoped to have gained altitude before attacking. Now they had to climb, which

The Lockheed P-38 "Lightning," selected as the instrument of Yamamoto's destruction.

(LOCKHEED-CALIFORNIA)

Thomas G. Lanphier, "credited" with shooting down Yamamoto's plane. (U. S. AIR FORCE)

placed them at a disadvantage. All aircraft released their belly tanks in preparation for the attack. Besby Holmes of the attack section, however, could not drop his tank. Raymond Hine stayed with him for protection—with auxiliary tanks the P-38 lost speed and could not maneuver properly in an air battle. Lanphier and Barber, at full throttle, roared in on the Japanese formation. Mitchell's top cover climbed to be on the lookout for possible Zero reinforcements.

The Japanese suddenly became aware of the P-38s; the two Bettys dived for the jungle and three of the Zeros turned upon Lanphier's plane. The Lightning was by this time on a level with the lead Betty and met the assault of the lead Zero head on. Both pilots exchanged wasted shots and then, more calmly, Lanphier took careful aim and the Zero spun into the jungle burning and minus a wing. The other two Zeros flashed by the P-38 as Lanphier made a sharp turn away. He was next aware of the shadow of one of the Bettys moving rapidly over the treetops.

Lanphier lunged the P-38 into a full power dive, then realized he would overshoot the bomber. By this time the duo of Zeros had whipped around to attack him again. To Lanphier it seemed that all were on a collision course, with all four aircraft des-

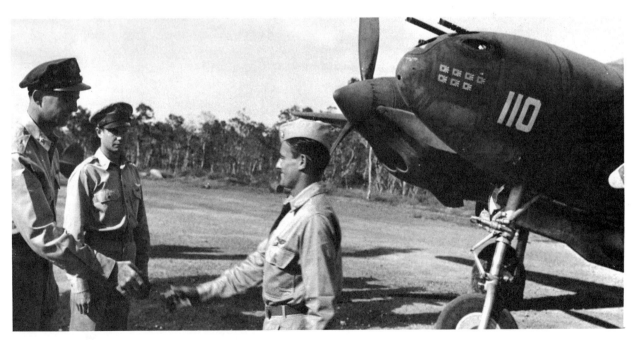

Lieutenant Besby Holmes, center, is congratulated by Brigadier General Dean G. Strother, commander of

Thirteenth Air Force Fighter Command, after the Yamamoto mission. (U. S. AIR FORCE) tined to meet at an imaginary point over the jungle. He maintained his course, however, eyes upon the Mitsubishi, racing in almost at right angles to the Betty's flight path. When it came into his sights he pushed the gun release button. In an instant the right engine of the Betty burst into flame; seconds later the entire wing was ablaze. The two Zero pilots, seeing that the Betty was doomed, no longer considered suicide. They pulled up sharply and away from Lanphier's Lightning.

The stricken Betty, dripping flame, suddenly lost its wing and crashed into the jungle. The ball of fire erupted into a savage explosion and only thick black smoke and red flame remained of the Betty.

The other Mitsubishi, carrying Ugaki, was attacked by Barber, who pursued it over the jungle toward the sea. Ugaki had observed the crash of his chief's Betty and knew that within minutes he too must share Yamamoto's fate. Barber's gun's decimated the crew, spattered the interior of the plane with bits and pieces of metal, killing the passengers also. A cannon hit in the right wing crippled the Betty so that the pilot brought it into the water at full speed. Only three men, one of them the injured Ugaki, survived the attack. With the aid of Mitchell's top cover, the Zeros, which attempted to avenge the attack, were driven off. Holmes, having finally dropped his tanks, shot a Zero off Barber's tail.

Lanphier and Barber raced from the vicinity of the crashed bombers by hedgehopping, dodging, and skidding. Of the sixteen aircraft which participated in the mission, only one, Lieutenant Raymond K. Hine's, failed to return. He had assisted Holmes in driving the Zeros away from Barber's P-38. (Although Lanphier was credited at the time with the victory over the Betty carrying Yamamoto, this victory was questioned by Barber, who thought he had shot down the critical Betty. Holmes also claimed a Betty, the one which fell into the sea, and thought that the bomber which fell into the jungle had been shot down by Barber. Lanphier, however, also claimed a Betty which fell into the

jungle. Unless there was a third Betty, which the Japanese claim there was not, the victory claims cannot be clarified.)

Whatever the dispute over the honors of having assassinated Admiral Yamamoto—honors which should be shared by all pilots who participated in the remarkably executed raid—there is no doubting that his loss was grievous to the Japanese. Their most gifted strategist was gone—and there was no one of equal stature to replace him. The one man who might have, Yamaguchi, had, in an excess of vainglory, chosen to go down with the *Hiryu* at Midway.

Yamamoto was succeeded by Admiral Mineichi Koga (who died within a year in an air accident), but the Japanese fleet had long since stopped "running wild." After Midway, a battle in which not one surface ship exchanged a shot with another, and yet which was the most decisive naval battle of the Second World War, the doom which Yamamoto had predicted for Japan should the war be prolonged was inevitable. After Midway, also, Yamamoto spoke of his own death, which he predicted with a curious wistfulness. Shortly before the interception near Kahili, Yamamoto composed a poem, a sequel to one he had written on the day of the Pearl Harbor attack. In the earlier quatrain he expressed contempt for the world's opinion of the brilliant attack he had engineered; even his own life was insignificant except as "the sword of my Emperor." In his final poem, translated by John Deane Potter, Yamamoto rhapsodized

> *I am still the sword*
> *Of my Emperor*
> *I will not be sheathed*
> *Until I die.*

The sword of the Emperor had been sheathed at Midway by a small band of courageous men in their Buffalos, Vindicators, Marauders, Wildcats, and Dauntlesses. No one knew that better than the wise Yamamoto.

BOOK II
The Big League

Hitler built a fortress around Europe but he forgot to put a roof on it.

—FRANKLIN DELANO ROOSEVELT

5

MILLENNIUM

Winston Churchill arrived in Washington within two weeks of the Pearl Harbor attack for the "Arcadia" conferences with President Franklin D. Roosevelt and other political and military chiefs. On the day of Churchill's arrival—December 22, 1941 —Japanese troops landed on Luzon in the Philippines to begin the inexorable crushing of Mac-Arthur's outnumbered and ill-equipped Filipino and American troops. By New Year's Day 1942, when Arcadia ended, the Allies agreed that, despite the Japanese conquests, Nazi Germany prevailed as the prime enemy.

But until the United States was capable of joining the British in the offensive, it would be necessary for the Empire to carry on alone as before. True, the situation had brightened somewhat: the Battle of Britain had proved abortive and now the Germans had embarked upon Barbarossa, the attack upon Russia which Hitler, with a love for coining phrases, termed the "eight-week war." The nightly terror which had fallen upon Britain was pretty much over by 1942. Hitler's neat little timetable was off a bit in the east so that he was forced to drain off much of the Luftwaffe strength from France and the Low Countries to pour it into the Balkans, north Africa, and the capacious Russian maw. Nearly half of the Luftwaffe was in Russia by the spring of 1942. A quarter of the Luftwaffe's strength remained on the Western Front and in Ger-

many. Although the bombers of Luftflotte 3 were few and aging, the fighters were modern and formidable. Among these were the late-model Messerschmitt 109 and the new Focke-Wulf 190. Some of the latter were converted eventually into fighter-bombers which made harassing "tip and run" raids upon Channel shipping and English seaside towns. These raids were not decisive, merely bothersome and deadly on a small scale. It was, in effect, a kind of stalemate.

Although the Russians clamored for a "Second Front," the only means by which the Allies could possibly bring the war directly to Germany in the spring of 1942 was via British Bomber Command. In February 1942 a new commander in chief, Air Marshal Arthur T. Harris, was appointed to replace Sir Richard Peirse, who had endured a hard and frustrating year as Chief of Bomber Command. Bomber crew losses had increased; bombing accuracy, primarily because of inadequately trained crews, had decreased. During the same period Bomber Command's forces were diverted to the Middle East and effective bombing missions into Germany became more academic than real. Without men and aircraft equal to the task such missions were hardly better than the German tip and run raids—and wasteful in terms of men and machines. So although he was not responsible for the situation, Peirse as commander in chief must serve as scapegoat. But it by no means improved the state of Bomber Command simply because Peirse was dispatched to the Pacific to head the all but non-existent Allied Air Forces there.

Harris had been absent from the battle scene since May of 1941, when he had been placed at the head of an RAF delegation and was sent off to Washington. It was the function of the delegation to acquire American aircraft for the RAF, but the attack on Pearl Harbor, for some time at least, quickly placed the American Air Force high on the priority list, and Harris had little to do.

When he was recalled to command the bomber offensive, Harris had inherited not only the afflictions of the depleted Bomber Command, but also an outstanding senior air staff officer, Air Vice-Marshal Robert H. M. S. Saundby, an old friend from early flying days. Both men were advocates of the "strategic bombardment" concept—the direct attack upon the enemy's warmaking facilities. In less guarded language: an attack upon Germany's industrial cities. If such assaults could be made regularly and in force, both Harris and Saundby believed, they would have a serious effect upon the future of the war.

The job facing Harris was a tough one indeed. He had been handed the task of dealing with several of Germany's greatest industrial concentrations at a time when his forces were being drained away to fight in the critical Battle of the Atlantic and to be used by the Army for close support in north Africa. In brief, while Bomber Command was expected to operate with greater impact than before, almost at the same time this was made difficult, or even impossible, by denying its expansion. Just three days after Harris had taken over, Sir Stafford Cripps, then Lord Privy Seal, spoke in the House of Commons touching upon the subject of whether or not "the building up of this bombing force is the best use that we can make of our resources." It being wartime, Cripps refrained from encouraging a public debate on the subject; he hinted, however, that if "the circumstances warrant a change, a change will be made."

While the semipolitical arguments proceeded and reams of paper were consumed for memos and minutes, Air Marshal Harris went on with his own plans undisturbed. He realized that only decisive accomplishment could save Bomber Command from

High Command conference at Bomber Command: Air Vice-Marshal R. Graham, Air Vice-Marshal Robert Saundby, and, seated, Air Marshal Arthur T. Harris, Commander in Chief. Harris and Saundby planned the Bomber Command attacks on Germany's war industries from 1942 until the end of the war.

(IMPERIAL WAR MUSEUM, LONDON)

complete dispersal and, in his view, waste. He believed too that unless a target was saturated with a series of concentrated blows, there would be little result from several scattered missions. Saturation could be achieved only if a target were correctly identified and bomb loads concentrated within a reasonably small area. By using "Gee," a new electronic navigational device, and by employing both advance aircraft to drop flares to mark the target and other early-wave planes to follow with incendiaries, the area would be clearly, even accurately marked for the succeeding waves of the main force bombers carrying high-explosive and incendiary bombs. It was a page torn from the book of the Luftwaffe, but the system was applied with greater intensity.

By early March Harris had initiated his campaign, although the first targets were not primary ones necessarily. The Renault works near Paris, which supplied war materials to the Germans, was struck by 235 bombers using Gee, which succeeded in knocking it out for about four months. A few days later Essen, home of a giant Krupp arms complex, was bombed using Gee for navigation and the flare system (later to be known as "pathfinder"); in all, 211 bombers were dispatched, but Harris found, upon studying the post-raid photographs, that the mission was not a success. The Krupp works was barely touched (many incendiaries were not dropped until after the flares had burned out; the resulting fires, scattered as they were, misled the succeeding waves of bombers). One bomber, struck by flak, had jettisoned its bomb load, which fell upon Hamborn, not Essen, causing fires which appeared to following bomber crews as signals for a target area. By pure accident many of the bombs intended for Krupp fell instead upon the Thyssen steelworks.

But Harris could not operate on such luck and he soon learned that Gee was not a foolproof device. Within limitations it was fine, but in order to work properly a good clear moonlit night was essential. It could bring a bomber force within reasonable proximity to a target, but the rest of the mission depended upon the human eye.

It was not until the end of March 1942 that Bomber Command could claim a truly successful raid. This was the March 28/29 strike upon the city of Lübeck, a Baltic port of great importance to the German supply system. The dwellings in Lübeck were predominantly wood and Air Staff pressed Harris upon the use of incendiaries. In the resulting attack nearly half of Lübeck was destroyed. Bad weather interfered with subsequent missions dispatched to Essen, Dortmund, Cologne, and Hamburg.

Hitler, meanwhile, issued his Baedeker order on April 14, in which the term *Terrorangriffe* ("terror attacks") appears. These, the Führer pointed out, were to be made upon targets which might "have the greatest possible effect on civilian life." Thus such raids were aimed at undefended, or lightly defended, cathedral cities such as Bath, Norwich, and York, beginning late in April. As Goebbels confided to his diary, Hitler "shares my opinion absolutely that cultural centers, health resorts and civilian centers must be attacked now. . . ." So much for philosophy and morality.

Harris contributed to Hitler's fury with a series of attacks upon Rostock beginning on the night of April 23/24 and continuing through the following three nights. Rostock was, like Lübeck, a port city on the Baltic and also the site of a Heinkel aircraft factory. Over the four nights a total of 521 aircraft were sent to bomb (468 claimed they had succeeded; twelve aircraft were lost) and severely crippled the city, besides damaging the Heinkel works and devastating nearly three quarters of Rostock.

Throughout these tentative, almost experimental early weeks of his tenure, Harris pondered a daring plan. What with the "successes" obtained upon Lübeck and Rostock, which greatly improved the morale of the bomber crews besides giving Hitler a jolt, what might be accomplished by a truly massive force concentrating upon a major target? Say a thousand bombers over a city like Hamburg or Cologne. He spoke of this fancy to Saundby, who immediately and quietly undertook the research to learn if it was not so much a fancy after all.

The next time Harris broached the subject, Saundby informed him that it was indeed feasible at that time, in May 1942. Harris was skeptical, though he continued to listen to Saundby's statistics. If they put up all of their first-line operational units plus training units and borrowed a few aircraft and crews from Coastal Command and perhaps from the Army, a total of a thousand bombers could be dispatched against a single target. Thus assured of at least one aspect of the plan, Harris turned to the others.

These would include target selection, weather, the use of Gee, the risk of collision, and, of course, the inevitable political backing. Harris was quite aware of the implications of failure; but if successful, the "result of using an adequate bomber force against Germany would be there for all the world to see, and I should be able to press for the aircraft, crews and equipment we needed with far more effect than by putting forward theoretical arguments, however convincing, in favour of hitting the enemy where it would hurt him most. . . ." In addition, "from such an operation we should also learn a number of tactical lessons of the greatest possible value, lessons which could not be learned any other way and without which we could not prepare for the main offensive."

By a main offensive Harris visualized hundreds of such massive raids upon the industrial cities of

Germany, which might possibly eliminate the need for an invasion of Europe.

However much exhilarated by the concept, Harris (who was no dreamer) realized also that "if anything went seriously wrong . . . then I should be committing not only the whole of my front-line strength but absolutely all of my reserves in a single battle." Using instructors and trainees from the Operational Training Units further risked, if the losses were great, the crippling of the training program for years to come. But then, since Bomber Command was being picked to pieces and dwindling away anyway, the dramatic conception of a thousand planes over a single target in one raid might make the impression that could save the Command.

To obtain official backing Harris approached his chief, Sir Charles Portal, who guardedly approved, although cautioning that Air Staff also must recognize its "usefulness" and that proper political backing was important. Harris immediately found his backer: Winston Churchill. The Prime Minister's home, Chequers, was but a ten-minute drive (at the high speed at which Harris generally drove his battered old Bentley) from Harris's home, Springfield. This was a handsome Victorian mansion situated near High Wycombe, headquarters of Bomber Command, about twenty miles directly west of London.

The two men, the flamboyant Churchill and the reserved but tough Harris, got along very well. After dinner on a Sunday evening in mid-May 1942, Harris broached the subject of a thousand-bomber raid. The very grandeur of the conception impressed Churchill. For all the romanticism, however, Churchill pressed for concrete details. The target? Hamburg or Cologne. Why not Essen (then regarded as the most important target in Germany)? Because of the limitations of Gee, it was necessary to strike at an easily identified city, Hamburg because it lay on the estuary of the Elbe River (although out of Gee range), and Cologne because of its location on the Rhine River.

There was the delicate point: How many aircraft did Harris expect to lose? Even this eventuality was taken into consideration. Fifty aircraft, or about 5 per cent of the force.

"I am prepared for the loss of a hundred," Churchill told Harris.

The Thousand Plan (Operation Millennium) was on.

II

On May 19 Harris received a letter from Portal informing him that the Prime Minister "warmly approved" of the plan and that it seemed that there was all likelihood of "the co-operation of Coastal Command unless they have special operations on hand." Within two days Harris had a letter from Sir Philip Joubert, Chief of Coastal Command, telling him that "I can go your 250 . . ." in answer to Harris's request for 250 aircraft. Thus Coastal Command would supply one quarter of the total force.

Rapid planning and preparation became essential, for the raid had to take place within the next period of full moon (May 26–30), a week away. Counting Coastal Command's promised 250 planes, Harris had by this time accumulated via his four operational groups, two bomber training groups, and Flying Training Command (with 21 aircraft) a total of 1081 planes and crews. With a force of this size, consisting of a large number of inexperienced crews, a serious possibility of many collisions over the target had to be faced. Although much was to be gained by concentrating a large force over a small space in a short time, there was still this nagging problem.

He asked Dr. B. G. Dickins, head of Bomber Command's Operational Research Section, to work out the probabilities scientifically. He quickly learned that with a single aiming point the risk of collision was very high, but that with three, which divided the forces into three parallel streams, the risk came down to just a little more than one an hour. There were chances also of aircraft being hit by the bombs of other aircraft because the different waves would come in at staggered altitudes, which to some extent lessened the chance of collision. But, theoretically at least, even these possibilities were less than those of being hit by flak or being shot down by night fighters.

With so great a concentration over the target in so short a time—if Cologne, which Harris had already decided would be the target, it would be for ninety minutes—it was hoped that the defenses would be saturated. Radar plots would pile up, gun crews would become confused, and the entire defense system in the area of Cologne would be swamped.

The night of May 27/28 was set for the attack, a night which promised a good moon. But it was just before this that Harris suffered his first blow. Coastal Command was forced to defect from the raid on orders from the Admiralty. A quarter of the total force was gone. Clearly the Admiralty did not wish to place so large a proportion of their planes in jeopardy. If Harris failed, they too would fail; if Harris carried off his scheme, the Admiralty would lose also. Harris would have proved his point and the Admiralty, which clamored for a diminished Bomber Command, would lose their appeal for bombers in the Battle of the Atlantic. There was little that Harris could do but curse the Admiralty. The Bomber Command planes, by May 26, stood ready at fifty-three airfields; training had ceased and the mission must go on.

The weather next turned on Harris. Thunderstorms and clouds over northern Germany made the mission impossible. The next night it was the same. Meanwhile hundreds of bombers and thousands of men waited for something to happen. The mission was postponed for a third time. In order not to make the Germans suspicious of an impending large mission, Harris sent a force to bomb targets in France and another to lay mines. As each wasted day went by, the chance of a security leak became greater.

The extra days, however, gave the ground crews the opportunity to put more aircraft on the Operational Forms. By the morning of Saturday, May 30, thanks to the hard work of these men, Harris actually had his thousand aircraft; more, in fact. On that morning, with good weather promised on home bases, there were 1046 bombers awaiting the signal to take off. Other planes, from Army Co-operation Command and Fighter Command, although not participating directly in the raid, would provide diversionary attacks along the way.

But the full moon period was drawing to a close, and unless the force took off that night, it would have to wait another month before the Thousand Plan could be attempted again. The continental forecast—again thunder and cloud, with chance of clearing—was less than ideal. Hamburg was curdled over with cloud. However, Harris's weather expert, Magnus Spence, predicted that Cologne might clear around midnight. Also, by the time the bombers returned to England some of their bases would undoubtedly be fogged in. But planes from those bases could be diverted to the still clear fields. It was the weather over Germany which most troubled Harris. With cloud over the target, the mission might very well prove fruitless, and with fog over England, with hundreds of milling aircraft, the mission could be disastrous. Still, to Harris, who had but that night and the next before the favorable moon period ended, Spence's prediction sounded better than any they had had so far.

Harris was alone now. It was up to him, however much Saundby sympathized, and he did, for Harris had seen it in an instant in which their eyes met as he lit a cigarette, stalling for time perhaps. He placed the cigarette into a holder, which he clenched in his teeth, and then leaned over the map that lay on his desk. Harris said, "Thousand Plan tonight. Target Cologne."

The word was flashed out immediately to the fifty-three bases scattered northward from London along the east coast of England, with a few farther inland and west of the capital. Unless the weather changed considerably during the remainder of the day, Operation Millennium would take place. With incredible efficiency the more than a thousand aircraft were readied for the mission—the English countryside, especially in East Anglia, resonated to the "dreadful note of preparation." There were shouts and curses; engines shuddering into life barked, snorted, and died, inspiring more curses and activity. Bomb loads ranged from 4-pound and 30-pound incendiaries to be used by the advance force marking the target area (nearly 500,000 incendiaries would fall on Cologne that night) through 4000-pound high-explosive bombs. In between were 2000-pound, 1000-pound, 500-pound, and 250-pound high explosives —about 1300 of these assorted bombs to sow destruction in the marked areas and to disrupt firefighting attempts by German Civil Defense units.

Nearly half of the force consisted of the Vickers Wellington, the "Wimpy" to crews (named for the "Popeye" cartoon character J. Wellington Wimpy). The Wellington was a favorite among aircrews because of its rugged ability to absorb battle damage and remain airworthy. It was reliable, tough, and a good plane to fly. The Wimpy, though designated

Vickers "Wellington," the "Wimpy," favorite of Bomber Command pilots. Its remarkable geodetic construction, the conception of Barnes N. Wallis of Vickers, made it a rugged aircraft capable of withstanding battle damage. Nearly six hundred Wellingtons participated in the thousand-plane raid on Cologne (although not these pictured: Wellington 1s of No. 311 [Czechoslovakian] Squadron).

(IMPERIAL WAR MUSEUM, LONDON)

as a heavy bomber, was powered by two engines rather than four. So was the Avro Manchester, a few of which also participated in the raid. Also a heavy bomber, the Manchester proved to be underpowered, and when two additional engines were later added, it was transformed into the four-engined Lancaster, one of the best bombers of the Second World War. A few of the early Lancasters, fitted with their four engines (Rolls-Royce Merlin), also went to Cologne that night.

The Short Stirling, Bomber Command's first four-engined heavy bomber, delivered the 2000-pound bombs, hundreds of the 500-pounders, and thousands of the incendiaries. By 1942 the Stirling, not a very popular aircraft among pilots, was gradually being retired to such less hazardous operations as minelaying and glider towing. Bomber Command's second four-engined heavy, the Handley Page Halifax, was second in weight of numbers to the Wellington of the participating aircraft. The Halifax was assigned mainly to the incendiary force which initiated the raid.

The two-engined bombers, besides the Wellington and the Manchester, were the Armstrong Whitworth Whitley and the Handley Page Hampden, both early designs which had formed the backbone of Bomber Command during the early months of the war. Both took part in the target-marking phase of the operation. Both aircraft soon after Millennium were gradually withdrawn from heavy bombing operations. Training aircraft, such as the de Havilland Tiger Moth and the Avro Anson did not take part

"Short Stirling," the RAF's first four-engined heavy bomber. Designed in the late 1930s according to curious specifications (the wing span was determined by the width of RAF hangar doors: a hundred feet; the span of the Stirling was ninety-nine). The performance *of the plane was affected by the wing design, restricting its operational ceiling. On missions to Italy, Stirlings were forced to fly through the Alps, rather than over them.*

(IMPERIAL WAR MUSEUM, LONDON)

in the Thousand Plan, although popular legend has long contended so.

All through the morning and afternoon of Saturday, May 30, the 1046 Wellingtons, Stirlings, Whitleys, Hampdens, Manchesters, Halifaxes, and Lancasters—each with its own special bomb load—were serviced, armed, and standing ready for the signal to take off.

The aircrews, totaling about six thousand men, came from all corners of the Empire, from Australia and New Zealand to Canada, and even from the United States. The Americans ranged from the inevitable boy from Brooklyn (Charles Honeychurch; although he was not a boy, being then in his thirties) to the equally inevitable representatives of the "Royal Texas Air Force," Bud Cardinal of Fort

Worth and Howard L. Tate, Jr., of Dallas. Gunner-radio operator R. J. Campbell came from Pawling, New York. One American, Flying Officer Frank Roper, piloted a Lancaster of No. 207 Squadron.

The British crewmen characteristically ranged across the spectrum of personalities, ranks, attitudes, and ages. For example, flying in one of the leading waves was a fifty-year-old air vice-marshal, J. E. A. Baldwin, Air Officer Commanding, No. 3 Group. During the First World War Baldwin had bombed Cologne; he could not let the opportunity slip by in Millennium, for obvious reasons. "I'm going to see for myself," he announced simply. As AOC, No. 3 Group, he was not supposed to take part in operations, but since he received no definite order to that effect (possibly because he had never both-

H. M. King George VI, in RAF air marshal uniform, visits a Bomber Command base and inspects a typical Lancaster crew. (IMPERIAL WAR MUSEUM, LONDON)

ered to mention it at HQ), Baldwin flew as second pilot in a Stirling of No. 218 Squadron. The pilot was Wing Commander Paul Holder, a South African, who commanded the squadron.

Alongside such veterans as Baldwin and Holder, there were also young men still in their teens, some of them pilots, some gunners, others navigators. Many first pilots had only been promoted from second (in U.S. usage, copilot). By the curious workings of the British system, several pilots in command of aircraft were non-commissioned officers, technically outranked by navigators and bombardiers. Inevitably, most pilots were called "Skipper," a reminder of Britain's seafaring traditions. The pilot was in complete charge of the plane, whatever his rank.

Leslie Manser, with the rank of flying officer, was skipper of a Manchester. A gentle, sensitive young man of twenty, his appearance was deceiving. When first encountered by one of his crew, Manser

quickly came under suspicion: he was too pretty to be the skipper of a bomber. At the controls of his plane, however, the youthful Hertfordshire man was as tough as any man in his crew. A superb pilot, extremely cool, competent and at the same time fully dedicated to the safety of the other five in the crew, Manser left no doubt in their minds as to his authority and competence. His copilot was Sergeant Leslie Baveystock, older than Manser, married and the father of an infant daughter. The navigator was Flying Officer Richard Barnes, the radio operator Pilot Officer Norman Horsley. The latter had finished his tour of duty, but was ordered to make one more operation before being posted to a training unit as an instructor. Barnes was a pilot, but was also a skilled navigator (his nickname was "Bang On" because of his reputation for directing his aircraft bang on the target). Neither man had any misgivings about flying with Manser, although Horsley sensed that "making one more ops" might be stretching his luck a bit far.

The rest of Manser's crew was made up of the two gunners: in the Manchester's tail was B. W. Naylor and in the nose, A. M. Mills. Horsley, in addition to operating the radio, also manned the top-turret guns of the plane.

All five men would, by Sunday morning, owe their lives to Manser.

Rumor had spread early throughout Bomber Command that on that Saturday night the "Big Show" would be on. So long as Bomber Command's chief meteorologist Magnus Spence could promise a reasonably stable weather situation, Harris permitted the preparations to continue through the day. By six in the evening the formal briefings on the various stations could officially begin. The scene was similar in all fifty-three stations. The men jammed into the briefing rooms, some diffident, some boisterous, some silent, all apprehensive. At one station the briefing room was furnished with folding seats which had been salvaged from a bombed London movie theater. The station commander entered with what appeared to be a smile on his face. After quiet had settled upon the room, he told the men, "You may have guessed there's something special on tonight. Well, this is what it is. We're bombing Germany tonight with over a thousand aircraft."

The men sprang to their feet, cheering, pounding each other on the back, and danced about. The tension of the past few days was over—and all believed that they would take part in a worthwhile operation. When calm had been restored, the station commander read them a message from Harris.

The force of which you form a part tonight is at least twice the size and has more than four times the carrying capacity of the largest air force ever before concentrated on one objective. You have an opportunity, therefore, to strike a blow at the enemy which will resound not only throughout Germany, but throughout the world. In your hands lie the means of destroying a major part of the resources by which the enemy's war effort is maintained. It depends, however, on each individual crew whether full concentration is achieved. Press home your attack to your precise objective with the utmost determination and resolution in the foreknowledge that, if you individually succeed, the most shattering and devastating blow will have been delivered against the very vitals of the enemy. Let him have it—right on the chin!

While the incendiary vanguard, primarily consisting of Gee-equipped Wellingtons and Stirlings from several squadrons of No. 3 Group, began taking off for Cologne, aircraft of the intruder forces also took off. These were the Blenheims of No. 2 Group and of Army Co-operation Command as well as Bostons,

Havocs (American-built Douglas A-20s), and Hurricanes of Fighter Command. Altogether these totaled eighty-eight aircraft, which were to "intrude" along the route to Cologne, bombing night fighter airfields, hopefully to draw the night fighters away from the main bomber stream. The Luftwaffe fields in northern France, Belgium, and Holland lay adjacent to the route of the thousand bombers. During this phase of the operation the weather proved to be a formidable hindrance. Coming in low over the Continent the men in the intruder aircraft found the German airfields hidden under heavy cloud and all but impossible to find. In some instances the bombers were unable to find the airfields at all, and if they did, the small bombs they dropped (250- and 40-pounders) had little permanent effect upon the targets.

All through the hours of the mission, from the time the first bomber took off for Cologne until the final bomb fell upon Cologne (theoretically at 2:25 A.M. Sunday morning), the intruders did all they could to harass the Luftwaffe, but with no great success. Of the eighty-eight aircraft which took part, however, only three were lost.

Nor did the major part of the operation proceed

Avro "Manchester," the predecessor of the four-engined Lancaster. The Manchester was regarded as a failure and plagued with engine problems until powered by four Merlins, which led to the highly successful Lancaster, Britain's most potent bomber. The Manchester pictured has not had an upper gun turret installed; this was done at about the point where the letter "E" is painted. "EM" is the code for No. 207 Squadron; an American, Frank Roper, was a pilot in this unit on the thousand-plane raid.

(IMPERIAL WAR MUSEUM, LONDON)

Handley Page "Hampden," an advanced aircraft for its time—it first flew in 1936—but afflicted with short-comings by 1942. A few Hampdens carried bombs in the Cologne mission, as well as other succeeding thousand raids, but it was not retained as a night bomber and went into Coastal Command operation as a tor- *pedo bomber. These aircraft, of No. 185 Squadron (which by the night of the raid had been converted into an operational training unit and did not participate), illustrate why the Hampden was frequently called "the Frying Pan."*

(IMPERIAL WAR MUSEUM, LONDON)

according to plan. Many heavily laden bombers struggled to achieve altitude and their pilots found themselves all but blind in the cloud. Icing too became a serious problem, rendering the planes sluggish and straining the already laboring engines even more. Some planes were forced to turn back before getting away from England because of straining engines, inability to gain altitude, or other mechanical problems. The first planes of the incendiary force, the Wellingtons and Stirlings of No. 3 Group, began lumbering down the flare paths of their runways around 10 P.M. Within a half hour all aircraft were ready to begin the flight to Cologne. Very soon it was clear that there would never, in actuality, be a thousand bombers over the target. Boomerangs, the planes with various mechanical problems, began to return with crestfallen and genuinely disappointed crews. About a hundred planes were thus forced to return.

Others were stopped by other mishaps. A Wellington of No. 12 Squadron, obviously suffering engine trouble, simply burst into flame and crashed in Norfolk, killing all aboard. Others, unable to gain the altitude and the safety of the larger formations, ran

into German night fighters and were shot down over Holland. Or, despite overheating engines, pilots continued on, hoping for the best—such a pilot was Pilot Officer Reece Reed of No. 101 Squadron—only to lose an engine and be forced to bail out.

Flying on Gee, the leading Wellingtons pushed on through the disconcerting overcast toward Co-

Wellingtons, which flew in the vanguard of the thousand-plane attack on Cologne.

(IMPERIAL WAR MUSEUM, LONDON)

logne. The conditions promised little success. The air was bumpy and with so many planes in the air, pilots became especially sensitive to the chance of collision. Around midnight the leading bombers were within less than an hour's flying time from Cologne and the cloud was still dense and rough.

In Cologne, veteran of 106 bombings, the routine Yellow Alert had been sounded; minutes later, one minute before midnight in fact, the Red Alert was flashed. It was still too early to tell where the British bombers were heading, but the efficient Warning Control of Cologne was on the job as usual. There was still no reason to sound the sirens.

When the vanguard Wellingtons approached within sixty miles west and slightly north of Cologne, the weather miraculously began to clear. In minutes the night sky flooded with moonlight and below the force glistened the Rhine. Germany lay in darkness, except for the glimmer of a lake and the bright curling Rhine pointing toward Cologne. The river, running generally north and south, intercepted the flight path of the bombers, coming from almost due west now, at right angles. The two lines crossed at the Hindenburg Bridge. About a mile to the west of the bridge lay that quarter of the city known as the Neumarkt, in the center of the Old City on the left bank of the Rhine. The Neumarkt was the aiming point for the first of the incendiaries.

At seventeen minutes after midnight the sirens

Night Mission to Germany: Lancasters await the signal to start engines. (IMPERIAL WAR MUSEUM, LONDON)

keened in Cologne. The dutiful, the experienced, the expectant, and the cynical moved into shelters. They had done it before—so many times, it was becoming a bore. And Göring had promised them that there would be no English bombers. . . .

Two Stirlings of No. 15 Squadron, one piloted by Wing Commander J. C. Macdonald and the other by Squadron Leader R. S. Gilmour, approached Cologne at an altitude of fifteen thousand feet. They had first skirted the city, turning north, in order to make the bombing run on the Neumarkt from the north. Off their starboard wing the Rhine glittered in the bright moonlight, the river gracefully arching eastward above the Hindenburg Bridge. The moonlight and intense shadows brought out the city's details. Less than a half mile northeast of the Neumarkt lay the famous cathedral of Cologne, begun in the thirteenth century and completed six hundred years later. The cathedral was not a target. However, just above it lay the main station on the rail line which crossed the Rhine over the Hohenzollern Bridge. The other two aiming points lay a mile to the north and a mile to the south of the Neumarkt.

As the two Stirlings settled on their bomb runs the first burst of flak came up. They were neither accurate nor numerous. Precisely, one half hour after the air raid sirens sounded in Cologne—at 12:47 A.M.—the first incendiary bombs fell from the two Stirlings and spattered across the Neumarkt. The fires these 4-pound and 20-pound bombs ignited would serve as aiming points for the bombers of the main force. During the next hour and a half Cologne would suffer bombing attacks by no less than nine hundred bombers—not the spectacular thousand perhaps, but tragically sufficient.

When the bombers in the train of Macdonald and Gilmour started on their bombing runs, the Germans had already lit dummy fires away from the critical centers of Cologne, hoping to confuse the attackers. In addition, the midnight sky was sliced with heavy flak and blindingly vivid with searchlights. If there was a beginning of terror on the ground, it was as terrifying at eighteen thousand feet. Within minutes after the initial bomb drop, even before the first conflagrations erupted in the Old City, the bombers had begun to take antiaircraft hits; some flared and fell out of the crisscross of the searchlights. The atmosphere bounced with flak, tossing the planes around as pilots, flying on instru-

Night Mission II: A Handley Page "Halifax" (105 attacked Cologne in the night of May 30/31, 1942) gets *the signal to begin its takeoff.*
(IMPERIAL WAR MUSEUM, LONDON)

ments to keep from being blinded by the lights, weaved to distract the flak-directing instruments, dodged lights, and worried about collision. Quite soon pilots discarded the carefully laid plans for the operation and proceeded under the desperation of the moment. Bombers struck by flak jettisoned bombs as quickly as possible; others, awed by the lights, the flak, and the sight of Cologne burning, bombed directly rather than proceeding according to the briefings on definite bomb runs. Some pilots, even after bombing, circled Cologne to watch in horrified fascination the great sheets of flame which appeared to engulf the city.

Aircraft, therefore, converged over the target area from many directions at different altitudes, some assigned and some enforced by the bomb loads and overtaxed engines. The first collision occurred during the incendiary phase. As one pilot approached the aiming point in a confusion of light, noise, and concussion, he saw one bomber nearby suddenly dissolve in one burst of flame, a great orange ball which remained in place for a moment as small pieces of dripping metal scattered away from it. Keeping directly on his run to give his bombardier the highest chance of accuracy, the pilot found him-

self dangerously close to a Stirling just above and ahead. There were about four hundred yards between him and the Stirling, so he kept a wary eye on his airspeed as well as the Stirling. From below, almost directly under the Stirling, loomed the form of a Wellington.

Night Mission III: Halifax lifts off the runway. Later "Marks" (Halifax III et seq.) were powered with air-cooled Rolls-Royce "Merlins" in place of liquid-cooled "Vultures." (IMPERIAL WAR MUSEUM, LONDON)

Night Mission IV: Lancaster I of No. 61 Squadron; sixty-seven Lancasters bombed Cologne the night of the raid. The only known collision over the target involved a 61 Squadron Lancaster and a Halifax.
(IMPERIAL WAR MUSEUM, LONDON)

"There were aircraft everywhere," one bombardier later reported. "The sky over Cologne was as busy as Piccadilly Circus. I could identify every type of bomber in our force by the light of the moon and fires."

The Stirling and the Wellington flew on toward

Night Mission V: A No. 50 Squadron Lancaster, barely off the ground, has already retracted its undercarriage. (U. S. AIR FORCE)

the center of the fires, their crews oblivious to the hazardous proximity of their aircraft. Besides "jinking" (taking evasive action) they were also being bounced by the slipstreams of the planes which had preceded them. The Stirling dropped down and the Wellington rose, but nothing happened and they continued flying with only a few yards separating them. And then they came together again. The Stirling had gained a fraction in speed so that, with a dazzling shower of sparks, the Wellington's propellers cut off its tail section. For a moment the two great planes hovered in unreal suspension; the next moment the Wellington blew out of existence; the four-engined Stirling gyrated down into the holocaust of Cologne, taking its crew with it.

When the incendiary force concluded its job of seeding with flame, there was no doubt as to the location of the target. The stricken city could be seen as far as two hundred miles away. "It was almost too gigantic to be real," one pilot observed. "But it was real enough when we got there. Below us in every part of the city buildings were ablaze. Here and there you could see their outlines, but mostly it was just one big stretch of fire. It was strange to see the flames reflected on our aircraft.

Night Mission VI: A Stirling heads for Germany—
seventy-one bombed Cologne.
                    (IMPERIAL WAR MUSEUM, LONDON)

It looked at times as though we were on fire ourselves, with a red glow dancing up and down the
wings."

The airspace over Cologne churned with the heat
of the fires, aircraft slipstreams, and the sporadic
burst of antiaircraft fires. Under the unremitting onslaught—about eleven planes crossed over the city
every minute—the defenses had indeed been saturated. The guns ringing Cologne could not keep up
with the great numbers of aircraft. Night fighters
operating on the edge of the flak areas could deal
with but a few of the bombers—and these frequently only after the bomb load had been dropped
into Cologne's inferno. Halfway through the attack
crews noticed a decided confusion and debilitation
on the part of Cologne's flak guns—of which there
were around five hundred.

The bombers of the main force, scheduled to follow the incendiary force, came over and bombed
for an hour. The first plane to arrive was a Wellington of No. 103 Squadron (of No. 1 Group), whose
pilot, a giant New Zealander, Clive Saxelby, brought
it in along the Rhine and without opposition re-

leased the bombs into the marked area. Saxelby
then pulled away and headed for England. It had
been an easy drop and the engines of the Wellington sang beautifully as it cruised over Holland. Out
of the dark came strange flashes which punctured
the fuselage, shattered bits of equipment, and
erupted into a fire in the plane's midsection. The
oxygen system went out immediately, controls went
out of order, and the fire spread.

Saxelby pulled off his oxygen mask, opened the
side window of the cockpit, and for a fleeting moment saw a Messerschmitt 110 in the gloom. They
had been found by a night fighter. With the hydraulic system shot up, the wheels of the Wellington
had come down and the bomb bay doors had
opened, making control of the plane difficult in
addition to slowing it up. Saxelby dived away from
the German fighter while the navigator attempted
to beat out the midsection fire with his bare hands.
Fabric shriveled and pulled away; the tail too caught
fire and lost much of its fabric. The radio operator joined the navigator in fighting the fire, which
in time was extinguished, leaving wide patches of
exposed framework showing. But the controls were
almost too much for Saxelby (his copilot, a man unknown to him before that night, had been killed in

Night Mission VII: A Whitley of No. 10 Squadron airborne. Employing the obsolescent Whitley was an op- *erational barrel scraping; only twenty-three bombed the target during Millennium.* (U. S. AIR FORCE)

the attack by the Me-110). By lashing the control column with rope, Saxelby managed to maintain a near-level flight across the rest of Holland and the North Sea and to the first base they found in England—Honington.

Leslie Manser's Manchester was one of the main force bombers. Like so many of the heavily loaded two-engined bombers, the Manchester could not climb to a safer altitude without dangerously overheating the engines. Manser was forced to bring the plane in under the other bombers at around seven thousand feet. Although he could take some comfort in assuming that the flak would be concentrating on the greater number of aircraft, in truth the overladen radar operators found it simpler to select strays.

On the approach to the drop point the Manchester seemed poised upon the fingers of several searchlights. Just as flak accuracy decreased with altitude, it inversely improved the lower a plane dropped. With the main force up at least twice the height of Manser's Manchester, the stray was quickly boxed in by flak bursts. Manser, the pilot

so many had regarded as "too pretty" to be a pilot, selected an area within the target zone still untouched by fire. Bang On Barnes peered through the bombsight and centered on the area as Manser guided the Manchester across Cologne in even flight.

"Bombs gone," Barnes announced. The Manchester elevated upon losing its burden and, almost instantaneously, recoiled under a direct flak hit. The controls threatened to tear out of Manser's hands as he fought to keep the tumbling and rocking plane under control. But he realized, too, that they must get away from the searchlights—for the flak had plotted their range. Manser heaved forward on the control column and dived away from the lights. When they entered blackness he eased the plane out of the dive. It responded beautifully and came out at less than a thousand feet. They could not remain at that height either, for even ground machine-gun fire could reach them. Pulling back on the controls Manser guided the plane up to two thousand feet; should they have to jump it was a safer altitude also. The plane had taken a hit in the bomb bay, luckily after the bombs had been dropped. The fire had gone out, but that proved only a temporary blessing. The strain on the left engine had been too much. The instruments flickered strangely and then a flash of fire shot out of the engine.

Manser coolly ordered copilot Baveystock to feather the left engine and to activate the fire extinguisher. The rest of the crew, including rear gunner Naylor, who had been wounded by the flak, began to make ready to jump. As Manser and Baveystock watched, the flames from the engine swept back along the wing. The question was: How long before the fire reached the fuel tank in the wing and blew them all over the sky?

But Manser only said, "Let's wait." And they did, for like their skipper the men in the aircraft wanted most of all to get back to England. The eerie flames consumed the fabric of the wing, burned the engine mount, and then, after about ten minutes, the fire went out. Manser had been right. He turned the Manchester toward home as the crew attended to other important details. Naylor lay in a rest bed in the rear of the plane, attended to by radio operator Norman Horsley. But the plane continued to lose altitude and it seemed unlikely that they could ever reach England. All possible equipment which could be spared and torn loose was flung from the plane to lighten it—even guns. The Manchester, despite this, continued to lose air speed. The engine must soon give up—or blow up. Manser found it more and more difficult to keep the plane under control.

Reluctantly he ordered the crew to jump. Mills, the nose gunner, left through the front exit, followed by Barnes, the navigator. Horsley helped the wounded Naylor through a side exit and followed soon after. The plane by this time shuddered and wheezed and was dangerously near stalling point.

Baveystock returned to the cockpit to make certain that Manser had his parachute. He attempted to clip it on the pilot. But he was stopped by Manser, who ordered him to jump immediately. Baveystock went forward to the forward hatch and jumped. But the plane at this time was scarcely a hundred feet above the hedgerow- and dike-crossed countryside of Belgium. In remaining behind to check Manser's parachute Baveystock had all but canceled his chances of survival. He leaped into the darkness, pulled his chute ring—and plunged into the water of a drainage ditch. Although the

parachute had not opened completely, it had decelerated Baveystock's falling speed and the water in the dike did the rest.

The Manchester continued on for only a few hundred feet before striking the ground with a terrific explosion. When he climbed out of the dike Baveystock tried to get to the burning wreck, but the heat of the flames—and the ammunition still aboard detonating—made it impossible. Manser had died in the aircraft; he had kept it aloft long enough to save his entire crew. Baveystock, Horsley, Naylor, and Mills, with the aid of the Belgian underground, finally returned to England. Navigator Barnes, injured in his parachute jump, was captured by the Germans. When the others eventually returned to England and told their story, Manser was posthumously awarded the Victoria Cross—the only participant in the Thousand Plane raid to receive it.

The final fifteen minutes of the raid involved the heavies, the Halifaxes and Lancasters of Nos. 4 and 5 Groups, which followed the main force to which Manser's Manchester belonged. Their function was to drop the 1000- and 4000-pound bombs into the furious chaos. These last two hundred planes would deliver the finishing touches to the destruction besides hindering whatever fire fighting was still possible in Cologne. By 2:25 A.M., Sunday morning, May 31, 1942, Cologne was a man-made hell. To the mystical Leonard Cheshire, who had completed a tour of duty and was then commanding a conversion unit (i.e., a training unit which prepared pilots accustomed to two-engined planes to operate four-engined craft), the hundreds of aircraft pointing toward the crimson glow which was Cologne was "the most monstrous sight in all the history of bombing." As he brought his Halifax in on the bomb run and the city came into view "there was a sudden silence in the aeroplane. If what we saw below was true,

_____

Night Mission VIII: A typical German flak and searchlight concentration over a German city (not Cologne). Flak was responsible for most losses over the target. Of the twenty-two British bombers lost over Cologne, sixteen fell to antiaircraft fire, four to night fighters, and two to a collision.

(ALIEN PROPERTY CUSTODIAN, NATIONAL ARCHIVES)

Cologne was destroyed. We looked hastily at the Rhine, but there was no mistake; what we saw below was true."

The orders had been that all bombing was to cease at two twenty-five precisely; all planes which had not bombed were to turn back. This was to ensure the returning planes as much darkness as possible. The German night fighters were problem enough without having to contend with the day fighters also.

When he took off at 1:15 A.M., Flight Lieutenant George Gilpin had scant hopes of reaching Cologne by two twenty-five. The other aircraft of No. 61 Squadron had left an hour ago. His Lancaster, of the squadron's conversion flight, had been ignored while the rest of the squadron's Lancasters—sixteen altogether—were made ready. Though he pleaded, Gilpin had little luck until the regular planes had been bombed-up and armed. Then all joined in, including himself and his crew, to get the plane ready. The bombing had been progressing for nearly an hour before Gilpin trundled the Lancaster to the runway, half expecting not to get the takeoff light. But it came and he gunned the engines and got away before anyone changed his mind.

Gilpin put the Lancaster into a climb and pulled away over England. They should have little trouble finding Cologne, for there were two navigators aboard the Lancaster. When Gilpin had been granted permission to go on the raid it was with the proviso he could scratch together a crew, for most of the men at his station were assigned to the regular squadron bombers. Gilpin had all positions filled, having assigned the role of navigator-bombardier to an old school friend, John Beach. But there was still need of a nose gunner. It was while he was out seeking a gunner that Gilpin found Flight Officer D. H. Brewer, who, having never flown in a Lancaster, jumped at the chance to go. But Brewer was not a gunner in fact, but a navigator.

They crossed the North Sea at about seventeen thousand feet and below them saw streams of returning bombers of the first wave. Their Lancaster was the only plane flying toward Germany. Gilpin consulted with Beach, asking for an estimated time of arrival over the target.

"0305."

"Forty minutes late?"

This would be counter to orders and Gilpin was not anxious to break rules. Nor was he anxious to waste the effort. He asked Beach for a heading toward another target. But it never came; there was a curious silence on the intercom, an eloquent testimonial to the wishes of the crew. Gilpin let it go at that, for as they crossed over Holland the glow of Cologne lit up the eastern horizon like a premature sunrise.

The Lancaster, then, at three in the morning, was the only plane in the air over Cologne, shimmering below. A pillar of smoke reached up to fifteen thousand feet. It seemed ludicrous for a single bomber to drop its load into the carnage which hundreds of bombers had wreaked. But Beach, lying in the nose, guided Gilpin assiduously on the bomb run. Although there were no fighters now over Cologne, the searchlights stabbed into the air, holding the Lancaster in their blinding light. Then the flak came hurtling up, leaving drifting puffs in the sky. Carefully Beach centered on the aiming point in the center of the burning mass.

Since he was in the nose serving as a scratch "bomb aimer," Beach was not seated in his regular position in the navigator's seat behind Gilpin. On the bomb run a piece of flak tore through the cabin and ripped out the navigator's seat—luckily unoccupied. The impact shook up Gilpin a little but he continued with the run until he heard Beach's quiet "Bombs gone." Gilpin immediately dived the Lancaster out of the beams of light, and although the flak continued to track them, they left Cologne and made for the sea.

When they reached the Dutch coast for the flight over the North Sea and home, the Lancaster was flying on three engines, one having given up on the way. Day had come as they approached England —luckily there had been no fighters. Gilpin brought them all home safely. Millennium was over.

Perhaps with the landing of Gilpin's Lancaster, it could be said that the operation was concluded, but in fact it was not. Even before the great bomber, coming in on three engines and with one propeller feathered, touched down gently at the base at Syerston, a single twin-engined aircraft raced into the air before dawn from its base at Horsham Saint Faith in Norfolk. This was a de Havilland Mosquito of No. 105 Squadron, one of the units which had served with the Advance Air Striking Force in France during the early weeks of the war. Called the "Wooden Wonder" or the "Termite's Delight," the Mosquito was of practically all-wood construction, which eluded radar detection. It was also faster than the German fighters of the period.

On the mission to Cologne, the Mosquito was dispatched to drop bombs (for this highly versatile plane could be used as a bomber as well as fighter, among other functions) and to photograph the destruction of the Millennium bombing. The pilot brought the Mosquito over Cologne at twenty-three thousand feet during the early morning, but although his bombardier could release their bombs, the smoke made it impossible to photograph the damage. Three additional Mosquitos left Horsham Saint Faith at later intervals, and of the two which returned, it was with the same result: too much smoke—for a vast fire cloud rose up to fifteen thousand feet—to take photographs. Only the survivors in the city below realized the extent of the effect of Millennium.

III

German propaganda quickly sneered at British claims of a thousand bombers over Cologne, claiming that the figure was closer to seventy and that the defenses had accounted for nearly half that number. Early British estimates of the impact of the raid were naturally exaggerated. Upon viewing the devastation, however, five days after the attack when

Night Mission IX: de Havilland "Mosquito," which flew a reconnaissance mission to Cologne the morning *after the thousand-plane raid and found smoke rising fifteen thousand feet into the air over the city.*
(DE HAVILLAND PHOTOGRAPH)

Night Mission X: A Stirling coming in for a landing in England. (IMPERIAL WAR MUSEUM, LONDON)

Night Mission XI: A Lancaster, engines warming up and wheels chocked, ready for the next mission.
(IMPERIAL WAR MUSEUM, LONDON)

reconnaissance photographs could be taken, it was clear that more than six hundred acres of the city had been eradicated.

Dismay was the mood in Cologne. Although the official Luftwaffe view was that a few English bombers had broken through the defenses, the city's police president reported that the "number of enemy aircraft over the city could not be estimated." Hitler's toady, Gauleiter Joseph Grohé, supplied his leader with his estimate of a "thousand or more," which Hitler used in a screaming attack upon the Luftwaffe.

The raid had killed 469 people and wounded 5027; more than 45,000 were bombed out of their homes. The incendiaries accounted for the most terrible aspects of the raid, spreading wildly and burning buildings and destroying life and property. This single attack caused the death of more people than all previous attacks upon Cologne combined.

Other than some spectacular figures, had the Thousand Plan accomplished what Harris had wished for? What had been the cost? And what would the future of this kind of warfare be?

The Millennium losses, considering the ambitiousness of the undertaking and the fact that so many inexperienced crews participated, were reasonably low. Forty-one aircraft were listed as missing on the morning after the raid; 3 planes of the intruder force were also missing. Thus it was officially noted that of the total aircraft involved in Millennium, 44 out of 1134 (combined bombing force and intruders) were missing.

And yet Churchill would have been prepared to defend the loss of a hundred aircraft and crews, if necessary, on the floor of the Parliament. Harris had predicted a loss of forty planes; he was a realistic professional. The casualty rate had been 3.8 per cent—a not unacceptable proportion. It was Harris's belief that "we should never have had a real bomber offensive if it had not been for the thousand-bomber attack on Cologne, an irrefutable demonstration of the power of what was to all intents and purposes a new and untried weapon." Another professional, Herr Goebbels, although no soldier, took his own realistic view of the raid when he noted in his diary that he could not "believe that the English have the power to continue such bombing attacks. . . ." Still he was nagged by the possibility of a number of such large-scale attacks, which

he admitted (to himself at least) "can damage us considerably." It was true that Harris would not be able to continue such attacks, risking his regular squadrons, his reserves, instructors, and trainees night after night. In fact, only one more raid of such scale took place in 1942 (June 25/26; the target was Bremen); an earlier attack upon Essen did not achieve the magical magnitude of a thousand. Not until the full weight of the U. S. Eighth and Fifteenth Air Forces came to operate over Europe could thousand-bomber raids become a daily and nightly procedure.

But Harris had made his point—the Thousand Plan had not failed. Cologne had suffered and, if not knocked out of the war, was thrown into confusion and industrial inaction for several weeks. The price of war, too, was brought home to the hapless civil population. The importance of morale under fire is always a questionable point—the human spirit endures under incredible adversity—but before the thousands of evacuees left Cologne they were compelled to sign a statement promising not to discuss the situation in Cologne. Though not readily measurable, the impact upon the German spirit was no less real. Harris had saved his command from the depletion it had suffered during the weeks before he was given its leadership. He had not "destroyed Cologne," as he had asserted, but he had saved Bomber Command and its continued existence and growth would have its effect upon the German war machine.

There were eventual changes in the Luftwaffe brought about by the Cologne attack; it was clear that aircraft would have to be siphoned away from the Russian front. There would be a greater need for more fighter protection over the cities of the Fatherland. Consequently, the German Army would lose some of its air cover. These were subtle yet far-reaching consequences.

There was an even more subtle, sublime might even be the word, sequel, the effect of which was pernicious to the Luftwaffe. This may have been the most important of all the "fruits" of Cologne. While the raid developed in all its fury, Hitler fumed at his headquarters at Rastenberg. His mind was saturated with the conquest of Russia and this sudden, full-scale onslaught from the west exasperated him. Göring was at that moment living the good life in his castle at Veldenstein. When the noon conferences took place on the Sunday following the attack, it devolved upon Jeschonnek and Bodenschatz (Göring's personal aide) to represent the Luftwaffe before the Führer.

Having heard reports from a representative of the Navy and the Army, Hitler turned to the young chief of staff. Jeschonnek did not begin immediately and was prodded by the Führer. "General Jeschonnek, I am waiting. . . ." Clearly Hitler was in a mood, although the devoted, naïve Jeschonnek appeared to be unaware of it.

"There was an RAF attack on Cologne," Jeschonnek began hesitantly, "a pretty heavy attack."

"How heavy?"

Jeschonnek shuffled some papers. "According to preliminary reports," he answered, "we estimate that two hundred aircraft penetrated our defenses. The damage is heavy . . . we are still waiting for final estimates."

"You are still waiting for final estimates . . ." Hitler mocked and shouted, "and the Luftwaffe thinks there were two hundred enemy aircraft!" His voice cracked and rose shrilly. "The Luftwaffe was probably asleep last night! But I was not asleep—not when one of my cities is under fire!"

The Luftwaffe, Hitler intimated, deceived him as usual. Thank God he could depend upon such reliable men as Gauleiter Grohé in Cologne.

"Let me tell you what Gauleiter Grohé has to say! Listen—I ask you to listen carefully—[shouting] there were a thousand or more English aircraft—you hear!—a thousand, twelve hundred, maybe more!" Hitler stopped, his face a livid, apoplectic study in wrath. Composed, but no less furious, Hitler then spoke in a cold tone. "Herr [not Reichsmarschall] Göring, of course, is not here; of course not. . . ."

Bodenschatz had slipped out of the room during the speech, upon assessing the situation. He reached Göring at Veldenstein by phone. "Chief," he said, "you had better come at once. There is trouble."

That he was *persona non grata* was obvious to Göring as soon as he entered the Führer's headquarters later that day. He had gone into the room briskly, but wearing an appropriate air of earnest sobriety. Göring was visibly shaken when Hitler disregarded his outstretched hand. The former corporal had never actually trusted flying men and he had been proved right. If he had failed to appreciate the potential of air power, from that moment on he would refuse even to attempt to understand it. The inner deterioration of the Luftwaffe was assured. Suspicion, vilification, abuse of function, and, even more damaging, the estrangement of Göring and Hitler, sealed the fate of the "Air Weapon."

Harris had not only won the battle; philosophically and morally at least, he had won the war.

6

X-SQUADRON

Lookouts in the small convoy of ships plying the night-shrouded North Sea quickened to the thick rumble of several aircraft engines bearing down from the direction of England. Immediately gunners brought their gun barrels around and waited; a challenge signal vaulted from the convoy commander's ship. Three dark, massive forms came hurtling toward the ships; the planes were barely fifty feet over the water and must have been doing better than two hundred miles an hour.

A Very pistol was fired from a side window in the lead plane and all the men in the convoy relaxed. The signal color was correct for the night, May 16, 1943; the aircraft were British. As was the custom, the convoy's skipper acknowledged recognition with the message "Good hunting" by Aldis lamp. From the lead plane another Aldis flashed as the plane grew smaller in the night. The seamen read the message as the light became a pin point:

We are going to get damn drunk tomorrow night.

As they pondered this curious intelligence two more groups of the same aircraft (Lancasters, they appeared to be) swept over the convoy toward Holland, probably on the way to Germany.

The pilot in the lead Lancaster was the young, stocky veteran of three tours of duty (bombers, night fighters, and bombers again) who was frequently referred to by his men as "the baby skipper," Guy Penrose Gibson. Not many weeks before

—in mid-March—he had returned from his 173rd sortie—a mission to Stuttgart—bringing his Lancaster back on three engines, expecting to take a much needed rest. Gibson hoped to have a few days' leave, the first in about a year, which he would spend with his wife in Cornwall relaxing. He would smoke a pipe, take walks with his dog, and forget about the war for a while. Instead he found himself leading a fantastic night mission.

At twenty-four, Gibson had served as squadron commander of No. 106 Squadron, had been awarded the Distinguished Service Order (with bar) and the Distinguished Flying Cross, and had acquired the reputation in Bomber Command as one of the finest minds in the service. Gibson had been born in 1918 in Simla, India, where his father had served as Conservator of Forests. He grew up in Kent, however, in the area which would serve as the setting for the Battle of Britain, and went to St. Edward's School, Oxford. Though powerfully built, Gibson never grew much taller than slightly over five feet. Whether or not this accounted for his physical drive is beside the point, for as recollected by the warden at St. Edward's, he "was one of the most thorough and determined boys I have ever known. . . ."

By the time he was well into his teens, Gibson had become air-minded and hoped to seek work as a test pilot. When he approached Vickers-Armstrong

Guy Gibson, who led one of the most daring bombing missions of the war during the Battle of the Ruhr. A born pilot and leader, Gibson earned a Victoria Cross for his part in the Dam Busters raid.
(IMPERIAL WAR MUSEUM, LONDON)

(who would later manufacture the Wellington), Gibson was told to join the RAF "to get all the flying time you can." However, upon applying Gibson was informed that his "legs were too short." But the determined Gibson had made up his mind and after exercising and stretching, he returned to the RAF and apparently, by sheer dint of will power, passed the physical requirements. In 1935 Guy Gibson began training with the RAF, hoping that when he had completed his courses, he might return to Vickers for a job as test pilot. The stocky youngster fell into the routine very well—he had a taste for pretty girls and drink and a love of animals. He also revealed a flair for flying and a mind which absorbed, classified, and retained details.

The political situation kept Gibson in the RAF after his enlistment expired and when war finally came he was a pilot of a Hampden in No. 83 Squadron based at Scampton in Lincolnshire. Gibson took part in the frustrating operations during the "Phony War," as well as more profitable strikes upon targets in the occupied countries and the Sealion barges during the Battle of Britain. Upon completing his tour with the bombers, Gibson was stationed—for "a rest"—with No. 29 Squadron, Fighter Command. While serving with this night fighter unit, Gibson succeeded in shooting down three enemy aircraft. Following his "rest" tour Gibson was sent to an Operational Training Unit, which did not please him at all. But it was a good post, for Gibson had married Evelyn Mary Moore, a young and pretty actress, and he spent much time at home. Even so, Gibson did not like the role of flying instructor and made it fairly obvious. Not long after Arthur Harris took over Bomber Command Gibson managed to get an interview with him and within days (two, in fact) was posted, in February 1942, to No. 106 Squadron as Wing Commander (Acting). Upon completing his tour with the squadron, its "baby skipper" looked forward with longing to the easy days with Eve at Cornwall.

But he had barely unwound from the Stuttgart mission when he was informed the following day that he would not go on leave; he was to be posted at Headquarters, No. 5 Group instead.

Air Officer Commanding of No. 5 Group was Air Vice-Marshal the Honorable Sir Ralph Cochrane, like Saundby an old prewar squadron mate of Harris. Cochrane, scion of a noble Scots family, was a lean, no-nonsense, crisply decisive man whose aviation experience dated back to the First World War. When Gibson reported to him at group headquarters at Grantham, it was with the gloomy expectation of being assigned to write a textbook on bombing. Having barely finished congratulating Gibson on the bar to his DSO, Cochrane immediately came to the point.

"How would you like the idea of doing one more trip?"

Visions of fighters and flak came into Gibson's mind. He had hoped all of that was over, at least for a while. But all he could do was ask, "What kind of trip, sir?"

"A pretty important one, perhaps one of the most

devastating of all time," Cochrane replied. "I can't tell you any more now. Do you want to do it?"

The urgency seemed so pressing that Gibson had begun trying to remember where he had left his flying kit. Certainly the trip of which the AOC spoke was scheduled for that very night. His answer reflected the state of his mind: "I think so, sir." Gibson was then sent away mystified.

But the trip was not scheduled for that night, or the next. On the third day after the first interview Gibson was once again ordered to Grantham's main office. Seated in Cochrane's office was a man Gibson knew, stocky, thirtyish, experienced Group Captain Charles Whitworth. Cochrane was cordial, even offered Gibson a cigarette before he broached the subject of "the trip." He began by warning Gibson that it would not be an "ordinary sortie. In fact, it can't be done for at least two months."

"Hell," Gibson thought, "it's the *Tirpitz*. What on earth did I say yes for?" The great 45,000-ton battleship, launched just six months before the war began, was a major source of anxiety to the British at this time (the *Tirpitz* did not prove as formidable in action as it promised, but this was not apparent in 1943). The battleship was then lying in Trondheim Fiord in Norway, all but impossible to reach by air and a threat to convoys to Russia.

Cochrane went on, without slipping Gibson the least hint of the nature of the target or of the mission itself beyond telling him that Harris regarded the training for the raid so important "that a special squadron is to be formed for the job. I want you to form that squadron. . . ."

Stressing the importance of the training and the little time in which it must be done, Cochrane suggested that Gibson go immediately to the personnel section to begin assembling his crews and arranging for aircraft and other equipment as well as ground crews. All Gibson knew actually was that he was to undertake some important mission or other and that his special squadron was to be based at Scampton, where Group Captain Whitworth was commander and where Gibson had begun his active career with No. 83 Squadron less than four years before.

When he left Cochrane's office for the personnel section Gibson's head swam and his ears rang with the order, "I want to see your aircraft flying in four days' time."

What aircraft, with what crews? Gibson wondered as he climbed the stairs to begin selecting pilots and crews and to start all the other gears meshing for the mysterious trip. Whatever it all ultimately would lead to, the trip was obviously of highest priority, for within two days a squadron of seven hundred men was formed and ordered to report to Scampton. In fact, its formation had come so quickly that the Air Ministry was itself not prepared for it and called it temporarily X-Squadron. Finally it was assigned the number 617.

II

That it was an elite unit was patent in the beribboned crews that began arriving at Scampton on March 21, 1942. "These were the aces of Bomber Command," Gibson noted. He had selected pilots he knew personally or by reputation; the rest were suggested by Bomber Command. It was a standing order, another tribute to X-Squadron's uniqueness, that the other squadrons must surrender requested crews on demand. This did not always work out to perfection. "Some of the squadrons which had been told by the SASO [Senior Air Staff Officer] to supply us with tip-top men had taken the opportunity to get rid of some of their duds. . . . Then another squadron supplied me, rather unkindly, with two pregnant WAAFs [Women's Auxiliary Air Force]. They were married, of course, but they weren't any use to me because they had to leave the service, anyway. There were other little games played on us which I won't mention." Gibson, however, managed to assemble twenty-one crews, some of them from his own No. 106 Squadron—all of them veterans with thousands of sorties to their credit.

When he called the 147 men of the aircrews together for their first official meeting, Gibson was still at a disadvantage. There was little of a solid nature which he could tell these 147 knowledgeable men. "You're here," he told them, "to do a special job, you're here as a crack squadron, you're here to carry out a raid on Germany which, I am told, will have startling results. Some say it may even cut short the duration of the war. What the target is I can't tell you. Nor can I tell you where it is. All I can tell you is that you will have to practice low flying all day and all night until you know how to do it with your eyes shut. . . ."

It would be some days before Gibson was to meet the gentle, white-haired man—a civilian—who had initiated all of this inexplicable activity. He was Dr. Barnes N. Wallis, an outstanding designer and aeronautical engineer employed by Vickers-Armstrong. Wallis, who had designed the structure of the airship R-100, had contributed also to the design of the Wellington bomber (in which work he had teamed up with Vickers' chief designer, Rex K. Pierson). Wallis's major conception was the geodetic system of construction, which made the Wimpy a rugged though comparatively lightweight aircraft.

A brilliant mathematician, the fifty-year-old engineer began to consider the problem of bombs as

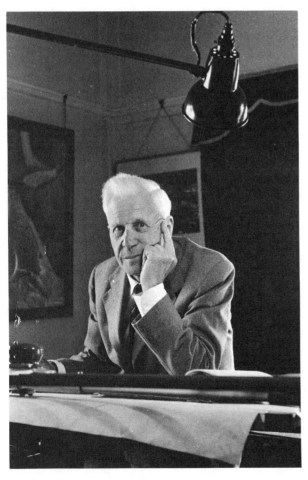

Dr. Barnes Wallis, inventor-engineer-designer, who made many contributions to Britain's war effort as well as to aviation. (VICKERS LIMITED)

soon as the war started. Wallis, in his own way, was a proponent of strategic bombardment. When war came he believed that the standard bombs then available to Bomber Command lacked the power to destroy important industrial targets: the five-hundred-pounders then in use would not do. Also, unless targets were selected with care, what bombs were dropped would accomplish little more than temporary damage. Wallis, in short, began to visualize a superbomb to be dropped upon a super target. It followed that his mind would consider the Ruhr, the great center of Germany's heavy industry. Within this highly defended area lay a complex of great dams, targets which could not be dispersed like a factory, nor even very easily camouflaged.

Wallis studied the situation closely and selected three of the dams as primary targets: the Möhne, the Sorpe, and the Eder. The first two, as Wallis later explained to Gibson when finally the young wing commander was permitted to know what he was about to attempt, held back "about 76 per cent of the total water available in the Ruhr Valley. If they were to be breached, the consequent shortage of water for both drinking and industrial purposes might be disastrous. Of course, the damage done by floods if they were breached quickly would result in more damage to everything than has ever happened in this war." The Möhne Dam alone, holding back a lake about twelve miles in length, would release about 140 million tons of water, if breached, into the Möhne Valley.

The Eder Dam was not a water supply dam as were the other two, but a source of hydroelectric power. It was somewhat larger than the Möhne, with a capacity of about 200 million tons of water.

Such were the targets, but there were no bombs then existing that could burst them. An object which could hold back 200 million tons of water would not breach under the impact of a mere five-hundred-pound high-explosive bomb. It was to this problem that Wallis applied himself next, studying the structure of dams and of the nature of explosion: shock, tension, and dozens of other variables. When he felt he had the answers to all of the problems, Wallis took his idea to the Air Ministry. He was not greeted with open arms and cries of recognition. Although Wallis's idea had been conceived early in the war, it was not until Harris took over Bomber

Command that it trickled down to him. Nor did the astute Harris seize upon the Wallis plan with joy and expectation.

The various ministries had come to be all but besieged by hundreds of inventors, idea men, armchair generals, and just plain screwballs with thousands of schemes and gadgets for winning the war. Wallis's device for a big bomb (an "earthquake bomb," he sometimes called it) would require a large aircraft to carry it (he called that a "victory bomber"). Neither bomb nor aircraft existed when he submitted his plan. Because of his reputation in the industry, Wallis's idea was not completely dismissed, as were so many others at the time. But, depite that, it took a long time before anyone in the Ministry of Aircraft Production read his paper with any understanding. This was Sir Henry Tizard, who had championed Watson-Watt's radar. A committee was formed to study Wallis's formulations (among which the dams project was but one) and soon after, another committee was formed known as "The Air Attack on Dams Committee." It took months before the idea took on any definite form, depending not only upon the accuracy and validity of Wallis's computations, but also upon the advent of a bomber which could lift and deliver a bomb of tremendous weight. Meanwhile, new very high explosives were being developed. So it was that when the high-capacity bombs became feasible—according to Wallis's figures it would have to be about ten thousand pounds in weight, explosive as well as casing—the Lancaster was on hand to carry it.

Months of experimentation followed, with Wallis practicing on small models of dams and bombs and filling pages with computations. Quite simply, it was Wallis's idea that in order to breach so sturdy an object as the Möhne Dam, the special bomb would have to be released at low altitude, with the aircraft traveling at a specific speed. Before the bomb—which was shaped like an oil drum—was dropped, it must be made to revolve. Upon release it was supposed to skip and jump along the water's surface until it struck the dam. Then it would, because of the spin, roll down the face of the dam to the proper depth and only then explode. The tremendous forces, magnified by water pressure, would have the force of an earthquake and would, theoretically, burst the dam. That is what Wallis's figures said and that is what he believed.

Eventually, with models and with test bombs Wallis proved that it could be done. However, when he finally took his idea to Harris, the latter was skeptical. He had heard of the little man with the dams idea. Another crackpot with what Harris termed a "panacea target," single targets that everyone—except the Germans—would assume might end the war in a single blow. These targets, often as not, were difficult to hit, well defended, and, even if hit, might very well prove not so conclusive after all. They were costly in terms of crew losses, spectacular, even dramatic—but wasteful. Harris had his own plan for ending the war—a city by city erasure of German industries with large forces of heavy bombers. Wars were not decided with single panacea blows. Harris regarded Wallis with misgiving and doubt.

He told Wallis he found the idea a bit beyond belief and, further, he was not ready to risk a squadron of Lancasters on it. One of Wallis's champions was Joseph "Mutt" Summers, chief test pilot at Vickers, who had been assisting Wallis in testing the dummy bombs in a converted Wellington off the coast of England. At the point where the two stubborn men, Wallis and Harris, were about to clash, Summers interceded and promised Harris that they could prove that the bomb worked.

"Prove it," Harris snapped, "and you'll get your squadron."

The two men brought out the film that Wallis had been shooting over the past half year and with Saundby operating the projector, the four men observed the results of Wallis's experiments.

When the film ended all Harris would say was, "Very interesting. I'll think it over."

This was not very encouraging. Wallis found that others also were less than enthused and he had even been asked to stop "making a nuisance of yourself at the Ministry." Exhausted, depressed, and fed up, Wallis offered to resign from all war work. This only aroused an outcry of "Mutiny!" Wallis seemed to have come to a dead end. But other forces had been at work, for approval of the idea had come down from the Chief of the Air Staff, Sir Charles Portal; Churchill had voiced his approval and others had chimed in. The date was February 26, 1943; the operation must take place sometime in May, when the water level of the dams was at maximum. That left three months in which to select and train

The objective: the Ruhr dams, in this instance the Möhne, holding back more than a million tons of water. (IMPERIAL WAR MUSEUM, LONDON)

crews, make and test the bomb, and modify the Lancasters to carry it.

It was Mutt Summers who brought Gibson finally to meet Wallis after No. 617 Squadron had begun training at Scampton. By coincidence, it had been Summers who had advised Gibson, so many years before, to enlist in the RAF. The trip from Scampton had been exceedingly cloak and dagger. Gibson was driven south, past London, and left at a small country railway station. He took a train for Weybridge, where he was supposed to meet someone. The someone turned out to be Summers, who then drove Gibson to Wallis's home in the peaceful southern countryside. Gibson found Wallis "neither young nor old, but just a quiet, earnest man who worked very hard. He was one of the real back-room boys of whom little can be told until after the war. . . ."

An awkward situation arose immediately, for Gibson admitted that to date he had not been informed of the target or of the "Wallis bomb." Wallis checked a list of names of persons with whom he could discuss the project and did not find Gibson's there.

"This is damned silly," Summers said. But Wallis would not discuss the plan except in general terms. He did run a film he and Summers had made which revealed something to Gibson. He saw a Wimpy come in within two hundred feet of the sea and drop a strange cylindrical object. Gibson was certain that if that were a bomb, the detonation would blow the plane sky-high, but instead the cylinder bounced along as the Wellington pulled out of the way of danger.

Clearly, they were to come in low over a target situated on or near the water. Was it the *Tirpitz*, Gibson wondered, or was it the U-boat pens?

Wallis explained that the cylinder was, indeed, his special bomb, the placement of which would require exceptional skill. However, the test bomb was but a quarter of the size of the real thing, so that further testing would be necessary. Gibson asked if any full-scale bombs existed.

"No, not yet," Wallis admitted, "the first will be ready in about a week's time with a modified Lancaster to carry it. Avro's is doing a great rush job to get the special fittings put on; I believe they're working twenty-four hours a day. Now what I want to know from you is this. Can you fly to the limits

I want? These are roughly a speed of two hundred and forty miles an hour at a hundred and fifty feet above smooth water, having pulled out of a dive from two thousand feet, and then be able to drop a bomb accurately within a few yards."

Although still mystified, Gibson left Wallis knowing just a bit more about their proposed mission. He promised to see if it would be possible to meet the requirements for the bomb drop, but that was all. So it was that the two men worked, in their separate spheres, concurrently toward a date in the middle of May, the younger man without concrete information and the older one still uncertain that the weapon he had invented would actually work.

Gibson assigned his crews the unpleasant task of flying low over lakes, rivers, and reservoirs. Within days the complaints began coming in—reports of low-flying aircraft. Even Gibson's own maintenance crews complained of leaves and branches jammed into the radiators.

"This means you are flying too low," Gibson told his flight leaders "You've got to stop this or else someone will kill himself. And I might also tell you that the provost marshals have already been up to see me about reported dangerous low flying. We all know we've got to fly low, and we've got to get some practice in, but for God's sake, tell your boys to try and avoid going over towns and aerodromes and not to beat up policemen or lovers in a field, because they'll get the rocket if they do."

The following day Gibson was summoned to Cochrane's office. On the floor stood three large packing cases. Cochrane handed Gibson a screwdriver and promised he would show him the targets —although he would not tell him either what they were or where they were located. Gibson removed the lids and peered into the boxes—there perfectly scaled were models of three dams, obviously very large and sturdy. But Gibson's first reaction upon seeing them was a fleeting thought: "Thank God, it's not the *Tirpitz*."

Without revealing much more, Cochrane told him to take a plane and fly down to see Wallis in Weybridge. At least now the men could discuss the problem intelligently. It was Wallis who informed Gibson that the three dams lay in the Ruhr Valley— "Happy Valley" to the bomber crews because of the deadly flak barrages they never failed to encounter there.

Gibson wondered why the special bombs, and why the stringent conditions—altitude, speed—for the attack. Wouldn't any large bomb hitting the dams knock them out?

Wallis explained the difference between a vault dam—the curved type which held back water by its configuration "much the same as the arch of a bridge"—and the dams they were after, which were called gravity dams and which retained water by their own weight. "As these are a hundred and forty feet thick, of solid concrete and masonry, a hundred and fifty feet high, you can see that there is a colossal amount of masonry to shift." Wallis further explained that the attack would have to take place when the water level was at its highest. At that moment it was twelve feet from the top of each dam; they would attack when the level reached four. This would give them the proper water capacity and also leave the four-foot space against which the bomb would strike after its last bounce carrying it over the floating torpedo nets which protected the dam, and then permitting it to roll down the dam toward the base before detonating. This was precision at its most precise. Gibson looked doubtful. They were to do this at night in addition to all the other contingencies.

"I have calculated," Wallis continued, "that the water level will be suitable during the week May 13–19, that is, in about six weeks' time. This, as it happens, is a moon period—I think you will have to do it at night or dawn—you couldn't get into the Ruhr by day, could you?"

"God, no!"

That was settled. There was another point. In order that the bomb could make the correct number of skips before striking the lip of the dam, it must be released at just the right point. Otherwise it might bounce over the dam (which might prove fatal to the Lancaster which had dropped it) or might fall short of the dam and merely sink into the water and detonate without effect. It was just one more detail which needed attention. There was a sense of urgency about the entire project which Gibson found unsettling, but he returned to Scampton to continue the training. He promised to see Wallis in two weeks, on April 16, to observe the test drops of the first two full-scale prototypes of the Wallis bombs.

Early in April Wing Commander C. L. Dann from the Ministry of Aircraft Production casually dropped in on Gibson at Scampton. With breath-taking abruptness Dann broached the subject of getting the correct sighting of the Möhne and Eder dams. Considering the few people in on the project —Gibson was the only man in the squadron who knew of the targets—it came as a shock that a man could walk in off the street, so to speak, and begin talking about a most ticklish subject.

"How the hell do you know all this?" Gibson demanded. Dann explained that he was a bombsight expert and had been asked to help solve the problem in connection with the dams. A mathematician, Dann had studied the aerial photos of the Möhne and Eder dams and found that each dam had towers at either end two hundred yards apart. Using these as the base of a triangle, Dann very quickly devised a simple bombsight which could be made of a few pieces of wood. The bombardier simply lined up two nails with the towers through a peephole. When all came in line, it was—provided the speed of the plane was correct—the drop point. Within hours the device was tested and found to be remarkably accurate.

Dann's little gadget solved that problem, a skilled pilot could manage the problem of air speed, but neither man nor instrument could make certain that the plane was flying at the correct height. Flying over water was especially deceiving. Also, they would be down low in a darkened valley, surrounded by hills. It was a serious problem indeed.

III

While Wallis worried over the casing of his bomb, which did not stand up to the strain of the test drops, Gibson continued with the training of No. 617 Squadron. They had progressed beautifully in all areas but the sticky one of height—how to find 150 feet and how to stay there? One solution seemed to be trailing a weight from a wire. The weight would be placed at the 150-foot mark. When it struck the surface of the water they would be at the proper height. Upon testing it was found that the wire and weight trailed almost directly behind the plane. Judging by eye was completely useless. There seemed to be no solution to the problem.

One day another "back-room boy" appeared out of the depths of the Ministry of Aircraft Production.

He was Sir Ben Lockspeiser, KCB, FRS, and he had a suggestion—an old one really, which had been employed in the Great War. Altimeters then were even more primitive than those of 1943, so it might be possible to employ classic trigonometry instead. Place spotlights in either wingtip so angled that when they converged on the surface of the water the distance from the aircraft to the water would be exactly 150 feet. This made sense and was almost as simple as the little wooden bombsight that Dann had conceived.

Gibson dispatched a Lancaster to Farnborough (Royal Aircraft Establishment), where Aldis lamps were fitted into the nose and near the tail (this was Gibson's slight variation on the idea). This task Gibson had assigned to Squadron Leader Henry Maudslay, who commanded B Flight of the special unit. Upon his return the following day, Maudslay took the Lancaster up at dusk and demonstrated the device for Gibson. When the beams of light merged beneath the low-flying plane Maudslay found that he could maintain the correct height with a little help from the navigator. Within days all the Lancasters were fitted with fore and aft Aldis lamps and practiced using the "spotlight altimeter calibrator" under observation of ground instruments. It was found to work with amazing accuracy. As Gibson watched the demonstrations he could not help but wonder about how much flying around with Aldis lamps on would aid the German gunners.

Late in April Gibson had an urgent summons to meet with Wallis. The little man's face was lined and he was visibly tired when he told Gibson, "The whole thing is going to be a failure unless we jiggle around with our heights and speed."

What could this possibly mean?

Wallis explained that he had continued experimenting with the bombs, shattering most of them. Upon studying the films and graphing the results Wallis had come up with one more set of conditions: Could they approach the dams at 60 feet and at a speed of 232 miles an hour? "If you can't," Wallis added, "the whole thing will have to be called off."

Dire thoughts raced through Gibson's mind. If 150 feet was low, 60 feet was very low. At that height you would only have to hiccup and you would be in the drink.

He promised, however, to try that night. The deflection of the Aldis lamps was changed and although the big aircraft seemed to be moving along awfully close to the ground, accuracy was excellent. It could be done and on May 1 Gibson called Wallis to reassure him. When another test was run at the new height and speed the bomb worked. But the time drew nigh, for from April 17 through May 1 the water level in the Möhne had risen five feet, within ten feet of the lip. The high-level period would soon be upon them; all the modified aircraft would be required and the bombs were yet to be manufactured.

The first special Lancaster had been flown into Scampton on April 18, another nineteen following at intervals—the last arrived on May 13. Around the same time lorries delivered the Wallis bombs to Scampton; the bombs were factory-fresh and still warm. The odd devices, weighing 9250 pounds, carried a charge of RDX, a very high explosive, weighing 6600 pounds. The cylinder itself was five feet long and fifty inches in diameter. The bombs were not cranked into the aircraft as was normal, but the Lancasters were lifted at the tail by a crane and lowered onto the bombs. These were fitted into the special cutout in the fuselage with the axis of the bomb at right angles to the centerline of the Lancaster's fuselage. The effect, since the bomb bay doors had been removed, was as if a garden roller had been installed into the aircraft. When the bomb was about ready to be dropped a hydraulically operated motor attached to pulley by a belt drive was activated and the bomb would begin to spin (backward toward the tail). At the point of release the spin would reach five hundred revolutions per minute. It was this rotation which carried the bomb skipping over the surface of the water and then, with the remaining momentum, rolled it down the face of the dam to explode at the correct depth. At least, that was the plan.

Gibson delegated the job of checking the modified aircraft to his engineering officer, the "plumber," Flight Lieutenant C. C. "Capable" Caple, and the handling of the bombs to his armament officer, Flight Lieutenant "Doc" Watson. There were still the routes to plot—coming and going to the dams— which would best avoid flak concentrations and night fighter fields; there was the question of communications. This last problem was solved when it was decided that in addition to the standard radios, all of the Lancasters were to be equipped with Very High Frequency Radio Telephones. This enabled the men to communicate with each other directly and would make it possible for Gibson to direct the operation in the target area. Such intercommunications had never been used before on bombers.

As the middle of May approached the pressures increased and Gibson himself showed the strain. He was irritable, impatient, and quickly lost his temper. A large carbuncle blossomed on his face; when he saw the base doctor (who knew nothing of the impending mission), Gibson was informed that he was "overworked. You will have to take two weeks off." Gibson burst out laughing and left. In two weeks it would all be over.

On May 15 Cochrane dropped by and told Gibson that, weather permitting, the squadron would take off the next night. After two and a half months, it seemed almost like good news.

During this period of training Gibson had divided the squadron into two flights, but for the raid itself there were to be three waves. The first, led by Gibson, consisted of nine Lancasters, which were to attack the Möhne Dam first; if successful, and if any bombs remained, they would continue on to the Eder Dam. These two dams were to be attacked from 60 feet and at 232 miles an hour, as had been calculated by Wallis. A second wave—which in fact would take off first—was made up of five bombers and would attack the Sorpe Dam (which was of a different construction than the other two) from the lowest possible height and at 180 miles an hour. The third wave, five Lancasters, was to be a mobile reserve and under control of No. 5 Group headquarters (Cochrane) and not Gibson. Since all reports of the success or failure would come into Group HQ, the mobile reserve aircraft could be sent by Cochrane to any unbreached dam or to other dams in the area. It was hoped that, in addition to the Möhne, Eder, and Sorpe dams, Gibson's crews might also deal with such smaller dams as the Lister, Schwelm, and Ennepe.

Of the original twenty-one crews, nineteen therefore would carry out the raid. One of the special Lancasters had been damaged five days before the raid during a training mission (spray had shot up against the low-flying aircraft and damaged the underside badly enough to put the plane out of action).

The other eliminated plane was forced to stand down because of an illness among the crew. In all, the nineteen Lancasters carried 133 men.

IV

The first Lancaster to take off from Scampton was piloted by Flight Lieutenant R. N. G. Barlow of the second wave (which took off first because of the greater distance to its target); it was nine twenty-eight in the evening of May 16, 1943. Within two minutes the second plane took off, Sergeant V. A. Byers, pilot; then, one minute after him, Pilot Officer G. Rice in the third aircraft; within eight minutes Flight Lieutenant K. L. Munro lifted his heavy Lancaster off the runway and vanished into the east. (At this moment—9:39 P.M.—Gibson's first wave (Möhne) began taking off.) The fifth and last plane of the second-wave force (Sorpe), piloted by a blond giant from Brooklyn, Flight Lieutenant Joseph C. McCarthy, did not get away on schedule. In fact, there was a delay, infuriating to McCarthy, of more than a half hour.

"Our favourite Yank, F. L. McCarthy, caused quite a disturbance," the squadron diary [written by squadron adjutant Flight Lieutenant H. R. Humphries] noted. "He arrived at his aircraft and after finding she had hydraulic trouble came dashing back to our only reserve aircraft. When inside he noticed he had no compass card and came rushing back to Flights frantically screaming for one. He had also pulled his parachute by mistake and the white silk was streaming all over the ground, trailing behind him. With perspiration dropping off his face, good old Mac ran back to his aircraft with everyone behind him trying to fix him up with what he wanted."

Of the five aircraft of the second wave only McCarthy's actually dropped its bomb on the target. The first two planes, Barlow and Byers, were lost. The latter was hit by flak at Texel as he crossed over the Dutch coast, and Barlow fell (whether by accident or by flak is unknown) into the Zuider Zee. Rice too had trouble at the Zuider Zee, for the Lancaster was down too low and the plane struck the water; two engines fluttered out and the Wallis bomb ripped off the plane. Rice could do nothing else but return to Scampton on the remaining two engines. The fourth plane, Munro, was hit by flak also, just as it crossed into Holland at Vlieland,

knocking out the intercommunications systems. It was pointless to continue on the mission, so Munro also returned to Scampton.

By the time McCarthy finally took off, so "browned off" (as the current expression went) that he was ready to leave without a parachute, all of Gibson's first wave had already left. McCarthy continued on alone, unaware of the fate of Byers and Barlow and that Munro and Rice had been forced to return to base. His navigator, Flight Sergeant D. A. McLean, plotted a dog-leg course, across the North Sea almost due east to Vlieland, then south across the Zuider Zee, an eastward turn where the course intercepted the Rhine. Slightly north of the Möhne, McLean set them on a southerly leg; the Sorpe lay just a few miles southwest of the Möhne.

McCarthy eased the Lancaster into the misty valley, hoping to get as low as possible. He had to be especially wary of the hills at each end of their run; it would mean dive in, slow up to the prescribed 180 miles an hour, drop bomb, and pull out before piling up against the farther hill. Warily, McCarthy circled the target—which looked just like the model they had studied during the final briefings. There was no flak at least. Coming down low through the mist, however, almost put them in the water. They were low enough. The bombardier, Sergeant G. L. Johnson, zeroed in on the aiming points as McCarthy held the Lancaster in a steady run.

"Bomb gone," he called out; almost at the same instant, McCarthy pulled back on the throttles and the control column to get away from the target and to avoid the looming black hills. He was leveling out over the hills when the bomb shattered against the dam wall. Circling back, the crew saw that the bomb had hit the parapet and had caused damage. But the dam had not burst. They wired the message back to No. 5 Group—where Wallis, Harris, and Cochrane awaited all scraps of information about the raid. McCarthy then turned "T for Tommy" for home.

Gibson took off at nine thirty-nine (the same time as the hapless Munro) in company with the aircraft of pilots Flight Lieutenants John V. Hopgood and H. B. Martin. Just as they were about to leave Gibson had said to Hopgood, "Hoppy, tonight's the night; tomorrow we will get drunk." It had been a long-standing tradition to say this just before a mis-

Crew of G George, special Lancaster ED 932/G (the G suffix denoting that the aircraft carried special equipment and must be constantly under guard): Flight Lieutenant R. D. Trevor-Roper, the squadron gunnery leader and mid-upper gunner of G George; Sergeant J. Pulford, flight engineer; Flight Sergeant G. A. Deering, *rear gunner; Pilot Officer F. M. Spafford, bombardier —"bomb aimer" in RAF terminology; Flight Lieutenant R. G. Hutchinson, the squadron's signals leader and radio operator of George; Wing Commander Guy Gibson; and Pilot Officer H. T. Taerum, navigator.*

(IMPERIAL WAR MUSEUM, LONDON)

sion, dating to their days together in No. 106 Squadron. Earlier Squadron Leader Melvyn Young (known as "Dinghy" because he had been twice saved from the sea) had also contributed another standing "joke." As they enjoyed the traditional luxury before takeoff (repeated after a mission) of bacon and eggs, Young asked Gibson, "Can I have your egg if you don't come back?"

"Sugar off," Gibson replied banteringly and then "told him to do something very difficult to himself."

Young led the second three-plane element (the other pilots: William Astell and David Maltby) and Squadron Leader Henry E. Maudslay led the third, consisting of his plane and those flown by David Shannon and L. G. Knight. The latter's plane was air-borne by ten o'clock.

The first-wave aircraft took a different course from that of the second wave; it was a more southerly route crossing over the Dutch coast south of Rotterdam, almost skirting the northern boundary of Belgium. They had crossed over the North Sea without incident, except for a brief meeting and an exchange of messages with a small British convoy. As they approached the coast, all gunners took their positions and Gibson, still holding the Lancaster to an altitude of less than a hundred feet, zigzagged around the known flak positions. He was assisted in this delicate operation with directions from the navigator, Canadian H. T. "Terry" Taerum. Gibson's plane, *G George,* followed by the eight others in the first wave, thus threaded its way across Holland and Germany. The route twisted and turned at irregular intervals to confuse the German defenses, which were having a difficult time of it also because the bombers flew too low to be picked up by radar.

The frequent shifts in route were complex and required concentration. Over Holland an airfield not on their maps suddenly sprang out of the night. It was heavily defended, although no fighters rose to challenge them. Near it was a check point for another turn in the route. Gibson radioed the two formations following closely behind him to look out for the nest of guns near Gilze-Rijen. The others made their turns, but Flight Lieutenant William B. Astell's Lancaster, in the second element, came within flak range of the airfield. The Lancaster lifted away for a moment, then flew into the ground, burned for a few seconds, and shattered when the Wallis bomb detonated.

After crossing the Rhine the eight remaining planes of Gibson's force passed into the Ruhr—Happy Valley. Flak barges along the river opened up with gunfire and followed the aircraft with searchlights, but lost the British planes among the trees. Gunners in the planes exchanged fire with the German gunners, disrupting their aim and at times even putting out the blinding lights. But all eight Lancasters flew past Dortmund, Hamm, Soest—all known flak centers. Just beyond Soest were the Ruhr hills over which lay Möhne Lake, at the end of which squatted their first target. Gibson studied it and found that the dam "looked grey and solid in the moonlight as though it were part of the countryside itself and just as immovable. A structure like a battle-ship was showering out flak all along its length, but some came from the powerhouse below it and nearby. There were no searchlights."

The effect of the flak over the water was curious, for the varicolored reflections on the smooth black surface doubled the actual number of shells spurting out at them. Gibson estimated the number of guns as twelve firing from five different positions on and around the dam. The shells were either 20 or 37 millimeter—"nasty little things."

Pulling away from "those bloody-minded flak gunners" Gibson circled the area, orienting himself and planning the next move. Over the intercom he heard the crew chattering.

"Bit aggressive, aren't they?"

"Too right they are."

"God, this flak gives me the creeps," Gibson interjected.

"Me too."

Gibson called in the other planes and found all answered but Astell. *Had Bill got the hammer?* "Well, boys," Gibson said with no enthusiasm whatsoever, "we had better start the ball rolling. Hello, all Cooler aircraft. I am going to attack. Stand by to come in to attack in your order when I tell you."

As the others dispersed out of range of the flak, Gibson circled to get into position for a run on the dam. He called John Hopgood: "Hello, *M Mother.* Stand by to take over if anything happens."

"OK, Leader. Good luck."

Gibson, now two miles from the dam, put the plane into a flat dive. The features of the Möhne stood out clearly in the light of the moon. In sharp relief stood the two towers on which the bombardier would set his little wooden sight. He was an Australian, Pilot Officer F. M. "Spam" Spafford, who reacted to the setting with professional interest. "Good show," he said. "This is wizard!"

But as they came down toward the surface of the lake, Spafford, in the "bomb-aimer" position in the nose, said excitedly, "You're going to hit them. You're going to hit those trees!"

"That's all right, Spam," Gibson told him, "I'm just getting my height."

Then to navigator Taerum, "Check height, Terry."

Flight Engineer Sergeant J. Pulford managed the throttles and flaps to maintain the precise air speed. Spafford lined up the sight with the two towers at either end of the dam and flicked on the fusing switches. The Wallis bomb began to revolve. Taerum gave directions for height, the searchlights in the fuselage having been turned on. When the two beams met he called out "Steady," and they were

The Wallis bomb as it was released from the specially converted Lancaster. The cradle that held the bomb actuated the bomb's backward revolution, which caused the bomb to skip over the surface of the water. The cut-out fuselage to accommodate the bomb and the gear may also be seen. The Lancasters thus equipped were called the "Steamrollers of Scampton."

(IMPERIAL WAR MUSEUM, LONDON)

at sixty feet. The gunners at the dam opened up on the illuminated target. The flak came twisting through the darkness as Gibson raced for the dam. The two gunners in the plane returned the fire as Gibson, almost certain they were flying into oblivion, bore down upon the target taking directions from both Taerum (height) and Spafford (distance and line).

The air reeked with cordite and the plane shuddered under the vibration of the guns firing. The sky was crisscrossed with spent tracers. A Very light popped out of the Lancaster in the hope of blinding the flak gunners. Suddenly Spafford's voice came over the intercom: "Mine gone."

Someone said, "Good show, Leader. Nice work." Gibson gunned the Lancaster up and away from the flak and from the explosion. There was a thunderous booming behind them and when Gibson turned the Lancaster, a thousand-foot water column hung in the air. Spafford had placed the bomb exactly right, but except for churning water, there seemed to be no real damage. Gibson studied the effect and waited until the surface calmed down before ordering the next attack. The spotlights would not work unless the surface was smooth. The eight planes circled as far from the guns as they could,

waiting. Gibson spoke to Hopgood. "Hello, *M Mother*. You may attack now. Good luck."

Hopgood brought his plane in from the same direction as had Gibson. The gunners were now alert to the direction of the attack and concentrated heavily on the approaching plane. Hopgood speared into the flak. About a hundred yards from the dam a flash of fire shot behind an inboard engine. The bomb did not drop until too late (possibly because the bombardier had been hit), so it fell onto the powerhouse, overshooting the dam. Hopgood's Lancaster staggered on as if the pilot were attempting to gain altitude. At around five hundred feet *M Mother* flared and crashed into the ground.

"Poor old Hoppy," a voice said over the intercom. Although the plane burned furiously, two men actually escaped, the bombardier, Flight Sergeant J. W. Fraser, and the rear gunner, Pilot Officer A. F. Burcher. The other five men, including Gibson's old friend Hopgood, died in the crash.

Still the Möhne Dam stood intact. Gibson ordered the third attack, by Squadron Leader H. B. "Mickey" Martin in *P Popsie*. The run was repeated, again with heavy flak fire. Gibson had drawn off some of the flak by bringing *G George* into range and shooting at the German gun positions. Martin's bomb fell a few yards short and had little effect upon the dam. The Lancaster itself was rather badly shot up; a fuel tank in the right wing—luckily empty—was punctured and the aileron shredded. But Martin brought the Lancaster away without further damage.

He added his plane to Gibson's as a decoy when the fourth plane, Squadron Leader Melvyn Young's *A Apple*, attacked. The bomb seemed to fall exactly right but the dam continued to stand. The next plane was piloted by Flight Lieutenant D. J. H. Maltby; this was number five. Again the area lit up with flak and machine-gun fire as the great bomber, seemingly held to the surface of the lake by two streams of light, bore down on the dam. The bombardier, Pilot Officer J. Fort, placed the bomb with uncanny accuracy. The squat barrel-like object bounced along the surface of the water, struck the wall, and then rolled down. A great geyser of water shot up and again the water roiled and churned.

Waiting for the disturbance to subside, Gibson swung around to get another view. He alerted the next pilot, Flight Lieutenant David Shannon, to prepare for his run. As Gibson came down he saw unusual eddies in the water and it appeared that the dam had moved. He heard someone shouting, "I think she has gone!" when the dam gave way. It was a massive rent of a hundred yards through which a mountain of water spilled into the valley below. Gibson's radio operator wired the news to Group headquarters at Grantham that the Möhne Dam had been successfully breached. The time was just four minutes before one o'clock in the morning of May 17, 1943.

Wallis had listened to the report of each released bomb with increasing misgiving. He had hoped one good strike would do the job, but on and on the raid went: *G George, M Mother, P Popsie, A Apple,* and then *J Johnny*—Maltby's plane—and the signal that the Möhne had burst. Wallis stood still for but a moment before throwing his arms over his head and literally danced around the room. Harris and Cochrane stopped him long enough to shake his hand in congratulations. At the same time the men in the seven Lancasters orbiting the Möhne burst into cheers, "to shout and scream and act like madmen. . . ."

From where he circled the frightful scene, Gibson saw not only the wall of water ramming through the valley, destroying everything in its path and overtaking fleeing automobiles, but also the still burning wreckage of Hopgood's plane just beyond the dam. *Hoppy has been avenged,* Gibson thought and then, after ordering Mickey Martin and Dave Maltby to return to base, led the way south- and eastward to the Eder. Only three aircraft still carried bombs—Henry Maudslay's, David Shannon's and L. G. Knight's. Melvyn Young as deputy leader made up the fifth plane, though his bomb had been expended on the Möhne.

The five aircraft encountered much fog as they flew through the valley leading to the Eder Dam. Although there were no antiaircraft defenses at the Eder, the hills surrounding it, plus the fog, made it an exceptionally difficult target to find. Gibson had arrived first and succeeded in locating the fog-enshrouded target, but until he had fired a Very light over the dam, the others had not been able to pick it out.

Shannon began moving in for the attack, which would be the same as those upon the Möhne. But there were complications. The Eder was more inaccessible than the Möhne. A castle stood in the bomb run. The plane would have to dive in over the castle, from about a thousand feet to the required sixty, zero in on the target, drop the bomb, and pull up before crashing against the cliffs of a mountain just about a mile beyond the dam. Shannon made at least five attempts but always something happened and he zoomed away without dropping the bomb. Finally, giving up for the moment, Shannon decided to circle the area to become better acquainted with it.

While Shannon studied the terrain, Gibson sent in *Z Zebra,* Henry Maudslay's Lancaster. Maudslay too found it a difficult run and made two attempts without dropping the bomb. On the third all eyes watched as the big Lancaster slipped down over the castle, leveled out on the lake. The spotlights converged under the plane on the water and soon a red Very light arced out above *Z Zebra.* The bomb had been dropped. But something had gone wrong; the bomb had been released too late. It fell, struck the parapet, and caught Maudslay's plane in the blast. The whole valley erupted in a glaring flash. Gibson was stunned. *Henry had disappeared.* There was no burning wreck on the ground. Desperately Gibson called, "Henry—*Z Zebra*—are you OK?"

The Möhne Dam before and after: an aerial reconnaissance photograph taken before the mission (left) shows the dam wall and, faintly, the protective torpedo nets. The bombs had to be dropped at the correct speed and altitude to be able to bounce over the net, *strike the wall, roll down the wall under the water, and burst against the face of the wall. The effects of the blast may be seen in a photograph taken the day after the raid—the Möhne breached; lower water level exposes sand of the banks.*

(IMPERIAL WAR MUSEUM, LONDON)

Although no plane was in sight, all were certain they heard Maudslay's voice faintly: "I think so, stand by." And then there was nothing.

Shannon returned again and, after a test run, came in for the second time (on his second round of attempts). The plane dropped the bomb perfectly as Flight Sergeant L. J. Sumpter, the bombardier, brought the towers into line and pressed the release. The bomb detonated against the face of the dam, but it continued to stand.

There was only one more left; unless it worked Gibson would have to ask for aid from the mobile reserve planes. Lester Knight, an Australian, brought his Lancaster in for a practice run. It went wrong and he pulled away and circled, with Gibson giving him advice over the radio telephone, and came in for another try. Carefully Knight brought the Lancaster in, down to sixty feet and straight for the dam; bombardier Flying Officer E. C. Johnson guided Knight toward the drop point and the bomb fell when all imaginary lines of the mathematical problem converged. The bomb struck the wall, rolled down, and then from out of the depths a terrific boom erupted, shooting water a thousand feet into the air. As if shaken by a great earthquake the Eder Dam cracked, spouting tons of water into the sleeping valley below. To Gibson the rushing waters seemed more destructive than those of the Möhne, ripping through the countryside, uprooting everything in their path, and even as he watched he "saw them extinguish all the lights in the neighborhood as though a great black shadow had been drawn across the earth."

With no bombs remaining, Gibson ordered the four surviving Lancasters to return to base. The Eder had been breached at one fifty-four in the morning. Dawn was on the way and they would do well to get away before the fighters came out in droves. They had been air-borne for more than four hours, fuel would be low, and with the coming light, the fighters would be thick. On the homeward flight they again passed over the Möhne. The geography of the valley had been completely changed. They continued flying down low to confute fighter passes.

The Lancasters droned over Germany and Holland and strove for home. But over Holland, just as he passed over the coast, Young's plane was hit by flak. He could not nurse it all the way to Scampton, and for the third—and last—time Dinghy Young ditched. No one survived the crash into the sea. So it was, then, that of the nine planes which Gibson had led into Germany that night, he returned leading only Shannon and Knight—to join those of Martin and Maltby, which had come back earlier.

When Gibson had radioed that he had no additional bombs, the five aircraft of the mobile reserve, the third wave, were directed to their targets by Group headquarters. These Lancasters had taken off shortly after midnight and by the time Gibson had turned for home the bombers were being dispatched to their targets. The first plane off was *C Charlie,* guided by Pilot Officer W. H. T. Ottley, who was ordered to attack the Lister Dam; the radio operator, Sergeant J. Guterman, acknowledged the message. That was the last heard from Ottley's crew. It may have been his plane that Gibson, then on his flight home, saw flying at five hundred feet in the vicinity of Hamm. "He got the chop," Gibson noted, wondering who it had been. He and his crew believed that it might have been a German night fighter which had been tracking them, hit by its own antiaircraft fire. But it was probably Ottley's *C Charlie,* for the wreckage of his plane was found near Hamm the next day.

Three planes were dispatched to the Sorpe Dam to add to the destruction which McCarthy, of the ill-fated second wave, had accomplished. These were *S Sugar* (Pilot Officer L. J. Burpee), *F Freddie* (Flight Sergeant K. W. Brown), and *Y Yorker* (Flight Sergeant L. T. Anderson).

S Sugar never got beyond Bergen op Zoom, Holland, where it fell to flak or a fighter. *F Freddie* had trouble finding the Sorpe because of the thickening mist, but Brown dropped down low and released some incendiaries which illuminated the area. Bombardier Sergeant S. Oncia was then able to place the bomb precisely on the target, although

this second strike did not add to the damage—the Sorpe remained standing. When *Y Yorker,* which had taken off one minute behind *F Freddie,* came upon the target area pilot Anderson found the valley completely filled with mist. Neither Sergeant L. Nugent, the navigator, nor Sergeant S. Green, the bombardier, could find any landmark upon which to base a bomb run. *Y Yorker,* crewed with disappointed men, was forced to make the return trip to Scampton still carrying the Wallis bomb.

O Orange (Flight Sergeant W. C. Townsend) was sent to the Schwelm Dam, which was found despite the early morning mist. Townsend made three runs on the target before bombardier Sergeant C. E. Franklin released the bomb. It was a perfect drop, but the single bomb had little effect upon the dam. The time was then 3:37 A.M., and when *O Orange* crossed the Dutch coast for the final leg of the flight daylight was breaking over the North Sea. When Townsend set his plane down at Scampton his was the last of the Lancasters which would return from the dams mission. Eight would never return; of the fifty-six men aboard these aircraft only two survived. Nearly half of the superb crew which had made up No. 617 Squadron was lost. It was, in the phrase of historians Charles Webster and Noble Frankland, "a costly success."

v

The "Dam Busters," as the squadron was popularly called, had furnished bomber chief Arthur Harris with a demonstration of the fallacy of attacking panacea targets, but on the other hand proved him wrong when he insisted that the Wallis bomb (or any bomb then available) could actually breach a well-built dam. Wallis had been proved correct in his theoretical conceptions of bomb design and the effects of certain bombs upon dams —but his strategic thinking had been optimistic. The major catastrophe he had expected—which was also expected by those more militarily oriented than he—did not result. The havoc was serious enough and for many it was total tragedy, but despite the inundation, the rupture of the Möhne and Eder dams had no long-range or even long-lasting effects upon the German war effort.

Goebbels admitted that the "attacks of the British bombers on the dams in our valleys were very successful. The Führer is exceedingly impatient and angry about the lack of preparedness on the part of the Luftwaffe." It was true—a single blow by so few aircraft had had a decided impact. Nearly a thousand people drowned (many caught in air raid shelters) and more than two hundred were listed as missing. About half of the casualties, however, were slave laborers from the east—they were easily replaced from Germany's store of prisoners from Poland and Russia. Livestock too perished in the flood and thousands of acres of agricultural land were despoiled. Seventy per cent of the harvest in

the Ruhr and Möhne valleys was ruined, as was all of the root crops, such as potatoes.

Industrial stoppages resulted with the washing out of railroads, the blacking out of electrical power, and, most of all—as a result of the Möhne breach —because of the shortage of water. A critical lack of water for drinking purposes afflicted about four and a half million people in the area; also industries requiring water, such as the coking plants in Dortmund, were forced to operate at a loss in production for two months.

The effects were extensive but not decisive. Within weeks, or at most within two or three months, the Germans had cleared away much of the dam-

Post-mission debriefing: Bomber Command Chief Harris and Air Officer Commanding, No. 5 Group, Air Vice-Marshal Sir Ralph Cochrane (standing) get a first-hand report of the dams raid while members of G George talk with a Bomber Command intelligence officer (left seated); bombardier Spafford speaks as navigator Taerum and gunnery officer Trevor-Roper listen. These three men of Gibson's crew, like their leader, were later killed in other missions.

(IMPERIAL WAR MUSEUM, LONDON)

age and the Ruhr remained the major industrial center of the Third Reich for the rest of the war. Had all dams been breached that night of the Dam Busters' raid (a physical impossibility, of course, in terms of men and bombs), the tale would have been different and much sadder for Germany. If the Sorpe (which was in fact immune to the Wallis bomb because of the dam's structure) had gone, the effects would have been more serious. Following the night of May 16/17, 1943, all important German dams were allotted heavier defenses. Further attempts upon them would have meant simple suicide—and none were made.

As he had promised the now dead Hopgood,

Gibson and the survivors got drunk. Gibson, however, left early to begin writing to the next of kin of the fifty-six men who had not returned. Wallis, though elated by the success of his bomb, was depressed at the thought of the loss of the young men. He stood around with the survivors that early morning, an untouched drink in his hand and tears in his eyes, saying, "If I had known, I wouldn't have started this."

In wartime, however, the exchange of fifty-four young lives for victorious headlines, for a setback for the enemy, seemed worth it. No one would question the attack, its costs, or the result: not when the very spirit of the moment seemed permeated

The Queen and King visit No. 617 Squadron after the mission to award decorations. In the background the Queen speaks with an airman. In the foreground the King exchanges views with "Our favourite Yank,"

Flight Lieutenant Joseph C. McCarthy of Brooklyn. Gibson is to the King's left, back to camera.

(IMPERIAL WAR MUSEUM, LONDON)

with destruction, sacrifice, death, and "good show." It was as normal as being alive.

Eve Gibson, who had assumed that her husband had been, as she had been informed, having an easy time of it at a training school, learned from the newspapers that he was an international hero. Gibson joined her for a rest after he had completed writing his letters. When he joined Eve, Gibson was a very old young man.

No less than thirty-three decorations were awarded for the dams raid. This was unusual, for the British are parsimonious with their decorations. Gibson was given the Victoria Cross. Among those who received the Distinguished Service Order was the Brooklynite Joseph McCarthy. The squadron was the most celebrated in Britain by then. Harris, despite his distaste for special units, decided to keep No. 617 Squadron together as a unit, and to employ it upon highly specialized targets demanding high precision. Although it was all but impossible to replace the lost crews immediately, No. 617 Squadron did operate as a precision night unit during the rest of the war. In fact, among other amazing feats—such as blasting a railroad tunnel in northern France with another Wallis bomb, the "Tallboy"—it was No. 617 Squadron which eventually finished the *Tirpitz,* which had so haunted Gibson.

But by this time the brilliant young commander was dead. After the raid he was sent to the United States, accompanying Churchill, on a kind of goodwill tour. When he returned in the spring of 1944 Gibson, who it was thought had already done his bit, was offered work as an executive with commercial firms—which he readily turned down. He was even asked to run for Parliament, an idea with which he toyed for a while, but he withdrew from that also. He grew restless, for he had been a year "off Ops." and he was unhappy. Finally he went directly to Harris and bullied his way back into active duty with No. 627 Squadron.

Gibson was base operations officer of the squadron, which like No. 617 was in No. 5 Group. The squadron began operations as a Pathfinder force (with No. 8 Group), marking targets with the Mosquito. Attached to No. 5 Group, the squadron took part in various special operations—bombing, target marking, dropping of "window"—the metallic ribbon which disrupted German radar—and minelaying.

On the night of September 19/20, 1944, Guy Gibson voluntarily assigned himself the task of master bomber on a raid to the Ruhr. He would fly around the target, a factory at Rheydt, directing the operations of the attacking Lancasters. When the attack was over, Gibson radioed the bombers. "OK, chaps. Now beat it for home." It was the last time his voice was heard, for over Holland something occurred and the Mosquito smashed into a hill. The men were buried by the Germans in a common unmarked grave near Bergen op Zoom. It was there that Burpee in *S Sugar* had "got the hammer" too a year before when Gibson and his X-Squadron had made history.

7

TIDAL WAVE

At Casablanca, French Morocco, Winston Churchill and Franklin Roosevelt met in January 1943 to outline the future Grand Strategy of the war. In this beautiful setting facing on the sea, following the successful launching of Operation Torch, the invasion of north Africa under Lieutenant General Dwight D. Eisenhower, the Allied leaders and their Combined Chiefs of Staff came to several key decisions. Uppermost in their minds, though they did not always agree upon details, were aid to Soviet Russia, sustained pressures on the Mediterranean flank, a future cross-Channel invasion of Europe, and the question of the Pacific war.

Among the objectives to be gained before the larger strategies could be achieved, at least in Europe, was control of the German submarines so effectively menacing Allied shipping. Another was the Luftwaffe, which stood in the way of strategic bombardment and any hopes for an invasion of Europe in 1944. Both these obstacles could be dealt with by air power. When he came to the Casblanca conference it had been Churchill's intention to persuade Roosevelt to get the American Air Force to give up its devotion to strategic bombardment by day and join the Bomber Command nighttime area assault. After five months of bombing, the U. S. Eighth Air Force had not yet dropped a single bomb on Germany proper. The first mission of the Eighth Air Force's Bomber Command was a modest—only a dozen B-17s participated—strike upon the marshaling yards at Rouen-Sotteville, France, on August 17, 1942. All twelve bombers returned safely and it was at least a sign that bombers in formation could bomb pin-point targets in daylight and make it back to their bases. Such high-altitude attacks, it was believed, would make it difficult for flak-gun accuracy, and the combined gun strength of the formation itself would make fighter opposition costly.

The British had found in their experience that daylight operations were deadly; and the Germans had learned this also. But the Americans persisted in clinging to the concept of precision daylight bombardment. This was not mere bullheadedness, although it was believed that a heavy bomber with its massive firepower (the Flying Fortress was armed with a dozen .50-caliber machine guns and the Consolidated B-24 Liberator with ten) and protective armor could withstand attack by fighters. The best argument in favor of American daylight precision bombardment was simply that the aircraft were designed for it and the Americans were trained for it. A change in operational technique would entail a prolonged retraining of crews, modifications in the aircraft, and a consequent delay. Even under "normal" wartime conditions, it had taken long enough to mount the Rouen-Sotteville attack, small as that was. Assembling men and equipment was a complex matter, considering the demand for both.

Casablanca: Franklin D. Roosevelt and Winston Churchill meet to plan the future strategy of the war with their chief military advisers. Standing behind them are (from left) Lieutenant General Henry H. Arnold, Ad- *miral Ernest J. King, General George C. Marshall, Admiral Sir Dudley Pound, General Sir Alan Brooke, and Air Chief Marshal Sir Charles Portal.*

(U. S. AIR FORCE)

Until the United States could contribute its full share to the offensive the operations of the Eighth Air Force from the United Kingdom were, of necessity, circumscribed. Up until the Casablanca conference, the heavy-bomber missions were, in a sense, experimental pinpricks, experimental because there was a good deal to learn under combat conditions and pinpricks because Major General Ira C. Eaker, who commanded Eighth AF Bomber Command, did not have sufficient numbers of planes and crews to do anything else. An effective attack force which could strike deep inside Germany and still be able to fight its way in, bomb, and return must contain about three hundred heavy bombers. The largest force Eaker had been able to muster in the half year from August 1942 to the January 1943 Casablanca meetings was but a third of that number.

In that half year one of the major lessons learned was that if German fighter pilots proved aggressive enough, there really was no such thing as a true "Flying Fortress." Although Eighth Air Force losses

had not been excessive in the half year of operations, there had been losses and interferences with bombing runs. These were not spectacular, but planes and crews were lost and targets could not be eliminated because they had not been accurately bombed. What was needed, then, was an Allied fighter plane which could escort the bombers to and from target areas to engage the German fighters. At the time of Casablanca no such fighter with the range say to go to Berlin and back was in action. The P-40 could not do it, nor could the Hurricane or Spitfire. Thus the British preferred their major bombing raids to take place at night and the Americans went out during the day. The advent of the Thunderbolt (Republic P-47) and the Mustang (North American P-51) was yet almost a whole year away. In the interim the skies over Europe would be lacerated in the most monstrous air battles in history.

At Casablanca Eaker convinced Churchill of the efficacy of the American plan and the Prime Minis-

The Boeing B-17 "Flying Fortress," on which the U. S. Army Air Force based its "precision daylight bombardment" concept—and which British Bomber Command rejected as inviting the disastrous possibility of high casualties and aircraft losses. Because of the bristling heavy armament of the B-17 it was believed it could stand off German fighter attacks. This did not prove to be true in combat; Luftwaffe pilots developed a hazardous technique of head-on attack that was most effective. The B-17F (left), the first Lockheed-built B-17, though an improvement on the earlier models still lacked firepower in the nose. This was later resolved with the addition of twin guns in the "G" model. The other photo, a view from the port waist-gun position, shows one of the nine .50-caliber machine guns (plus one .30) carried by the Flying Fortress. (ERIK MILLER; LOCKHEED/U. S. AIR FORCE)

The Consolidated B-24 "Liberator," which came after the B-17 and which would join it in bombing Germany. The B-24 was not as easily flown as the B-17, nor could it achieve the altitude of the Boeing. It did, however, have a greater range and could carry a heavier bomb load. The prototype (left), the XB-24 was initially flown in 1939 (the first B-17 flew in 1935) and had no gun turrets. Top view of a B-24D clearly shows the high-aspect ratio wing designed around the low-drag Davis airfoil as well as the nose-gun position (before the nose turret was installed in the B-24G), top and tail turrets.

(CONVAIR/GENERAL DYNAMICS; U. S. AIR FORCE)

Standing in the way of the American daylight attacks upon German industry were the German fighters such as this Messerschmitt Bf-109G; engine-mounted 20-mm. cannon could rip a wing off an enemy bomber. Though formidable, the cannon had a tendency to jam; as did the wing-mounted cannon of the Bf-109F.
(ALIEN PROPERTY CUSTODIAN, NATIONAL ARCHIVES)

In effect, therefore, the Directive left the interpretation of how this was to be accomplished up to General Eaker and Air Chief Marshal Harris. Although the Directive implied precision attack, it did not deny the area attack. Harris, with his experience, had little respect for plans on paper and continued to go his way. "The subject of morale had been dropped," Harris noted, "and I was now required to proceed with the general 'disorganisation' of German industry, giving priority to certain aspects of it such as U-boat building, aircraft production, oil production, transportation and so forth, which gave me a very wide range of choice and allowed me to attack pretty well any German industrial city of 100,000 inhabitants and above. But the Ruhr remained a principal objective because it was the most important industrial area in the whole of Germany, which was why it had been originally chosen for morale-breaking attacks; the new instructions therefore made no difference."

Eaker by April 1943 had formulated what the British refer to as the Eaker Plan, but which was more officially known as "The Combined Bomber

The most potent adversary of the American daylight bomber streams, the Focke-Wulf 190 (in this instance the FW-190A of JG 26). Nicknamed the Würger ("Butcher-bird"), the 190 was heavily armed—two machine guns on upper cowling, two cannons in the wing roots, and two more machine guns farther out on the wings. The major weakness of the FW-190 was that its performance fell off above twenty thousand feet (the B-17s operated above this altitude). It was still a tough fighter when dealing with enemy escort planes as well as bombers. Although superior to the Me-109, the Focke-Wulf was not built in the quantities the Messerschmitt was.
(IMPERIAL WAR MUSEUM, LONDON)

ter, though reluctantly, dismissed his own plan of suggesting to Roosevelt that the American daylight approach be abandoned. Out of this came what was called the Casablanca Directive, outlining in effect the joint future operations of British and American Bomber Commands. Operating as before, British by night and Americans by day—thus giving Churchill his cue for the phrase "bombing around the clock"—the bombing offensive was to be based upon a system of target priorities. These were agreed upon by the Combined Chiefs of Staff, advised by industrial analysts such as Britain's Ministry of Economic Warfare. The targets, in order of priority, were the German submarine construction yards, the aircraft industry, transportation, oil installations, and other targets in enemy war industry.

Offensive, from the United Kingdom" (April 12, 1943). A month later a modified version of the plan, code word "Pointblank," was approved by the Combined Chiefs of Staff. This defined the mission of the U. S.-British Air offensive, which, in general terms, was aimed at weakening German resistance so "as to permit initiation of final combined operations on the Continent." It called for an expansion of the American bombing forces in Europe, pointing out that "at least 800 airplanes must be in the theater to dispatch 300 bombers on operations." Until such a force existed, there would be little point in attempting precision attacks upon the German aircraft industry, which remained second on the priorities list.

Lest there be misunderstandings and consequent resistance from certain strong-minded air marshals, it was emphasized that "This plan does not attempt to prescribe the major effort of the R.A.F. Bomber Command. It simply recognizes the fact that when precision targets are bombed by the Eighth Air Force in daylight, the effort should be complemented and completed by R.A.F. bombing attacks against the surrounding industrial area at night."

Under the section entitled "Intermediate Objective" another important point was made: "The Germans, recognizing the vulnerability of their vital industries, are rapidly increasing the strength of their fighter defenses. The German fighter strength in western Europe is being augmented. *If the growth of the German fighter strength is not arrested quickly, it may become literally impossible to carry out the destruction planned and thus to create the conditions necessary for ultimate decisive action by our combined forces on the continent.*" In other words, the invasion of Europe would be stalled unless the Luftwaffe could be "neutralized."

Eaker, however, almost immediately had to give up some of his planes to the Mediterranean when the Northwest African Air Force was formed to assist Eisenhower's ground troops in the invasion of north Africa; more would go when "Husky," the invasion of Sicily which had been decided upon during the Casablanca meetings, went into effect. It would be extremely difficult for the Eighth Air Force to mount the Pointblank operations if its forces continued to be drained off to other theaters. At the moment when Eaker hoped for "at least 800 airplanes" in order to mount raids of three-hundred-bomber

strength, he was aware of the fact that in the three months since Casablanca the average American bomber attack force consisted of a mere eighty-six planes.

II

Sometime between the end of June and the Fourth of July, Eaker lost his two veteran B-24 groups, the 44th and the 93rd. These were soon joined by the newly formed, inexperienced 389 Bombardment Group—also equipped with Liberators. They combined with two units already in the Mediterranean's Ninth Air Force: the 98th and 376th Bombardment Groups (B-24s). All units began operations against various Husky targets, including, on July 19, Rome. On the following day all were ordered off operations to begin intensive training near Benghazi in Libya.

The curious feature of this training, besides the heavy security precautions, was the fact that the airmen were being trained to fly the Liberator at an extremely low level. This was a worrisome feature considering the flying characteristics of the Liberator and the danger of passing through prop wash near the ground. Also mystifying was that very few knew what the assignment was all about. The answer lay in that parenthetical phrase (referring to "attacks upon Ploesti") which had appeared following "Oil" in the Combined Bomber Offensive paper.

This Rumanian city was situated in the south central section of the country known as the Wallachian plain, in the heart of the oil-producing regions. Ploesti lay in the center of vast fields, refineries, cracking plants, great complexes which supplied Nazi Germany—thanks to dictator Ion Antonescu—with more than half of its crude oil supply. A full third of Germany's petroleum needs came from Ploesti; the other two thirds came from other sources including its own synthetic plants, which extracted petroleum products from coal. Without oil Germany could not function militarily, a fact of which Hitler was acutely aware even before Pearl Harbor. There were pitiable outcries from the Navy, the Luftwaffe, and the panzer-dependent Wehrmacht. Even with Germany's synthetic plants increasingly productive, Ploesti remained the major source of oil. And oil, if the Combined Chiefs and their Committee of Operations analysts had been aware of the critical situation

Liberators practicing for a low-level mission over the Libyan Desert near Benghazi, north Africa.
(U. S. AIR FORCE)

in Germany, would have been placed first on the priorities list, not fourth.

To Harris Ploesti represented another despised panacea target. Besides, it was not within reach of Bomber Command in England. He continued to concentrate upon the Ruhr. Eaker complied with the spirit of the Combined Bomber Offensive whenever he could muster enough planes to strike at the sub pens or other high-priority targets within reach of the Eighth Air Force. But his resources had dwindled so much because of the diversion of several of his heavy-bomber groups to Africa.

These purloined groups came into the province of Major General Lewis H. Brereton, a cocky bantam of a man who commanded the Ninth Air Force. Brereton, who had been in command of the Far East Air Force in the Philippines when the Japanese struck, had moved out of the Philippines into Java. When Java fell Brereton worked his way across Burma and India until he arrived in Egypt late in June 1942. His nine battered Flying Fortresses became the United States Army Middle East Air Force. In close co-operation with the RAF, the Middle East Air Force assisted in the war upon Rommel by bombing Mediterranean supply ports and convoys at sea. Prior to the breakthrough at El Alamein, the force attacked the harbors of Tobruk and Benghazi, among others, and when Rommel was driven out of Africa, it set up bases around Benghazi—although by this time the unit was called the Ninth Air Force. Brereton's forces by then had been joined by the Northwest African Air Forces

Lewis H. Brereton (here a lieutenant general), commander of the Ninth Air Force at the time it made its attack on Ploesti. (U. S. AIR FORCE)

(Major General Carl Spaatz) to work with RAF, Middle East. The missions of all these air forces were co-ordinated by Mediterranean Air Command under Air Chief Marshal Sir Arthur W. Tedder. It was a complex international co-operative effort which, despite differences, worked very well.

This was because ultimate command of all units actually continued under normal national division. Americans served under American leaders and British under British; no attempt was made to intermix the units. At the high levels of command there was a good deal of give-and-take, a willingness to co-operate, and mutual respect, so that despite the command complexities—a concession to political needs—operations came off remarkably well.

So it was that on June 11, 1943, Brereton received a message from Tedder "concerning Operation SOAPSUDS. It will be mounted from the Middle East, and three more heavy groups are en route to join the Ninth Air Force." Soapsuds was the initial code name for the Ploesti bombing, later changed to "Tidal Wave." Coincidentally, exactly one year before to the day of Brereton's diary entry American bombers had taken off to bomb Ploesti. This was done by the "Halverson Detachment," led by Colonel Harry A. Halverson. Originally equipped with twenty-three B-24Ds, the Halverson Detachment was to have been sent to Chinese bases for bombing missions against Japan. However, delays en route found Halverson in north Africa at a critical moment, and his Liberators were pressed into service there. Taking off on June 11, 1943, Halverson led thirteen Liberators toward the oil fields of Ploesti. One plane was forced to turn back and a dozen succeeded in reaching the target after a long over-water flight, crossing over neutral Turkey. Although accomplishing little damage, the Halverson Detachment planes had struck the first American blow against the Axis. No American life was lost, although one aircraft crash-landed and four, short of fuel, landed in Turkey, where their crews were interned. But the implications of the remarkable mission were lost in the excitement of the news from Midway, which still dominated newspaper space. Those planes which returned from Ploesti remained in the Middle East and were absorbed into Brereton's Ninth Air Force.

Colonel Jacob E. Smart, of Arnold's staff, had conceived the idea of a low-level mission against Ploesti. Surprise, it was hoped, would thus be achieved despite the fact that the Liberator was not designed for low-level performance. A large force, it was assumed, coming in low could deal much damage to the oil complexes. There was another assumption: that except for sporadic Russian attacks upon Ploesti, no large-scale attempt had been made since the Halverson mission, and therefore the German defenders might be caught off guard and unprepared.

Although it was soon proved by aircrews that the Liberator could indeed operate at zero altitude, the assumption that the Luftwaffe was unprepared at Ploesti was ill founded. It was, in fact, one of the best defended targets in all of Europe. The heavy antiaircraft concentrations ringing the city were under the efficient control of Oberst Alfred Gerstenberg, a former faculty member of the Russian-based Luftwaffe air center at Lipesk. In addition to Gerstenberg's guns, several Luftwaffe units were within calling distance of the oil fields—three fighter groups equipped with the Me-109 and a night fighter group with the Me-110. The Rumanians too could supply fighters, but the Germans did not count upon them. Although some were given Messerschmitts, most Rumanian pilots were saddled with inferior Rumanian and Bulgarian fighters.

As commander of 9th Bomber Command, Brigadier General Uzal G. Ent was entrusted with the detailed planning of the mission. Like Brereton, Ent had his serious reservations about a low-level attack; likewise, so did the group commanders leading the mission. But when a conference was held by Brereton in Benghazi on July 6, he "invited no discussion whatsoever among the commanders" and "stressed the necessity for absolute ruthlessness in the immediate relief of any Commander who at any time during the training period showed lack of

Colonel Jacob E. Smart, who believed that Ploesti could be hit by a surprise low-level bombing to throw off what was also believed to be weak defenses.

(U. S. AIR FORCE)

Brigadier General Uzal G. Ent, chief of 9th Bomber Command, and upon whom the planning of the Ploesti mission devolved. Ent did not care for Smart's concept of the low-level mission. (U. S. AIR FORCE)

caught up in the grandeur of the conception. Perhaps he was conscious of the historic impact of such an undertaking when he told the crews, "You should consider yourself lucky to be on this mission." More than three hundred of his auditors would not have agreed; they were dead the following day.

III

The cast for this historical drama included a number of iron men. The leading one was undoubtedly the unpopular, but tough, Colonel John R. Kane, leading the 98th Bomb Group ("Pyramiders"). A hard-driving professional warrior out of Texas, Kane carried the nickname of "Killer." Whether this applied to his attitude toward the Germans or his own men—or himself—is disputable. That he was obsessed with making war upon the Germans could not be denied. When the mission to Ploesti was activated Kane rescinded the orders which would have enabled men in the 98th who had completed their tour of duty to return to the United States. This did not endear him further to his men, who had

leadership, of aggressiveness, or of complete confidence."

It had been Brereton's decision, selected from two suggested plans, a high-level attack launched from Syria or the low-level attack from Benghazi, to attempt the low attack. Once he had decided he adhered to the decision whatever his personal feelings and those of the men actually given the job of carrying it out. Even a petition signed by the group commanders and by Ent made no difference. Late in July Tedder had suggested postponing the attack or canceling it in favor of attacks upon aircraft factories at Wiener Neustadt near Vienna. But now Brereton opposed Tedder on the grounds that "the Ploesti refineries are more important to the Axis war effort than the Messerschmitt factory and because training had almost been completed for Tidal Wave and to call it off now would seriously impair the morale of the entire Bomber Command." Would a cancellation have been as bad for morale as much as knowing your commander (Ent) believed the mission would be a success "even if none returned"?

Despite his misgivings Brereton was certainly

John R. "Killer" Kane (here seen as an air cadet), who would lead his "Pyramiders" (98th Bomb Group) to Ploesti despite a number of hitches. (U. S. AIR FORCE)

never loved him. Kane was as courageous as he was coldly ruthless. He was one commander Brereton would have never replaced. It was also unlikely that Kane would have fulfilled the requirements of "officer and gentleman," but he was an amazing war leader.

Another fine leader was Colonel Leon Johnson, leading the 44th Bomb Group (nicknamed the "Eight Balls"), a businesslike, quietly efficient veteran; Lieutenant Colonel Addison Baker led the 93rd Bomb Group, known as the "Traveling Circus," originally "Ted's Traveling Circus." This was in honor of the commander, Colonel Edward J. Timberlake, who had preceded Baker as group leader. Timberlake was involved with the Ploesti raid as an operational planner because of his experience with B-24 operations, most of it earned in the north African campaign. In turning over his Traveling Circus to Baker, Timberlake was acknowledging Baker's capabilities as a superb leader.

Colonel Keith K. Compton ("K.K."), a Missourian, led the 376th Bomb Group ("Liberandos"). Described by a former squadron mate as "a real gung ho type," Compton had served with Timber-

Keith K. Compton, "a real gung ho type," commander of the "Liberandos" (376th Bomb Group); mission leader Ent would fly in Compton's aircraft to Ploesti —and back. (U. S. AIR FORCE)

lake and was placed by the latter in command of the Liberandos. This group would lead the mission and General Ent would fly in Compton's plane.

The fifth group, the recently activated 389th Bomb Group, was led by Colonel Jack Wood. These unseasoned men had taken the name of "Sky Scorpions." Although a detachment of the 389th had arrived in Libya as early as July, most men participating in the raid would not have had any combat experience.

Major Ramsay D. Potts, Jr., a Tennessean, who "wanted to fly and wanted to fight Hitler," was a twenty-six-year-old deputy commander in Addison Baker's 93rd. A brilliant young leader, Potts had guessed long before he was told that the target for which they trained would be Ploesti. During this period, Potts recalls that the weather at Benghazi "was absolutely frightful." The air was so filled with fine sand (which ruined engines and other parts of aircraft) that at times it was impossible to see five feet ahead. Aircraft became so hot that touching them resulted in serious burns. Dysentery afflicted one and all, from colonel to sergeant.

Leon Johnson, commanding officer of the "Eight Balls" (44th Bomb Group), a superb battle leader.

(U. S. AIR FORCE)

Scale map (1:5000) of Ploesti built for the Air Force by RAF technicians in England in a week and flown to Africa. It was transported from group to group for study in a truck. Top (just left of center line) is Concordia Vega, largest production unit at Ploesti; counterclockwise, in wedge-shaped area, is Xenia, one of the smaller installations; almost directly below, near bottom, Columbia Aquila; to immediate right below is Astra Romana; to far right near center (i.e., directly east of Ploesti) is Romana Americana, owned by American Standard Oil; although a target, it would not be hit during the mission. (U. S. AIR FORCE)

But training continued despite the hardships. A dummy target area, duplicating in full scale the dispersed installations at Ploesti, was built by engineers. Practice missions at zero altitude were made upon the target. One mission, on July 28, wiped out the desert Ploesti in two minutes. The RAF provided a beautifully made table-top, three-dimen-

sional map of Ploesti which was studied by pilots, navigators, and bombardiers. Special films were made based upon the most recent, though outdated, intelligence. The smooth, confident voice of John "Tex" McCrary, an ex-newspaperman turned Air Force public relations expert, assured the crews of the weaknesses of Ploesti's defenses. "The fighter defenses are not strong and the majority of the fighters will be flown by Rumanian pilots who are thoroughly bored with the war." As for antiaircraft, it was estimated that there were a mere "eighty heavy AA guns and 160 light AA guns," but these were "largely disposed for a night attack" and the "heavy ack-ack should not trouble you at low altitude." Besides, all "the antiaircraft guns are manned by Rumanians, so there is a pretty good chance there might be incidents like there were in Italy at the beginning of the war—when civilians could not get into shelters because they were filled with antiaircraft gunners."

But there were forty batteries of the wicked 88s (88-mm. rifles which were employed against tanks and ships as well as aircraft)—240 guns in all, besides the smaller 37-mm. and 20-mm. guns: hun-

Edward Timberlake, former commander of the "Traveling Circus" (93rd Bomb Group), assisted in the planning of the Ploesti mission. The photograph was taken while the group was still stationed in England.

(U. S. AIR FORCE)

dreds of guns ringing Ploesti and many of them manned by Luftwaffe gun crews, not Rumanians. It was not deception, merely wishful thinking based on the best and latest intelligence reports. But it was the basis for one of the more horrible realizations to be met in the target area by the men in the five groups of Liberators.

At dawn on Sunday, August 1, the first of 178 Liberators, *Wingo-Wango,* piloted by First Lieutenant Brian Flavelle and carrying the mission navigator Lieutenant Robert Wilson, lifted out of the Libyan dust and pointed for the island of Corfu, a three-hour flight across the Mediterranean. At this point the mission would bear northeast across the mountains of Albania and Yugoslavia and eventually the Danube River. This led into the Wallachian plain and Ploesti. The trip would cover, for those who made it both ways, a distance of roughly twenty-seven hundred miles.

The cumbrous, slab-sided "pregnant cows," swollen with fuel for the long trip (additional tanks were installed in the bomb bay of each plane), seemed to struggle to rise off the ground. Although the extra fuel meant sacrificing pay load—1000-

Aircrew: men who would fly the mission to Ploesti; 93rd Bomb Group. (RAYMOND C. WIER)

pound and 500-pound bombs as well as incendiaries —each Liberator carried more than 4000 pounds of explosives: a total of 311 tons of destruction in the entire striking force. All planes were overloaded, some of them made heavier by extra nose guns (in formation lead planes which were to attack flak-gun installations on their bomb runs) and armored crew stations protecting the men from ground fire.

The bombs carried delayed fuzes; the first two waves would thus drop bombs timed to detonate after a period of from one to six hours. This would make it safe for the planes which followed to drop their bombs, theoretically, without flying into the bursts of the preceding aircraft or through the fires the early bombs might have set. There were seven major target areas. Five were situated at Ploesti; another was at Brazi, which was almost adjacent to Ploesti and just to the south; the seventh target was at Campina, about eight miles northwest of Ploesti.

Aboard the 178 Liberators were 1725 Americans and one stowaway, an Englishman. RAF Flight Lieutenant George C. Barwell, a gunnery expert, had been given unofficial permission to fly as topturret gunner in the plane of Major Norman C. Appold, leading B Section of the leading group, the Liberandos (376th). Led by Compton, the

Pre-mission pep talk: General Brereton addresses the 376th Bomb Group before its men boarded their Liberators for Ploesti. Curious portent: as he spoke a sudden wind came up and Brereton was blown off the platform. (U. S. AIR FORCE)

376th Bomb Group put up twenty-nine B-24s; at the head of the formation flew Flavelle's *Wingo-Wango,* leading the bombers to Ploesti. Tucked into the 376th formation was Compton's plane, *Teggie Ann,* carrying the mission command pilot, General Ent.

Following the Liberandos came Baker's Traveling Circus (93rd) with thirty-nine aircraft and Killer Kane's Pyramiders (98th) with forty-seven tawny (almost moth-eaten in appearance) B-24s; the Eight Balls, Johnson's 44th Bomb Group, came up with thirty-seven bombers; behind Johnson were the Sky Scorpions (389th), led by Wood, with twenty-six Liberators. Each group, some divided into two forces, had its assigned targets; all were scheduled to approach their targets in the order in which they had taken off. A strict radio silence was maintained in order not to alert German detection stations. Unknown to the men aboard the Liberators, the Germans were aware of a large force taking off from Libya, although the destination was not known.

"The very first news of the Ploesti operation was bad," Brereton noted in his diary. *Kickapoo,* which had taken off with Kane's Pyramiders, developed trouble shortly after pilot First Lieutenant Robert Nespor had it air-borne. With flame shooting out of an engine, Nespor turned around and headed back for the field. In coming in he was forced to attempt a landing upon a runway still obscured by clouds of red desert dust. *Kickapoo* came in, settled onto the runway, roughly bounced along, and rammed into a concrete telephone pole. Only two men survived the burning wreck.

But the armada, led by *Wingo-Wango,* continued on its way. From time to time over the Mediterranean a Liberator here and there feathered a propeller—a sign of engine malfunction—wheeled out of the formation, jettisoned bombs and fuel into the sea, and headed back for Africa. Before they came within sight of Corfu, ten Liberators had gone; six of these came from Kane's Pyramiders.

The remaining 167 planes were bearing down on Corfu when the lead plane began to behave peculiarly. As the other craft in A Section scattered out of harm's way, *Wingo-Wango* swooped and dived, climbed and dived directly into the sea. Even during these shocking moments radio silence was not violated and no one could know what had oc-

Wingo-Wango, Brian Flavelle's Liberator, has silently fallen into the Mediterranean, taking "Tidal Wave's" lead navigator Robert Wilson with it.

(RAYMOND C. WIER)

rurred in the lost plane. Only a tall column of smoke rose from the Mediterranean marking the spot where the aircraft had plunged. The formation was supposed to continue on its way—and it did, except for Flavelle's wingman, First Lieutenant Guy Iovine. Unable to leave the stricken ship, he dipped his B-24 down and circled over the spot hoping to find survivors to whom he might drop rafts. But there was no one, and then to his dismay Iovine found that he was unable to get the heavy plane back up to formation altitude. There was nothing to do but head back to Benghazi.

The mission navigator was lost in Flavelle's plane; the deputy navigator was in Iovine's. John Palm, in *Brewery Wagon,* moved into the lead spot; his navigator, young William Wright, was now chief navigator of the mission to Ploesti.

Now 165 of the original 178 planes turned north-east over Corfu. Spotters, still uncertain of the formation's destination, kept close watch on the B-24s and telephoned various Luftwaffe stations in the area. But there was some suspicion in Bucharest that the target might be Ploesti.

The formation had hugged the sea for the first leg, but as it approached Albania the Pindus Mountains would necessitate a climb. The mountains peaked to nine thousand feet, but a build-up of cloud massed up to seventeen thousand feet. Compton led the 376th through at sixteen thousand feet, followed by Baker's 93rd. Kane elected to go through at twelve thousand feet leading his 98th, which had spread out according to procedure for passing through cloud, and was followed by Johnson's 44th and Wood's 389th Groups. At sixteen thousand feet a tail wind hurried the two lead groups toward Ploesti while at twelve thousand the three other groups bucked winds through the soup. Thus when the five groups finally emerged from the cumulus, Compton's and Baker's formations were out of sight of Kane, Johnson, and Wood's Liberators. Radio silence made it impossible for the force to reassemble for the final attack. By this time also men in the American bombers had seen enemy planes hovering below them, unable to climb to the height at which the bombers flew without proper oxygen equipment. These were Bulgarian pilots in antiquated fighters. Leon Johnson then realized that all hopes for surprise had come to nothing. And with the three groups trailing the two lead groups, all chances of making a concerted attack upon the seven target areas were likewise lost.

About sixty-five miles west of Ploesti lay the first IP (Initial Point), the city of Pitesti. It was here that the formations were to assume attack altitude, about five hundred feet, and the 389th would leave the other groups to attack the Campina targets. The final IP was the town of Floresti, about thirteen miles northwest of Ploesti. Turning southeast at Floresti would bring the four remaining groups in over Ploesti for their low-level bombing runs.

Brewery Wagon, the lead plane of the 376th Group, carrying William Wright, the new mission navigator, continued on past Pitesti. Slightly behind was *Teggie Ann,* flown by Captain Ralph Thomp-son, as copilot to Compton and carrying mission leader Ent as a passenger. *Brewery Wagon* passed over Targoviste on the way to the final IP, Floresti; here the most fatal incident of the mission occurred. Mistaking Targoviste for Floresti, Compton ordered Thompson to make the southeast turn for the final run on the target. Palm's *Brewery Wagon* continued on the correct flight path, but all planes following saw the command ship turn and turned in train. *Brewery Wagon* wavered, seemed about to join in the wrong turn, but convinced that Wright was correct, Palm continued directly on to the target alone. But *Teggie Ann,* meanwhile, pointed both the 376th and 93rd at Bucharest instead of Ploesti.

Ramsay Potts, among the first to realize that the lead plane with Compton and Ent had made a wrong turn, broke radio silence to warn of the error. But too late; Potts was forced to turn also because of being boxed in by the formation. (U. S. AIR FORCE)

Major Ramsay Potts, leading B Section of the 93rd, realized instantly that the turn had come too soon. So did Major Norman Appold of the 376th. It was too much for both men and they broke radio silence—it no longer mattered—shouting, "Not here!" (Appold) and "Mistake!" (Potts). The latter hoped to break away from the formation, but was "boxed in and had no choice but to turn."

The two lead groups were now heading into Gerstenberg's most potent flak-gun concentration—and for the capital city of Rumania, a city of no military consequence. Within minutes the spires and steeples of Bucharest came into view. To the men in the racing Liberators, now around fifty feet above the ground, it did not at all look like the target for which they had been briefed. Alerted gun crews ran to their 88s and alarms rang in fighter bases for miles around. Why the Americans should attack Bucharest was a total mystery, but Rumanian and German alike ran to his gun station or to waiting fighter aircraft. The Battle of Ploesti had been prematurely ignited.

Addison Baker, leading the 93rd, which had followed the 376th on the wrong course, was aware also of the wrong turn. So was, by then, Ent and Compton in *Teggie Ann*. But it was Baker who reacted first. Seeing the church spires of Bucharest ahead instead of the stacks of Ploesti, which stood to his left, without breaking radio silence Baker executed an almost right-angle turn toward the target. With near miraculous skill and remarkable discipline the rest of the Traveling Circus followed: Lieutenant Colonel George S. Brown leading A Section swinging to Baker's right, and Ramsay Potts, with B Section, wheeling to Brown's right. Now in a broad frontal formation the 93rd approached Ploesti from the south instead of from the west as it had been briefed. Ploesti looked strange to the navigators and bombardiers as its stacks loomed up out of the ground.

IV

The one plane on the correct course, John Palm's *Brewery Wagon,* all but embraced the earth as it charged for the target. Almost on Ploesti *Brewery Wagon* took a direct .88 hit in the nose, killing young William Wright, who had led the formations

The payment for Ploesti begins: the antiaircraft guns, having been forewarned by the wrong turn, are ready for Brewery Wagon, *which had not made the error— thanks to the navigation of William Wright, whom Ent overruled—and which continued "as briefed" for Ploesti until struck in the nose by a German .88 shell.* (RAYMOND C. WIER)

The 93rd, having swung back on course because of Potts's realization of the navigational error of Teggie Ann, *passes by a burning Liberator.*

(RAYMOND C. WIER)

A view from the cockpit of Kenneth O. Dessert's Liberator; flame billows up from an oil tank. To the right, in the lower left-hand corner of the windscreen may be seen Hell's Wench, *carrying Group Commander Addison Baker and mission planning assistant John J. Jerstad. Struck by an .88 shell and burning, the plane continued on its run over the target and crashed; no one survived, not even the two men who parachuted from the burning plane.* (RAYMOND C. WIER)

Lieutenant Colonel Addison Baker, commander of the 93rd Group, here photographed in his office using the public address system, while the group was still stationed in England. Baker died in the crash of Hell's Wench *and was awarded a Medal of Honor for his role in the mission to Ploesti.* (U. S. AIR FORCE)

so brilliantly, and bombardier Second Lieutenant Robert W. Merrell. Palm too had been hit; his right leg was all but blown away. With three engines gone—two of them gushing flame—there was nothing to do but salvo the bombs and try to land. Half in shock upon learning that his leg remained attached to him by the merest shred, Palm had been unaware of the attack of a Messerschmitt on *Brewery Wagon* as it came crunching into the ground. Copilot William F. Love foamed the engines and the distressed plane came in without further burning. Palm, who later had his right leg amputated below the knee, and the seven other survivors were taken prisoner by the Rumanians and Germans.

Having turned for Ploesti, leaving the 376th still on the wrong course to Bucharest, Baker's 93rd ran into the muzzles of flak guns awaiting them. The alarms which had alerted the capital's defenses also quickened the rings of guns around the true target area. Baker flew directly into an inferno: the planes were so low that gun crews simply bore-sighted and used instantaneous fuzes. So it was that *Hell's Wench,* Baker's plane, with young Major John J. Jerstad, one of the important assistants to Timberlake in the planning of the mission, as co-pilot, bore down upon the target area. One of the first obstacles was the balloon barrage. *Hell's Wench* flew into a cable, which luckily snapped, freeing the balloon. But then an .88 shell smashed into the nose of the Liberator and more hits followed, into the wings and the cockpit. Aflame, *Hell's Wench* proceeded toward the target; but Baker knew it would not remain aloft with the bomb load and he jettisoned the explosives. The plane continued leading the rest of the 93rd toward the target. A chute or two blossomed out of *Hell's Wench,* and it appeared that Baker had attempted to bring it up high enough to enable the men to have sufficient altitude from which to drop.

Hell's Wench, still burning, continued to lead the force into the target area, attempting to clear the stacks which spiked up into its path. To observers it appeared to be completely afire in the cockpit area although still seemingly under control. About three hundred feet above the ground *Hell's Wench* suddenly veered into the earth with a splashing flame. Baker had succeeded in bringing his group over the target, but everyone—including the few men who had been able to leave the doomed plane —died.

Those who followed placed the first bombs into the Ploesti target area. The first bomb fell from Walter Stewart's *Utah Man,* only survivor of Baker's three-plane wave. However, the bombs rained down upon targets assigned not to the 93rd, but to the 44th (still coming up, though late, but, as briefed, in company with Kane's 98th). Liberators had begun dropping out of the force before Ploesti was reached as point-blank antiaircraft fire smashed into the low-flying aircraft. Black funeral pyres dotted the route to the target. Gunners in the aircraft engaged in duels with the enemy machine gunners and antiaircraft crews. Some of the machine-gun fire from the planes ignited the unimportant tank farms, smudging the area with leaping flames and dense, black smoke, introducing just one more hazard into the affrighted air.

It was an unimaginable scene as the thirty-four (of the original thirty-nine) 93rd Bomb Group planes swept through at more than two hundred miles an hour and barely off the ground. Their attack could only have taken minutes, but lifetimes ended and complex actions occurred in those few minutes. More than half of the attacking planes did not come out of the fiery target area. Some struck balloon cables; some were hit by flak or other gunfire; some, flying through the turbulence of earlier planes, simply slammed into the ground. Hidden guns popped out of fake haystacks or special mobile flak nests on railway cars with drop sides. Liberators trailed sheets of flame and crashed into fields of wheat or corn even before arriving at the target.

Ramsay Potts, in *Duchess,* led the final 93rd element, Target Force 3, into fumid Ploesti. Deeply fearful that the wrong turn had "wiped out our chance for a successful mission," Potts knew his small force would not be able to hit its target. Having weathered a murderous sequence of flak guns, it would be difficult enough to find an alternate target. Potts and his wingmen turned to find their assigned target but with Astro Romana directly in their line of flight began dropping bombs; this target in the original planning had been assigned to Kane's 98th. The planes behind and around *Duchess* began shredding parts of fuselage or wing,

some continuing on but others smashing to earth in fiery, gashing crashes. One of Potts's wingmen, *Jersey Bounce,* with nose shot away, engine trailing flame, painfully rose over various obstacles until pilot Worthy Long managed to skid it into a clearing, where it burst into flame. Half the crew managed to get out of the plane.

Rumanian fighters, which had vaulted into the air from near Bucharest, initiated attacks on the harassed 93rd Liberators. As one of Potts's B-24s emerged out of the target area, a low-winged monoplane clung to the big aircraft. Apparently in distress, the Liberator roared above the streets of Ploesti with the little Rumanian fighter underneath (all but scraping the street) firing into its belly. With a massive boom the American bomber crashed into the women's prison, in which not only the crew of the plane but around sixty prisoners died trapped in the flames.

As Potts led the remnants of the 93rd away from Ploesti, he was on a near-collision course with planes of the 376th, now coming in to bomb. Ent and Compton had faced the frightful truth: they had led the force into a wrong turn. During the run from Targoviste to the outskirts of Bucharest they had, indeed, "served their time in hell." And there was more to come. Ent spoke into the command channel and ordered the 376th away from Bucharest, turning north and following a railroad linking the capital with Ploesti. The question now was: Should they circle to come in from the briefed course or should they bomb from a completely unfamiliar approach?

This vexing question was answered when Ent, observing the savagery of the antiaircraft fire, ordered the men to hit "targets of opportunity." The B-24s had been flying north, directly into heavy flak, and most then swerved away to the east, to strike at whatever targets they could find. According to the original plan the target of Compton's planes was the Romana Americana refinery—deliberately selected because of its onetime (i.e., before the Germans took over) American ownership. There must be no favoritism displayed in the Ploesti attack. Because of the confusion, as well as the heavy flak reception, the Romana Americana complex was not hit at all that day.

Major Norman Appold led his five Liberators of

Norman C. Appold, who had like Ramsay Potts realized Teggie Ann *had made a wrong turn, but who pressed on toward Ploesti and saw a mass confusion over the target. Despite this, Appold bombed his target of opportunity, Concordia Vega.* (U. S. AIR FORCE)

the 376th directly into Ploesti instead of spreading out as did the other planes. Appold had selected what appeared to be an untouched target of importance (it was: Concordia Vega, which had been assigned to Baker's 93rd). But even as he approached on the bomb run, Appold was disconcerted to see other B-24s flying through the smoke directly toward him; these were the survivors of Potts's force leaving the target. But there was more for Appold to see: as he bore down on Concordia Vega more B-24s appeared to be converging upon him. These were Killer Kane's Pyramiders, somewhat late after joining up upon emerging from the cloud mass, and now on the proper target run.

If ever there was a demonstration of just how a carefully planned military operation could go awry thanks to the simple introduction of human error, Ploesti became a classic.

There is a classic Army axiom: when in doubt

do everything. Appold, however, was not in doubt. He had selected his target and went for it; blind good fortune would have to see to the rest. His five bombers groped through the hail of fire and smoke and dropped their bombs directly into the target area. Only then did he lead his planes up and over Potts's planes rushing away from Ploesti. Appold turned also and, while Barwell in the top turret engaged in duels with various low-lying gun positions, pulled away from the nightmare in noontime Ploesti.

The other 376th aircraft, seeking targets of opportunity, scattered in sweeping turns to the west of Ploesti. Compton's *Teggie Ann* salvoed into a small complex of buildings, not one of the briefed targets. Other planes followed suit, dropping their loads to the north and west of Ploesti before veering south near Floresti—where they converged with Jack Wood's Sky Scorpions, which had bombed at Campina.

v

It was at Floresti, the third IP and correct turning point for the run into Ploesti, that Kane's 98th and Johnson's 44th began their massed approach. The dividing line between the two forces was a railroad track running from Floresti to Ploesti. A heavily armed flak train ran along this track, firing at Kane's Pyramiders to the north and Johnson's Eight Balls to the south as the two forces, flying abreast, came upon Ploesti.

While Kane's Pyramiders and sixteen of Johnson's Eight Balls bore down upon their Ploesti targets, Colonel James Posey, also of the 44th, led an additional twenty-one Eight Ball Liberators toward his target, Brazi, about five miles southwest of Ploesti. Here was located the Creditul Minier refinery, production center for high-octane aviation fuel.

Leading in *V for Victory,* piloted by veteran John H. Diehl, Posey swept into Brazi in the first wave. Diehl had to pull the plane up to avoid chimneys, but the bombs fell precisely into the target area. Brazi had not been struck by any of the earlier planes which had scattered over Ploesti seeking targets. This part of the mission occurred exactly as planned—and the Brazi refinery was totally destroyed at a cost of two Liberators.

Kane's Pyramiders come in over Ploesti to find that their targets have already been hit by Baker's Traveling Circus. (JERRY JOSWICK: U. S. AIR FORCE)

But the fate of the remaining Eight Balls and the Pyramiders was totally different. As they approached Ploesti, it seemed that they would be further hindered by murky rain clouds low over the target area. Several Liberators in both Kane's and Johnson's forces had been damaged by the flak train, and the dark cloud was but one more unforeseen hitch. But as they charged down upon Ploesti it became clear that the "rain" was in fact smoke, the effusion of the bombings by the 93rd Group. This smoke, now rising above bombing height, not only added turbulence, but also secreted chimneys, barrage balloon cables, and bracing wires of the chimneys. Intense flame, too, shot into the air intermittently throughout the entire target area.

It was at this point that both Johnson and Kane could have swerved off course and fled. Their targets, obscured by smoke and livid with flame, had already been struck. They could turn back and no one would question their decision. It is unlikely that the thought so much as flickered through the minds of these two quite opposite men. Johnson expressed their attitudes when he said that "we had all agreed ahead of time that we weren't going that far without trying to get our targets. . . ." Kane had come to bomb Ploesti and he would not leave until he had. So he led his decimated Pyramiders into the inferno. One of his crew, Raymond B. Hubbard, recalled that the "fire wrapped us up. I looked out of the side windows and saw the others flying through smoke and flame. It was [like] flying through hell. I guess we'll go straight to heaven when we die. We've had our purgatory."

"It was more like an artist's conception of an air battle than anything I have ever experienced," Johnson later told Brereton. "We flew through sheets of flame, and airplanes were everywhere, some of them on fire and others exploding. It's indescribable to anyone who wasn't there."

Kane, at the controls of *Hail Columbia,* churned up the target area with his fixed front guns and led the way into Ploesti. The heat was so intense at his attack altitude that his left arm was singed; *Hail Columbia* also received a hit in an engine and when the smoke- and flame-blacked B-24 escaped from the inferno it was flying on three engines. Of the forty-one planes which had begun the target run at Floresti, only nineteen followed Kane out of the smoke. But their bombs lay in the assigned target zone, compounding the destruc-

The 98th Bomb Group flies over an already burning Astra Romana. Stacks in the heavy smoke were as much a danger as German flak.

(JERRY JOSWICK: U. S. AIR FORCE)

tion laid on by the distracted 93rd. There had been, however, just one more hazard—the explosions of the delayed-action bombs.

Johnson's "White Five" target force of sixteen Liberators flew directly into a curtain of black smoke, evidence of the earlier visit of Baker's Traveling Circus. The great B-24s, twisting and turning to avoid balloon cables and chimneys, wallowed like so many winged whales in a fiery sea. With shocking regularity the leviathans foundered to the bottom of the murky ocean, spurting red, bloodlike flame. Of the sixteen planes which entered the "White Five" (Colombia Aquila refinery) target area only seven, with Johnson's *Suzy-Q* in the lead, came out.

But leaving the area of the target did not conclude the nightmare, for both Kane's and Johnson's survivors came under severe fighter attack—mainly Luftwaffe men in Me-109s. As he raced away with all the power his three straining engines could muster, Kane's *Hail Columbia* was laced by fighter fire, with punctures in the wing (with a resultant buckled wing spar), the tip of a propeller shot away, and a holed blade on another. Knowing he could never make it back over the planned with-

Leon Johnson's 44th approaches Columbia Aquila, only to find it burning; of the sixteen planes that flew in, only seven came out.

(JERRY JOSWICK: U. S. AIR FORCE)

drawal route to Benghazi, Kane set course for Cyprus, throwing out all excess weight on the way.

The Sky Scorpions (389th) were led with only the slightest hitch by Jack Wood to their target at Campina ("Red Target"). Wood too had inadvertently led his formation into a wrong turn; he corrected it by a smoothly executed turnabout and a vault over a small ridge. The Scorpions came in in two forces, Wood leading a dozen B-24s and Major John A. Brooks, his deputy, leading seventeen. With forward firing guns chattering, Wood led the forces into the until then untouched Steaua Romana complex. Like Posey's attack upon Brazi, Jack Wood's attack upon Campina was "as briefed." His group had the least losses of all involved. Of the twenty-nine attacking planes, six were lost, one of them flown by Second Lieutenant Lloyd Hughes, the only man of the Ploesti mission below the rank of major to receive the Medal of Honor.

Hughes's Liberator had been struck by flak as it approached the drop point. A wide stream of fuel poured out of a ruptured bomb bay tank, twist-

One of the targets hit "as briefed," Steaua Romana, the objective of the green "Sky Scorpions" (389th Group) led by Jack Wood.

(JERRY JOSWICK: U. S. AIR FORCE)

Lieutenant Lloyd Hughes (as an air cadet), one of the Sky Scorpions who did not leave the target area; Hughes was awarded the Medal of Honor for the mission. (U. S. AIR FORCE)

dos (376th), they came under fighter attack. From the dropping of the first bomb by *Utah Man* just before noon, until the last—placed by the 389th's *Vagabond King*, piloted by John B. McCormick—less than a half hour had elapsed. But for the survivors, most of them spread across the skies of Rumania with damaged planes, wounded, dying, and dead aboard, there were still the fighters to contend with until the German and Rumanian planes ran out of fuel. Keeping the tattered, scorched Liberators air-borne was an epic in itself.

The plan, having gone so completely astray, no longer held. On paper it had been intended that all targets would be hit simultaneously and that all survivors of the attack should return to the Libyan bases together. Thus would they be able to defend each other in formation with massed guns. The withdrawal from Ploesti was not orderly as different groups in various stages of distress left the target areas. Some planes were badly damaged and could not keep up with a formation, others came away under fighter attack.

An attempt was made to form ragged groupings

ing and flashing under the big plane like a liquid ribbon of fuze. Now on his bomb run, Hughes did not attempt to land or to evade the wall of flame which stood in the path. In an instant Hughes's Liberator was set afire. The bombs fell into the target, but the stricken plane, a white sheet of pure fire streaming from the left wing, had no chance. Obviously still under control, Hughes seemed headed for a stream bed for an emergency landing. A bridge loomed in the path of the burning plane, but the plane rose above the obstruction, lowered again—and then a wing tip brushed the riverbank. The blazing Liberator whirled across the earth, spattering molten wreckage and scarring the meadow in its scorching death throes; all but two men in the plane died in the crash.

The Sky Scorpions were the last to bomb in the Ploesti area, and in addition to dodging the target-of-opportunity seekers of Compton's Liberan-

"Getting the hell out": a Liberator at treetop level rushes away from burning Ploesti. Some bombers nearly scraped the earth and returned with cornstalks in their bomb bays.

(JERRY JOSWICK: U. S. AIR FORCE)

for the sake of survival. Some aircraft, not badly damaged, throttled down to remain with others which could not keep up and thus became easy targets for fighters. A trail of ammunition belts, radios, guns, seats—anything no longer required and which added weight to a struggling plane—followed the Liberators from Ploesti to the sea. The least hurt groups, the 376th (Liberandos) and the 389th (Sky Scorpions), managed to form up and head for home over the planned route, although not as a single unit. Some of the 44th and 98th (the worst hit Eight Balls and Pyramiders) joined together for the flight back, but the Pyramiders' leader, John Kane, with other planes in tow, made for Cyprus. It was a shorter flight than to Africa, although not without its Bulgarian mountain barrier. Planes which could not make it even that far landed in neutral Turkey, where crews were interned. In all, seven Liberators came down in Turkey, and one ditched into the sea off the Turkish coast; twenty-three came down at Allied bases in Malta, Sicily, or Cyprus.

It was nighttime before Kane brought *Hail Columbia* into the RAF base at Nicosia, Cyprus. Although the flare path was lighted, the exhausted

In the wake of "Tidal Wave," Rumanians fighting the fires at Ploesti. Although smoke and flame were impressive, the attack did not knock out the target. (U. S. AIR FORCE)

Journey's end: a Liberator sets down in north Africa after the Ploesti mission. (U. S. AIR FORCE)

iron man brought the wheezing Liberator in a little short, snagging the landing gear in a ditch which the British, with characteristic perversity, placed at either end of runways. The main wheels snapped and the Liberator came in on its nose and with tail threatening to rise and upend them. Kane and copilot John S. Young pulled on the controls to prevent flipping onto their back. The tail came down as the battered aircraft bellied screechingly along the runway. Bumping along, Kane was surprised to see two wheels and a propeller racing ahead. The plane twisted to a halt, and for the first time in more than twelve hours, Killer Kane left his seat.

On the return flight to Benghazi more planes were lost to the last fighter attacks and fell into the sea; two aircraft flying in formation entered a cloud and never came out—they had collided. Finally, after nearly twelve hours of waiting, the men at Benghazi heard the first of the survivors approaching. Brereton awaited the arrival of Compton and Ent, from whom he had had no word since around noon, when the simple message "Mission Successful" had been radioed from Ploesti.

In the deepening African twilight the giant bombers fluttered back, their engines whining from strain, the planes themselves whistling because of bullet- and flak-riddled surfaces. Planes came in without brakes, without proper control, some crash-landed with dead and wounded aboard. When the dispirited Ent revealed to Brereton the story of the mission, the latter realized that he had no triumph on his hands. The extent of damage to Ploesti would not be known until reconnaissance photographs were taken. From eyewitnesses it was clear that Ploesti had been hard hit, so that Ent's curiously premature and wildly optimistic "Mission Successful" message seemed less ironic.

But the ravages of the toll began to come in, intimated by the condition of men and aircraft as they landed at Benghazi. Ramsay Potts brought *Duchess* down and his feet had barely touched the ground before he was telling Timberlake of a military nightmare.

Of the 164 Liberators which had gained the target area, 41 had been lost to enemy action. An additional 14 (including the 8 interned in Turkey) were lost through other causes, such as the takeoff accident of *Kickapoo,* the inexplicable dive into the sea of Flavelle's plane near Corfu and the collision in the clouds over Bulgaria. Thus the total plane loss added up to 54. (And of those which had returned to Benghazi, barely 30 were still flyable.) This would mean too the loss of 540 men.

The final death toll of the Ploesti raid, according to Air Force files, came to 310. The number of wounded was initially given as 54 (3 of whom were in Turkey), but that number plus 20 lay in hospitals in Rumania. More than 100 prisoners, also, spent the rest of the war in Rumania.

The cost to the Ninth Air Force for less than a half hour's work was, indeed, high. This was implicit in the awarding of no less than five Medals of Honor (the highest number for any single air action) to Ploesti raiders, to the quick—Leon Johnson and John Kane—and the dead—Addison Baker, John Jerstad, and Lloyd Hughes.

On August 4, 1943, following the preliminary estimates, Brereton noted in his diary, "While the TIDAL WAVE operation was extremely successful, I was somewhat disappointed because we failed to hit White No. 1 and 2 at all." White No. 1 was Romana Americana, the American-leased section of Ploesti; No. 2 was Concordia Vega, which had, in fact, been hit by the determined Appold with his five planes that had not swerved away, as had the others of the 376th, to seek targets of opportunity. Brereton assigned his discomfiture to the fact that the 65 to 75 per cent destruction he had hoped for had not been achieved. Still, he believed that a 60 per cent figure had been reached and had "put a serious dent in Germany's oil supply." As reported centuries before by Plutarch, it had been another victorious warrior, Pyrrhus, who had said, "Another such victory . . . and we are finished."

In truth, the extent of damage was closer to 40 per cent, and while bombs and fire (as well as crashing aircraft) did knock out some facilities for four to six months, no "serious dent" was put in Germany's oil supply. In fact, Ploesti had never produced to full capacity, so that other units could be activated to make up the loss. With slave labor in plentiful supply, the Germans very quickly restored the damaged facilities, and Ploesti, instead of being knocked out of the war, was as potent as ever. It was not until late in the spring of 1944 that any more attempts could be made upon the heavily defended target. When the U. S. Fifteenth Air Force, based at Foggia, Italy, was formed and powerfully armed with B-17s and B-24s, Ploesti could be struck en masse from high level. By that time, too, long-range American fighter planes could escort the bombers to and from the target.

But Ploesti was never to be an easy target, with its heavy flak concentration, and many men died attempting to put a stopper to Hitler's oil supply. By the end of August 1944, a little over a year after Tidal Wave, the oil fields did stop functioning. In September the Russians moved in and occupied the ruin. It had taken thousands of bombers (and a further expenditure of more than 350 bombers lost). In short, the men who undertook and carried through Tidal Wave had attempted the impossible. Their true achievement could be measured only in courage and not decisive results. For the tragedy of Ploesti is that there were no decisive results.

8

SCHWEINFURT

OVER another panacea target, ball bearings," Air Chief Marshal Sir Arthur Harris exclaimed with undisguised scorn, "the target experts went completely mad." The outspoken Briton, it is true, was speaking from the vantage point of hindsight, but he was no less critical and skeptical at the time. He resisted all pleas, suggestions, and even demands which had initiated with the "panacea mongers" despite their quite accurate information that about half of Germany's supply of ball bearings, so essential to the machines and instruments of war, was produced in the Bavarian city of Schweinfurt.

Harris rejected the claims for Schweinfurt's importance (in which rejection he was not correct), stating that even if Schweinfurt were entirely destroyed the effect upon German war production would not be as disastrous as was "so confidently prophesied." The fiery Bomber Command leader, standing firm against his own chiefs of the Air Staff, argued that Schweinfurt was a relatively small city and would therefore be difficult to find at night, that it was heavily defended, and that even several full-scale attacks would achieve, in his firm but considered opinion, only dubious results.

For months the doughty Harris endured the pressures of his chiefs, who in general agreed with the American policy of concentration upon selected targets. They argued that massive destruction in a few key industries would naturally be more effective than

widespread small destruction in many. Harris preferred the larger population centers, for such cities were easier to locate—and they housed many, many Germans. These were the cities to destroy, not little Schweinfurt with its population of sixty thousand. While the crisis boiled in Bomber Command, the American Eighth Air Force, committed to the spirit and letter of the Combined Bomber Offensive, a major objective of which was the crippling of the German aircraft industry, prepared to spring upon Schweinfurt.

Eighth Air Force Bomber Command (more correctly VIII Bomber Command) had, since its initial modest mission to the Rouen-Sotteville marshaling yards (August 17, 1942), concentrated its slowly expanding forces upon such ungrateful targets as submarine pens, besides various industrial targets in the occupied countries and Germany and Luftwaffe airfields. By the beginning of 1943 it was grievously clear that the German Air Force was indeed a formidable enemy. As German pilots gained experience against the American bomber formations, composed mainly of the Flying Fortress and the more recent Liberators, tactics were devised to interfere seriously with bombing missions. The early Fortresses and Liberators were weak on frontal armament, so German pilots learned eventually to attack in small formations, ranging from single aircraft to a half dozen, from the front. The head-on

Aircraft of British Bomber Command and the American Eighth Air Force, by night and by day, shared the menace of German flak guns in occupied Holland. Flying Fortress Lady Liberty *falls toward Flushing after being cut in half by a direct hit.* (U. S. AIR FORCE)

must be eliminated. This did not preclude attention to other targets. Weather, the number of operational aircraft, the range limit of escort planes also played a part in the planning.

The force that Eaker was capable of dispatching in the year which separated Mission No. 1, when a dozen B-17s flew to Rouen-Sotteville, and Mission No. 83, when 237 bombers struck various German operated airfields in France, had grown. But postholing runways, wrecking operations buildings and barracks, and destroying parked aircraft could only be defined as tactical—warmaking with an immediate, short-range objective. The more strategic aspect was notable in missions toward the end of July 1943—Missions 78, 79, 80, for example— when the Fiesler aircraft components factory at Kassel, the Focke-Wulf plant at Oschersleben, and the Heinkel works at Warnemünde (all of which

Colonel Curtis E. LeMay, commander of the 3rd Air Division (right), who led the first shuttle bombing mission from England to Regensburg to north Africa. To LeMay's right: Brigadier General Haywood S. Hansell, commander of the 1st Bombardment Wing (units of which later comprised the 1st Air Division). When this photograph was taken LeMay was commander of the 305th Bomb Group. Later in the war both Hansell and LeMay were to play important roles in the development of the B-29 as an air weapon.

(U. S. AIR FORCE)

attack, considering the double closing speed of the two aircraft, the always present danger of collision, and the sight of twinkling wing guns and cannon, was unnerving, to say the least. Although aggressive Luftwaffe fighter attacks did not succeed in turning back any of the American bomber forces, they did succeed in knocking aircraft down and, with the head-on attack, in interfering with the accuracy of bombing. Flak was another problem, but a more impersonal one, and one which depended to some extent upon chance. A German pilot in an Me-109 or an FW-190 was out to get you, specifically, and this was rattling.

It was true, then, as noted in the Combined Bomber Offensive document, that before the major target systems could be dealt with, the Luftwaffe belonged to the complex which turned out the formidable FW-190) were heavily hit. They were also zealously defended; the three days' missions cost forty-four heavy bombers. And, if the Eighth had not succeeded in erasing the factories from Germany's war economy, it did initiate serious thought among the German High Command about dispersing such factory complexes, which dispersal promised to disrupt production as critically as damage.

The first anniversary of the Eighth's first mission from Britain was to be celebrated with Mission No. 84, the most impressive up to that moment. It sparkled with superlatives: more aircraft than ever before, more bomb tonnage than ever before; the deepest penetration into Germany ever attempted and a strike against the then two most critical targets: the Messerschmitt factories at Regensburg and the ball-bearing plant at Schweinfurt.

"It was a bold strategic concept," Lieutenant General Ira C. Eaker has written of the Regensburg-Schweinfurt mission. "It was the first shuttle bombing mission of the war. The 3rd Air Division, the

Aircrew quarters, Grafton-Underwood, England. Men of the 384th Bomb Group hug the stove between missions. Galoshes are a concession to England's muddy airfields. The steel helmet was not an affectation; it was worn by aircrews in combat. (ROBERT CHAPIN)

force attacking the Messerschmitt fighter factory at Regensburg, took off from English bases and landed in fields in North Africa. The decisions by the VIII Bomber Commander, Major General Frederick L. Anderson [who replaced Eaker, now head of the Eighth Air Force], and the 3rd Air Division Commander, Colonel Curtis E. LeMay, to proceed to Regensburg with but part of the force, when the 1st Air Division [led by Brigadier General Robert Williams] was delayed in take-off due to weather, were *two* of the most dramatic and courageous command decisions of the air war in Europe. This battlefield was a thousand miles long and five miles above the earth. It was fought in sub-zero temperatures and the gladiators, friend and foe, wore oxygen masks."

Brereton's Ninth had bled at Ploesti; now, less than a month later, it would be the turn of Eaker's Eighth.

II

By June of 1943 about ten heavy bombardment groups had arrived in England, taking over ex-RAF

Major General Frederick L. Anderson, commander of the Eighth Air Force's Bomber Command during the Schweinfurt missions. (U. S. AIR FORCE)

With a jack raising the wing, 384th Group ground crew men prepare to remove a wheel from a B-17. (ROBERT CHAPIN)

stations in East Anglia and the Midlands. One of the most recent arrivals was the 384th Bombardment Group (H) based at Grafton-Underwood, from which the first heavy bomber strike had been made the previous August. In time the 384th adopted the slogan "Keep the Show on the Road," the contribution of Major S. L. McMillan, deputy group commander, who went down on the group's second mission—a strike upon the docks at Hamburg. Writing from a German prisoner of war camp, McMillan provided the heartening phrase, the philosophy of which the men in the group might have found ironic. In its first four days in combat the 384th lost ten aircraft on the wrong side of the Channel.

These losses, as well as the others decimating 8th Bomber Command, were more a tribute to the Luftwaffe's assertiveness than a reproach to the capabilities of the 384th Group. Even if bomber formations had grown larger during the critical first year of 8th Bomber Command's operations (thus massing defensive firepower), numerous German

fighter bases dotted the routes to and from the targets. Allied fighter planes could not venture beyond a certain point because of limited range. From that point on, it was a running battle of unexampled destructiveness and terror.

Obviously one solution, until the advent of the fighter capable of escorting the bombers round-trip, was to rid the sky of the Luftwaffe. So it was that the Regensburg-Schweinfurt mission was visualized as a double blow: directly upon the Messerschmitt factory itself and indirectly by striking at Schweinfurt's anti-friction-bearing complex which supplied ball bearings for several war industries.

"The plan of attack," Eaker has written, "called for the 3rd Air Division with 150 Flying Fortresses to cross the Channel at 8 A.M., fly to Regensburg, more than three hours away from English bases, attack the fighter factory there, and proceed to landing fields in Africa, fuel being insufficient for return to England.

"The 1st Air Division with 150 heavy bombers would follow 30 minutes later and bomb the ball-bearing complex at Schweinfurt, returning to English bases. It was visualized the 3rd Air Division would bear the brunt of German fighter reaction on the way in, and the 1st Air Division would have to fight its way out. Such long-range U.S. fighters as were then available would escort the 3rd Division in and the 1st Division out."

The 384th was one of the groups belonging to

B-17F of 384th Bomb Group; triangle on tail signifies that the group belonged to the 1st Air Division; "P" was the group's code letter. (ROBERT CHAPIN)

The airman's English enemy: the weather. Sudden changes made takeoff and assembly difficult and frequently led to collision over bomber bases. After a mission bad weather added to the toll when distressed aircraft attempted to land. (U. S. AIR FORCE)

the 1st Air Division and was alerted by a field order the evening before the mission was scheduled. Speculations about the nature and location of the target for what was rumored to be a "big one" had begun six weeks before. Would it be Berlin, or Hitler's private fortress in Berchtesgaden? Berlin seemed likely, for the Eighth had not yet struck at the capital of the Third Reich. Each group was ordered to pick their best navigator-bombardier team and to detach them to headquarters for special training. "We didn't know where the target was," Malvern Sweet, navigator of *The Ex-Virgin,* admitted, "but we could draw pictures of what it looked like."

During this same period of waiting, partly to recuperate from previous mission losses and partly to await a good turn in the weather, LeMay, commander of the 4th Combat Bombardment Wing (later the 3rd Air Division) placed his crews on bad-weather practice. The foresighted commander's reasoning was characteristically clear-cut: it was unlikely that they would have clear weather over both the bases and the target. Practicing blind takeoffs would take care of the poor visibility over England, LeMay calculated. Once above the clouds—and provided target visibility was good—all would be

as well as could be. LeMay planned to lead the force to Regensburg and then to Africa. But his foresightedness, as it eventuated, led to an ominous twist in the outcome of the mission.

The 1st Bombardment Wing (later the 1st Air Division) was preparing for the mission in its special training of navigator-bombardier teams. It was not, however, unlike LeMay, giving due consideration to the weather contingencies.

After several scrubbings, the mission was finally "laid on" for August 17, 1943. As was its capricious wont, English weather contributed its set of unknown factors. "It was so foggy," Curtis LeMay recalls, "that we had to lead the airplanes out with flashlights and lanterns, in order to get them onto the runway." The weeks of instrument takeoff paid off; LeMay managed to get all 146 B-17s of the 3rd Division off the ground and above the clouds. As division leader, LeMay flew in the lead aircraft of the 96th Bombardment Group and found to his consternation that there were no escort fighters to be found in the sky. Then there was a further hitch: the 1st Division too was socked in by fog but could not get off the ground as scheduled (this was timed for ten minutes after LeMay's force had crossed the enemy coast). With the approach of the Schweinfurt force, some of the German fighter attack, it had been hoped, would be drawn off the Regensburg force; and friendly fighters—eighteen squadrons of American P-47s and sixteen squadrons of Spitfires—could take on the Luftwaffe as planned.

Because he had to arrive at the African bases before dark, LeMay could not wait for the fogbound 1st Division, nor could he spend time hoping for the arrival of the fighters. So he proceeded on to Regensburg. "Our fighter escort," LeMay has written, "had black crosses on their wings." In truth, American and British fighters did arrive to protect some of the other groups, although not the 96th with which LeMay flew—for the bombers stretched across miles of air—but had to turn back when fuel ran low. They returned to their bases to refuel and rearm in order to take off again to escort the Schweinfurt bombers.

LeMay meanwhile hurtled through a ferocious air battle. Flak had begun coming up at Woensdrecht, within minutes after the B-17s had crossed the North Sea. Eight minutes later German fighters ripped through the formations and the battle was on. For almost two hours, until Regensburg was reached, the violent battle ensued and both German and American aircraft fell. LeMay and his surviving men placed the bombs neatly into the Messerschmitt factories, hitting every important building besides destroying a number of finished aircraft awaiting delivery to the Luftwaffe.

"I lost twenty-four out of my hundred and twenty-seven planes which attacked the target at Regensburg," LeMay has noted. His battered formations, however, pushed onward from Regensburg for North Africa. This confused the German fighters, who expected the B-17s to return over the same route flown on the way in. It was on this final leg of the mission that six of the Regensburg force's twenty-four losses occurred, some falling over Italy and others splashing into the Mediterranean. LeMay landed at the base at Telergma in Africa and found facilities more than primitive. His losses had been the second highest (the first: the June 13 attack on Bremen, which cost twenty-six planes) sustained by the Eighth Air Force in its year of operations. There had not been any fighter protection, so far as he could see, and upon arriving at Telergma he found that no arrangements has been made to house his men or to service the B-17s. Though he had gone to Africa himself a month before to arrange for the shuttle mission, the war had moved on in North Africa, taking LeMay's arrangements with it. LeMay was not in a good mood when he reported on the first, historic shuttle mission from England to Africa: and he was not shy about letting this be known.

LeMay's Regensburg groups had gotten away around 9:35 A.M. But the Schweinfurt force, unable to take off in the heavy fog, was "stood down." This was a hopeful development for the waiting men; perhaps, like all the others, this mission too would be scrubbed.

During the early morning briefing, when the cover was removed from the large wall map and the men had a chance to see their route and target, there was an audible reaction. That it would be a long mission had already been gleaned by many from the bomb load and the fuel they carried. Berlin remained the favorite of the rumor mongers. Whistles, indrawn sighs, and several "Wows!" greeted the map unveiling in the briefing room of the 546th Squadron of the 384th Bombardment Group. There was a seemingly interminable ribbon running from the base at Grafton-Underwood across the North Sea, over occupied Holland, and deep into Germany. There had never been so long a ribbon before.

Considering the probabilities which the crews must face, a special effort was made by the briefing officers to stress the importance of Schweinfurt as a target; why they carried a mixed bomb load of five-hundred-pound general-purpose bombs and incendiaries: the ball-bearing factories at Schweinfurt were floored with wood. This was, they were informed, so that if a bearing dropped to the floor it would not be damaged. No detail was too minute, apparently. The GPs would open up the factories and the incendiaries would set them ablaze. A thorough job must be done, for "we don't want to have to go back there."

Lieutenant Frank A. Celentano, ex-Cornell law student, and a navigator in the 546th Squadron, sat through the briefing in a state of unease. He had been assigned to a strange ship, *Lucky Thirteen,* because his regular plane, *Battle Wagon,* was under repair. But that was not the worst of it. The squadron had been assigned the low position in the 384th Group's formation—low and at the rear: "Coffin Corner." In this most vulnerable position in the formation, German fighters generally struck with most telling effect.

And then the waiting followed. "If you didn't get off right away," Celentano recalls laconically, "you lost enthusiasm." The longer the wait, the more apprehensive the crews became; tension set in. The longer they waited, the more likely the Germans would guess the target. "Word had gone out that the mission was bound to be called off. We were hoping it would be, particularly because of the weather. The danger of collision was ever-present. There was nothing quite so chilling as pulling up above the clouds into the clear air and seeing a column of black smoke rising up from the clouds. It was always a sign that two planes had come together in the overcast."

For more than three hours Celentano and the other crews of 230 Flying Fortresses had a good deal to think about: from the soupy English weather to the long ribbon on the map. And then, unexpectedly, about one in the afternoon, a green flare shot up from the control tower and it was time to crank engines. Celentano settled in his position in

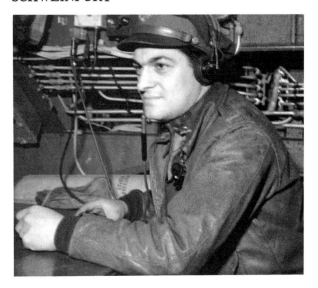

Lieutenant Frank Celentano, navigator of the 546th Squadron, 384th Group, who went to Schweinfurt for the first time in Lucky Thirteen *in the low rear position in the bomber stream—"Coffin Corner" to airmen.*

(FRANK CELENTANO)

the nose of *Lucky Thirteen* as pilot Lieutenant Philip M. Algar gracefully lifted the heavy B-17 off the runway and climbed, without incident, through the clouds. He tucked the plane into Coffin Corner at the end of the 384th's bomber stream, the eighteenth plane in the formation. Major Thomas P. Beckett, leading the group that day, brought them into the wing formation, which then joined the division, led by Brigadier General Robert Williams.

Even before they arrived over Germany, *Lucky Thirteen*'s luck had gone bad. Over Holland the formation had come under 20-mm. attack and *Lucky Thirteen* rocked to the blast of a hit in the plane's center section. Both waist gunners, Loring C. Miller and John Schimenek, were hit. Miller, unaware of his own injury—a sliver of shell had punctured his lung—called in to inform Algar that Schimenek had been hit. He said nothing about himself. But soon Miller was too busy to think about the pain in his chest.

"There were at least 200 enemy fighters attacking us," Celentano was later quoted in the London *Daily Herald.* "F.W. 190's, some with the old yellow noses, some painted black and some half black and white. Some were painted just like our P.47s and maneuvered like them but they did not fool us.

"It's a lot of ballyhoo to say that Germany's first-line fighters have all been shot down. They came at us four abreast and fought like hell."

"When we got over the enemy coast we had to lose altitude because of the lowering overcast," Beckett in the lead plane related later. "That's where the fighters got to us. Although we had fighter support, enemy fighters kept hitting us anyhow."

During the fighter attack, mainly by FW-190s, Miller manned his waist gun, but the seriousness of his wound began to show. He remained, however, at his gun, firing at the countless attackers. Algar ordered radio operator Francis Gerow to take over Miller's gun and Miller was forced to lie down. Even then he indicated to Schimenek that he was all right and need no attention and that Schimenek must remain at his own gun.

"After the fighters left," Beckett continued, "we climbed back to altitude. When we got to the target there were no fighters there." But by this time there were a number of 384th planes gone too. Celentano found that *Lucky Thirteen* had graduated from Coffin Corner during the battle to squadron lead—and that there remained only two or three planes to lead.

Lead navigator of the 384th was Lieutenant Edward J. Knowling, who brought the survivors of the

A Flying Fortress neatly tucked into formation—in "Coffin Corner."

(ERIK MILLER/LOCKHEED-CALIFORNIA)

The 384th encounters flak over the target; bombs have begun to descend through the overcast and the flak comes up. German fighters generally pulled away at this point to let the radar-directed antiaircraft guns do their work. (ROBERT CHAPIN)

A B-17 falls over Schweinfurt after a fighter attack. (U. S. AIR FORCE)

hour-long fighter assault over Schweinfurt. A squadron commander of one of the other groups, the 305th, formerly commanded by LeMay, observed bitterly, "Our navigator has an easy job today. All he has to do is follow the trail of burning Fortresses and parachutes from the task forces ahead of us."

The 384th's lead bombardier was Second Lieutenant Joseph W. Baggs, who found the target area partially obscured by a smoke screen. As he came in, eye peering through the bombsight, he picked what appeared to be the target. "At that time it was about the only thing I could see that resembled the target as described," he said at the debriefing later. "But as we got closer I could see our target at the right. I saw the race track and knew where I was. . . ." Correcting and adjusting his sight, Baggs led the 384th to the target. "As we got over the target we noticed that the first building on the target was on fire," Baggs said.

In *Lucky Thirteen* it was obvious that if Loring Miller was to have any chance for life, the plane would have to get below an altitude at which an oxygen mask was required. As soon as the bombs were dropped into the ball-bearing factory area, Celentano plotted the shortest course for Grafton-Underwood. Algar then began an immediate but gradual descent to a lower altitude; he also throttled to maximum speed. From time to time, until normal breathing could be resumed, the now unconscious Miller had to have his oxygen mask removed to empty it of blood. Otherwise he might have drowned in his own blood.

Celentano had plotted their route so skillfully that *Lucky Thirteen* skirted most of the heavy flak areas, and, as luck would have it, there were no further fighter attacks. By this time, perhaps, the German fighter pilots were exhausted, after fighting LeMay's Regensburg force earlier and the Schweinfurt aircraft coming and going. *Lucky Thirteen* thundered in over Grafton-Underwood shooting red flares from the side windows, indicating wounded aboard, and as Algar touched the runway an ambulance trailed the bomber until it stopped. Schimenek and the grievously wounded Miller were rushed to the hospital. The shell fragment was removed from Miller's lung and he recovered. For his "gallantry and devotion to duty," Sergeant Loring Corwin Miller of Stockton, California, was awarded the Silver Star.

The Focke-Wulfs and flak were not the only weapons employed by the Germans that day over Schweinfurt. Teutonic genius for destruction seemed unlimited to the point of creativity. Some of the fighter bombers, Ju-88s and Me-110s, were equipped with rocket launchers and spread terror through the bomber formations when their smoking missiles pierced them. A direct rocket hit snapped a B-17 in half and trapped the entire crew in the gyrating pieces of the falling aircraft.

The sky was transformed into swiftly moving, soaring debris- and smoke-glutted battleground: tracers interlaced in beautifully intricate but mad patterns, smoke of various shadings floated among the clouds, pieces of exploded or collision-shredded aircraft fell to earth, and the sky was dotted with white (American) and yellow (German) parachutes.

Observing the battle from his perch in the nose of *Lucky Thirteen,* Frank Celentano had found it difficult to fathom; as he watched in fascinated helplessness a crewman leaped from a badly burning Fortress. The figure fell away from the distressed plane toward the safety of the earth; but when the chute opened it too was aflame. In an instant the airman's brief refuge had ended and he had a 25,000-foot fall in which to consider the fortunes of war.

Other German aircraft introduced another innovation. They actually flew over the American bombers and dropped bombs upon them timed to detonate within the bomber formations. While neither accurate nor effective, the tactic was unnerving to the American crews, and now and then a B-17 actually fell to the air-to-air bombing.

There was yet another curiously fiendish device. German fighters, FW-190s, trailing cables from which bombs dangled, approached the American bombers from above—which incidentally brought the fighter under attack from the top-turret guns of the Fortresses. When the German pilot brought his plane with the bomb dangling in the proper position, he electrically detonated it. This method was not very effective either, but during the fighting some

Back at Grafton-Underwood, ground crews anxiously search the sky for returning aircraft.

(ROBERT CHAPIN)

actually worked. As one tail gunner, Sergeant Thomas Murphy of the 381st Bombardment Group, watched, an FW blew the wing off a B-17 with the cable device.

If the German High Command did not understand its own air weapon and if the Luftwaffe High Command was remarkably ineffectual in its strategy, there was no denying the courage of the Luftwaffe's pilots or the imaginativeness of their tactics.

Despite the unrelenting ferocity of that German opposition, however, the bomber formations fought through to Schweinfurt, dropped their bombs, and then fought as tenaciously to get back to England. It was a monotony of terror. But then the German fighters began to withdraw as fuel and ammunition depleted, and the Fortresses, some of them hardly more than a pile of flying wreckage, struggled to get back home.

At Grafton-Underwood the last of the 384th's strays had begun to straggle in. Five of the eighteen planes which had taken off would never return: *Deuces Wild, Snuffy, M'Honey, Vertical Shaft,* and *Powerhouse II.* Fifty men: of these forty were taken prisoner, four escaped and made their way back to England eventually, and six were killed. One plane which circled Grafton-Underwood was *El Rauncho,* piloted by colorful Randolph Jacobs. Like *Lucky Thirteen, El Rauncho* had trouble almost from the start of the mission. Over the enemy coast a 20-mm. shell holed the left wing; that was followed by a flak burst in the wing which interfered with aileron control. The fuselage was struck, the top-turret gun simply stopped operating, and the oxygen supply of the ball turret gunner leaked. There was a gash in the tail. But no one, luckily, was hit, and Jacobs completed the mission and brought the plane home. When he lowered the landing gear and the air spun the wheels, Jacobs saw that a piece of flak had lodged in one of the tires. Suddenly, too, the two port engines sputtered out and the plane fell thousands of feet before Jacobs brought it under control about eight hundred feet over the field. The landing gear came up but there was no time to feather the windmilling propellers as he brought *El Rauncho* in for a wheels-up, belly-scraping landing.

"The *El Rauncho* pointed steeply down, then levelled off at the tree-tops and began feeling for the runway," Walter E. Owens, historian of the 384th, has written. "She must have been going a hundred and fifty miles an hour when the friction of aluminum on concrete began throwing off sparks. The plane slid at a terrific pace the full length of the runway, screeching all the way and leaving a shower of sparks behind. At the far end she whirled abruptly about and careened over an anti-aircraft emplacement, finally coming to a stop only twenty-five yards from a parked aircraft."

With studied calm Jacobs climbed out of the wreckage. After begging a light for his cigar, he turned to look at the pile of junk which had once been a Flying Fortress and said, "I guess they didn't want us to get at their nut and bolt factory."

There were thirty-six 1st Air Division B-17s missing testifying to that fact. The day's total losses, then, added up to a total of sixty Flying Fortresses lost on the Schweinfurt-Regensburg mission, more than twice the toll of any previous mission. And this does not count those planes like *El Rauncho* which, although they had returned to England, would never fly again. Six hundred men too were lost—dead, wounded, and missing—in Germany, France, and Holland. To these could be added the wounded, like Loring Miller, who would be out of action for a long time. Other planes carried severely wounded men who died days or weeks after the battle; some men were dead on arrival. In short, mere numbers of aircraft lost do not fully reveal the full extent of losses.

The bombing at Regensburg had been excellent, but that at Schweinfurt not quite so good. The Germans reported that eighty high-explosive bombs had fallen into the two major bearing plants; in one more than six hundred machines were destroyed or damaged. A drop in production followed, which gave the Germans pause. They must seek out other sources of high-quality bearings, of Swiss or Swedish manufacture if need be, and consideration would have to be given to the dispersal of ball-bearing facilities. While this would make the industry a less neat panacea target, it also produced a loss in production which was almost equally effective.

But two facts were underscored by the hard-fought missions. One was expressed bluntly by the 384th's Frank Celentano, in direct contradiction to popular newspaper reportage, when he said, "It's a lot of ballyhoo to say that Germany's first-line fighters have all been shot down." The other, hanging like a gloomy cloud over the Eighth Air

A wounded airman of the 384th Bomb Group is lifted into an ambulance after returning from a mission in a shot-up B-17. (ROBERT CHAPIN)

Force, was that they had not not wiped out Schweinfurt.

They would have to go back.

III

Meanwhile, however, small missions were "laid on" to relatively nearby targets in France and the Low Countries to which the bombers could be escorted by the P-47s. It was not until September 6 that the Eighth had recovered enough to attempt another large-scale mission—this time to bomb aircraft and friction-bearing factories in Stuttgart. The three B-24 groups which had been detached to North Africa for the Ploesti mission had returned to England and what operational strength remained of these groups was added to the B-17 divisions. Replacements made it possible finally on September 6 to dispatch no less than 407 bombers, of which 69 were B-24s. The Liberators were employed in a diversionary sweep over the North Sea while the Fortresses aimed at Stuttgart. Weather once again interfered with the operations and only 262 bombers succeeded in bombing—and most of these targets were targets of opportunity. The day's losses, however, were high: 45 Flying Fortresses.

Most of September 1943 was notable for its poor bombing weather, so experiments were made with blind-bombing equipment in certain lead aircraft. At first there were only twelve radar (H2X) sets available, which were scattered through the bombing divisions. With these few sets in lead planes, the divisions could be led directly, more or less, over a target obscured by cloud. Specially trained operators manned the equipment, and reasonably good, if not excellent, results were obtained in the early attempts. These missions marked the initiation of what would eventually be called "Pathfinder" bombings. The lead plane of each group equipped with H2X found the target, and when this plane dropped its bombs, all other planes in the group did the same. Eventually exceedingly accurate blind bombing by radar became a common practice.

However, if the Allies could find targets electronically through the overcast, so likewise could the Germans find enemy aircraft. In order to confuse gun-directing radar, various devices were used, such as "window," strips of metal-coated paper which when dropped from aircraft made it difficult for antiaircraft radar to distinguish, so to speak, the wheat from the chaff. Another device was called "carpet," a transmitter carried in aircraft for jamming radar receivers.

But in September 1943 these were experimental attempts and did not always contribute much to the Combined Bomber Operation plan. Early in October it was possible, with new planes and crews, to concentrate on industrial targets inside Germany. On October 4 more than 360 heavy bombers took off for assorted targets in the vicinity of Frankfurt, as well as French airfields and marshaling yards in western Germany.

The second week of October 1943 proved to be one of the most critical in the history of the Eighth Air Force. On the eighth a large force (more than 350) bombed Bremen and Vegesack (with a loss of thirty planes). The next day another sizable force (a total of 352) bombed various targets, ranging from naval targets in Poland to the Focke-Wulf factories at Marienburg. This last was a superb demonstration of the efficacy of Eaker's confidence in daylight precision bombardment. The factory area was blanketed by five-hundred-pound general-purpose (GP) bombs plus incendiaries and all but wiped out. The damage was so severe that

THE FLIGHT IS DROPPING "WINDOW," WHICH CREATES THE SO CALLED "WINDOW CLOUD".
THE SCOPE OF THE RADAR ON THE RIGHT SHOWS THE RESULT.

THE PLANES MUST REMAIN IN THE "CLOUD". OTHERWISE THEY WILL REGISTER ON THE RADAR SCOPE.

PLANES A AND B ARE EQUIPPED WITH CARPET. PLANE C WILL ALSO BE "HIDDEN" AS IT IS IN
THE SAME AREA. THE SCOPE AT THE RIGHT SHOWS THE RESULT.

THE PLANES HAVE MOVED CLOSER TO THE RADAR SET. PLANES B & C ARE STILL "HIDDEN"
BUT PLANE A IS TOO CLOSE AND STICKS OUT ALTHOUGH IT IS STILL JAMMING.

The workings of "window" and "carpet" as explained to airmen of the Eighth Air Force. Both devices con- *fused German detection and flak-gun-aiming devices.*
(ROBERT CHAPIN)

no attempt was made to repair the factory. Losses for the day amounted to twenty-eight planes. The next day, October 10, the bombers attacked rail and waterway targets at Münster. The Luftwaffe swarmed out in full fury that day, concentrating on a single group in the formation, decimating that before going on to another. Of the 236 planes bombing Münster, it was the thirteen of the 100th Bombardment Group, in the lead, which took the worst of the new tactic. Of the day's thirty losses, twelve belonged to the 100th (a turn of fate which gave rise to the legend of the "Bloody Hundredth"), the single exception being Robert Rosenthal's *Rosie's Riveters,* which alone returned to England.

The total losses of those three consecutive days in October were eighty-eight planes. At such a rate, 8th Bomber Command could be eliminated from the war in a week. The Münster mission was officially Number 114; following that a three-day pause permitted the bomber forces to recuperate for the next one.

erudite though unsophisticated radio-gunner offer the intelligence that the city they were to attack that October 14 was "named afer a very special pig."

Apparently, to the unseasoned airman the name of Schweinfurt had little other significance.

To Budd Peaslee it had more than etymological portent. His old command, the 384th, had bled over Schweinfurt in August. It meant, too, that as air commander of the 40th Wing, he would lead them again along with the rest of the 1st Division deeply into Germany and, he hoped, back. The hope was that the "first" Schweinfurt had proved so rough a mission because of chance; the second might very well prove to be a "milk run" (an easy mission).

As air commander Peaslee was to fly as copilot in the lead aircraft, flown by Captain James K. McLaughlin of the 92nd Bombardment Group. At different points over England the 92nd would be joined by the 305th (Curtis LeMay's old command) and 306th Groups. These three groups constituted

IV

Colonel Budd Peaslee, who had served as a popular commander of the 384th during its first missions, had been made deputy wing commander of the 40th Wing (the 92nd, 305th, and 306th Bombardment Groups) of the 1st Air Division. When Mission 115 was "laid on" it was Peaslee's turn to act as 1st Division air commander for the mission.

"From the beginning," Peaslee has written, "Mission Number 115 was in doubt. A persistent low overcast had hung over the English bases for three days." To the mission-scarred men, the day broke propitiously. "There was considerable speculation that the mission would be scrubbed and they could return to their sacks till noon. This was a happy thought but it was not to be."

Briefings were held in the dank, bone-chilling darkness as crews assembled to learn of the day's target. A dull silence invariably descended when the map was uncovered showing the black ribbon stretching from England into Germany. *Yank* staff correspondent Walter Peters attended one of these briefings; he was detailed to fly that day in the first combat mission of a B-17 newly named *Yank.* Upon leaving the briefing room he overheard an

Budd Peaslee, air commander of the 1st Division on Mission 115 (Schweinfurt), October 14, 1943.

(ROBERT CHAPIN)

A B-17 of the 303rd Bomb Group in an East Anglian wheat field near Molesworth before the Schweinfurt mission. (U. S. AIR FORCE)

the 40th Combat Bombardment Wing. Also participating would be the 91st and 381st Groups (under supervision of the 1st Combat Bombardment Wing) and the 41st Wing (303rd, 379th, and 384th Groups). These three wings made up the striking force of the 1st Air Division, which was to contribute 149 Flying Fortresses to the striking force.

The 2nd Air Division, B-24s of the 93rd and 392nd Groups, was also to bomb Schweinfurt. Their sixty Liberators, however, did not get to the target.

The 3rd Air Division was to contribute seven groups (also combined into wings for command purposes): the 94th, 95th, 96th, 100th, 385th, 388th, and 390th. This division would provide a total of 142 Flying Fortresses.

Theoretically, if all went as planned, a total of 291 Fortresses and 60 Liberators were to go to Schweinfurt. But it was not to be. The Liberator bases, for example, were so badly fogged in that only 29 even managed to get off the ground. Unable to form up in the dense, swirling fog, 8 returned to their bases and the remaining 21 made a diversionary sweep toward Emden, hoping thus to draw away some of the German fighters from the B-17s, if they ever got off.

Peaslee sat in the left-hand seat of McLaughlin's Fortress, eyes on the control tower. There was still a question of whether or not Mission 115 would actually take place. But a weather plane, having crossed over Schweinfurt, radioed back that the target area was clear. The green flare went up and

the mission was on. McLaughlin throttled up the great plane and with Peaslee keeping an eye on the runway (to assure that the plane remained on the fog-enshrouded concrete), McLaughlin took off on instruments; at intervals, eighteen other 92nd Group B-17s followed. Above the clouds, in the brilliant sunlight, the planes assembled into combat boxes, proceeded to the assembly point, where the 306th Group joined them.

But where was the 305th? On this mission the group had been assigned the low position in the wing. However, in the confusion of attempting to assemble above the clouds, the 305th was unable to find the planes in the 40th Wing. Rather than scrub the mission, and thus deny the formation its sixteen aircraft, Major G. G. Y. Normand, in the lead B-17 of the 305th, attached to the 1st Wing. This left Peaslee's 40th Wing short an entire group. According to SOP (Standard Operating Procedure), he would have been justified in aborting; instead Peaslee relinquished command of the mission to Colonel Archie J. Olds, Jr. (then commander of the 45th Combat Wing). Peaslee then ordered his two groups to join up with the three groups of the 41st Wing.

One of the components of the 41st Wing was his old group, the 384th. On this Thursday Frank Celentano was acting as lead navigator for the group; he was in his regular plane, *Battle Wagon,* also carrying the 384th's air commander, Major George W. Harris. They lifted carefully through the haze, formed up, and proceeded toward Schweinfurt. Above the clouds it was a welcome sight to see the other B-17s of the group as well as the P-47s of the 56th and 353rd Fighter Groups (about a hundred in all), assigned to escort the bombers part of the way. On the return, also, they were to be waiting to protect the bombers.

Not so welcome, however, was the loss of several B-17s, forced to turn back because of engine trouble or some other mechanical malfunction. Twenty-six Fortresses returned to their bases for such reasons. The combined forces of the two air task forces were reduced from 291 to 265 Flying Fortresses. Once the bombers crossed the enemy coast the German fighters began pouncing on them. The American Thunderbolts swept down to intercept, and although many succeeded, they did not prevent some of the Me-109s and FW-190s from sweeping through the bomber formations. And when the P-47s were forced to turn back near Aachen because of their limited fuel supply, the Luftwaffe smashed down upon the B-17s in the most savage aerial assault of the war.

It was the first Schweinfurt all over again, with deadly interest. The interceptions by German fighters were so finely co-ordinated and timed that a suspicion arose (never actually confirmed, however) that the Luftwaffe had been forewarned of the mission. Whether or not this was true, the Germans were very well prepared for the invaders. Every possible technique employed in the past —unnerving head-on fighter attacks, cannons, rockets lobbed into the formations from the rear, and air-to-air bombing, as well as flak—was unleashed that day. If Ploesti represented a burning, low-level inferno, the second Schweinfurt was a freezing, high-level (above twenty thousand feet) inferno.

Wave after wave of German fighters, their guns winking in the wings, tore at the formations again and again. As at Münster, there was an attempt to concentrate upon a definite portion of the bomber stream. The 1st Division received the brunt of the attacks, with special attention to the lead planes, for the Germans knew that the air commander, lead

Fortresses of the 91st Bomb Group over Schweinfurt.
(U. S. AIR FORCE)

navigator, and lead bombardier flew in this plane. Likewise, the group in Coffin Corner was attacked ferociously. In this spot in the 1st Division it was the 305th Group, which had missed the rendezvous with Peaslee over England and had attached itself to the 1st Combat Wing. The Thunderbolts had barely turned for England when the 305th planes took their first mauling—and it continued all the way to Schweinfurt. Curiously, the battle let up over Schweinfurt itself, partly because the German fighters had to return to their bases to refuel—and to give the flak a chance. About two-forty in the afternoon the first bombs of the 1st Division fell upon Schweinfurt and continued to fall for about six minutes. Six minutes after that, at 2:52 P.M., the first bombs of the 3rd Division began tumbling from the bomb bays. The sky filled with 1000-pound and 500-pound high-explosive as well as 100-pound incendiary bombs, a total of 395 tons of the HE and 88 tons of incendiaries. And despite the ordeal through which the survivors had passed, the bombing was remarkably accurate and, as was later learned, effective.

But of the 291 bombers which in the original plan were to have set out for Schweinfurt, only 228 actually succeeded in placing their bombs on the target. The rest, other than those planes which had aborted, lay burning along the penetration route of the two air divisions. On the return flight, too, German fighter attacks were relentlessly pressed. The fighting was swift, concentrated, and confused; Fortress gunners claimed 186 German planes that day (although the more accurate total may have been closer to 35). Even if the claims had been realistic, it would still have been a costly exchange.

Sixty Flying Fortresses were lost over the Continent and 5 others were abandoned over England, making a total of 65 B-17s totally destroyed. In addition, 140 planes had returned in various stages of damage, 17 beyond possibility of repair. The human toll was even more depressing: 600 men were missing, the fate of many never to be known. Many died in exploding planes, or were trapped in gyrating B-17s, or were killed in fighter attacks or by flak.

The orphan 305th Group lost twelve of its sixteen aircraft before reaching Schweinfurt; three B-17s of the 305th dropped bombs on Schweinfurt—and only two returned to their English base at Chelveston

Bomb run: 91st Bomb Group Flying Fortress Bomb Boogie *now under the control of the bombardier in the nose as he zeroes in on the target. The bomb bay doors are open awaiting the moment of "bombs away."* (U. S. AIR FORCE)

(one had aborted earlier in the mission). The 306th Group lost ten planes, which made it the second in losses. The 92nd Group, the third component of the 40th Wing, lost six B-17s (plus another which crash-landed in England), so that Peaslee's 40th Wing lost twenty-nine planes over the Continent, about half of the total of the entire mission.

High losses in individual units had a despairing effect on the survivors in those units and rendered them less potent while replacement crews were trained.

Schweinfurt revealed the terrible workings of chance in aerial warfare (always present in the form of flak), for not all units came under strong fighter attack. In part, the fate of an individual aircraft depended on its position in the formation. Although every group in the 1st Air Division lost at least one plane, there were three in the 3rd Division which did not lose a single B-17 (the 100th, 385th, and 388th). Bruce R. Riley, pilot of *Riley and Crew,* flew to Schweinfurt with the 3rd Air Division and found that "from the standpoint of the 390th Bomb Group, [it] was a rather routine mission. . . . During the short times I was

Strike photo of the 100th Bomb Group, Schweinfurt, Thursday, October 14, 1943. (U. S. AIR FORCE)

"Now we have got Schweinfurt," *General Arnold said after Mission 115, and so it had appeared to the crews that left it burning. Schweinfurt was hard hit, but it was* *not finished. But so had the Eighth Air Force been hard hit, if not finished.* (U. S. AIR FORCE)

able to glance away from our formation, I saw at least three Forts blow up ahead over the target, probably due to direct hits by flak. Our one loss was due to a fighter attack that ruptured three out of four fuel tanks on the plane that went down."

If chance, luck, fortune, or whatever that unknown but ever present factor present in every air battle was operative, so was truth. Despite the frightful and wholesale onslaught and the withering sight of blasted, burning, and falling planes, the bomber crews thrust on through the opposing German fighters, despite their various gadgets of destruction. There were no aborts over Germany; aircraft continued over the targets on less than full engine power, some made bomb runs (the average time was six minutes) while burning, during which time it was likely that a B-17 would explode. Some did.

That truth was the fact of American courage. A second truth was more difficult to face. The losses over Schweinfurt, added to those losses already accumulated during the early weeks of October, proved clearly that such deep penetrations into Germany without fighter escort were self-defeating. The cost in men and aircraft was not worth it, however strategically important the target.

The October 14, 1943, Schweinfurt attack was, in fact, the most effective upon that target made

SCHWEINFURT
K: 1785
Neg. No. 32020

during the entire course of the war. There were fifteen others, however, which would mean fourteen sequels to the mission which Martin Caidin so aptly called "Black Thursday." It would appear, therefore, that when General Arnold announced to the newspapers, "Now we have got Schweinfurt," he was being overoptimistic. He was also being honest, insofar as he knew. Secret reports from inside Germany via neutral Sweden hinted at great devastation at Schweinfurt. Reconnaissance photographs, as well as the strike photos, sustained this belief. The Air Force informed its crews, via the official publication *Impact,* that "All five plants—representing about 65 per cent of the ball- and roller-bearing capacity of Germany—were so heavily damaged that *our bombers may never have to go back."*

And they did not go back to Schweinfurt, not for another four months. The truth is that they could *not* go back. Air superiority over Germany had reverted to the Luftwaffe. But when they did go back, in the spring of 1944, in conjunction with the RAF's Bomber Command—the British bombed Schweinfurt for the first time on February 24, 1944 —many wondered why it was necessary if such devastation had been wrought in October.

Schweinfurt had suffered heavy destruction, which had interfered with production. But not forever, as intimated in the optimistic reports, but for a month and a half. Since Schweinfurt was granted four months of grace, there was time to repair the damage and to reorganize the anti-friction-bearing industry, which, as reported in the *United States Strategic Bombing Survey* (September 30, 1945), "precipitated, also, the disperal of the industry from Schweinfurt, forced the expansion or construction of old and new plants, and accelerated the program of substitution and redesign in order to reduce the excessive and often luxurious use of bearings in many types of equipment."

Under the organizing genius of Hitler's armament czar Albert Speer and more directly under Speer's special commissioner for ball bearings, Philip Kessler, the co-ordination of the industry was undertaken to disperse the installations as well as to in-

Crew of Battle Wagon *of the 384th Bomb Group assemble for a debriefing after the "rugged" mission to Schweinfurt. The group lost a total of nine B-17s on the mission, six over enemy-held territory and three battle-damaged planes abandoned over Britain.*

(FRANK CELENTANO)

ventory stock. The latter contained surprises for all, including the Germans. It was discovered that large surpluses of anti-friction bearings were stored in Germany by the millions and that, however effective the raid upon Schweinfurt had been, many industries requiring ball bearings continued to operate normally; redistribution of surplus stock made up for any losses.

The RAF and Eighth Air Force bombers joined eventually to eliminate Schweinfurt from the war map, but by then, because of dispersal, Schweinfurt was no longer a vital military target. By October 9, 1944, when the Eighth Air Force dropped more than eight hundred tons of bombs upon Schweinfurt, it was "a city which was less than one-half as important industrially as in August 1943," according to the *United States Strategic Bombing Survey.*

"Now we [had] got Schweinfurt," but it no longer mattered. Bomber crews viewed the Schweinfurt mission with characteristic dark humor but with more realism when they spoke of Black Thursday as the day when "We took out 150% of the ball-bearing industry."

It would be inequitous to assert bluntly that the two Schweinfurt missions accomplished nothing— despite the failure of the second, for all its pre-

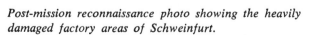

Post-mission reconnaissance photo showing the heavily damaged factory areas of Schweinfurt.

(U. S. AIR FORCE)

cision, to "take out" the ball-bearing industry. In purely objective terms, numbers, percentages, the missions were frightfully expensive in loss of life and aircraft, but they were not total failures. The second mission to Schweinfurt, especially, has become a symbol of both courage and failure. That the one was not enough to prevent the other lay in the nature of the target itself and in the fact that long daylight flights without escort were doomed to terrible opposition.

Schweinfurt was not the greatest loss suffered by the U. S. Air Force in the course of the war; later battles over Berlin claimed more bombers. It was the worst to date.

It was, in a word current at the time, "rugged." But any mission whatever the number or percentage of loss, was "rugged" if your plane did not return or did return badly chewed up by the Luftwaffe. Airmen who fought in the two major theaters of operations invariably referred to Europe as "the Big League" because of the potency of Luftwaffe fighters during the waning days of 1943 and the flak. Heavy bombardment during daylight, without massive formations and fighter protection, seemed to be at an impasse.

But inside Germany, unknown to Allied air leaders arguing about the cost of daylight missions and the foolishness of panacea targets, there was serious consternation. The bombing was taking on a serious pattern, no longer the derring-do of knocking out a dam, or a foolhardy low-level attack on an oil field. The bombing was beginning to look more businesslike, less haphazard.

"The Luftwaffe leaders knew that they could not stop our bombers," Eaker has observed, "and save their weapons-making establishments." A subtle, almost sudden twist had come—at great cost perhaps, but it had come.

"For Germany," Eaker concluded, "it marked the beginning of the end."

Index TERROR FROM THE SKY

Note: References to illustrations are in italics

INDEX

INDEX

INDEX

Index TRAGIC VICTORIES

Note: References to illustrations are in *italics*

INDEX

INDEX

INDEX

INDEX

INDEX

INDEX

INDEX